LEONARDO
DA VINCI

PHAIDON

LUDWIG GOLDSCHEIDER

LEONARDO

PAINTINGS AND DRAWINGS

WITH THE LEONARDO BIOGRAPHY
BY VASARI·1568·
NEWLY ANNOTATED·
114 ILLUSTRATIONS
INCLUDING 41 IN COLOUR

PHAIDON PRESS·LONDON

FIRST EDITION 1943
SEVENTH EDITION 1964
EIGHTH EDITION 1967

© 1959 PHAIDON PRESS LTD · LONDON SW7
MADE IN GREAT BRITAIN
TEXT AND COLOUR PLATES PRINTED BY HUNT BARNARD & CO · LTD · AYLESBURY · BUCKS
PHOTOGRAVURE PLATES PRINTED BY CLARKE & SHERWELL LTD · NORTHAMPTON
BOUND AT THE PITMAN PRESS · BATH
BOOK DESIGN BY THE AUTHOR

CONTENTS

FOREWORD

THE PRESENT WORK is not a book on Leonardo, it is rather a book by him.
It contains large-scale reproductions of all his paintings, together with a few which are reasonably
ascribed to him; it also shows some sculptures which by some students are thought to be his;
and eighty of his drawings, most of which are given in their actual sizes.

In addition to the reproductions of Leonardo's work, there is his biography by Vasari, who was
a boy of eight when Leonardo died. The two other biographies, which follow, are even earlier.
The one was written by a man who studied surgery at Milan while Leonardo was occupied there
with his anatomical researches. The third biography in this volume was compiled about eight
years before the publication of the first edition of Vasari's *Vite*, but remained unprinted for three
hundred years. The unknown author, a Florentine, probably never met Leonardo, though he was
acquainted with Michelangelo and other artists of his time. These three early Leonardo biographies,
translated into English, form the nucleus of the present book, which also contains a number of
documents – letters by Leonardo and communications from his contemporaries. These documents,
translated from the Italian, Latin and French, combine to show how Leonardo's work appeared to
those who lived and worked with him.

A systematic bibliography and the notes on the plates will help readers to find their way through
the maze of Leonardo discussions, if they are eager or curious enough to wander so far. In fact,
the plates, the master's biography by Vasari and the passages from the biographies of other artists
enable everyone to make up his own book on Leonardo by reading this one. He will see what
Leonardo did, he can study firsthand information from the Master and from his contemporaries
– and he probably does not want more.

None the less, I found it necessary to add notes to the text, and notes on the plates, to acquaint
the reader with modern judgements on Leonardo; and as I quite often disagree with those judgements I could not help giving occasionally my own opinions and saying a few things that are
new. Thus, to cite two instances, I have ventured an explanation of the 'knots', the *fantasie de
Vinci*, and commented upon the words on the scroll of the Ambrosiana *Musician*.

In the Notes on the Plates I have taken care to say which paintings and drawings are disputed;
I have also pointed out which paintings are damaged and which drawings retouched by a later
hand.

*　　　　*

The first edition of this book was prepared during the initial years of the last war, and published
in 1943. It was a volume in a rather large format. The format changed in subsequent editions;
the size of the illustrations remained the same. The choice of plates also changed a little every time
the book was reprinted in the last twenty years. The present edition, with all its shortcomings, is,
I am afraid, to be regarded as final.

L.G.

LIFE OF LEONARDO DA VINCI
PAINTER AND SCULPTOR OF FLORENCE
BY GIORGIO VASARI · 1568

LIONARDO DA VINCI

LIONARDO DA VINCI PITT.
E SCVLTOR FIOR.

VITA DI LIONARDO DA VINCI
PITTORE, ET SCVLTORE
FIORENTINO.

THE heavens often rain down the richest gifts on human beings naturally, but sometimes with lavish abundance bestow upon a single individual beauty, grace and ability, so that whatever he does, every action is so divine that he distances all other men, and clearly displays how his genius is the gift of God and not an acquirement of human art. Men saw this in Leonardo da Vinci, whose personal beauty could not be exaggerated, whose every movement was grace itself and whose abilities were so extraordinary that he could readily solve every difficulty. He possessed great physical strength, combined with dexterity, and a spirit and courage invariably royal and magnanimous; and the fame of his name increased not only during his lifetime but also after his death.

This marvellous and divine Leonardo was the son of Ser Piero da Vinci.[1] He would have made great

1. The little town of Vinci is situated in Tuscany between Empoli and Pistoia, about 20 miles from Florence. Vasari calls Leonardo's father 'Ser' Piero, a title borne by notaries. Ser Piero was engaged from 1451 onwards in his profession, mainly in Florence, where he became one of the most sought-after notaries. Leonardo, the illegitimate son of Ser Piero and the peasant maid, Caterina, was born on the 15th of April, 1452. Caterina lived at Anchiano, a hamlet outside Vinci. She married some labourer when Leonardo was five, and the child was received into his father's household where he was taken care of by a young, childless stepmother. (Ser Piero had married a rich girl aged sixteen, in the year Leonardo was born. By his third and fourth wives Ser Piero had eleven children. He died in 1504, aged 77.)

Portrait of Verrochio, by Lorenzo di Credi, c. 1480–83. Florence, Uffizi.
Leonardo was Verrocchio's pupil; but his favourite disciple was Lorenzo di Credi,
who finished for him the Pistoia altar-piece.

profit in learning had he not been so capricious and fickle, for he began to learn many things and then gave them up. [2] Thus in arithmetic, during the few months that he studied it, he made such progress that he frequently confounded his master by continually raising doubts and difficulties. [3] He devoted

2. Paolo Giovio, in his short biography of Leonardo, written in about 1527, judged similarly but more comprehendingly; after mentioning Leonardo's exertions 'in the sciences and the liberal arts', his optical and anatomical studies, he adds regretfully: 'But while he was thus spending his time in the close investigation of subordinate branches of his art he brought but very few works to completion, for his masterly facility and his fastidious disposition caused him to discard many works he had already begun.' Similar opinions were held by Sieur de Chantelou (who had a share in Du Fresne's edition of Leonardo's *Trattato della Pittura* of 1651). In his *Journal de voyage du chev. Bernin en France* we find, under the date of 24th August 1665, the following conversation. '*Chantelou:* The relationship between Leonardo and Francis I was based entirely on the admiration the King had for him, although Leonardo was rather a speculative thinker

than a creative artist. – *Bernini*: What you mean is Leonardo understood how to grow old working endlessly on one single composition. – *Chantelou:* The outcome of this is anyway that France possesses nothing from his hand but a few unfinished paintings. – *Bernini:* Naturally. Leonardo may have taken six years to paint just the hair.'
3. Edward McCurdy assumes that Leonardo's teacher in mathematics was Benedetto dell'Abbaco, the most famous man of his calling in Florence. Leonardo continued to cultivate the study of mathematics all his life, and about 1497 collaborated in *Divina Proportione*, the work of his friend, Fra Luca Pacioli; the geometrical figures in the 1509 edition are after Leonardo's drawings. Mathematics was for him the foundation of art, and on the back of a drawing (Windsor 19118) he wrote: 'Let no man who is no mathematician read the elements of my work.'

some time to music, and soon learned to play the *lira*, and, being filled with a lofty and delicate spirit, he could sing and improvise divinely with it. [4]

Yet though he studied so many different things, he never neglected design and working in relief, those being the things which appealed to his fancy more than any other. When Ser Piero perceived this, and knowing the boy's soaring spirit, he one day took some of his drawings to Andrea del Verrocchio, [5] who was his close friend, and asked his opinion whether Leonardo would do anything by studying design. Andrea was so amazed at these early efforts that he advised Ser Piero to have the boy taught. So it was decided that Leonardo should go to Andrea's workshop. [6] The boy was greatly delighted, and not only practised his profession, but all those in which design has a part. Possessed of a divine and marvellous intellect, and being an excellent geometrician, he not only worked in sculpture, doing out of clay some heads of smiling women, of which casts in plaster are still taken, and children's heads (*teste di putti*), also, executed like a master, [7] but also prepared many architectural plans and elevations, and he was the first, though so young, to propose to canalize the Arno from Pisa to Florence. [8] He made designs for mills, fulling machines, and other engines to go by water, and as painting was to be his profession he studied drawing from life. He would make clay models of figures, draping them with soft rags dipped in plaster, and would then draw them patiently on thin sheets of cambric or linen, in black and white, with the point of the brush. [9] He did these admirably, as may be

4. Paolo Giovio, the Anonimo Gaddiano, Luca Pacioli and Lomazzo, all mention Leonardo's musical talent, a gift which he shared with Piero della Francesca, Giorgione, and his teacher Verrocchio. Paolo Giovio relates: 'He sang beautifully to his own accompaniment on the *lira* to the delight of the entire Court of Milan.' The Anonimo Gaddiano (see the Biography on p. 30) says: 'Leonardo was an exquisite musician on the *lira* and was the teacher of the singer Atalante Migliorotti.' (See also note 7 on p. 30.)

5. Andrea del Verrocchio, born in Florence 1435, died in Venice 1488; pupil of Donatello (according to Baldinucci); best known through his bronze equestrian statue of Colleoni in Venice, which was not completed by him (but by Leopardi, 1496, and set up after the master's death).

6. It is uncertain at which date Leonardo was placed with Verrocchio; we only know that as late as 1476 Leonardo was still staying and working with him. Some authorities (including Müller-Walde, Thiis, Van Marle, and Heydenreich) assume that he came to the studio in 1466, when the boy was between fourteen and fifteen years; but others (Ravaisson-Mollien, Richter, Venturi, de Rinaldis, and Valentiner) suggest a date between summer 1469 and spring 1470. As Leonardo is still mentioned in the tax records of Vinci in 1469, the latter date is most probably correct. In July 1472 Leonardo became a master, a member of the Guild, as transpires from an entry in 'the red book of the Florence Guild of Painters'. (The usual term of apprenticeship for a painter in those days was six years; but sometimes it was only four, and when Michelangelo was placed with the brothers Ghirlandaio, it was stipulated that the term should be only three years. There is no fixed rule.)

On the 1st January, 1478, Leonardo received his first independent commission; in March, 1481, the contract for the 'Adoration of the Kings' was entered into, and at this time Leonardo was working in his own dwelling, and no longer with Verrocchio. By July, 1481, the model for the equestrian statue of Colleoni was finished in Verrocchio's workshop in Florence. A short time afterwards Leonardo removed to Milan, and not much later Verrocchio to Venice. His last payment to the Florentine Guild of Painters dates from 1481.

7. Lomazzo in his *Treatise on Painting* (Milan, 1584, p. 127) mentions a terracotta head of the infant Christ in his collection, 'by Leonardo's own hand'; also a clay relief of a horse by Leonardo, in the collection of the sculptor Leone Leoni. All these sculptural works of Leonardo's youth are lost, and all we know for certain about Leonardo as a sculptor is based on a few drawings; all the attributions are mere conjectures.

8. The aim of the plan was to procure for Florence direct access to the sea. Numerous drawings connected with this idea have been preserved. (Cf. e.g. Richter §§ 1001, 1006; Windsor Catalogue, Nos. 12279, 12659). Leonardo was particularly occupied with this idea in the summer of the year 1503.

9. A good and richly illustrated survey of these drapery drawings, which were executed in Leonardo's studio for study purposes, is to be found in Bernard Berenson's *The Drawings of the Florentine Painters*, amplified edition, Chicago 1938; particularly figs. 517–531. How such drawings were employed in painting is shown by our plate 43. Drapery drawings from clay models were, in the earlier Renaissance, rather usual, and not in Verrocchio's workshop alone. In the life of Piero della Francesca (about 1416–1492), Vasari says: 'Piero was in the habit of making clay models, covering them loosely with soft cloth in order to copy them and turn them to account.' In the *Life of Lorenzo di Credi* Vasari speaks of 'drawings copying clay models draped in waxed cloth'.

seen by specimens in my book of designs. He also drew upon paper so carefully and well that no one has ever equalled him. I have a head in grisaille which is divine. The grace of God so possessed his mind, his memory and intellect formed such a mighty union, and he could so clearly express his ideas in discourse, that he was able to confound the boldest opponents. Every day he made models and designs for the removal of mountains with ease and to pierce them to pass from one place to another, and by means of levers, cranes and winches to raise and draw heavy weights; he devised a method for cleansing ports, and to raise water from great depths, schemes which his brain never ceased to evolve. Many designs for these notions are scattered about, and I have seen numbers of them. He spent much

School of Leonardo: Knot, engraving, c. 1483. London, British Museum.
This 'fantasia dei vinci', a pattern of linked chains, is most probably a hieroglyphic signature of Leonardo.

time in making a regular design of a series of knots so that the cord may be traced from one end to the other, the whole filling a round space. There is a fine engraving of this most difficult design, and in the middle are the words: *Leonardi Vinci Academia.*[10] Among these models and designs there was one which he several times showed to many able citizens who then ruled Florence, of a method of raising the church of San Giovanni and putting steps under it without its falling down. He argued with so much eloquence that it was not until after his departure that they recognized the impossibility of such a feat.

His charming conversation won all hearts, and although he possessed nothing and worked little, he kept servants and horses; of which latter he was very fond, and indeed he loved all animals, and trained them with great kindness and patience. Often, when passing places where birds were sold, he would let them out of their cages and having paid the vendor the price asked, he let them fly away into the air, restoring to them the lost liberty. Wherefore Nature favoured him so greatly that in whatever his brain or mind took up he displayed unrivalled harmony, vigour, vivacity, excellence, beauty and grace.

10. Six of these engravings have been preserved. Albrecht Dürer copied them (Richter, vol. I, p. 387, n.). From the inscription on these knots it has been assumed that Leonardo was the director of a drawing academy (school) in Milan, but this supposition is now generally discredited. I should like to put forward the suggestion that these engravings represent tickets for scientific disputations, being either tickets of admission or prize tickets. By 'academia' was understood in the Renaissance a poetical or scientific tourney; 'academia coronaria' was the name of the poetical competition which Leon Battista Alberti organized in the Florence Cathedral on the 22nd October, 1441. Leonardo, Pacioli, and the Duke were present on 8th February, 1499, at a scientific tourney (*duello*) in the Castello Sforzesco. But why was a knot used as an emblem for Leonardo's 'Academia', and what is the reason for the interlacing ornaments on the dress of Mona Lisa and in other paintings? The explanation is a play on the words *vincire* (to fetter, to lace, to knot) and *Vinci*; being a cryptographic signature of Leonardo da Vinci. Niccolò da Correggio, who through Atalante (see note on plate 26) was in connection with Leonardo, designed in 1492 and 1493 dresses for Isabella and Beatrice d'Este with this pattern of interlaced links embroidered on silk. (See also Richter § 680.)

His knowledge of art, indeed, prevented him from finishing many things which he had begun, for he felt that his hand would be unable to realize the perfect creations of his imagination, as his mind formed such difficult, subtle and marvellous conceptions that his hands, skilful as they were, could never have expressed them. His interests were so numerous that his inquiries into natural phenomena led him to study the properties of herbs and to observe the movements of the heavens, the moon's orbit and the progress of the sun.[11]

LEONARDO was placed, as I have said, with Andrea del Verrocchio in his childhood by Ser Piero, and his master happened to be painting a picture of St John baptizing Christ. For this Leonardo did an angel holding some garments; and, although quite young, he made it far better than the figures of Andrea.[12] The latter would never afterwards touch colours, chagrined that a child should know more than he.

Leonardo was next employed to draw Adam and Eve, sinning in the Earthly Paradise, a cartoon for a door-hanging in tapestry, to be made in Flanders of gold and silk, to be sent to the King of Portugal. Here he did a meadow in grisaille, with the lights in white lead, containing much vegetation and some animals, unsurpassable for finish and naturalness. There is a fig-tree, the leaves and branches beautifully foreshortened and executed with such care that the mind is amazed at the amount of patience displayed. There is also a palm-tree, the rotundity of the dates being executed with great and marvellous art, due to the patience and ingenuity of Leonardo. This work was not carried farther, and the cartoon is now in Florence in the fortunate house of the illustrious Ottaviano de' Medici, to whom it was given not long ago by Leonardo's uncle.[13]

It is said that when Ser Piero was at his country-seat he was requested by a peasant of his estate to get a round panel of wood[14] painted for him at Florence, which he had cut from a fig-tree on his farm. Piero readily consented, as the man was very skilful in catching birds and fishing, and was very useful to him in such matters. Accordingly Piero brought the wood to Florence and asked Leonardo to paint something upon it, without telling him to whom it belonged. Leonardo, on taking it up to examine it one day, found it warped, badly prepared and clumsy, but with the help of fire he made it straight, and giving it to a turner, had it rendered smooth and even, instead of being rough and rude. Then, after preparing the surface in his own way by covering it with *gesso*, he began to think about what he should paint on it, and resolved to do the Head of Medusa to terrify all beholders. To a room to which he alone had access, Leonardo took lizards, newts, maggots, snakes, moths, locusts, bats, and

11. In the first edition of Vasari's *Life of Leonardo* (1550) followed here a sentence which is omitted in the second edition: 'Leonardo was of such a heretical frame of mind that he did not adhere to any kind of religion, believing that it was perhaps better to be a philosopher than a Christian.'

12. Albertini's description of Florence, 1510, already mentions Leonardo's share in this painting. (The angel on the left, see plate 43.) Not only the Angel, but also the Landscape (plate 87) has been painted over by Leonardo, and indeed with oil colours above Verrocchio's tempera. (A. Bayersdorfer, *Leben und Schriften*, 1908, pp. 72–76. Bode, *Leonardo-Studien*, 1921, pp. 10–14.) The tuft of grass beside the kneeling angel testifies to the same understanding of the life of plants as Leonardo's later plant studies.

13. Leonardo's father had only one brother, Francesco, who dwelt, as a countryman and silk-worm rearer, in Vinci. Allessandro degli Amadori, a brother of Ser Piero's first wife, also called himself Leonardo's uncle; in 1506 he interpreted to Leonardo the wishes of Isabella d'Este. (Beltrami, Documenti, Nos. 173, 174.) I believe that Messer Allessandro Amadori, Canonico di Fiesole, was the first owner of Leonardo's cartoon of Adam and Eve. This cartoon has disappeared.
   Suida surmises that Raphael's 'Fall of Man' in the Stanza della Segnatura of the Vatican is a free rendering of Leonardo's lost cartoon.

14. In the original *rotella*, which in fact means: a shield of a round form.

other animals of the kind, out of which he composed a horrible and terrible monster, of poisonous breath, issuing from a dark and broken rock, belching poison from its open throat, fire from its eyes, and smoke from its nostrils, of truly terrible and horrible aspect. He was so engrossed with the work that he did not notice the terrible stench of the dead animals, being absorbed in his love for art. His father and the peasant no longer asked for the work, and when it was finished Leonardo told his father to send for it when he pleased, as he had done his part. Accordingly Ser Piero went to his rooms one morning to fetch it. When he knocked at the door Leonardo opened it and told him to wait a little, and, returning to his room, put the round panel in the light on his easel, which he turned with its back to the window to make the light dim; then he called his father in. Ser Piero, taken unaware, started back, not thinking of the round piece of wood, or that the face which he saw was painted, and was beating a retreat when Leonardo detained him and said, 'This work is as I wanted it to be; take it away, then, as it is producing the effect intended.' Ser Piero indeed thought it almost a miracle, and he warmly praised Leonardo's idea. He then quietly went and bought another round panel with a heart transfixed by a dart painted upon it, and gave it to the peasant, who was grateful to Piero all his life.

Piero took Leonardo's work secretly to Florence and sold it to some merchants for one hundred ducats, and in a short time it came into the hands of the Duke of Milan, who bought it of them for three hundred ducats. [15]

Leonardo next did a very excellent Madonna, which afterwards belonged to Pope Clement VII. Among other things it contained a bowl of water with some marvellous flowers, the dew upon them seeming actually to be there, so that they looked more real than reality itself. [16] For his good friend Antonio Segni he drew a Neptune on a folio sheet of paper, with so much diligence that it seemed alive. [17] The sea is troubled and his car is drawn by sea-horses, with the sprites, monsters, and south winds; there are in it also some very fine heads of sea-gods. This drawing was given by Antonio's son Fabio to Messer Giovanni Gaddi with this epigram:

> *Pinxit Virgilius Neptunum, pinxit Homerus,*
> *Dum maris undisoni per vada flectit equos.*
> *Mente quidem vates illum conspexit uterque,*
> *Vincius ast oculis; jureque vincit eos.* [18]

Leonardo then had the fancy to paint a picture of the Medusa's head in oils with a garland of snakes about it, the most extraordinary idea imaginable, but as the work required time, it remained unfinished, the fate of nearly all his projects. [19] This is among the treasures in the palace of Duke Cosimo, together

15. This painting has disappeared.

16. Some critics identify Leonardo's *Madonna with the Glass Vase full of Flowers* with the painting in Munich, plate 63.

17. For a study to this lost drawing, see plate 46. For Antonio Segni Botticelli painted his *Calumny of Apelles*. Concerning the Gaddi Collection see J. Schlosser, *Ghiberti*, 1941, p. 142.

18. The meaning of this Latin epigram is roughly as follows: 'Virgil and Homer both depicted Neptune driving his sea-horses through the rushing waves. The poets saw him in their imaginations, but Leonardo with his own eyes, and so he rightly surpassed them.' There is a pun on the words *Vincius* (the man from Vinci) and *vincit* (he vanquished) which is untranslatable.

19. Lost. The panel in the Uffizi at Florence, which was once erroneously supposed to be Leonardo's Head of the Medusa, is a work of the 17th century, and actually an adaptation of the head on a shield in the *Fight for the Standard* (cf. plate 108; the fallen man in the centre foreground). But it may be that *The Head of the Medusa* by Rubens in the Vienna Museum (No. 846) is a free version of Leonardo's lost painting.

The Angel of the Annunciation. Detail of a black chalk drawing, corrected
in pen and ink, c. 1506. Windsor Castle, Royal Library (No. 12328).

Drawing by a pupil of Leonardo, with some retouchings by the master.
The head of the Angel is drawn on a larger scale than the arms and the hands.
(Compare also plate 55, which dates from about ten years later.)

with the Head of an Angel, who is raising an arm in the air, this arm being foreshortened from the
shoulder to the elbow, while the other rests on its breast.[20]

So marvellous was Leonardo's mind that, desiring to throw his things into greater relief, he endeavoured to obtain greater depths of shadow, and sought the deepest blacks in order to render the
lights clearer by contrast. He succeeded so well that his scenes looked rather like representations of the
night, there being no bright light, than of the lightness of day, though all was done with the idea of
throwing things into greater relief and to find the end and perfection of art.

Leonardo was so delighted when he saw curious heads, whether bearded or hairy, that he would
follow about anyone who had thus attracted his attention for a whole day, acquiring such a clear idea
of him that when he went home he would draw the head as well as if the man had been present. In
this way many heads of men and women came to be drawn, and I have several such pen-and-ink
drawings in my book, so often referred to. Among them is the head of Amerigo Vespucci,[21] a fine
old man, drawn in carbon, and that of Scaramuccia, the captain of the gypsies, which afterwards
belonged to Messer Donato Valdambrini of Arezzo, Canon of San Lorenzo, left to him by Giam-

20. The original is lost but there are several copies known,
of which one of the best belonged once to Jacob Burckhardt
and is now in the Basel Museum. Leonardo developed this
composition, about ten years later, to a *St John* (plate 55).

21. In the Uffizi there is a portrait of Amerigo Vespucci as
an old man. This portrait bears such resemblances to some
of the heads in Leonardo's *Adoration of the Kings*, and even
more to the Windsor drawing of *Judas* that the unknown

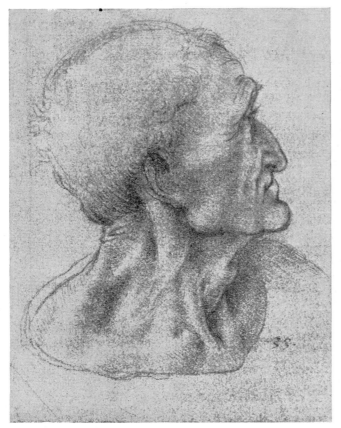

Leonardo: Study for the Judas in the Last Supper, red chalk on red paper, c. 1495. Windsor Castle, Royal Library (No. 12547).

Portrait of Amerigo Vespucci, by an unknown Florentine Painter, (copy after Leonardo?). Florence, Uffizi.

bullari.[22] He began a panel-picture of the Adoration of the Magi, containing many beautiful things, especially heads, which was in the house of Amerigo Benci, opposite the Loggia de' Peruzzi, but which was left unfinished like [most of] his other works.[23]

ON THE DEATH of Giovan Galeazzo, Duke of Milan, and the accession of Ludovico Sforza in the same year, 1494,[24] Leonardo was invited to Milan with great ceremony by the Duke to play the *lira*, in which that prince greatly delighted. Leonardo took his own instrument, made by himself in great part of silver, and shaped like a horse's head, a curious and novel idea to render the harmonies more loud and sonorous, so that he surpassed all the musicians who had assembled there. Besides this he was the best improviser of verse of his time. The Duke, captivated by Leonardo's conversation and genius,

painter of this portrait might be presumed to be familiar with Leonardo's charcoal-drawing. Amerigo Vespucci was born in 1454, and was therefore about the same age as Leonardo; he left Florence for Spain when he was forty, and never came back to Italy, as far as is known. Though I cannot discover where and when Leonardo could have drawn the likeness of the aged Amerigo Vespucci, the Leonardo-like portrait in the Uffizi would seem to corroborate Vasari's statement. (Cf. R. Langton Douglas, in *The Burlington Magazine*, February, 1944. But see also H. Brockhaus in *Forschungen über Florentiner Kunstwerke*, Leipzig, 1902, p. 83 f.)

22. There is a (much retouched) black chalk drawing at Christ Church, Oxford (B.B. 1050, fig. 536) of which Berenson thinks it might be the 'Scaramuccia', mentioned by Vasari.

23. Plates 49–53, and 103.

24. This date is certainly wrong. The Anonimo Gaddiano (see here, p. 30) says that Leonardo went to Milan when he was thirty years old; this means: in Spring, 1482. (See also Document I, p. 33.) In 1494, when Gian Galeazzo Sforza died, his uncle Ludovico had for already fourteen years been in full possession of all the power in Milan.

conceived an extraordinary affection for him. He begged him to paint an altar-piece of the Nativity, which was sent by the Duke to the Emperor.[25]

Leonardo then did a Last Supper for the Dominicans at Santa Maria delle Grazie in Milan, endowing the heads of the Apostles with such majesty and beauty that he left that of Christ unfinished, feeling that he could not give it that celestial divinity which it demanded.[26] This work left in such a condition has always been held in the greatest veneration by the Milanese and also by foreigners, as Leonardo has seized the moment when the Apostles are anxious to discover who would betray their Master. All their faces are expressive of love, fear, wrath or grief at not being able to grasp the meaning of Christ, in contrast to the obstinacy, hatred and treason of Judas, while the whole work, down to the smallest details, displays incredible diligence, even the texture of the tablecloth being clearly visible so that actual cambric would not look more real.

It is said that the Prior incessantly importuned Leonardo to finish the work, thinking it strange that the artist should pass half a day at a time lost in thought. He would have desired him never to lay down the brush, as if he were digging a garden. Seeing that his importunity produced no effect, he had recourse to the Duke, who felt compelled to send for Leonardo to inquire about the work, showing tactfully that he was driven to act by the importunity of the Prior. Leonardo, aware of the acuteness and discretion of the Duke, talked with him fully about the picture, a thing which he had never done with the Prior. He spoke freely of his art, and explained how men of genius really are doing most when they work least, as they are thinking out ideas and perfecting the conceptions, which they subsequently carry out with their hands. He added that there were still two heads to be done, that of Christ, which he would not look for on earth, and felt unable to conceive the beauty of the celestial grace that must have been incarnate in the divinity. The other head wanting for him to paint, was that of Judas, which also caused him thought, as he did not think he could express the face of a man who could resolve to betray his Master, the Creator of the world, after having received so many benefits. But he was willing in this case to seek no farther, and for lack of a better he would do the head of the importunate and tactless Prior. The Duke was wonderfully amused, and laughingly declared that he was quite right. Then the poor Prior, covered with confusion, went back to his garden and left Leonardo in peace, while the artist indeed finished his Judas, making him a veritable likeness of treason and cruelty. The head of Christ was left unfinished, as I have said. The nobility of this painting, in its composition and the care with which it was finished, induced the King of France to wish to take it home with him. Accordingly he employed architects to frame it in wood and iron, so that it might be transported in safety, without any regard for the cost, so great was his desire. But the King was thwarted by its being done on the wall, and it remained with the Milanese.

While engaged on the *Last Supper*, Leonardo painted on the end wall in the same refectory, where there is a *Passion* in the old style, the portrait of Duke Ludovico, with Maximilian, his eldest son, on the left; and on the right he did Duchess Beatrice with Francesco, her other son, both of whom afterwards became Dukes of Milan, the portraits being marvellous.[27]

25. See the note on plate 70.

26. Plates 71–75. See also plates 14–17; 89; and Appendix, plate IV.

27. The *Crucifixion* (which Vasari calls 'a Passion in the old style'), on the wall opposite Leonardo's *Last Supper*, is by Giovanni Donato Montorfano, dated 1495. The portraits which Leonardo, according to Vasari, introduced into Montorfano's *Crucifixion*, are reproduced here as plate II in the Appendix. In 1945, when these photographs were taken, the figures were better visible than fifty years ago, as most of the retouchings have flaked off. Unfortunately, in the meantime a good deal of the original paint has also crumbled away, e.g. the whole face of Duke Ludovico.

While thus employed, Leonardo suggested that the Duke should set up a bronze horse of colossal size with the Duke upon it in memory of himself. But he began it on such a scale that it could never be done.[28] Such is the malice of man when stirred by envy that there are some who believe that Leonardo, as with so many of his works, began this with no intention of completing it, because its size was so great that extraordinary difficulties might be foreseen in having it cast all in one piece. And it is probable that many have formed this opinion from the result, since so many of his things have been left unfinished. However, we can readily believe that his great and extraordinary talents suffered a check from being too venturesome, and that the real cause was his endeavour to go on from excellence to excellence and from perfection to perfection. 'Thus the wish retarded the work', as our Petrarca says. In truth, those who have seen Leonardo's large clay model confess that they never beheld anything finer or more superb. It was preserved until the French came to Milan with King Louis of France, and broke it all to pieces. Thus a small wax model, considered perfect, was destroyed, as well as a book of the anatomy of horses, done by Leonardo.

He afterwards devoted even greater care to the study of the anatomy of men, aiding and being aided by Messer Marcantonio della Torre, a profound philosopher, who then professed at Padua and wrote upon the subject.[29] I have heard it said that he was one of the first who began to illustrate the science of medicine, by the learning of Galen, and to throw true light upon anatomy, up to that time involved in the thick darkness of ignorance. In this he was marvellously served by the genius, work and hands of Leonardo, who made a book about it with red chalk drawings outlined with the pen, in which he foreshortened and portrayed with the utmost diligence. He did the skeleton, adding all the nerves and muscles, the first attached to the bone, the others keeping it firm and the third moving, and in the various parts he wrote notes in curious characters, using his left hand, and writing from right to left, so that it cannot be read without practice, and only at a mirror.[30] A great part of the sheets of this anatomy is in the hands of Messer Francesco da Melzi, a nobleman of Milan, who was a lovely child in Leonardo's time, who was very fond of him, and being now a handsome and courteous old man, he treasures up these drawings with a portrait of Leonardo.[31] Whoever succeeds in reading

28. See plates 106 and VIII. The statue was not intended for Ludovico, but for his father, Francesco Sforza. The bronze horse is mentioned in Leonardo's famous letter to the Duke Ludovico, written probably in 1482: 'Again, the bronze horse may be taken in hand, which is to the immortal glory and eternal honour of the prince your father, of happy memory, and of the illustrious house of Sforza.' But the first sketches for this statue can be dated after 1485, and so it would seem that Leonardo did not begin this work immediately after his arrival in Milan.

The bronze horse was indeed planned to be of 'colossal size', about 24 feet high, twice as large as Verrocchio's *Colleoni*. According to Fra Luca Pacioli, Leonardo's friend, about 200,000 lb. of metal would have been required for the casting of the horse without the rider.

29. Marcantonio della Torre was professor of anatomy at the University of Padua and Pavia (1511); he died, when only thirty years old, in 1512. Leonardo's anatomical studies are in Windsor Castle (cf. Clark, pp. L–LIII. Richter II, 83). The earliest inventory of the Leonardo drawings in the Royal Collection confirms the collaboration therein of Marcantonio della Torre (Richter II, 399). The first scientific appreciation

of Leonardo's anatomical researches came from William Hunter, *Two introductory Lectures to his last course of anatomical lectures*, London, 1784. (See Prof. William Wright, in *Burlington Magazine*, May, 1919.) The best introduction to Leonardo's anatomical studies, is for English readers, J. Playfair McMurrich's *Leonardo da Vinci, the Anatomist*, Baltimore, 1930. See also Elmer Belt, *Leonardo the Anatomist*, Lawrence, Kansas, 1955.

30. As Leonardo was left-handed (which is also confirmed by two of his contemporaries, Luca Pacioli and Sabba da Castiglione) he shaded his drawings from left to right.

31. Francesco Melzi, a nobleman of Milan, born 1493, died in his villa at Vaprio d'Adda near Milan in 1570. He was a pupil and friend of Leonardo. He stayed with him in Rome (1513–16), and afterwards accompanied him to France. He was the executor of Leonardo's Will, and the Master bequeathed to him his library, his manuscripts, his instruments, some money, and even his clothes. In the Ambrosiana at Milan there are several drawings by Melzi; the 'Vertumnus and Pomona', in the Berlin Museum, the 'Columbine', in the Leningrad Hermitage, and some other paintings are attributed to him.

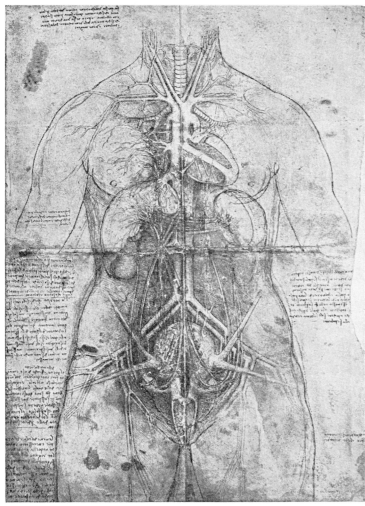

Leonardo: Anatomical study, pen and ink drawing over black chalk, c. 1513.
Windsor Castle, Royal Library (No. 12281).

these notes of Leonardo will be amazed to find how well that divine spirit has reasoned of the arts, the muscles, the nerves and veins, with the greatest diligence in all things. N.N.,[32] a painter of Milan, also possesses some writings of Leonardo, written in the same way, which treat of painting and of the methods of design and colour. Not long ago he came to Florence to see me, wishing to have the work printed. He afterwards went to Rome to put it in hand, but I do not know with what result.[33]

To return to Leonardo's works. When Leonardo was at Milan the King of France came there and desired him to do something curious; accordingly he made a lion whose chest opened after he had walked a few steps, discovering himself to be full of lilies.[34] While at Milan Leonardo took Salai[35] of that city as his pupil. This was a graceful and beautiful youth with fine curly hair, in which Leonardo greatly delighted. He taught him many things in art, and some works which are attributed in Milan to Salai were retouched by Leonardo.[36]

HE RETURNED to Florence,[37] where he found that the Servite friars had allotted to Filippino the picture of the high altar of the Annunziata. At this Leonardo declared that he should like to have done

32. Vasari does not give the owner's name. As the manuscript is not mentioned at all in the first edition of his *Vite*, he can only have seen it between 1551 and 1567. (The Milanese painter N.N. was either Lomazzo, or Aurelio Luini.)

33. The first printed edition was published in 1651 by Raphael du Fresne in Paris. The first English translation was issued (anonymously) in 1721, London. But the *Trattato della Pittura* is a mere compilation by some disciple. For Leonardo's Manuscripts, see Bibliography, p. 188.

34. An automaton, such as had been constructed ever since ancient times. Vasari's story is confirmed by Lomazzo (*Trattato dell'arte*, Milan, 1585, p. 106; and *Idea del tempio*, Milan, 1590, p. 17). Lomazzo states that he heard from Francesco Melzi that this lion was made for Francis the First. Similar sketches may be found on a sheet (fol. 179 recto) of the *Codice Atlantico* (published by Müller-Walde, *Prussian*

Jahrbuch, 1898, p. 233). Lomazzo was also told that Leonardo constructed artificial birds which flew through the air. (Similar automatons were made by the Emperor Charles the Fifth on his retirement to a monastery.)

35. Giacomo Salai came to live with Leonardo as a boy of ten, on the 22nd July, 1490. He was obviously a child of bad character—Leonardo called him 'thief, liar, glutton'. But the Master kept him for twenty-five years, gave him expensive presents, including a cloak of silver brocade, trimmed with green velvet, and a pair of rose-coloured tights; nor did he forget him in his Will. Emil Möller (*Salai und Leonardo*, in the *Vienna Jahrbuch, NF II*, 1928, p. 139 et seq.) attributed a number of beautiful paintings to Salai, also our Plate 19.

36. A letter from the White Friar, Pietro da Novellara, to Isabella d'Este, 1501, states that Leonardo corrected and retouched the paintings of his pupils. (See here p. 37.)

37. April 1500.

a similar thing. Filippino heard this, and being very courteous, he withdrew. The friars, wishing Leonardo to paint it, brought him to their house, paying all his expenses and those of his household. He kept them like this for a long time, but never began anything. At length he drew a cartoon of the Virgin and St Anne with a Christ, which not only filled every artist with wonder, but, when it was finished and set up in the room, men and women, young and old, flocked to see it for two days, as if it had been a festival, and they marvelled exceedingly.[38] The face of the Virgin displays all the simplicity and beauty which can shed grace on the Mother of God, showing the modesty and humility of a Virgin contentedly happy in seeing the beauty of her Son, whom she tenderly holds in her lap. As she regards Him, the little St John at her feet caresses a lamb, while St Anne smiles in her great joy at seeing her earthly progeny become divine, a conception worthy of the great intellect and genius of Leonardo. This cartoon, as will be said below, afterwards went to France.[39] He drew Ginevra, the daughter of Amerigo Benci, a beautiful portrait,[40] and then abandoned the work of the friars, who recalled Filippino, though he was prevented from finishing it by death.[41]

For Francesco del Giocondo Leonardo undertook the portrait of Mona Lisa, his wife, and left it incomplete after working at it for four years.[42] This work is now in the possession of Francis, King of France, at Fontainebleau. This head is an extraordinary example of how art can imitate Nature, because here we have all the details painted with great subtlety. The eyes possess that moist lustre which is constantly seen in life, and about them are those livid reds and veins which cannot be rendered without the utmost delicacy. The brows could not be more natural for the way in which the hairs issue from the skin, here thick and there scanty, following the pores of the skin. The nose possesses the fine nostrils, rosy and tender, as seen in life. The opening of the mouth, with its red lips, and the scarlet cheeks seem not colour but living flesh. To look closely at her throat you might imagine that the pulse was beating. Indeed, we may say that this was painted in a manner to cause the boldest artists to despair. Mona Lisa was very beautiful, and while Leonardo was drawing her portrait he engaged people to play and sing, and jesters to keep her merry, and remove that melancholy which painting usually gives to portraits. This figure of Leonardo's has such a pleasant smile that it seemed rather divine than human, and was considered marvellous, an exact copy of life.

The fame of this divine artist grew to such a pitch by the excellence of his works that all who delighted in the arts and the whole city wished him to leave some memorial, and they endeavoured to think of some noteworthy decorative work through which the State might be adorned and honoured by the genius, grace and judgment characteristic of his work. The great hall of the council was being rebuilt under the direction of Giuliano da San Gallo, Simone Pollaiuolo called Il Cronaca, Michelangelo Buonarroti and Baccio d'Agnolo, by the judgment and advice of the Gonfaloniere,[43] and leading

38. See Wilhelm R. Valentiner, *Über zwei Kompositionen Leonardos*, in the *Prussian Jahrbuch*, vol. 56, 1935, p. 213 f. This version of the St Anne was not carried beyond the stage of a cartoon (see note on plate 54). In 1503 the commission was transferred to Filippino Lippi, who painted a *Crucifixion* for the High-altar of S. Annunziata (now Uffizi, No. 8370), but died before he had finished it. Filippino's *Crucifixion* was finished by Perugino in 1505.

39. Suida, *Leonardo und sein Kreis*, p. 130. See Document XI.

40. Plates 23 and 88.

41. See footnote 38.

42. Plates 28–29.

43. Gonfaloniere di Giustizia, the 'standard-bearer of justice', the highest Florentine magistrate. In the *Life of Cronaca* Vasari says: 'At the same time it was proposed to make the great hall of the Signoria at Florence for the council of Fra Girolamo Savonarola, the famous preacher [July, 1495]. Upon this a consultation was held with Leonardo da Vinci, Michelangelo Buonarroti, then a youth, Giuliano da San Gallo, Baccio d'Agnolo, and Simone Pollaiuolo, called Il Cronaca. . . . After many discussions it was agreed that the hall should be made as it always stood until its restoration in our own day.' If this statement of Vasari's is correct, Leonardo was for some time in Florence before he started the work on the *Last Supper* in Milan.

citizens, as will be related at greater length in another place, and being finished with great speed, it was ordained by public decree that Leonardo should be employed to paint some fine work. Thus the hall was allotted to him by Piero Soderini, then Gonfaloniere of Justice. Leonardo began by drawing a cartoon at the hall of the Pope,[44] a place in Santa Maria Novella, containing the story of Niccolò Piccinino, captain of Duke Filippo of Milan.[45] Here he designed a group of horsemen fighting for a standard, a masterly work on account of his treatment of the fight, displaying the wrath, anger and vindictiveness of men and horses; two of the latter, with their front legs involved, are waging war with their teeth no less fiercely than their riders are fighting for the standard. One soldier, putting his horse to the gallop, has turned round and grasping the staff of the standard, is endeavouring by main force to wrench it from the hands of four others, while two are defending it, trying to cut the staff with their swords; an old soldier in a red cap has a hand on the staff, as he cries out, and holds a scimitar in the other and threatens to cut off both hands of the two, who are grinding their teeth and making every effort to defend their banner. On the ground, between the legs of the horses, are two fore-shortened figures who are fighting together, while a soldier lying prone has another over him who is raising his arm as high as he can to run his dagger with his utmost strength into his adversary's throat; the latter, whose legs and arms are helpless, does what he can to escape death. The manifold designs Leonardo made for the costumes of his soldiers defy description, not to speak of the scimitars and other ornaments, and his incredible mastery of form and line in dealing with horses, which he made better than any other master, with their powerful muscles and graceful beauty. It is said that for designing the cartoon he made an ingenious scaffolding which rose higher when pressed together and broadened out when lowered. Thinking that he could paint on the wall in oils, he made a mixture so thick for laying on the wall that when he continued his painting it began to run and spoil what had been begun, so that in a short time he was forced to abandon it.[46]

Leonardo had a high spirit and was most generous in every action. It is said that when he went to the bank for the monthly provision that he used to receive from Piero Soderini, the cashier wanted to give him some rolls of farthings, but he would not take them, saying that he was not a painter for farthings. Learning that Piero Soderini accused him of deceiving him and that murmurs rose against him, Leonardo with the help of his friends collected the money and took it back, but Piero would not accept it.

He went to Rome[47] with Duke Giuliano de' Medici on the election of Leo X, who studied philosophy and especially alchemy. On the way he made a paste with wax and constructed hollow animals which flew in the air when blown up, but fell when the wind ceased. On a curious lizard found by the vine-dresser of Belvedere he fastened scales taken from other lizards, dipped in quicksilver, which trembled as it moved, and after giving it eyes, a horn and a beard, he tamed it and kept it in a box. All the friends to whom he showed it ran away terrified. He would often dry and clean the guts of a bullock and make them so small that they might be held in the palm of the hand. In another room he kept a pair of smith's bellows, and with these he would blow out one of the guts until it filled the room, which was a large one, forcing anyone there to take refuge in a corner. The fact that it

44. *Sala del Papa* – thus called because this part of the Monastery was the abode of different Popes during the 15th and 16th centuries.

45. The Battle of Anghiari, 29th June, 1440; a victory of the Florentines over a Milanese army. See plates 108–110.

46. The original cartoon, on which Leonardo worked from October 1503 till February 1505, is lost, as also is the mural which had to give way to one of Vasari's murals when the room was redecorated from 1558 onward.

47. 24th September, 1513; in August 1516 he was still there.

had occupied such a little space at first only added to the wonder. He perpetrated many such follies, studied mirrors and made curious experiments to find oil for painting and varnish to preserve the work done.

At this time he did a small picture for Messer Baldassare Turini of Pescia, the Datary of Pope Leo, of the Virgin and Child, with infinite diligence and art.[48] But today it is much spoiled either by neglect or because of his numerous fanciful mixtures of ground and colouring. In another little picture he represented a boy, marvellously beautiful and graceful, both works being now at Pescia in the possession of Messer Giulio Turini.[49]

It is said that, on being commissioned by the Pope to do a work, he straightway began to distil oil and herbs to make the varnish, which induced Pope Leo to say: 'This man will never do anything, for he begins to think of the end before the beginning!'

There was no love lost between Leonardo and Michelangelo Buonarroti, so that the latter left Florence owing to their rivalry, Duke Giuliano excusing him by saying that he was summoned by the Pope to do the façade of San Lorenzo.[50] When Leonardo heard this, he left for France, where the king had heard of his works and wanted him to do the cartoon of St Anne in colours.[51] But Leonardo, as was his wont, gave him nothing but words for a long time. At length, having become old, he lay sick for many months, and seeing himself near death, he desired to occupy himself with the truths of the Catholic Faith and the holy Christian religion. Then, having confessed and shown his penitence with much lamentation, he devoutly took the Sacrament, leaving his bed, supported by his friends and servants, as he could not stand. The king arriving, for he would often pay him friendly visits, he sat up in bed from respect, and related the circumstances of his sickness, showing how greatly he had offended God and man in not having worked in his art as he ought. He was then seized with a paroxysm, the harbinger of death, so that the king rose and took his head to assist him and show him favour as well as to alleviate the pain. Leonardo's divine spirit, then recognizing that he could not enjoy a greater honour, expired in the king's arms, at the age of seventy-five.[52]

The loss of Leonardo caused exceptional grief to those who had known him, because there never was a man who did so much honour to painting. By the splendour of his magnificent countenance he comforted every sad soul, and his eloquence could turn men to either side of a question. His personal strength was prodigious, and with his right hand he could bend the clapper of a knocker or a horse-shoe as if they had been of lead. His liberality warmed the hearts of all his friends, both rich and poor, if they possessed talent and ability. His presence adorned and honoured the most wretched and bare apartment. Thus Florence received a great gift in the birth of Leonardo, and its loss in his death was immeasurable.

To the art of painting in oil he added a certain mode of deepening the shadows, by which the moderns have imparted great vigour and relief to their figures. He proved his powers in statuary in three figures in bronze over the door of San Giovanni on the north side. They were executed by

48. Lost.

49. Probably the Infant Jesus. The picture is lost; Rio thought that it was burnt in Whitehall. (See also the note on plate 7, p. 152.)

50. Michelangelo worked on the façade of San Lorenzo from 1516 to 1520 in Florence and made during this period only occasional visits to Rome. By the end of 1516, or perhaps in Spring 1517, Leonardo left for France.

51. See the note on Plate 68, painted about seven years earlier in Milan. But what the king probably wanted was a painting after the St Anne cartoon of 1501, which at that time was already in France. (See p. 20.)

52. Leonardo died on May 2nd, 1519, when sixty-seven years old. A letter from Francesco Melzi from Amboise, dated June 1st, 1519, to Leonardo's brothers, does not mention the King, who, on the day of Leonardo's death, was not in Amboise, but with the Court at St. Germain-en-Laye.

Giovan Francesco Rustici, but under Leonardo's direction, and are the finest casts for design and general perfection that have as yet been seen in modern times.[53]

To Leonardo we owe a greater perfection in the anatomy of the horse, and the anatomy of man. Thus, by his many surpassing gifts, although he laboured far more by words than by his deeds, his name and fame will never be extinguished.[54]

Giovan Antonio Boltraffio of Milan was a pupil of Leonardo, and a very skilful and intelligent man, who in 1500 painted a panel in oils in the church of the Misericordia, outside Bologna, with the Virgin and Child, St John the Baptist, and a nude St Sebastian, including a portrait of the donor kneeling.[55] To this fine work he signed his name, adding that he was a pupil of Leonardo. He did other works at Milan and elsewhere, but the one I have just referred to is the best. Marco Uggioni,[56] another pupil, painted the Death of the Virgin and the Marriage of Cana in Galilee in Santa Maria della Pace.[57]

53. See the illustrations p. 180 and p. 181.

54. Here follows in the original text an epigram by Messer Giovan Battista Strozzi in praise of Leonardo: 'Vince costo pur solo/Tutti altri, vince Fidia, vince Apelle/E tutto il lor vittorioso stuolo.' This play upon words – vincere, to vanquish, and Vinci – cannot be translated into English. The meaning of the epigram is roughly: 'Single-handed he vanquished all the others, Phidias, Apelles, and their whole victorious troop.'

55. Born 1467, died 1516. The picture, mentioned by Vasari, is now in the Louvre, No. 1169; painted in 1500, for the Casio family. Two kneeling donors, Giacomo and Giro-lamo Casio, are represented in this picture. According to an old tradition (Baldinucci), Leonardo himself helped with the painting. In the National Gallery, London, there are a Profile of a Man and a Madonna by Boltraffio's hand.

56. Marco d'Oggiono (or De Uglono), born about 1477 at Oggiono near Milan; worked in Leonardo's workshop from about 1490 to 1499; died in Milan about 1530. The copy he made of Leonardo's 'Last Supper', now at The Royal Academy, London, is well known. The National Gallery, London (No. 1149) owns one of his Madonnas. (See W. Suida, Marco d'Oggiono, in Raccolta Vinciana, 1939, pp. 127–155.)

57. The two pictures from Santa Maria della Pace in Milan are now in the Brera, Milan; Nos. 79 and 81.

Portrait of the Florentine poet *Bernardo Bellinzone*, engaged at the Court of
Ludovico Sforza. Woodcut, based (according to Amoretti and Kristeller)
on a drawing by Leonardo. From Bellinzone's *Rime*, Milan 1493.

ADDITIONAL REFERENCES CONCERNING
LEONARDO DA VINCI
TAKEN FROM SIX OTHER 'VITE' BY VASARI · 1568

In the 'Life of Giorgione':

Having seen and greatly admired some things of Leonardo, richly toned and exceedingly dark, as has been said, Giorgione made them his model, and imitated them carefully in painting in oil.[58]

58. *'Exceedingly dark' connects Giorgione's first style with Leonardo's 'chiaroscuro', mentioned in his Life by Vasari (p. 15). Leonardo passed through Venice in 1500 and perhaps also in 1503 and 1506. 'But in 1507', says Vasari in the Life of Titian, 'arose Giorgione, who began to give his works more tone and relief, with better style'. How far the young Giorgione made him his model can be seen from his 'Christ carrying the Cross' (cf. note on plate 88), but still more from his 'Judith' in the Hermitage, which seems to me more Leonardesque than all the copies of the standing 'Leda' attributed to the School of Leonardo. Leonardo's knot pattern is used as an ornament on the dress of the Brocardo portrait by Giorgione in the Budapest Museum.*

In the 'Life of Andrea del Verrocchio':

There are some of Andrea's drawings in our possession . . . among them being some female heads so beautiful and with such charming hair that Leonardo was always imitating them. [See also the illustration on p. 25.] We also own two [drawings of] horses, squared and measured proportions, by which method they can be increased to a large scale without error.[59]

59. *Some of Verrocchio's drawings are sometimes attributed to Leonardo; e.g. the famous silverpoint drawing in Dresden, connected with the Pistoia altar-piece (reproduced, Berenson, No. 672, Fig. 139); a Madonna head in Paris (repr. Suida, plate 4); and others. One of Verrocchio's drawings of a horse 'with measures and proportions' is in the Metropolitan Museum, New York (at one time attributed to Leonardo by Sirén).*

In the 'Life of Piero di Cosimo':

He practised painting in oil after seeing some things by Leonardo toned and finished with the extreme diligence characteristic of that Master when he wished to display his art. This method pleased Piero, and he strove to imitate it, though he was a long way behind Leonardo.[60]

60. *Piero di Cosimo borrowed from Leonardo's Madonna drawings. Suida contends that his painting 'Perseus and Andromeda' in the Florence Uffizi (No. 1536) is taken from a drawing by Leonardo, or even executed with his help. He was not the first to express this opinion. In the inventory of the Uffizi Gallery, made in 1580, the picture is mentioned as drawn by Leonardo and coloured by Piero di Cosimo. Morelli (Galleries in Rome, English ed., 1892, p. 120) said 'Several of the heads have not*

only Leonardo's sfumato, but recall the Gioconda in expression'. And Maud Cruttwell (A Guide to the Paintings in the Florentine Galleries, 1907, p. 98): 'The female crouched in the foreground with a strange-shaped musical instrument is worthy of Leonardo, who it is not impossible may have designed it.'

In the Chapter on 'Lombard Artists':

In the Mint at Milan there is a copy of a portrait of a smiling woman by Leonardo done by Fra Girolamo [Monsignori] and of a young St John the Baptist, very well imitated.[61]

61. *This passage from Vasari shows that even in the middle of the 16th century it was not easy to distinguish Leonardo's work from imitations.*

In the 'Life of Raphael':

In his childhood Raphael imitated the style of Pietro Perugino, his master, improving it greatly in design, colouring and invention. But in riper years he perceived that this was too far from the truth. For he saw the works of Leonardo da Vinci, who had no equal in the expression which he gave to his heads of women and children, while in the grace and movement of his figures he surpassed all other artists; this filled Raphael with wonder and amazement. As Leonardo's style pleased him more than any he had ever seen, he set to work to study it, and gradually and painfully abandoning the manner of Pietro, he sought as far as possible to imitate Leonardo; and, though some consider him superior in sweetness, and in a certain natural facility, yet he never excelled that wonderful ground-work of ideas and that grandeur of art, in which few have equalled Leonardo. Raphael, however, approached him more closely than any other painter, especially in grace of colouring.[62]

62. *How much Raphael borrowed from Leonardo cannot be told in a single note. He was indebted to Leonardo's Anghiari cartoon, his standing Leda with the Swan, and his Mona Lisa. From a drawing of the Mona Lisa, Raphael painted his portrait of Maddalena Doni. Raphael's 'Family with the Lamb' is copied freely from Leonardo's first St Anne cartoon; his Madonna with the Flower, his Esterházy Madonna, his Madonna Alba, in fact most of his Madonna paintings are either directly derived from drawings by Leonardo, or are variations of them. It may sound paradoxical, but it seems that Leonardo had only two true disciples: Raphael and Dürer.*

Verrocchio: *Marble bust of a Lady holding primulas.* About 1475–78. (By Mackowsky, Suida, and others, attributed to Leonardo.)
Florence, Bargello.

Leonardo: *Madonna Benois*. About 1478–80. (At one time attributed to Lorenzo di Credi, or Sogliani.)
Leningrad, Hermitage.

Verrocchio (and Lorenzo di Credi): *The Pistoia Altar-piece* ('*Madonna di Piazza*'). 1475–1486. Pistoia, Cathedral.
(Cf. Plate I, p. 169.)

In the '*Life of Lorenzo di Credi*':
His ambition rising, Lorenzo went to Andrea del
Verrocchio, whose whim was then painting. Under this
master he had as friends and companions, although
rivals, Pietro Perugino and Leonardo da Vinci, both
diligently studying painting. Leonardo's style greatly
delighted Lorenzo, who succeeded better than any
others in imitating his polish and finish.
Lorenzo's first work was a circular painting (tondo)
of a Madonna sent to the King of Spain, the design
being taken from one of Andrea del Verrocchio's. He
then did a far better picture, copied from one by
Leonardo da Vinci, and also sent to Spain. It could not
be distinguished from the original.[63]

63. *Some works of Lorenzo di Credi were sometimes ascribed to Leonardo,
and vice versa. Thus, for instance, the Liechtenstein portrait (plate 23),
the Benois Madonna (p. 26), the Uffizi Annunciation (plate 59) were
once attributed to Credi. On the other hand, the predella of the Pistoia
altar-piece, the Louvre Annunciation, and 'San Donato of Arezzo and
the Tax Collector' in the Worcester Art Museum, Mass., were thought
to be by Leonardo (Appendix, plate I). The Pistoia altar-piece was produced in Verrocchio's workshop, 1475–1486; it was begun by the Master
himself but finished by Credi. Leonardo had perhaps some share in it. About
eight years older than Credi, Leonardo was not only his co-pupil in
Verrocchio's workshop but his teacher as well.*

A NOTE ON
THE EARLIEST BIOGRAPHIES OF LEONARDO DA VINCI
PAOLO GIOVIO – ANONIMO GADDIANO – LIBRO DI ANTONIO BILLI –
AND SABBA DA CASTIGLIONE'S RICORDI

THE following two short accounts cannot compare in literary value with Vasari's pages on Leonardo; but they are earlier.

Paolo Giovio was born in 1483 at Como, not far from Milan, where at that time Leonardo lived; he studied at Padua and then practised surgery at Milan. In 1517 he went to Rome; but while doctor to Pope Leo X, he spent most of his time reading the classics and preparing his *Historia sui temporis* in forty-five parts (which was printed, 1548–52, in two folio volumes at Florence). After Giovio had lost all his books and papers during the sack of Rome in 1527, Pope Clement VII made him bishop of Nocera. He took great interest in the art of portraiture, and collected a large number of portraits of famous men and women. The 'Museum Jovianum' in Giovio's villa on the Lake of Como was a kind of National Portrait Gallery; there were so many portraits that it took Cristoforo dell' Altissimo twelve years to paint a selection of 240 copies for Grand Duke Cosimo I. Giovio died at Florence in 1552.

Giovio's three eulogies on famous men and women, of which the short Leonardo biography forms a part of the unfinished third eulogy, were written on the island of Ischia, where the author had retired for a short time after the sack of Rome in 1527. (Paolo Giovio, *De viris illustribus*, in Tiraboschi's *Storia della letteratura italiana*, Modena, 1781, vol. IX, p. 290 f.)

The translation from the Latin of Giovio's Leonardo biography is by J. P. Richter and was first printed in his edition of *The Literary Works of Leonardo da Vinci*, vol. I, p. 3, London, 1939. (I have added a few footnotes.)

The second biography is about fifteen years later and by an anonymous writer, called *Anonimo Gaddiano*, or *Magliabecchiano*. (The manuscript, now in the Biblioteca Nazionale at Florence, belonged before to the Biblioteca Gaddiana, and after that to the Biblioteca Magliabec-chiana.) The English translation of this biography is by Kate T. Steinitz and Ebria Feinblatt, and was first published in the Leonardo Exhibition Catalogue of the Los Angeles County Museum, 1949. (The footnotes are my own.)

The Anonimo made use of a page on Leonardo in the '*Book of Antonio Billi*', which was written in about 1518. Those thirty lines contain only one point of interest, namely the statement that Leonardo was cheated over the linseed oil which he used in painting the *Anghiari Battle*, and that this was responsible for the fast decay of the mural. ('*Dettesi la colpa, che lui fu ingannato nello olio del seme del lino, che gli fu falsato.*') Billi also says: 'Not many things did Leonardo in colour, because never and with nothing, not even the most beautiful he did, he was satisfied: and for this reason there are so very few paintings by him, as his great knowledge about errors in work prohibited him from working.' As to the rest, Billi gives a short list of Leonardo's works in the following order: The portrait of Ginevra de' Benci – A panel of the Madonna – A St John – An altar-piece which Ludovico Moro sent to the German Emperor – The Last Supper – The clay model of the huge Equestrian Monument for Francesco Sforza – A large number of marvellous drawings: a Saint Anne, that went to France; and the cartoon of the Anghiari Battle. As the author of the 'Book of Antonio Billi' mentions the *St Anne* amongst the drawings, he apparently means a cartoon, and not a painting (see also p. 31).

These three short biographies are earlier than Vasari's *Vita di Leonardo*; so are also the *Ricordi* by Sabba da Castiglione (Bologna 1546). Castiglione wrote as an old man who had known Leonardo; he mentions *The Last Supper*, and the Sforza monument, on which, he says, Leonardo worked for sixteen years; he also describes how the model was destroyed; he states that Leonardo was left-handed; and he thinks that Leonardo finished so very few works because he devoted most of his time to Architecture, Geometry and Anatomy.

I

THE LIFE OF LEONARDO DA VINCI
BY PAOLO GIOVIO

Leonardo, born at Vinci, an insignificant hamlet in Tuscany, has added great lustre to the art of painting. He established that all proper practice of this art should be preceded by a training in the sciences and the liberal arts which he regarded as indispensable and subordinate to painting. He placed modelling as a means of rendering figures in relief on a flat surface before other processes done with the brush. The science of optics was to him of paramount importance and on it he founded the principles of the distribution of light and shade down to the most minute details. In order that he might be able to paint the various joints and muscles as they bend and stretch according to the laws of nature, he dissected in medical schools the corpses of criminals, indifferent to this inhuman and nauseating work. He then tabulated with extreme accuracy all the different parts down to the smallest veins and the composition of the bones, in order that this work on which he had spent so many years should be published from copper engravings for the benefit of art. But while he was thus spending his time in the close research of subordinate branches of his art he carried only very few works to completion; for owing to his masterly facility and the fastidiousness of his nature, he discarded works he had already begun. However, the wall painting at Milan of Christ at Supper with His Disciples is greatly admired.[1] It is said that when King Louis saw it he coveted it so much that he inquired anxiously from those standing around him whether it could be detached from the wall and transported forthwith to France, although this would have destroyed the famous refectory. There is also the picture of the infant Christ playing with His mother, the Virgin, and His grandmother, Anne, which King Francis of France bought and placed in his chapel.[2] Moreover, there remains the painting of the battle and victory over the Pisans[3] in the Council Chamber at Florence which was extraordinarily magnificent but came to an untimely end owing to the defective plaster which persistently rejected the colours ground in walnut oil. It seems as if the very natural regret caused by this unexpected injury and interruption of the work was instrumental in making it famous. For Lodovico Sforza he made also a clay model of a colossal horse to be cast in bronze, on which was to be seated the figure of the famous condottiere Francesco, Lodovico's father.[4] The vehement life-like action of this horse as if panting is amazing, not less so the sculptor's skill and his consummate knowledge of nature. His charm of disposition, his brilliancy and generosity were not less than the beauty of his appearance. His genius for invention was astounding, and he was the arbiter of all questions relating to beauty and elegance, especially in pageantry. He sang beautifully to his own accompaniment on the *lira* to the delight of the entire court. He died in France at the age of sixty-seven[5] to the grief of his friends, which loss was all the greater for among the great crowd of young men who contributed to the success of his studio he left no disciple of outstanding fame.

1. Plate 73.
2. Did Paolo Giovio mean the late painting, now in the Louvre? (See note on Plate 68, p. 168.) Or did he mean the cartoon of 1501? (See pp. 19–20.) Or did he mean a painting after this cartoon? (See note 52 on p. 22.)
3. Plate 108 (a copy of the lost cartoon). Leonardo's *Battle of Anghiari* represented a victory of the Florentines over the Milanese, and not, as Giovio says, over the Pisans. (It was Michelangelo's *Battle of Cascina* that gave a scene from the Pisan war.)

4. See note on plate 106.

5. This is correct. The Anonimo Gaddiano and Vasari are giving wrongly Leonardo's age at the time of his death.

LEONARDO DA VINCI
BY THE ANONIMO GADDIANO
ALSO CALLED ANONIMO MAGLIABECCHIANO

A Florentine citizen who, although he was the illegitimate son of Ser Piero da Vinci, was born of good blood on his mother's side. He was so unusual and many-sided that nature seemed to have produced a miracle in him, not only in the beauty of his person, but in the many gifts with which she endowed him and which he fully mastered. Greatly talented in mathematics, he was no less so in the science of perspective, while in the field of sculpture and design he far surpassed all others. He made many excellent inventions, but because it was hard for him to be satisfied with his work we find but few paintings from his hand. An eloquent speaker, he was an exquisite musician on the *lira* and taught the singer Atalante Migliorotti.[6] He was delightfully inventive, and was most skilful in lifting weights, in building waterworks and other imaginative constructions, nor did his mind ever come to rest, but dwelt always with ingenuity on the creation of new inventions.

As a young man he was with Lorenzo de' Medici the Magnificent, and with his support he worked in the gardens of his palace in San Marco in Florence. When he was thirty years of age it is said that the Magnificent sent him to the Duke of Milan to present, with Atalante Migliorotti, the gift of a *lira*,[7] which the latter could play with rare execution. Later he returned to Florence where he remained for some time, but then, either because of some kind of indignation or other causes, while working in the hall of the Council of the Signoria,[8] he left and went back to Milan where he served the Duke for a few years. Afterwards he was with Cesare Borgia, the Duke Valentino, and then also in France in several places, before returning to Milan.[9] While preparing to cast his equestrian monument in bronze a revolution in the state brought him back to Florence, where for six months he stayed in the house of Giovanni Francesco Rustici, sculptor of the via Martelli.[10] Once more he returned to Milan, and then finally went to France in the service of the king, Francis I. He took with him enough of his drawings, leaving some again in the Hospital of Santa Maria Nuova, Florence, together with other household goods, and the greater part of a cartoon in the Council Hall, of which the design of a group of horses can be seen today in the Palace.[11] He died near Amboise, a French city, at the age of seventy-two,[12] in a place called Cloux, which he had made his home. He left in his testament everything to Messer Francesco da Melzi, a nobleman of Milan, all his money and clothes, books, writings, drawings, instruments, and his treatises on painting, art and his industriousness, and whatever else could be found, and made him executor of his will. To his servant Battista Villani he left half of his garden on the outskirts of Milan, and the other half to Salai, his pupil. He left four hundred ducats to his brothers, depositing the sum in the Hospital of Santa Maria Nuova in Florence, but after his death only three hundred ducats were found.

6. Atalante was famous as a maker of musical instruments, and also as an actor and a singing master. In 1490 he became the leading singer of the Ducal Festival Hall at Mantua. In 1513 he was in Rome where Leonardo must have met him again.

7. The *lira da braccio*, with five to ten playing strings and two humming strings (also called drone strings), played with a bow; described in G. M. Lanfranco's *Scintille di Musica*, Brescia, 1533, p. 137.

8. Working on the '*Battle of Anghiari*', 1503–06.

9. Leonardo was in the service of Cesare Borgia in 1502–03, for about eight months. He returned to Milan in 1506, where he served the King of France and his governor; a visit to France in the period 1503–06 is not known and is highly improbable.

10. See note on plate VI.

11. See note on plate 108.

12. Should read *sixty-seven*.

Among his pupils were Salai of Milan, Zoroastro of Peretola, Riccio Fiorentino of the Porta della Croce, Ferrando the Spaniard, who worked with him in the Hall of the Signoria Palace.[13]

In Florence he painted the portrait of Ginevra d'Amerigho Benci from nature, a work which was so finished that it seemed not a portrait but Ginevra herself.[14]

He made a panel of Our Lady, a most excellent work.

He also painted a Saint John.[15]

And again a Leda.[16] He painted Adam and Eve in water colour, today in the house of Messer Ottaviano de' Medici.

He made the portrait from nature of Piero Francesco del Giocondo.[17]

He painted . . . a head of Medusa with a wonderful and unique collection of serpents; today it is in the chamber of the most Illustrious and Excellent Signor Duke Cosimo de' Medici.

He was commissioned to paint in the great Council Hall of the Palace in Florence a cartoon of the battle of Florentines, during the time at Anghiari when they attacked Niccholo Piccin[in]o, the captain of Duke Filippo of Milan, and he began the work in that place as can be seen there today; and with varnish. . . .

He undertook to paint a panel in the same Palace, which was later finished after his design by Filippo di Fra Filippo.[18]

He painted an altar panel for Signor (the Duke) Lodovico of Milan, which those who have seen it declare to be the most beautiful and unusual work to be found in painting, and which the afore-mentioned lord sent . . . to the Emperor.

He also painted in Milan a Last Supper, a most excellent work.[19]

Again in Milan he likewise made a horse of immense grandeur, bearing upon it the Duke Francesco Sforza, a most beautiful work which was to be cast in bronze, a feat universally judged impossible, especially since he said he desired to cast it all in one piece; this work was never realized.[20]

He made innumerable drawings, all marvellous things, and among them a Madonna and a Saint Anne,[21] which went to France, and anatomical studies which he drew in the Hospital of Santa Maria Nuova in Florence.

13. About Ferrando de Llanos see Elizabeth du Gué Trapier, *Luis Morales and the Leonardesque influences in Spain*, New York, 1953; about the other pupils see W. Suida, *Leonardo und sein Kreis*, Munich, 1929, p. 167 f. and p. 250 f.

14. See note on plate 23.

15. This St John and the panel of Our Lady, both probably painted in Florence, are also mentioned in the *Libro di Antonio Billi* (see p. 28). The *St John* was perhaps a version of the *Angel of the Annunciation*, illustrated here on p. 15.

16. The manuscript reads here, according to Carl Frey, p. 369: 'Et anchora [una Leda] dipinse Adamo et Eva d'aquarello.' The two words put here in square brackets are crossed out in the manuscript. – See plate 37.

17. Carl Frey, p. 372, suspects here a slip of the pen and suggests: 'Ritrasse dal naturale moglie di Francesco del Giocondo'. This would mean the portrait of Mona Lisa (plate 28).

18. Contract, dated 1478, for the Chapel of San Bernardino in the Palazzo Vecchio. Valentiner accepted the statement of the Anonimo as correct and identified the San Bernardino altar-piece with Filippino Lippi's picture of a Madonna with four saints, dated February 20th, 1485 (now Uffizi No. 1568). – Another altar-piece was ordered first from Leonardo, and then from Filippino Lippi, by the monks of San Donato a Scopeto outside Florence. Leonardo received his commission in 1481 and left the picture unfinished (plate 49). Fifteen years later the order was transferred to Filippino Lippi (*Adoration of the Kings*, dated 1496, now Uffizi No. 1257). – There was a third encounter of the two artists, of which we know through Vasari (see footnote 38 on p. 20).

19. Plate 73.

20. See note on plate 111.

21. Probably the cartoon of 1501; see also note on plate 54.

THE ANONIMO GADDIANO

The following supplement to the biography is introduced by the words Dal Gav. *This is supposed to refer to Giovanni da Gavina, a Florentine painter and friend of Leonardo, who related it to the Anonimo Gaddiano. Carl Frey and J. Wilde, however, read* Dal Cav. *and explain it as Cavaliere Bandinelli.*

Leonardo da Vinci was a contemporary of Michelangelo, and from Pliny he took the recipe for the pigments with which he painted, but without fully understanding it. The first time he demonstrated it upon a wall in the Hall of the Pope, where he was working, he placed a great fire of burning coals in front of it, whereby through the heat the material would be dried and fixed. After that, desiring to put the work in the Hall (of the Council), it turned out that the fire dried and joined the lower part of the fresco, but was unable to reach the upper section, due to the great distance, and this part did not come together and the colours ran.

Beautiful in person and aspect, Leonardo was well-proportioned and graceful. He wore a rose-coloured cloak, which came only to his knees, although at the time long vestments were the custom. His beard came to the middle of his breast and was well-dressed and curled.

Leonardo, in the company of Giovanni da Gavina of Santa Trinita, passed the benches of the Palazzo Spini one day, where a group of gentlemen were disputing over a passage in Dante. They appealed to Leonardo to explain the lines to them. Exactly at this moment Michelangelo passed by and Leonardo replied to the questioners, 'Michelangelo will explain it to you'. Michelangelo responded with anger, since it seemed to him that Leonardo was making mock of him, 'You made a design for a horse to be cast in bronze, and, unable to cast it, have in your shame abandoned it'. And saying this, he turned his heels to them and left the street. And Leonardo remained at these words and blushed.

And to annoy Leonardo, Michelangelo called after him: 'And those Milanese idiots did believe in you!'

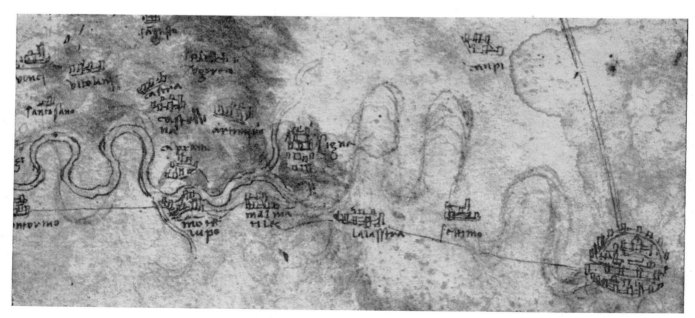

The country between Vinci and Florence. Pen and ink drawing by Leonardo da Vinci, c. 1503. Windsor Castle, Royal Library
No. 12685 r. detail: In the upper left corner *Vinci*, in the lower right corner *Florence*).

(32)

LETTERS AND OTHER DOCUMENTS

I. DRAFT OF A LETTER FROM LEONARDO TO LUDOVICO SFORZA, IN WHICH HE OFFERS HIS SERVICES AND STATES HIS ABILITIES; c. 1482.

Most Illustrious Lord, Having now sufficiently considered the specimens of all those who proclaim themselves skilled contrivers of instruments of war, and that the invention and operation of the said instruments are nothing different from those in common use: I shall endeavour, without prejudice to any one else, to explain myself to your Excellency, showing your Lordship my secrets, and then offering them to your best pleasure and approbation to work with effect at opportune moments on all those things which, in part, shall be briefly noted below.

(1) I have a sort of extremely light and strong bridges, adapted to be most easily carried, and with them you may pursue, and at any time flee from the enemy; and others, secure and indestructible by fire and battle, easy and convenient to lift and place. Also methods of burning and destroying those of the enemy.

(2) I know how, when a place is besieged, to take the water out of the trenches, and make endless variety of bridges and covered ways and ladders, and other machines pertaining to such expeditions.

(3) Item. If, by reason of the height of the banks, or the strength of the place, and its position, it is impossible, when besieging a place, to avail oneself of the plan of bombardment, I have methods for destroying every turret or other fortress, unless it were founded on a rock, &c.

(4) Again, I have kinds of mortars, most convenient and easy to carry; and with these I can fling small stones almost resembling a storm; and with the smoke of these cause great terror to the enemy, to his great detriment and confusion.

(5) Item. I have means by secret and tortuous mines and ways, made without noise, to reach a designated [spot], even if it were needed to pass under a trench or a river.

(6) Item. I will make covered chariots, safe and unassailable, which, entering among the enemy with their artillery, there is no body of man so great but they would break them. And behind these, infantry could follow quite unhurt and without any hindrance.

(7) Item. In case of need I will make big guns, mortars, and light ordnance of fine and useful forms, out of the common type.

(8) Where the operation of bombardment might fail, I would contrive catapults, mangonels, *trabocchi*, and other machines of marvellous efficacy and not in common use. And in short, according to the variety of cases, I can contrive various and endless means of offence and defence.

(9) And if the fight should be at sea I have many kinds of machines most efficient for offence and defence; and vessels which will resist the attack of the largest guns and powder and fumes.

(10) In time of peace I believe I can give perfect satisfaction and to the equal of any other in architecture and the composition of buildings public and private; and in guiding water from one place to another.

Item. I can carry out sculpture in marble, bronze, or clay, and also I can do in painting whatever may be done, as well as any other, be he who he may.

Again, the bronze horse may be taken in hand, which is to be to the immortal glory and eternal honour of the prince your father of happy memory, and of the illustrious house of Sforza.

And if any of the above-named things seem to any one to be impossible or not feasible, I am most ready to make the experiment in your park, or in whatever place may please your Excellency – to whom I commend myself with the utmost humility, &c.

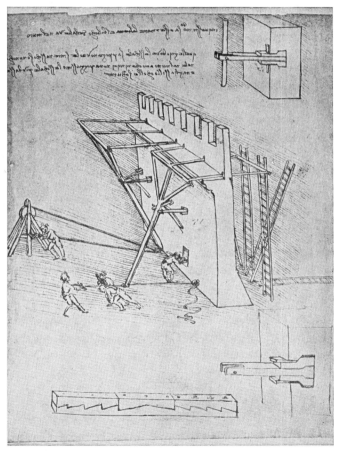

Device against storm ladders. Pen and ink drawing by Leonardo
(Codex Atlanticus, 49 v.–b).

II. A Letter from the Florentine Ambassador in Milan to his master, Lorenzo de' Medici, 22 July, 1489; concerning the Sforza Monument.

The Duke Ludovico is planning to erect a worthy monument to his father, and in accordance with his orders Leonardo has been asked to make a model in the form of a large horse (to be cast in bronze), ridden by the Duke Francesco in full armour. As His Highness has in mind something wonderful, the like of which has never been seen, he has directed me to write to you and ask if you will kindly send him one or two Florentine artists who specialize in this kind of work. For, although the Duke has given the commission to Leonardo, it seems to me that he is not confident that he will succeed.

III. From Leonardo's Note-books, concerning the Sforza Monument.

'On the 23rd of April, 1490 . . . I started the horse afresh.'

IV. From the draft of a letter by Leonardo to the Duke Ludovico Sforza, c. 1498.

. . . It vexes me greatly that having to earn my living has forced me to interrupt the work and to attend to small matters, instead of following up the work which your Lordship entrusted to me. But I hope in a short time to have earned so much that I may carry it out quietly to the satisfaction of your Excellency, to whom I commend myself; and if your Lordship thought that I had money, your Lordship was deceived, because I had to feed 6 men for 36 months, and have had only 50 ducats.

V. Ercole I d'Este, Duke of Ferrara, to his agent in Milan, 19 September, 1501; Concerning the model of the Sforza Monument.

Seeing that there exists at Milan a model of a horse, executed by a certain Messer Leonardo, a master very skilful in such matters, one which the Duke Ludovico always intended to have cast, we think that, if the use were granted us of this model, it would be a good and desirable thing to make a casting from it. Therefore, we wish you to go immediately to the most illustrious and reverend the Lord Cardinal of Rouen, and acquaint him with our desire, begging his reverend lordship, if he do not need the said model himself, to be so good as to make it over to us. We would not deprive him of anything that he holds valuable, yet we are persuaded that he cares but little for this work. You may add, like-wise, that this will be very agreeable to us for the reasons aforesaid; and that we would gladly be at pains to remove it, bearing in mind that the said model at Milan is, as you have told us, falling daily into decay, there being no care taken of it. If the very reverend lord will gratify us, as we hope, in this matter, we will send persons to bring the said model hither with all care and due precaution, so that it come by no hurt. Do not fail to employ all your good offices that our petition may be granted by his very reverend lordship, to whom we proffer our offers of service and our humble duty.

The Cardinal of Rouen was an uncle of the French governor of Milan. – A model of the equestrian monument was exhibited in 1493, on the occasion of the marriage of the Emperor Maximilian with Bianca Maria Sforza in Milan. When the French entered the town, the Gascon bowmen used this clay model as a target and 'destroyed' it, as Sabba da Castiglione and Vasari have recorded. But, as two years later the Duke of Ferrara asked for the model of the horse, we may assume that there existed a cast of it in plaster or wax.

VI. From the answer of Giovanni Valla, the agent of Ercole I d'Este, Milan, 24 December, 1501.

With reference to the model of the horse erected by Duke Ludovico, as far as he is concerned, his reverend lordship perfectly agrees to its removal; yet as his Majesty the King had himself seen the statue, his lord-ship dare not grant the Duke's request without pre-viously informing the King.

VII. The Duke, Ludovico Sforza, to his secretary Domino Marchesino Stanga; concerning the 'Last Supper'.

We have entrusted to you the carrying out of the matters mentioned on the enclosed list; and, although our orders were delivered to you by word of mouth, it shall add to our comfort that we set them down in these few words to inform you how extraordinary is our interest in their execution.

Ludovico Maria Sfortia

Milan, the 29th of June, 1497.

The 'memoriale' appended to this letter mentions twelve different matters, the greater portion referring to works of art. One of the points is:

'Item. Of Leonardo of Florence it is to be solicited that he finish the work in the Refettorio delle Gratie, when he must set to work upon the other front wall* thereof, which if he can do, the agreements previously signed by him respecting its completion within a given time will be cancelled.' (*See pl. 73, and Appendix plate II.)

VIII. Concerning the 'Last Supper'. From a tale by Matteo Bandello ('Novelle', Lucca 1554).

In Ludovico's time, some gentlemen living in Milan

Madonna with the laughing Child. Terracotta. About 1472–78. (Attributed to Leonardo by Carotti, Sirén, Valentiner, Middeldorf, Venturi, Heydenreich, and John Goldsmith Phillips.) London, Victoria and Albert Museum.

The Madonna with the Yarn-winder. Composed in 1501. (Attributed to Leonardo by Emil Möller, 1926, and by Cecil Gould, 1957.)
Drumlanrig Castle, Scotland, The Duke of Buccleuch.

were met one day in the monks' refectory of the convent delle Grazie, where with hushed voices they watched Leonardo da Vinci as he was finishing his marvellous picture of the *Last Supper*. The painter was well pleased that each should tell him what they thought of his work. He would often come to the convent at early dawn; and this I have seen him do myself. Hastily mounting the scaffolding, he worked diligently until the shades of evening compelled him to cease, never thinking to take food at all, so absorbed was he in his work. At other times he would remain there three or four days without touching his picture, only coming for a few hours to remain before it, with folded arms, gazing at his figures as if to criticize them himself. At mid-day, too, when the glare of a sun at its zenith has made barren all the streets of Milan, I have seen him hasten from the citadel, where he was modelling his colossal horse, without seeking the shade, by the shortest way to the convent, where he would add a touch or two and immediately return.

Matteo Bandello was a nephew of Vincenzo, the prior of the Dominican monastery of Santa Maria della Grazie. In 1495, when he was about fifteen, he came to Milan and was placed in the care of his uncle; two years later he became acquainted with Leonardo, who was then painting the 'Last Supper' in the refectory of the Church belonging to the monks whose prior was Bandello's uncle.

IX. LEONARDO IN VENICE. A LETTER FROM LORENZO GUSNASCO, MAKER OF MUSICAL INSTRUMENTS, TO ISABELLA D'ESTE.

Most illustrious Lady, I am sending you by this courier an excellent lute of walnut wood, made in the Spanish fashion, which seems to me to have the finest tone I ever heard. I have been ill and unable to finish the other lute . . .

Leonardo da Vinci, who is in Venice, has shewed to me a portrait of your Highness, which is in every way a most truthful likeness. Indeed it is so well executed that nothing could be better. This is all that I write by this post, and with the repeated assurance of my respect,

I beg to subscribe myself,
Your Highness's faithful servant,

Venice, 13th March, 1500   LORENZO DA PAVIA

Leonardo's portrait of Isabella d'Este is mentioned by Père Dan (Trésor des merveilles de Fontainebleau, 1642) as being in the collection of Francis the First, King of France.– Cf. plate 24.

X. FROM A LETTER OF ISABELLA D'ESTE, 27 MARCH, 1501, TO FRA PIETRO DA NOVELLARA; CONCERNING A MADONNA PAINTING AND A PORTRAIT.

Ascertain whether he is inclined to paint a picture for our studio. If he consents, we will leave the invention and the time to his decision. If he is reluctant, try at least to induce him to paint for us a small picture of the Madonna, pious and sweet, as is his style. And then ask him to send us a new sketch of our portrait. For his Highness, our consort, has given away the one he left for us here.

The 'studiolo' of the duchess was on the ground floor of the Castello di Corte at Mantua. For this studio Mantegna, Correggio, Perugino and Costa painted nine pictures. Leonardo did nothing. In 1504, however, he accepted the commission to paint an Infant Christ for Isabella (see note on plate 7, p. 152).

XI. A LETTER FROM FRA PIETRO DA NOVELLARA TO MARCHESA ISABELLA D'ESTE OF MANTUA, 3 (?) APRIL 1501; CONCERNING 'THE CARTOON OF ST ANNE'.

Leonardo's life is changeful and uncertain; it is thought that he lives only for the day. Since he has been in Florence, he has worked just on one cartoon, which represents an infant Christ of about one year, freeing himself almost out of his mother's arms and seizing a lamb and apparently about to embrace it. The mother half rising from the lap of St Anne is catching the child to draw it away from the lamb, that sacrificial animal which signifies the Passion. St Anne, just rising from her seat, as if she would wish to hinder her daughter from parting the Child from the lamb; which perhaps signifies the Church that would not wish the Passion of Christ to be hindered. The figures are life-size, but they fill only a small cartoon, because all are seated or bent, and each one is placed before the other, to the left. The sketch is not yet complete. He has done nothing else, except that he now and then lends a hand to one or another of the portraits which his two assistants are painting. He is entirely wrapped up in geometry and has no patience for painting.

Novellara describes a lost cartoon of St Anne. See the note on plate 54. Concerning his important remark on Leonardo's touching up portraits by his pupils, compare plate 27.

XII. A LETTER FROM FRA PIETRO DA NOVELLARA, TO MARCHESA ISABELLA D'ESTE OF MANTUA, 14 APRIL, 1501; CONCERNING 'THE MADONNA WITH THE YARN-WINDER'.

I have this week heard, through his pupil Salai and other of his friends, of Leonardo the artist's decision, which led me to visit him on the Wednesday of Passion Week in order to assure myself that it was true. In brief, his mathematical experiments have made painting so distasteful to him that he cannot even bear to take up a brush. However, I tried all I could, using first every art in order to get him to accede to your highness's wishes; and when I saw that he seemed well-disposed to place himself under obligation to your Eminence, I frankly told him everything, and we came to the following understanding, viz.: that, if he should be able to release himself from his engagement with the King of France without thereby forfeiting that monarch's goodwill (which he hoped might be managed in, at the most, a month's time), he would serve your Eminence in preference to any one else in the world. In any case, however, he will at once paint the portrait and forward it to your Eminence, as the small picture which he had to paint for one Robertet, a favourite of the King of France, is now finished. The little picture represents a Madonna seated, and at work with a spindle, while the Infant Christ, with one foot upon the basket of flax, holds it by the handle, and looks with wonder at four rays of light, which fall in the form of a cross, as if wishing for them. Smilingly, he grasps the spindle, which he seeks to withhold from his mother. Thus much I was able to fix with him. I preached my sermon yesterday. God grant that it may bring forth rich fruit, for the hearers were numerous.

I commend myself to your Eminence.
FRATER PETRUS DE NUVOLARIA
Vice-General of the Carmelite Monks.
Florence, April 14th, 1501.

See Burlington Magazine, vol. XLIX, August 1926, pp. 61-68, Emil Möller, 'The Madonna with the Yarn-winder', in the possession of the Duke of Buccleuch (see the illustration on p. 36). Another copy is in the collection of Robert W. Reford in Montreal, Canada. As of the 'St Anne', Leonardo designed two versions of the 'Madonna with the Yarn-winder', one with the Christ Child on the left, and one with the Child on the right. Copies of both versions are extant.

XIII LETTERS PATENT ISSUED TO LEONARDO BY CESARE BORGIA. PAVIA, 18TH AUGUST, 1502.
To all those of our *locotenenti, castellani, officiali* and *subditi*, whom it may concern, we herewith charge and command them, that they everywhere and in every place give free entrance to our highly-esteemed court architect Leonardo da Vinci, the bearer of this, who has been commissioned by us to inspect the fortresses and strongholds of our states, and to make such alterations and improvements as he may think needful. Both he and his followers are to be received with hospitality, and every facility afforded him for personal inspection, for measurement and valuation, just as he may wish. For that purpose a band of men is to be placed at his disposal, which is to give him all the help that he may require. With reference to the state works already in

course of completion, we desire that every engineer be prepared to further any undertaking which he may find necessary.

XIV. A LETTER FROM FRANCESCO PANDOLFINI, FLORENTINE AMBASSADOR AT THE FRENCH COURT, FROM BLOIS, 12 JANUARY, 1507.
Finding myself this morning in the presence of the most Christian King, his Majesty called me and said: 'Your lords must render me a service. Write to them that I desire to make use of their painter, Master Leonardo, who is now at Milan, and that I wish him to do certain things for me. Do this in such a way that their lordships enjoin him to serve me promptly and tell him not to depart from Milan before my arrival. He is a good master, and I desire certain things by his hand. Write to Florence at once, and in such a way as to obtain the desired result, and send me the letter.' All this came from a little painting by his hand that has recently been brought here, and which is judged to be a very excellent work. In the course of conversation I asked his Majesty what works he desired from him, and he answered, 'Certain small pictures of Our Lady and others, according as the idea occurs to me; perhaps I shall get him to paint my portrait.'

XV. DRAFT OF A LETTER FROM LEONARDO TO THE DUKE OF NEMOURS, GIULIANO DE' MEDICI, THE BROTHER OF LEO X.
I was so greatly rejoiced, most Illustrious Lord, by the desired restoration of your health that it almost had the effect that my own health recovered. . . . But I am extremely vexed that I have not been able completely to satisfy the wishes of your Excellency, by reason of the wickedness of that deceiver, for whom I left nothing undone which could be done for him by me and by which I might be of use to him; and in the first place his allowances were paid to him before the time, which I believe he would willingly deny, if I had not the writing signed by myself and the interpreter. And I, seeing that he did not work for me unless he had no work to do for others, which he was very careful in soliciting, invited him to eat with me, and to work afterwards near me, because, besides saving of expense, he would acquire the Italian language. (He always promised, but would never do so.) And this I did also, because that young German who makes the mirrors, was there always in the workshop, and wanted to see and to know all that was being done there and made it known outside blaming what he did not understand and because he dined with those of the Pope's guard, and then they went out with guns killing birds among the ruins; and this went on from after dinner till the

evening; and when I sent Lorenzo to urge him to work he said that he would not have so many masters over him, and that his work was for Your Excellency's Wardrobe; and thus two months passed and so it went on; and one day finding Gian Niccolo of the Wardrobe and asking whether the German had finished the work for your Magnificence, he told me this was not true, but only that he had given him two guns to clean. Afterwards, when I urged him further, he left the workshop and began to work in his room, and lost much time in making another pair of pincers and files and other tools with screws; and there he worked at reels for twisting silk which he hid when any one of my people went in, and with a thousand oaths and mutterings, so that none of them would go there any more.

Written in Rome, c. 1514, while Leonardo was living in the Belvedere of the Vatican. There is another draft for the same letter extant, showing the same nervous irritation.

XVI. THE VISIT OF THE CARDINAL LUIGI D'ARAGONA, PAID TO LEONARDO, ON 10 OCTOBER, 1517; TOLD BY HIS SECRETARY, ANTONIO DE' BEATIS.

On the 10th of October, 1517, Monsignor and the rest of us went to see, in one of the outlying parts of the Amboise, Messer Leonardo Vinci the Florentine, a grey-beard of more than seventy years, the most eminent painter of our time, who showed to his Eminence the Cardinal three pictures: one of a certain Florentine lady, painted from life, at the instance of the late Lord Giuliano de' Medici; the other of the youthful St John the Baptist; and the third of the Madonna and the Child in the lap of St Anne, the most perfect of them all. One cannot indeed expect any more good work from him, as a certain paralysis has crippled his right hand. But he has a pupil, a Milanese, who works well enough: and although Messer Leonardo can no longer paint with the sweetness which was peculiar to him, he can still design and instruct others. This gentleman has written a treatise on anatomy, showing by illustrations the members, muscles, nerves, veins, joints, intestines, and whatever else is to discuss in the bodies of men and women, in a way that has never yet been done by any one else. All this we have seen with our own eyes; and he said that he had dissected more than thirty bodies, both of men and women of all ages. He has also written of the nature of water, and of divers machines, and of other matters, which he has set down in an endless number of volumes, all in the vulgar tongue, which, if they be published, will be profitable and delightful.

St Anne, plate 68(?); St John, see plate 55. The portrait of 'a certain Florentine lady' was probably not the Mona Lisa (plate 28) but rather a portrait of Costanza d'Avalos (now lost). The 'Milanese pupil' is Francesco Melzi.

XVII. LETTER FROM FRANCESCO MELZI TO THE BROTHERS OF LEONARDO, ABOUT THE DEATH OF THE MASTER.

To Ser Giuliano and his honoured brothers –

I believe that the death of your brother, Maestro Leonardo, has already been certified to you. He was to me the best of fathers, and it is impossible for me to express the grief that his death has caused me. Until the day when my body is laid under the ground, I shall experience perpetual sorrow, and not without reason, for he daily showed me the most devoted and warmest affection.

His loss is a grief to everyone, for it is not in the power of nature to reproduce another such man. May the Almighty accord him everlasting rest. He passed from the present life on the 2nd of May with all the sacraments of holy Mother Church, and well disposed to receive them. The reason that he was able to make a will, leaving his goods to whom he liked, was on account of his possessing a letter from the king, exempting him *quod heredes supplicantis sint regnicolae*. Without such a letter he would not have been able to will away anything he possessed here, this being the custom of the country. Maestro Leonardo accordingly made his will, which I should have sent you sooner had I been able to confide it to a trustworthy person. I expect that one of my uncles who has been to see me will soon return to Milan. I will dispose it in his hands, and he will faithfully remit it to you. Up to the present time I have not found other means of sending it. In so much as concerns your part in the will, Maestro Leonardo possessed in the [hospital of] Santa Maria Nuova, in the hands of the treasurer, four hundred gold crowns (*scudi di sole*) in notes which have been placed out at five per cent for the last six years counting from last October. He had also an estate at Fiesole that he wished to be distributed equally among you. There is nothing more concerning you in the will, and I will say no more except to offer you my most willing service. You will find me ready and anxious to do your will.

I recommend myself continually to you.

Given at Amboise, the 1st of June, 1519.
Please reply by the Gondi,
Tanquam fratri vestro,
Franciscus Meltius

Leonardo's father, and later on his brothers, lived in a house belonging to the Gondi family who were rich merchants in gold filigree and had connections with many towns in Italy. (See Richter, vol. II, note to § 1450.)

CHRONOLOGY OF LEONARDO'S LIFE

I. FIRST FLORENTINE PERIOD: 1452–1481

1452 (15 April) Leonardo born in Anchiano, outside Vinci, near Florence; the illegitimate son of Ser Piero da Vinci and Caterina, a peasant girl. Leonardo's father marries in the same year a young woman of a rich family.

1457 Leonardo's mother marries a lime-burner. The child is taken into Ser Piero's household, where he lives with his grandparents, and a married uncle, and is nursed by a childless stepmother. (Leonardo's father married four times and had eleven children by his third and fourth wives.)
Leonardo is mentioned in the 1457 taxation return of his grandfather as an illegitimate son of Ser Piero.

1469 Leonardo is mentioned again in the taxation return of the Vinci family.
Ser Piero becomes notary to the Signoria and moves with his family to Florence; Leonardo enters Verrocchio's workshop. Three years later he is admitted a member of the Painters' Guild.

1472 Leonardo's name appears in the Red Book of Painters of Florence, as a member of the Compagnia di San Luca. He is now entitled to accept commissions of his own but stays as an assistant in Verrocchio's workshop.
The '*Annunciation*' (plate 59).

1473 Dated Landscape drawing (plate 81). The '*Kneeling Angel*' (plate 43).

1476 Leonardo accused of sodomy with a model, Jacopo Santarelli. This accusation is dismissed (7 June, 1476) with the condition that it might be brought up again on further evidence. He is mentioned twice in this year as living in Verrocchio's house. Verrocchio competes for the commission of the Forteguerri monument; his model is accepted. (Valentiner claimed that Leonardo collaborated in this sculpture.)

1478 (10 January) Leonardo receives a commission for the altarpiece of the St Bernard chapel in the Palazzo Vecchio.
(14 March) First payment for this painting (which he soon abandons).
(Autumn) Drawing with note by Leonardo: '. . . *bre* 1478 *inchominciai le 2 S. Vergine Marie . . .*' (which means that Leonardo began two Madonna paintings or reliefs in autumn 1478). Underneath is a line of which half is torn off; we can just read, '. . . *e chompa in Pistoia*' (the meaning is probably that the one Madonna was begun in Florence, the other in Pistoia).
The '*Madonna di Piazza*' for the Duomo in Pistoia is painted in Verrocchio's workshop (illustrated, p. 27). Verrocchio works (with the help of Leonardo?) on the '*Careggi Resurrection*' relief (plate VII).

1479 Leonardo's drawing of Baroncelli hanging by his neck from a window of the Bargello. (The commission to paint in fresco the hanging of the murderers of Giuliano de' Medici was given to Botticelli.)
Leonardo '*in casa propria*', his own lodgings; he does not stay any longer with Verrocchio or Ser Piero.

1481 (March) Leonardo is commissioned by the monks of San Donato a Scopeto to paint *The Adoration of the Kings* for the high-altar of their monastery (plate 49). He also decorates their clock; the monks buy him some ultramarine for this job.
(28 September) Last payment for the *Adoration of the Kings*; the picture remains unfinished.
Leonardo offers in a letter his services (as engineer, architect and sculptor) to Ludovico Sforza, the ruler of Milan (Document I, p. 33).
Verrocchio sends his model for the horse of *Colleoni* to Venice.

II. FIRST MILANESE PERIOD: 1482–1499

1482 Leonardo moves to Milan. (The Anonimo Gaddiano says: 'When he was thirty'.) He brings a *lira*, a present from Lorenzo de' Medici, and is accompanied by the musician Migliorotti.

1483 (25 April) Contract for the '*Virgin of the Rocks*', given by the Confraternity of the Immaculate Conception in S. Francesco Grande at Milan to three painters – Leonardo, and the brothers Evangelista and Ambrogio de Predis (plate 64 and plate 65).
Leonardo paints the portrait of Cecilia Gallerani, the mistress of Ludovico Sforza (plate 22).
Leonardo begins his work on the equestrian monument for Francesco Sforza (on which, according to Sabba da Castiglione, he worked for sixteen years).

1485 (26 March) Leonardo studies the total eclipse of the sun.
(13 April) Ludovico Sforza commissions Leonardo to paint an '*Adoration of the Child*' for Matthias Corvinus, King of Hungary.

1487 Payments to Leonardo for a wooden model for the tambour of the dome of the Cathedral in Milan.

1488 Death of Verrocchio in Venice, before the casting of his *Colleoni* is carried out.

1489 Anatomical studies (MS. B.).

1490 (13 January) Leonardo designs dresses for the Court on the occasion of the marriage of Gian Galeazzo Sforza, and other decorations, including even horse-trappings. '*Il Paradiso*' by the court poet Bernardo Bellinzone (also spelled *Bellincioni*) is performed; the stage design is by Leonardo.
A note by Leonardo's hand (in MS. C, folio 15): '*A di 23 aprile 1490 cominciai questo libro e ricominciai il cavallo*' (I have started this book and re-started to work on the equestrian monument).
(8 June) In Pavia with Francesco di Giorgio, consulted in connection with the Duomo. He admires the 'Regisole', the equestrian monument at Pavia (Richter §1445).
(22 July) Salai, a boy of ten, joins Leonardo as his servant and pupil; he remains with him for twenty-five years.

1491 (26 January, and the following days) 'Tournament', staged by Galeazzo Sanseverino in honour of the wedding of Ludovico Sforza and Beatrice d'Este; designed by Leonardo.

(2 April) Boltraffio mentioned as in Leonardo's studio.

1492 A short visit to Rome.

Death of Lorenzo de' Medici.

1493 (30 November) Leonardo's huge clay model for the horse of the Sforza monument is exhibited during the marriage festivities for Bianca Maria Sforza and Emperor Maximilian.

1494 A French army invades Italy. The Medici expelled from Florence. (They return in 1512.)

Luca Pacioli publishes his 'Summa arithmetica'.

1495 Leonardo working on *The Last Supper* (plate 73). He teaches himself Latin.

(Summer) Short visit to Florence.

1496 (31 January) In the Palazzo of Gian Francesco Sanseverino at Milan, in the presence of the Duke, a play on Danaë, by Baldassare Taccone, is performed. Leonardo designed the scenery. Luca Pacioli, professor of mathematics, moves to Milan and becomes friends with Leonardo.

Baldassare Castiglione, the 'complete gentleman', moves from the Court of Mantua to the Court of Milan.

1497 (29 June) Leonardo still working on *The Last Supper*. He paints in oil, on the opposite wall, the portraits of Ludovico Sforza and his family (in the corners of Montorfano's Crucifixion fresco; plate II).

1498 Savonarola hanged, and then burned on the stake. Leonardo's murals in the Sala delle Asse.

(2 October) Ludovico Sforza gives Leonardo a vineyard.

(December) Short visit to Mantua.

1499 (6 October) Occupation of Milan by a French army under Trivulzio; the Duke has fled from his town a few days earlier.

(14 December) Leonardo sends 600 gold florins for his account to Florence, and soon after that he returns there by way of Mantua and Venice. Luca Pacioli is in his company.

III. SECOND FLORENTINE PERIOD: 1500–1506

1500 (February) In Mantua; draws the portrait of Isabella d'Este (plate 24).

(March) In Venice. Lorenzo Gusnasco, a maker of musical instruments, writes to Isabella d'Este that he has seen her portrait, painted by Leonardo ('*molto naturale, tanto bene fatto, non è possibile meglio*'. See Document IX, p. 37).

(10 April) Ludovico Sforza, who had returned to Milan with an army of Swiss and German mercenaries, is defeated and taken prisoner.

(24 April) Leonardo, back in Florence, draws there 50 gold florins from his account at the Ospedale di S. Maria Nuova.

(Leonardo had left Florence when he was thirty, now he is forty-eight. There is a scarcity of good artists in Florence; Verrocchio, Luca della Robbia, Bertoldo, the brothers Pollaiuolo, Domenico Ghirlandaio, and Botticini are dead now; young Michelangelo is in Rome, where he has just finished his *Pietà* of St Peter's; the best artists in Florence are Andrea della Robbia, Piero di Cosimo, Fra

Bartolommeo, Botticelli, Lorenzo di Credi, and Filippino Lippi. Leonardo has to his credit hardly more than the *Last Supper* and the model of the large *Horse*. He will stay in Florence only seven years.)

1501 (April) Letters from Fra Pietro da Novellara to Isabella d'Este concerning Leonardo's cartoon of *St Anne*, a *Madonna with the Yarnwinder*, and about portraits painted by pupils and touched up by Leonardo (Documents XI and XII; and the illustration on p. 36).

1502 (probably from July onward, about eight months) Leonardo as military engineer in the service of Cesare Borgia on his campaign in Central Italy.

1503 (4 March) Leonardo has returned to Florence and draws some money from his account at the Ospedale di S. Maria Nuova. His luggage is still at the custom-house (Richter §§ 1420, 1444, 1454); he is in connection with several artists – Lorenzo di Credi, Filippino Lippi, Piero di Cosimo, and others –, and he also mentions in these notes Lorenzo di Pierfrancesco de' Medici (who died later in this year, 20 May). Leonardo, now over fifty, needs spectacles (mentioned three times in these notes). In the same notes Leonardo mentions "my map of the world which Giovanni Benci has", and the name "Piero dal Borgo", which could mean Piero della Francesca and his manuscript on perspective.

(8 October) Rejoins the Guild of Painters in Florence. A mural *The Battle of Anghiari* commissioned by the Signoria of Florence (plates 108–110).

The portrait of *Mona Lisa* (plate 28).

1504 (25 January) Leonardo – together with Botticelli, Cosimo Rosselli, Piero di Cosimo, and other artists – in a committee appointed to decide the best position for Michelangelo's *David*.

De Sculptura by Pomponius Gauricus is published in Florence; Leonardo, 'Verrocchii discipulus', is mentioned in this book, and as his works *The Last Supper* and the unfinished *Sforza Monument*.

(9 July) Death of Leonardo's father.

Young Raphael in Florence.

1505 (30 April) The Signoria pays 11 Lire for ochre, gypsum and sponges: Leonardo has finished the cartoon for *The Battle of Anghiari* and begins the painting of the mural.

The Signoria pays at the custom house in Florence the expenses for the transport of some garments which have come from Rome and belong to Leonardo.

Leonardo studies the flights of birds and stereometry.

(31 August and 31 October) Last payments for materials for the Anghiari mural.

1506 (20 May) Leonardo has spent 450 gold florins, out of the savings of 600 he had made in Milan.

Leonardo invited to Milan by the French Governor Charles d'Amboise, Count de Chaumont.

IV. SECOND MILANESE PERIOD: 1506–1513

1506 (June) Leonardo in Milan. He paints a small picture of the Madonna which enchants the King.

He is appointed painter and engineer to Louis XII.

He begins, assisted by pupils, the second version of *The Madonna of the Rocks* (plate 65).

1507 (20 April) The vineyard, once given by Ludovico Sforza to Leonardo, is restituted to him.

(September) Leonardo returns to Florence; stays for about six months in the Casa Martelli and aids the sculptor Rustici in his work (plate V).

1508 (Spring) Back in Milan.

Studies for the Trivulzio monument (plate III; the last sketches for this monument date from 1511).

1509 Luca Pacioli's *Divina Proportione*, issued in Venice, with 60 illustrations, probably after designs by Leonardo.

1510 Leonardo occupies himself mainly with anatomy and other scientific studies.

1511 Leonardo meets the anatomist Marc Antonio della Torre, who helps him with his researches.

Milan at war with the Pope and Venice.

(Spring) Leonardo back in Florence; writes to Melzi. Letter to Charles d'Amboise, telling him that he will return to Milan at Easter and bring two Madonna paintings for the King.

(Late summer, or autumn) Returns to Milan.

(18 December) Windsor drawing No. 12416: Two studies of a fire in Milan.

1512 The restoration of the Medici in Florence. The French lose Milan; Massimiliano Sforza, son of Ludovico, supported by a coalition of the Pope, Venice and Spain, returns to Milan.

1513 (24 September) Leonardo moves to Rome, accompanied by Melzi, Salai, and two other pupils.

(October) He passes through Florence and deposits some money for his account at the Ospedale di S. Maria Nuova.

V. THE LAST SEVEN YEARS : ROME AND CLOUX
1513–16; 1517–19

1513 (1 December) Leonardo in the service of Giuliano de' Medici, Duke of Nemours, brother of Pope Leo X.

He lives in the Belvedere of the Vatican.

Raphael on the peak of his fame, working on his *Stanze di Vaticano*. Michelangelo, who has already finished his *Sistine Frescoes*, works on the large marble statue of *Moses*.

1514 Leonardo draws, in black chalk and ink, the visions of the '*Deluge*' (a set of ten drawings at Windsor Castle, Nos. 12377–86; see Plate 85).

1515 (9 January) Leonardo reports that his patron, Giuliano de' Medici, Duke of Nemours, has left Rome. (Richter, vol. II, p. 345, § 1377).

(October) Francis I, successor of Louis XII, recaptures Milan.

(14 December) Leonardo probably present at a meeting of the Pope and the King of France in Bologna.

1516 (August) Leonardo's note on measurements in the church of S. Paolo, Rome.

(Autumn 1516, or perhaps Spring 1517) Leonardo accepts the invitation of Francis I and departs for France.

1517 Ascension Day in Amboise; May in Cloux.

Lives in the Manoir de Cloux, between the town and the Royal Castle.

(10 October) The Cardinal Luigi d'Aragona visits Leonardo and is shown illustrated manuscripts from Leonardo's hand, and three paintings – a portrait of a Florentine Lady, commissioned by Giuliano de' Medici, Duke of Nemours, a youthful John the Baptist, and a Madonna and Child in the lap of St Anne (Document XVI).

1517–18 Salary payments for two years to Leonardo, Melzi, and Salai.

1518 (19 June) Court festivals at Cloux, repeating Bellin-zone's pageant '*Il Paradiso*' of 1490, for which Leonardo made the designs.

1519 (23 April) Leonardo makes his Will (Richter § 1566). The Testator desires to be buried in the church of Saint Florentin at Amboise; he stipulates how many priests and monks should follow the body; he asks that three high and thirty low masses should be celebrated at Saint Florentin for the peace of his soul, and similar services in other churches at Amboise. To Melzi he leaves 'for services and favours done to him in the past' all his instruments and artist's tools, his manuscripts and paintings, also his clothes and money; everything else he bequeathes to Salai and other servants. He names the exact number of candles to be carried at the funeral and says how much wax should be donated to the churches; and he does not forget alms to the poor. To his half-brothers in Florence (with whom, twelve years before, he had fought in court over the division of an inheritance) he bequeathes all the money 'in the hands of the treasurer of Santa Maria Nuova in Florence'.

1519 (2 May) Death of Leonardo. (The King was on this day with the Court at Saint Germain-en-Laye, where he signed a decree on the 1st of May.)

(12 August) Ceremony of Leonardo's burial at the cloister of the church of Saint Florentin at Amboise.

THE PLATES

AN ASTERISK (*) IN FRONT OF THE NUMBER INDICATES THAT THE
REPRODUCTION IS IN THE SAME SIZE AS THE ORIGINAL

1. *Leonardo's Self-Portrait*. Red chalk. About 1512. Turin, Library

*2. *Five Grotesque Heads*. Pen and ink. About 1490. Windsor Castle, Royal Library

*3. *Antique Warrior*. Silverpoint on cream-coloured paper. About 1478. London, British Museum

4. *Heads of Girls, Young and Old Men*. Pen and ink. About 1478–80. Windsor Castle, Royal Library

*5. *Female Half-Figure*, seventeen studies. Silverpoint on red prepared paper. About 1478–80. Windsor Castle, Royal Library

*6. *Old Man thinking*. Pen and ink (slightly enlarged). About 1510. Windsor Castle, Royal Library

*7. *Head of a Pharisee*. Pen and ink, and wash. About 1504. Windsor Castle, Royal Library

*8. *Head of Christ*. Silverpoint. About 1500. Venice, Academy

9. *Head of Christ*. About 1495. Milan, Brera

*10. *Studies for the Leda*. Pen and ink. About 1506. Windsor Castle, Royal Library

*11. *Study for the Leda*. Pen and ink. About 1506. Windsor Castle, Royal Library

*12. *Head of a Warrior* (Study for the *Battle of Anghiari*). Red chalk. 1503. Budapest, Museum of Fine Arts

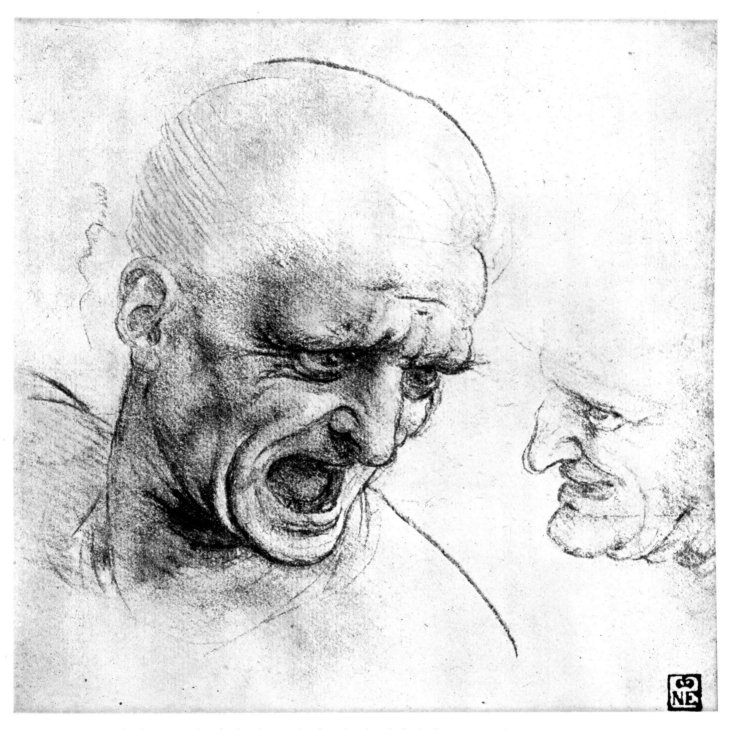

*13. *Heads of Warriors* (Study for the *Battle of Anghiari*). Black chalk. 1503. Budapest, Museum of Fine Arts

*14. *Apostle* (Study for the *Last Supper*). Pen and ink, and wash, on blue prepared paper.
About 1495. Vienna, Albertina

*15. *St. James the Greater* (Study for the *Last Supper*). Red chalk. 1495–96.
Lower left corner: *The Sforza Castel at Milan*. Pen and ink.
Windsor Castle, Royal Library

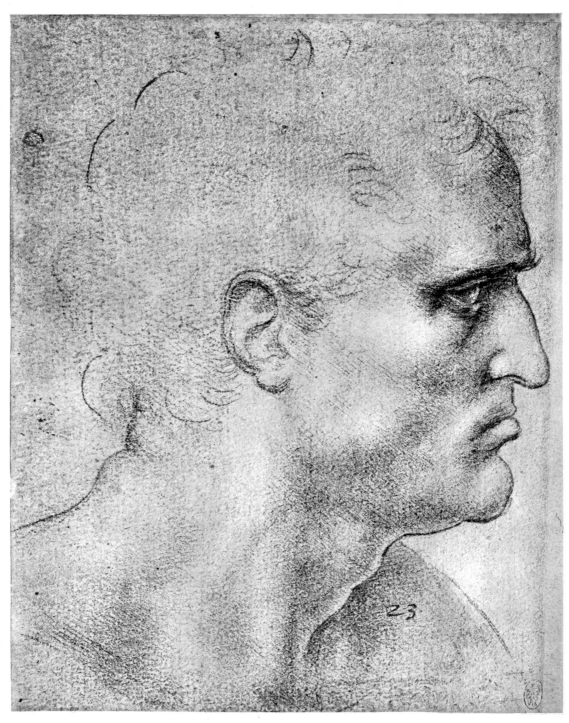

*16. *St. Bartholomew* (Study for the *Last Supper*). Red chalk on red paper. 1495–96.
Windsor Castle, Royal Library

*17. *St. Philip* (Study for the *Last Supper*). Black chalk. 1495–96.
Windsor Castle, Royal Library

*18. *St. Anne*. Red chalk on brownish paper, heightened with white. About 1501. Windsor Castle, Royal Library

*19. *Head of a Young Woman.* Silverpoint on blue prepared paper (partly worked over by a pupil). About 1486.
Windsor Castle, Royal Library

*20. *Study for the Angel's Head in the Virgin of the Rocks*, Louvre (cf. Plate 21). Silverpoint on light brown prepared paper, heightened with white. 1483. Turin, Royal Library

*21. *Angel's Head*. Detail from Plate 64

22. *Portrait of a Lady with an Ermine*. About 1483. Cracow, Museum Czartoryski

23. *Portrait of Ginevra de' Benci*. About 1474–78. Vaduz, Liechtenstein Gallery
Acquired in 1967 by the National Gallery of Art, Washington

24. *Supposed Portrait of Isabella d'Este*. Black chalk and pastel, touches of yellow in dress, red in hair, heightened with white. (Detail.)
About 1500. Paris, Louvre

25. *Portrait of a Girl with a Cap*. Silverpoint on pinkish paper. About 1493–95. Windsor Castle, Royal Library

26. *Portrait of a Musician*. Unfinished. About 1485. Milan, Ambrosiana

27. Ambrogio de Predis and Leonardo: *Portrait of a Lady*. About 1490. Milan, Ambrosiana

28. *Mona Lisa*. 1503. Paris, Louvre

29. *Mona Lisa*. Detail from Plate 28

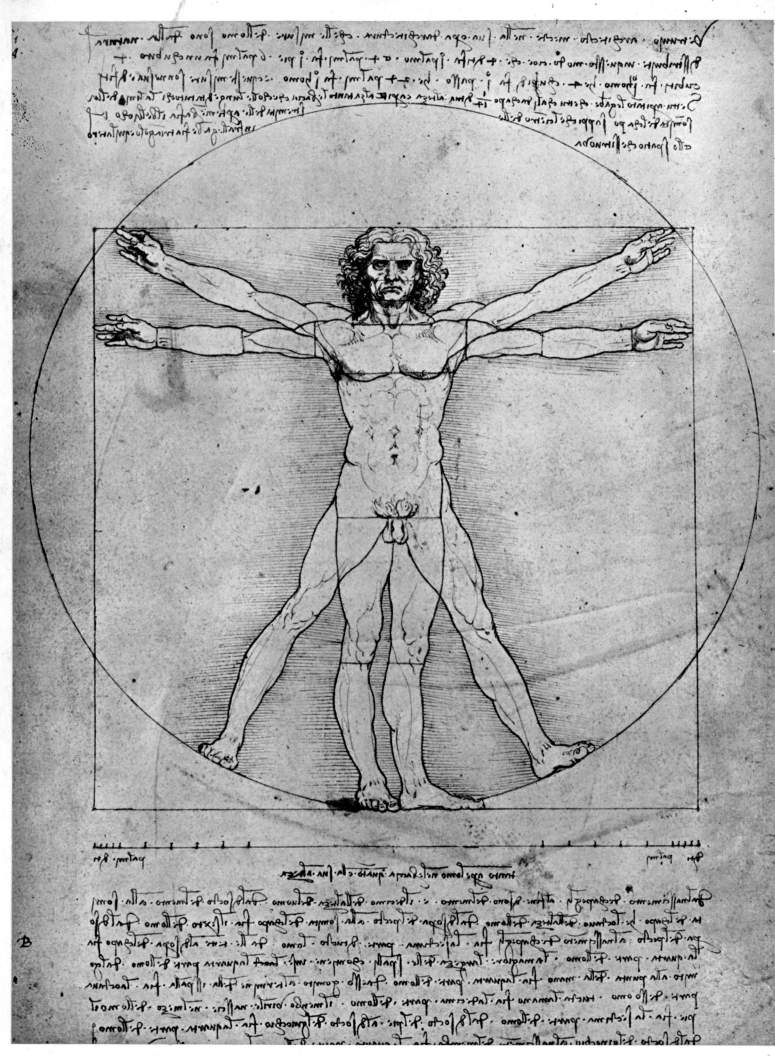

*30. *The Proportions of the Human Figure,* after Vitruvius. Pen, and ink. About 1492. Venice, Academy

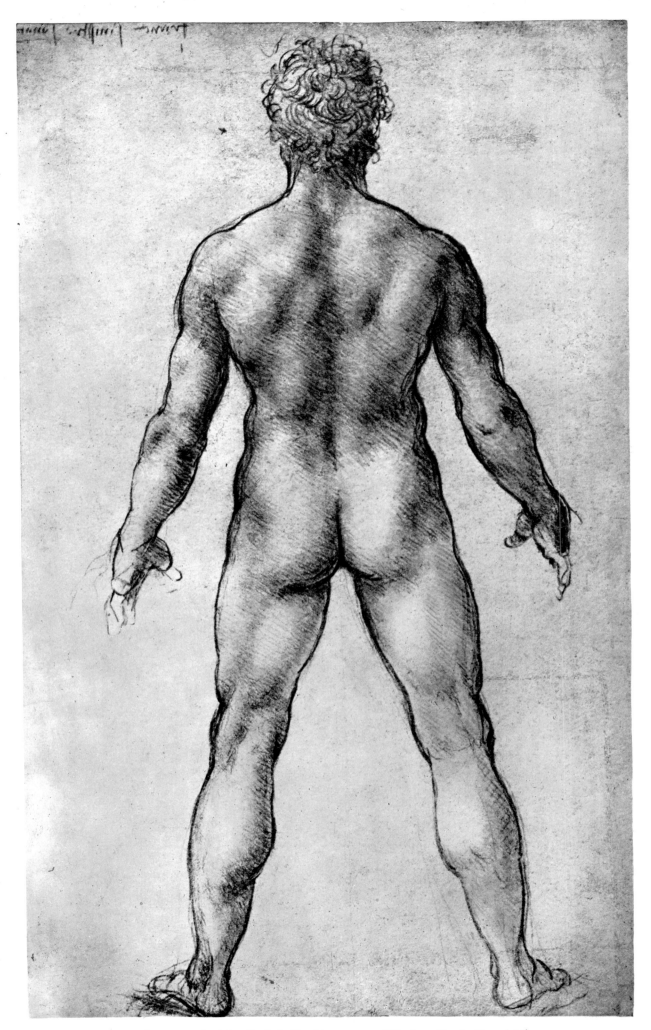

*31. *Nude Figure of a Man*. Red chalk. About 1503. Windsor Castle, Royal Library

*32. *Studies of Hands*. Silverpoint on pink prepared paper. About 1481. Windsor Castle, Royal Library

*33. *Study of a Woman's Hands folded over her Breast.* Silverpoint on pink prepared paper, heightened with white. About 1478. Windsor Castle, Royal Library

*34. *Pointing Woman in Landscape*. Brownish chalk. About 1513. Windsor Castle, Royal Library

*35. *Youth in a Masquerade Costume*. Pen and ink, wash, over black chalk. About 1506–7. Windsor Castle, Royal Library

*36. *Leda and the Swan*. Pen and bistre, and wash, over black chalk, about 1504–06.
Chatsworth, Devonshire Collection

37. *Leda and the Swan*. Free copy of a lost painting by Leonardo of about 1506. Rome, Spiridon Collection

*38. *Drapery Study for a kneeling Woman.* Brush drawing in black and white on blue paper. About 1483–86.
Windsor Castle, Royal Library

*39. *Drapery Study for a kneeling Woman*. Silverpoint, heightened with white, on red prepared paper. About 1477.
Rome, Corsini Gallery

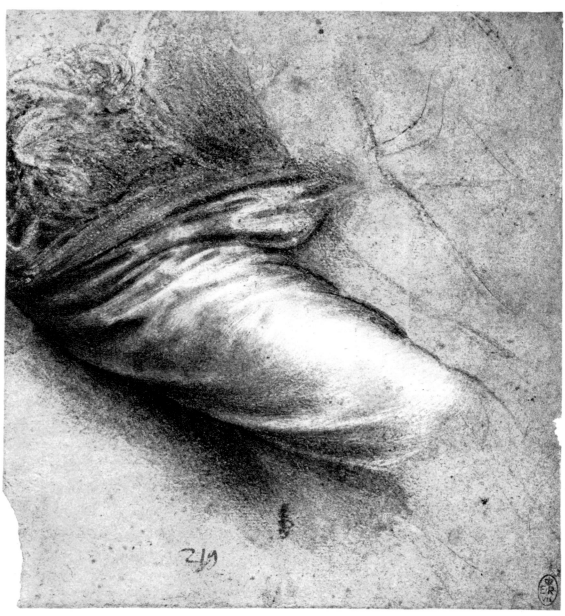

*40 and *41. *Drapery Studies* (for the Madonna in the *St. Anne* painting, Plate 68). About 1508.
Windsor Castle, Royal Library

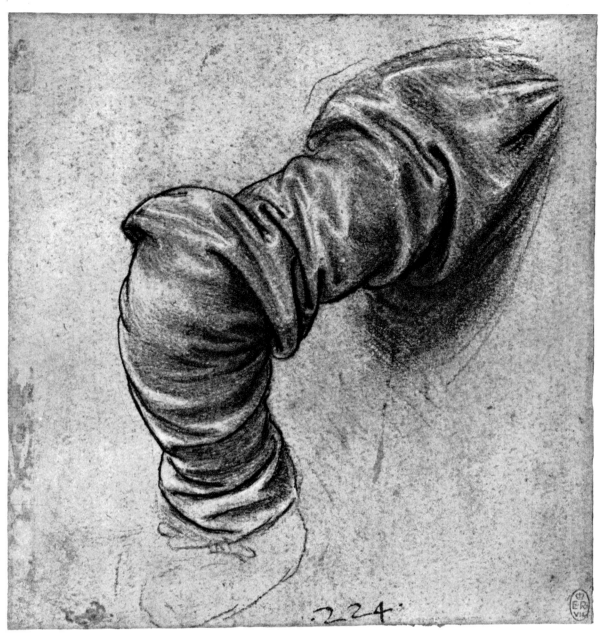

*42. *Study of Drapery* (for the right arm of St. Peter, Plate 73). Black chalk, heightened with white. About 1496.
Windsor Castle, Royal Library

43. *Kneeling Angel in Profile*. About 1473 (Contributed by Leonardo to Verrocchio's *Baptism of Christ*.) Florence, Uffizi

*44. *St. John the Baptist*. Silverpoint, heightened with white, on blue prepared paper.
About 1478. Windsor Castle, Royal Library

*45. *Three Dancing Maidens*. Pen and ink. About 1503. Venice, Academy

46. *Neptune*. Black chalk. About 1504. Windsor Castle, Royal Library

*47. *Allegory of Fortune*. Silverpoint, pen and ink, and wash. About 1483. London, British Museum

*48. *Study for the Adoration of the Kings* (Plate 49). Pen and ink. About 1481. Paris, Louvre

49. *The Adoration of the Kings.* (Unfinished.) About 1481–82. Florence, Uffizi

50. Detail from Plate 49

51. Detail from Plate 49

52. Detail from Plate 49

53. Detail from Plate 49 (Supposed Self-portrait of young Leonardo)

54. *Cartoon for the Virgin and Child with St. Anne and the Infant St. John*. Black chalk on buff paper. About 1499. London, National Gallery

55. *St. John the Baptist*. About 1509–12. Paris, Louvre

56. *Madonna with the Fruit-Plate*. Silverpoint, pen and ink, and wash. About 1481. Paris, Louvre

57. *The Adoration of the Child, with two Angels.* About 1470–72. (By Verrocchio and Leonardo). Detroit, Institute of Arts

*58. Study for the background of the Adoration of the Kings (Plate 49). Pen and ink over silverpoint. About 1481. Florence, Uffizi

59. *The Annunciation.* About 1472. Florence, Uffizi

60. Detail from Plate 59

61. Detail from Plate 59

62. Detail from Plate 59

63. Attributed to Leonardo: *Madonna with the Carnation*. About 1478. Munich, Ältere Pinakothek

64. *Madonna of the Rocks*. About 1483–85. Paris, Louvre

65. *Madonna of the Rocks*. About 1506–08. London, National Gallery

*66. *Study for the Head of the Madonna Litta* (Plate 67). Silverpoint on green prepared paper. About 1484. Paris, Louvre

67. Workshop of Leonardo: *Madonna Litta*. About 1485–90. Leningrad, Hermitage

68. *Virgin and Child with St. Anne*. Unfinished. About 1508–10. Paris, Louvre

69. Detail from Plate 68

*70. *Studies for an Adoration of the Child*. Pen and ink over lead point. About 1483. New York, Metropolitan Museum

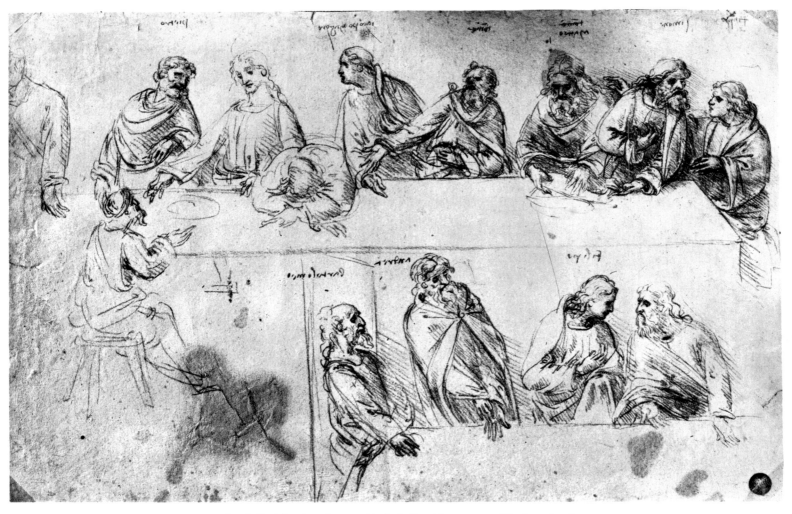

71. *Sketch for* The Last Supper. Red chalk. About 1495. Venice, Academy

72. Reconstruction of the above composition

73. *The Last Supper*. Wall-painting in oil tempera. 1495–98. Milan, Santa Maria delle Grazie

74. Detail from Plate 73

75. Detail from Plate 73

76. *St. Jerome*. Unfinished. About 1483. Rome, Vatican Gallery

77. *Rocky Landscape*. Detail from Plate 76

78. *Rocky Landscape*. Detail from Plate 64

79. *Rocky Landscape*. Detail from Plate 68

*80. *Ravine with Water Birds*. Pen and ink on pinkish paper. About 1478–80. Windsor Castle, Royal Library

*81. *Arno Landscape.* Pen and ink. 1473. Florence, Uffizi

-137-

*83. *Storm in the Alps*. Red chalk. About 1500. Windsor Castle, Royal Library

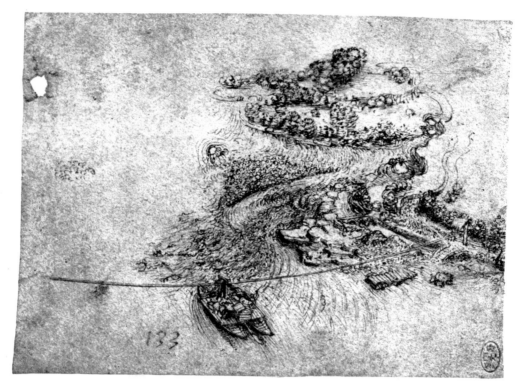

*84. *The Ferry*. Pen and ink on yellowish paper. About 1503. Windsor Castle, Royal Library

*85. *The Deluge*. Pen and ink and brown wash over black chalk. About 1514-16. Windsor Castle, Royal Library

86. *Landscape*. Detail from Plate 59

87. *Landscape*. About 1473. (Contributed by Leonardo to Verrocchio's *Baptism of Christ*.) Florence, Uffizi

88. *Plant Ornament.* About 1474–78. On the reverse of the *Portrait of a Lady* in the Liechtenstein Gallery (Plate 23)

89. *Fruit Garlands*. About 1498. Detail from the left lunette over the *Last Supper* (Plate 73). Milan, Santa Maria delle Grazie

90. *Plants*. About 1483. Detail from the *Madonna of the Rocks* (Plate 64). Paris, Louvre

91. *Flowering Plants*. Pen and ink over red chalk. About 1506. Windsor Castle, Royal Library

*92. *Anemones*. Pen and ink. About 1506. Windsor Castle, Royal Library

*93. *Studies of Flowers*. Pen and ink over metal-point, on brownish paper. About 1483. Venice, Academy

94. *Lilies*. Pen and ink and sepia wash, over black chalk. About 1479. Windsor Castle, Royal Library

95. *Undergrowth*. About 1506–08. Detail from the *Madonna of the Rocks* (Plate 65). London, National Gallery

*96. *Flowering Rushes*. Red chalk. About 1504. Windsor Castle, Royal Library

*97. *Oak Leaves with Acorns, and a Spray of Greenweed.* Red chalk, with touches of white, on pink paper. About 1506.
Windsor Castle, Royal Library

98. *Flowering Meadow*. About 1472. Detail from the *Annunciation* (Plate 59). Florence, Uffizi

99. *Irises and Wood Anemones.* About 1483. Detail from the *Madonna of the Rocks* (Plate 64). Paris, Louvre

*100. *A Dog*. Two sketches in red chalk. About 1498. Windsor Castle, Royal Library

*101. *A Bear*. Silverpoint sketches on pinkish buff prepared paper. About 1480–1482. New York, Lehman Collection

*102. *An Ox and three Asses*. Silverpoint and pen. About 1480. Windsor Castle, Royal Library

103. *Fighting Horsemen*. About 1481–82. (Detail from Plate 49.) Florence, Uffizi

104. *Dragon Fight*. Pen and wash. About 1482. London, British Museum

105. *Studies of a Dragon Fight*. Pen and ink. About 1506. Windsor Castle, Royal Library

*106. *Study for the Sforza Monument.* Silverpoint on blue prepared paper. About 1488–1490. Windsor Castle, Royal Library

*107. *Studies of Horses' Feet*. Silverpoint on blue prepared paper, heightened with white. About 1490. Turin, Royal Library

108. *The Fight for the Standard*. Copy by Rubens of the centre part of Leonardo's wall painting *The Battle of Anghiari*.
The Hague, Royal Collection

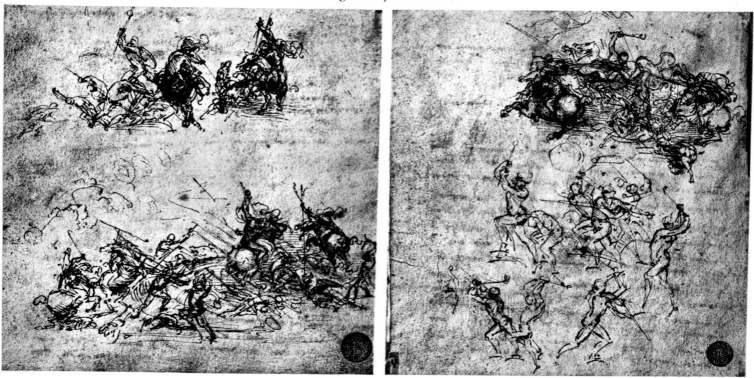

109–110. *Sketches for The Battle of Anghiari*. Pen and ink. About 1503. Venice, Academy

*111. *Studies for the Trivulzio Monument*. Pen sketches on grey paper. About 1511. Windsor Castle, Royal Library

*112. *Studies of Horses*. Silverpoint on blue prepared paper. About 1490. Windsor Castle, Royal Library

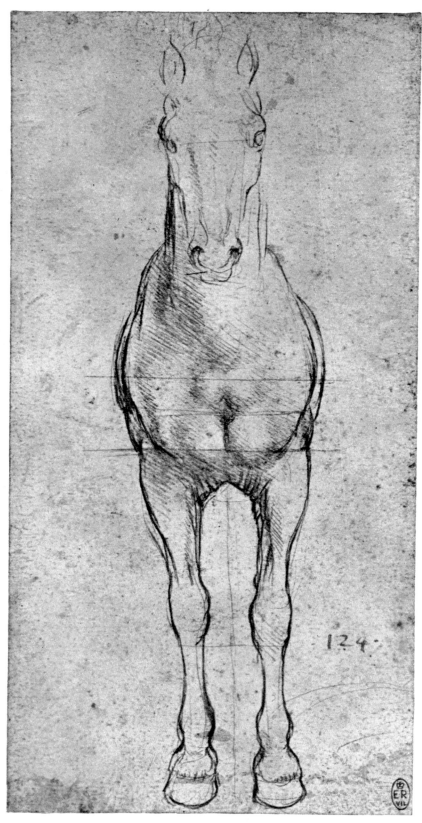

*113. *Study of a Horse*. Silverpoint on blue prepared paper. About 1490.
Windsor Castle, Royal Library

114. Leonardo's Workshop: *Horse and Rider*. Bronze statuette, perhaps after a wax model by the master of about 1506.
Budapest, Museum of Fine Arts

NOTES ON THE PLATES

The full titles of books, quoted in abbreviated form in the
Notes on the Plates, can be found in the 'Bibliography'.

Plates marked with an asterisk are reproduced in the original size;
therefore their measurements are not given in the following notes.

a   b   c   d

e   f   g

Supposed Portraits of Leonardo da Vinci. (a) Leonardo as the supposed model for St Michael. Detail from *Tobias and the three Archangels*, painted in about 1467–70 in Verrocchio's workshop, attributed to (his assistant) Francesco Botticini (Florence, Uffizi). – (b) Leonardo as the supposed model for David. Detail from Verrocchio's bronze statue, about 1473 (Florence, Museo Nazionale). – (c) Bust of an old Man, pen and ink drawing by Leonardo, supposed self-portrait of about 1514. (Amsterdam, Fodor Museum). – (d) Pen and ink drawing by Leonardo, about 1496. This sketch, showing the proportions of the head, was supposed to have been done in front of a mirror (Turin, Library). – (e) Pen and ink drawing by Michelangelo, about 1503, supposed portrait of Leonardo lecturing on anatomy (London, British Museum). – (f) Supposed portrait of Leonardo as Plato. Detail from Raphael's *School of Athens*, 1509–11 (Rome, Vatican). – (g) King David, Detail from Raphael's *Disputa Del Sacramento*, 1509–11 (Rome, Vatican).

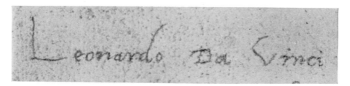

Leonardo's signature. Normal writing, from left to right, not inverted.
Black chalk, about 1492. London, Victoria and Albert Museum.
(SKM III, fol. 62– verso; Richter § 1341.)

NOTES ON THE PLATES

I

SELF-PORTRAIT. Turin, 1557[1]

According to Berenson (1083), retouched on nostrils and mouth. 33.3×21.4 cm.

The illustrations on p. 150 indicate the various opinions held on the appearance of Leonardo. The profile of the woodcut by Cristoforo Coriolano in Vasari's *Life of Leonardo* (p. 9), corresponds with a profile drawing at Windsor Castle (No. 12726, attributed to Ambrogio de Predis). Vasari himself had, in 1557, painted a likeness of Leonardo in the mural in the Palazzo Vecchio at Florence, *Leo X and his Cardinals*. On the other hand, the well-known 'Self-Portrait of Leonardo' in the Uffizi is a fake and the X-ray photographs show that it has been painted over a German picture representing a St Mary Magdalene, datable about 1620.

Berenson, Gronau and Calvi thought they had found a youthful self-portrait of Leonardo in the *Adoration of the Kings* (plate 53). Müller-Walde and Bayersdorfer suspected that Leonardo was the model for the St Michael in Botticini's *Tobias and the Archangels* (fig. a); the same suggestion has been repeatedly put forward for Verrocchio's *David* (fig. b). Beltrami contributed a little to the confusion by his idea that certain sketches of heads with measurements of proportions (e.g. fig. d) were drawn by Leonardo in front of a mirror. Beltrami and Nicodemi maintain that a sketch in Amsterdam (fig. c), representing an old man, or perhaps an Apostle, is simply another self-portrait of the master. (Adolfo Venturi and Valentiner thought that this drawing was freely copied by Leonardo from Michelangelo's *Moses*, which would date it rather late; Berenson took it for the sketch for a figure in an *Adoration*, which would date it rather early.) Marie Herzfeld and Müntz called a drawing at Windsor, plate 6, a self-portrait of Leonardo. Möller found a portrait of the master in a Michelangelo drawing (fig. e); this figure is of the same type as Raphael's *Plato*, or even his *David* (figs. f and g); and as all the *ciceroni* in Rome will tell you, Raphael's *Plato* is again a portrait of Leonardo!

2

FIVE GROTESQUE HEADS. Windsor, 12495

Sometimes called 'The temperaments'. The inscription on the reverse of the drawing, Richter § 1355. Kenneth Clark: 'This is the most important of all Leonardo's caricature drawings.' Old copies in the Louvre and at Weimar.

3

BUST OF A WARRIOR. British Museum, 1895-9-15-474, from the Malcolm Collection (Cat. 1950, No. 96).

Doubted by Morelli and others, and ascribed to Verrocchio. This drawing is done with the left hand, and it is certainly by Leonardo. It was always thought to be connected with two reliefs, 'Scipio' (or Alexander) and 'Darius', executed in Verrocchio's workshop and sent to Matthias Corvinus of Hungary. Of those two reliefs, as Bode contended, old copies and versions are preserved (*Leonardo-Studien*, p. 28); amongst others the Scipio relief in the Louvre from the Rattier collection, which is sometimes attributed to Leonardo himself (Möller, Valentiner, a.o.); a clay relief of an old warrior in the Berlin Museum, attributed to the Robbia workshop (No. 2014, Sch. 188), and a circular relief, with the same bust of an old warrior, in the Louvre (ill. Müller-Walde, 1889, p. 71). The *Alexander* relief in the National

Workshop of Verrocchio: *Scipio Africanus*. Detail of a marble relief, about 1478. Paris, Louvre (No. 668) from the Rattier Collection.

Gallery of Art, Washington (formerly in the Herbert N. Strauss collection, New York) is an original work by Verrocchio and has generally been accepted as one of the two reliefs sent by Lorenzo Magnifico to Matthias Corvinus. Vasari speaks, however, about 'due teste di metallo', and as the existing copies of the Darius relief give one rather the feeling that the original has been formed in clay and cast in bronze or silver, one cannot believe that Vasari has made a mistake about the material. The assumption is that Leonardo's drawing of an old warrior is freely copied from Verrocchio's Darius relief, or else, that it is a design for a similar relief, in imitation of Verrocchio's style. (See Planiscig, Verrocchio, Vienna, 1941, plates 36–38.)

Leonardo's warrior is obviously an ideal type similar to Verrocchio's Colleoni, and to the warrior in Verrocchio's silver relief of the Beheading of the Baptist, from the altar of San Giovanni, now in the Museo del Duomo, Florence. (About Verrocchio as the creator of this style, and about his influence on Leonardo, see Planiscig, pp. 8–10. Compare E. Jacobsen, in Kunstchronik, 1906–07, p. 194f.)

Very interesting is the fantastic armour of Leonardo's warrior, the armour alla romana. Armour of this kind was certainly produced in Verrocchio's workshop, and a helmet in the Florence Bargello shows the same bat wings, and the same circular ornament on the wings.

4

HEADS OF GIRLS AND MEN. Windsor, 12276 verso. 40.5 × 29 cm.

Recto of the same sheet contains a Madonna drawing. The youth in the centre closely resembles the Rattier Relief, as Bode observed (see illustration on p. 151). The type of the old man was repeated by Leonardo throughout his life.

5

SKETCHES OF THE HEAD AND SHOULDERS OF A WOMAN. Windsor, 12513

Six of these seventeen studies show the figure seen from the back; therefore they can hardly have been done directly for a Madonna composition; they are just studies of movement.

6

OLD MAN THINKING. Windsor, 12579. 15.2 × 21.3 cm.

The sheet is folded in the middle, and contains two separate drawings: the reproduction gives only the left half of the sheet. The right half shows sketches of swirling water and plaited hair, and a note (see Richter § 389).

7

STUDY FOR THE HEAD OF A PHARISEE. Windsor, 19106

W. von Seidlitz thought it a study for the Judas in the Last Supper (Leonardo, 2nd edition, 1935, p. 150). The sheet is folded in the middle, the left half containing little sketches of twigs and notes on physics; the right half (which alone is reproduced here) the turbanned head. (The two drawings on this folded sheet are not necessarily of the same date.) Kenneth Clark connects this drawing with a painting, Christ among the Doctors, for which Leonardo received a commission, in 1504, from Isabella d'Este of Mantua. A version of this picture is in the National Gallery, London (No. 18, 'seriously damaged', attributed to Bernardo Luini); a better version is illustrated below.

Christ among the Doctors (attributed to Leonardo by Bernard Seidlitz a.o.). New York, Cathy and Bobby Gregory.

According to Vasari, Leonardo painted (c. 1513) for Baldassare Turini da Pescia, who was Datary to Pope Leo X 'un fanciuletto, che è bello e grazioso a maraviglia'. Seidlitz (p. 375) and Heydenreich (p. 201) understand this as a Head of Christ as a Boy. Such a Head is in the Museo Lázaro Galdiano, Madrid, attributed there to Leonardo himself (apparently by Ambrogio de Predis).

8

CHRIST CARRYING THE CROSS. Venice, 231

This small drawing shows just the head of Christ crowned with thorns, and the hand of a beadle clutching the hair. It seems feasible that of this composition Leonardo executed not only one but two cartoons, which are lost and now known only by different imitations.

In the first cartoon Christ was turned to the left (as in the drawing), and I imagine that Leonardo took this

Christ carrying the Cross. Fresco by Sodoma, 1506–08.
Monteoliveto Maggiore.

Christ carrying the Cross. Attributed to Giorgione, about
1506. Boston, Isabella Stewart Gardner Museum.

cartoon with him to Venice, as most imitations I know of this version belong to the Venetian School.[1] I reproduce here the one which originated in the workshop of Giovanni Bellini, and of which at least three copies are extant; the best of the three, though the least Bellinesque, is thought to be a copy by Giorgione (though Philip Hendy ascribed it to Palma Vecchio).

In the other, and later, version Christ was turned to the right, and this composition was imitated only by Milanese painters. The most beautiful of these adaptations is Sodoma's fresco in the convent of Monteoliveto Maggiore (near Siena).

Charles Loeser (1903) called the attribution of this fine drawing (plate 8) to Leonardo a 'defamation'.

9

HEAD OF CHRIST. Brera, 280. 40×32 cm.
This drawing, a study for the Christ of *The Last Supper* (plate 74), is in the worst state possible, half destroyed and overpainted with chalks, and tempera, but it still retains its magic. I think it gives a much better idea of how the head of Christ in *The Last Supper* looked

originally than what is left of it in the wall-painting itself (plate 74). It has been doubted, of course, many times, e.g. by G. Carotti, who ascribed it to Cesare da Sesto; and it has been zealously defended, e.g. by Prof. Hildebrandt (in his *Leonardo*, 1927, pp. 98–101; see also Sirén, 1916, p. 109).

It is the ghost of a Leonardo drawing; worse still, it is a rouged and made-up ghost; but it remains the only visible thing we can take hold of if we want to dream how Leonardo painted the central figure of his masterpiece.

There are two notes by Leonardo which prove that he made studies from living persons, meaning to use their features as a model for the figure of Christ in *The Last Supper*. One of the notes reads, 'Christ. Count Giovanni, the one with the Cardinal of Mortaro' (S.K. M. II–1, 3a). The other, 'Alessandro Carissimo of Parma, for the hand of Christ' (same note-book, 6a).

According to Vasari (1568) and Francesco Bocchi (1584), Leonardo left the head of Christ in the wall-painting unfinished.

10 and 11

STUDIES FOR THE HEAD OF LEDA.
Windsor, 12516 and 12518
Leonardo made two different cartoons for a Leda painting, one for a Leda with the Swan in a crouching position, and one for a standing Leda. (Cf. notes on plates 36 and 37.) The latter was copied by Raphael

---

1. Leonardo was in Venice in the spring of 1500, the only sojourn of which we have documentary evidence. This happened when he travelled from Milan to Florence. When, in 1506, he travelled from Florence to Milan, he could have visited Venice again; at least, his influence on the art of Bellini and Giorgione is most apparent about this time.

during his stay at Florence, about 1506, in a pen and ink drawing which is now at Windsor Castle.

A sketch in oil, from Leonardo's studio, of a similar head was in Lord Melchett's possession, a repetition is in the Parma Gallery, and other copies in the William van Horne Collection, Montreal, and in the Johnson Collection, Philadelphia. Those four versions are painted on wooden panels. A brush drawing in umbra on linen, similar in technique to Leonardo's drapery studies on canvas, was in the Pietro del Giudice Collection, London (sold by Sotheby's in 1963).

12 and 13

HEADS OF WARRIORS. Budapest, Museum of Fine Arts, Nos. 344 and 343.

Studies for the helmeted figure on the right, and for the two central figures in the cartoon for the *Battle of Anghiari*. (See plate 108.) On the reverse of No. 12 is a sketch in metal-point, a helmeted man carrying a lance over his left shoulder; a rather weak drawing. According to Suida (p. 142), No. 12, and perhaps also No. 13, are copies; but neither Popham (1946), nor Heydenreich (1954), nor Kenneth Clark (1958) have agreed to this condemnation of the two particularly fine drawings.

14

STUDY OF AN APOSTLE. Vienna, Albertina, Cat. No. III, 18.

Pen over metal-point; some of the ink lines are perhaps by a later hand.

Usually regarded as a study for St Peter (plate 73, the head between Judas and St John), which is difficult to accept. It is probably a study for the Apostle Simeon in the first version of *The Last Supper* – see the second figure from the right in the upper row of plate 71.

15–17

STUDIES FOR HEADS OF APOSTLES IN THE LAST SUPPER. Windsor, 12552, 12548 and 12557.

For St James the Greater (No. 15) compare the head at the extreme right in plate 74; for St Bartholomew (No. 16) the head at the extreme left in plate 73; for St Philip (No. 17) the head at the extreme right in plate 75.

18

HEAD OF ST ANNE. Windsor, 12534

Study for the cartoon of St Anne, which Fra Pietro da Novellara described in 1501 (see Document XI, on p. 37). See also the note to plate 54. The face in the drawing much retouched by a later hand.

19

HEAD OF A YOUNG WOMAN. Windsor, 12512. 16.5×12.4 cm.

According to Kenneth Clark, 'the silver-point outline of the back of the head, neck, bust, etc., is so masterly and has so much Leonardo's rhythm of hand that we are tempted to say that the drawing originally was by him, and has been worked over by a pupil.' Some of the shading, although very little of it, is from left to right. This drawing appears to me a very important example of a workshop production, where a sketch by the master was made into a finished drawing by one of his pupils – perhaps by Ambrogio de Predis (according to Möller, by Salai). Compare the cartoon, plate 24, which is also worked over by a pupil.

20

STUDY FOR THE ANGEL'S HEAD IN THE VIRGIN OF THE ROCKS. Turin, 15572
Cf. plates 21 and 64.

21

ANGEL'S HEAD. Detail from plate 64, Madonna of the Rocks, Paris, Louvre. (The reproduction is in original size.)

22

LADY WITH AN ERMINE. Cracow, No. 180. Panel, 55×40.4 cm.

In ancient times ermines (Greek, *galéa*) were kept as mouse-hunters instead of cats.[2] This also appears to have been sometimes a custom in the Renaissance, as a big weasel is depicted in this portrait, and a small one in a lady's portrait from Titian's studio (Vienna Museum, and a variant in the John Ringling Art Museum, Sarasota, U.S.A.).

Leonardo used the ermine (*galéa*) as a speaking symbol in this portrait of Cecilia Gallerani, as he used the juniper, or ginevra, in the portrait of Ginevra de'Benci; a cock, or *gallo*, in the allegory on Gian Galeazzo Sforza; and the knots, the *fantasie dei vinci*, as a symbol for his own name.

Cecilia Gallerani became the mistress of Ludovico Moro

2. 'Professor Rolleston and others believed that the domestic animal of the Greeks and Romans, for which we now use the cat, was the white-breasted marten. The word *felis*, it is true, is commonly used for the weasel' (Watkins, *Natural History of the Ancients*, London, 1896, p. 63). Bode (*Leonardo-Studien*, p. 112) thought that Leonardo was depicting a marten, or rather a ferret (Mustela furo), as he never saw a real ermine. (See also G. Jennison, *Animals in Ancient Rome*, 1937, pp. 19 and 129.) The ermine was also the emblem of Ludovico Sforza.

in 1481, and the portrait was painted shortly after Leonardo arrived in Milan.

The ermine is the best part of the picture, as the critics, including Ochenkowski, Hildebrandt and Clark, are all agreed. Otherwise, the painting is not well preserved. The lower part of the hand has been repainted as well as the left shoulder and the part of the dress underneath the ermine, where Cecilia's left hand was originally sketched in. The dark background is new, and the outline of the figure spoilt by it. New also is the inscription in the upper left corner: 'La belle Feroniere Leonard d'Awinci,' which suggests that the picture had been in France before it came into the possession of Prince Adam Czartoryski during the French Revolution.

In spite of its doubtful preservation, this is Leonardo's most charming portrait painting. Seidlitz attributed this portrait to Ambrogio de Predis, Gronau and Sirén to Boltraffio. Berenson, Kenneth Clark, and Heydenreich give it to Leonardo, which is indeed correct.

23

PORTRAIT OF GINEVRA DE' BENCI. Vaduz, Liechtenstein Gallery, 32. Panel, 42×37 cm.

On the reverse a sprig of juniper encircled by laurel and palm forming a garland, with the inscription '*virtutem forma decorat*' (plate 88). The garland, in its mutilated shape, on the back of the panel proves that the painting has been cut by c. 8 inches; the lower part, originally containing the hands, is lost. The slit of the bodice has been overpainted; originally the fingers of the right hand, probably holding some flowers, were painted here. A drawing at Windsor (plate 33) might have been a study for the hands of this portrait.[3]

Compare the reconstruction, illustrated on p. 175.

Juniper (*ginepro* or *ginevra* in Italian) is the symbol for the name of the sitter. The *Libro di Antonio Billi* (c. 1518), the Anonimo Gaddiano (c. 1542) and also Vasari (1550 and 1568) confirm that Leonardo portrayed Ginevra de' Benci, and they praise the picture (See p. 31.)

24

PORTRAIT OF ISABELLA D'ESTE. Louvre, M.I. 753. (The reproduction is reduced to two-thirds of the original size.)

The drawing is pricked for transfer, but the painting done from it is lost. Leonardo painted Isabella in 1500 – see Documents IX and X. There were at least two portraits of Isabella, one which Leonardo left in Mantua (and which probably was later in Fontainebleau) and one which he had with him in Venice, as we know from a letter from Lorenzo Gusnasco to Isabella d'Este, dated March 13th, 1500. And it may be that Leonardo painted a third 'sketch', fulfilling Isabella's wish.

The cartoon reproduced here is of very poor preservation.[4] The reproduction gives only a part of the drawing, as the head only is by Leonardo, and the dress and hand by a mediocre pupil, who unfortunately was bold enough to redraw even the profile. The cartoon must have been famous, because there are several old copies of it, including one at Oxford, showing the hands in the right position resting on a book, and one at the Uffizi, the head only, probably by Ambrogio de Predis. Other copies are in the Munich Print-room, and in the British Museum.

25

PORTRAIT OF A GIRL. Windsor, 12505. 32×20 cm.

Chin and other parts of the face re-drawn, but probably by Leonardo himself.

26

PORTRAIT OF A MUSICIAN. Ambrosiana, sala E.19. Panel, 43×31 cm.

In Leonardo's List of Drawings (Richter § 680) of c. 1482 there is one item: '*una testa ritratta d'Atalante che alzava il volto*'. This probably means that Leonardo portrayed the musician Atalante Migliorotti, who had learned from him to play the *lira* (according to the Anonimo Gaddiano) and who went with him from Florence to Milan in 1482. Atalante moved in 1490 to Mantua; and in 1513, when Leonardo came to Rome, he found Atalante there as Superintendent of the buildings of Pope Leo X.

Nevertheless, Luca Beltrami, who saw in the Ambrosiana picture a portrait of Franchino Gaffurio, was probably right. In 1905, the picture was freed from overpaint, and the sheet was revealed with music notes and a half-effaced inscription line on it, reading CANT … ANG … Now Gaffurio, conductor of the Cathedral choir in Milan from 1483, was the author of an

---

3. Why has the lower part of the painting been cut off? No one painted hands more beautifully than Leonardo did. I suspect that the painting was unfinished, the hands only sketched in (as the left hand of the Lady with the Ermine, or the right hand of the Musician, plates 22 and 26). Ginevra was born in 1456, in 1473 she married Luigi Niccolini, in 1490 she was still alive.

4. Popham, p. 120: 'Of the authenticity of this it is difficult to speak; in its present state one cannot say that it represents much of the master's handiwork'. Nevertheless, he reproduces in his book this important cartoon (fig. 172).

Franchino Gaffurio, playing the organ. Woodcut (detail)
from his *Angelicum ac divinum opus musicae*, Milan, 1508.
(This block was first used in 1480.)

Franchino Gaffurio, teaching the theory of music. Woodcut
from his *De harmonia musicae disciplinae*, 1480.
(Inscribed: *Harmonia est discordiæ concors*.)

'Angelicum ac divinum opus', not published until 1508, but composed probably much earlier.[5] We may read the inscription on the sheet in the Ambrosiana musician's hand as 'canticum angelicum', which would be the title of a work by Gaffurio. According to Gerolamo Adda, Leonardo made the designs for the woodcuts in Gaffurio's 'Practica musicae', published at Milan, 1496. Gaffurio, born 1451, was of about the same age as Leonardo.

As a third possibility, the inscription could be read CANT(or) ANG(elo), which would make it a portrait of Angelo Testagrossa, who in 1496 was the singing-master of Isabella d'Este.[6]

This portrait is the only painting by Leonardo which is in a perfect state of preservation. Only the face and a part of the hair are finished; everything else, including the hand, is just sketched in. All the brush strokes, especially those on the cheek-bone and the neck, seem to me to be made by a left-handed painter. For the rather strange design of the eyes, compare the drawing of an angel, from the same period, plate 20.[7]

27

PORTRAIT OF A YOUNG LADY IN PRO-FILE. Ambrosiana, sala E, 8. Panel, 51 × 34 cm. Müller-Walde thought it a portrait of Bianca, a natural daughter of Ludovico Moro, for which painting Leonardo received a commission in 1491. Bode, Gronau and Beltrami[8] attributed it without any reservation to Leonardo; Suida thinks that Leonardo did the better part of the portrait; Kenneth Clark suggested that the master may have painted some of the details, especially the headdress.[9] But Morelli, Berenson, Bodmer, Sirén and other experts regard it as the master-piece of Ambrogio de Predis. R. Longhi is alone in attributing it to Lorenzo Costa (*Ampliamenti nell' officina Ferrarese*, 1940, p. 142).

I believe that it was designed by Leonardo in his workshop but not executed by him. Ambrogio de Predis is certainly responsible for some of the weaknesses of the painting, mainly for the insensitive, dark background, by which he even spoiled the outlines of the back of the head and the shoulder.[10] The flesh is much better

---

5. The woodcut representations of Gaffurio do not contradict the identification of this picture as a portrait of him. The woodcut from *De harmonia musicae* was first published in 1480; the other from *Angelicum ac divinum opus* was also first printed at Naples in 1480, and reprinted at Milan in 1492 and 1508. (See A. M. Hind, *History of Woodcut*, 1935, vol. I, p. 516.)

6. I am mentioning this although I am convinced that this is a portrait of Franchino Gaffurio, and of no one else.

7. Adolfo Venturi (1941) followed Morelli and Seidlitz in attributing this portrait to Ambrogio de Predis. A similar portrait in the Ambrosiana, Milan (inscribed '*vita si scias uti longa est*'), certainly a work of Ambrogio de Predis, shows the inferiority of the pupil's art.

8. Luca Beltrami, *Leonardo e i disfattisti suoi*, Milan, 1919, p. 64 f.

9. May we assume that Leonardo designed, for the Court jeweller, jewellery as worn by the Lady of this portrait? The golden *ghirlanda* or *ferronnière* round the brow, the net made of gold wire and pearls, and the interlaced wire ornament over the shoulder are of exquisite design. An engraving by Jaques Prévost de Gray, a portrait of Francis I (Bibl. Nat., Paris, reprod. Bouchot, *Pièces choisies de l'école Française*), shows the King with a neck-chain formed of shells and *fantasie dei vinci*, which looks as if designed by Leonardo.

10. From 1796 to 1815 the picture was in Paris where, apparently, it was restored. There are several pictures at the Louvre showing the same poor style of restoration.

modelled, softer and more lifelike than anything Predis ever painted, including the Archinto portrait with its sooty shadows in the National Gallery, dated 1494 (which is most probably by him), or the utterly disagreeable profile of Emperor Maximilian in the Vienna Museum, dated 1502.

Profile portraits by Leonardo are scarce; but compare, for example, plate 25; or plate 24; or the portraits of Ludovico Sforza and his family, plate II: which all belong to the 1490's.

28, 29

MONA LISA. Louvre, No. 1601. Panel, 77×53 cm. The only Leonardo portrait painting which has never been questioned. The sitter was Lisa Gherardini, born in 1479, married in 1495 to Francesco di Zanobi del Giocondo of Florence. Leonardo brought the painting to France (see Document XVI), where Francis I bought it for 12,000 francs.

The preservation of the painting is not too good; there are overpaintings in the dress, the veil, the right hand, in the sky and elsewhere. Part of the glazes is rubbed off, and the whole is covered by dirty greenish varnish. According to Wölfflin (Seidlitz, 1935, p. 268) the dress was originally green and the sleeves yellow. The picture is cut both sides, about 3 inches.[11]

The cleaning of the picture has often been considered, but the French artists, especially Degas, protested against it; and they were right.

Many pages have been written since Vasari's time on the 'Smile of the Gioconda'. A Frenchman (Robert de Sizeranne, 1896) has observed that Gioconda smiles with only the left part of her mouth – but this is in accordance with the advice given to women in Renaissance times as to how to look most graceful: we read in Agnolo Firenzuola's 'Della perfetta bellezza d'una donna', 1541: 'From time to time, to close the mouth at the right corner with a suave and nimble movement, and to open it at the left side, as if you were smiling secretly . . . not in an artificial manner, but as though unconsciously – this is not affectation, if it is done in moderation and in a restrained and graceful manner and accompanied by innocent coquetry and by certain movements of the eyes. . . .' This is a precept for ladies of fashion, and we should not overlook the fact that Mona Lisa – who plucked her eye-brows and the hair above her brow – was one of them.[12]

---

11. Concerning the state of preservation of the Leonardo paintings in the Louvre see C. Wolters, in *Kunstchronik*, 1952, p. 135 f.

12. Vasari describes Mona Lisa's eye-brows indeed in detail. Did he mean the eye-lashes? The excellent Milanese restorer Cavenaghi stated (Seidlitz, p. 509) that eye-brows have never been painted in this portrait.

[The *Mona Lisa* is probably the most popular portrait in the world. And its popularity was considerably enhanced when thirty years ago it was stolen from the Louvre and remained undiscovered for more than two years. The thief was an Italian house-painter, Vincenzo Peruggia, who did occasional work at the Louvre. On the 21st of August, 1911, at 8 o'clock in the morning he took the picture out of its frame, put it under his workman's blouse, marched through a backdoor and down to the quay. He was questioned by the Police, but they did not find the painting which he kept in a small storeroom at his lodgings. When two years later, in Florence, Peruggia offered the smiling Gioconda to an art-dealer, Alfred Gori by name, he was arrested, and the picture was surrendered to the French Ambassador on the 21st December, 1913. Peruggia declared he had taken this Italian picture to Italy, being himself a Lombard and a patriot. He was sentenced to seven months imprisonment.]

30

THE PROPORTIONS OF THE HUMAN FIGURE. Venice, 228. 34.3×24.5 cm. (A part of the text underneath the figure is not reproduced here.)

This drawing is an illustration to a passage in Vitruvius, book III, cap. 1 (Richter § 343), and Leonardo's writing on the sheet is a free rendering of what Vitruvius said; but Leonardo did not copy the sentences which he in fact illustrated, viz.: 'The navel is naturally placed in the centre of the human body, and if a circle be described of a man lying with his face upward and his hands and feet extended, it will touch his fingers and his toes. It is not alone by a circle that the human body is thus circumscribed, as may be seen by placing it within a square. For if we measure from the feet to the crown of the head, and then across the arms fully extended, we should find the latter measure equal to the former; so that the lines at right angles to each other enclosing the figure, would form a square.'

31

NUDE FIGURE OF A MAN, HIS BACK TURNED TO THE SPECTATOR. Windsor, 12596

Probably done in connection with the earliest studies for the Battle of Anghiari.

32

STUDIES OF HANDS. Windsor, 12616

For the *Adoration of the Kings*, Uffizi (1481, plate 49). The sheet is partly discoloured by damp and the fine silver-point lines are hardly visible on the pink pre-paration; this reproduction is based on a ultra-violet photograph which shows much more than one can see in the original drawing. (Cf. Popham, in *Burlington Magazine*, XCIV, pp. 127–132.)

33

STUDY OF A WOMAN'S HANDS. Windsor, 12558

See the note on plate 23: the drawing has been con-nected (by Müller-Walde) with the Ginevra portrait in the Liechtenstein Gallery, and with Verrocchio's marble bust of a *Lady with Primulas* (Florence, Museo Nazionale, attributed to Leonardo by Mackowsky, Bode, and, with some reservation, by Suida); see the illustration on p. 25; and the note on plate 23.

34

POINTING WOMAN IN A LANDSCAPE, NEAR A WATERFALL. Windsor, 12581

This drawing, probably done during Leonardo's late period in Rome and under the influence of Hellenistic reliefs, also shows how far Leonardo had returned to the style of his native Florence; Seidlitz (p. 215) felt re-minded of Botticelli.

The landscape – with the little waterfall in the left corner, the trees on both sides, the river, and the hills disappearing in the distance as in a grey haze – is barely indicated, but is as full of atmosphere as any late drawing by Rembrandt.

This drawing is dated sometimes too early (Seidlitz: c. 1491) and sometimes too late (Heydenreich: one of the last drawings). The technique of the drawing is the same as in the study for the Trivulzio monument, Windsor, No. 12354, of about 1511, and the Deluge series, Windsor, e.g. No. 12383, of about 1514. The *Pointing Woman* is later than No. 12354, and earlier than 12383.

35

YOUTH IN MASQUERADE COSTUME. Windsor, 12575

Malaguzzi Valeri, Seidlitz and Bodmer dated this draw-ing early, connecting it with a masquerade for Count Galeazzo Sanseverino, in 1491; Müller-Walde thought it was done in the first Florentine period, for the joust of Giuliano de' Medici in 1475. Calvi attributed it to the later Milan period. Popp attributed it to the French period, 1517–18, and Heydenreich accepted this date. Sir Kenneth Clark thought the drawing should be dated after 1513. Thus, the main problem of this drawing is its date.

In May, 1506, Leonardo was summoned to Milan by the Governor, Charles d'Amboise; he obtained three months' leave from the Signoria of Florence, and in September of that year the leave was prolonged, with-out the Signoria's consent. He stayed another full year in Milan, and he suspended his work on the painting of the Battle of Anghiari in the Sala di Gran Consiglio, and never resumed it. Why was Leonardo summoned to Milan? Certainly he would not have been granted leave merely to put the last touches to an altar-piece for an obscure monastery. I think this leave was granted because Louis XII was expected in Milan, who actually entered the town on the 23rd May, 1507, when three triumphal arches were erected in his honour and two hundred youths in costumes of blue silk welcomed him.[13] I imagine Leonardo's masquerade drawings (Windsor, 12573–77) were done in this year.

All Leonardo's late drawings are marked by a profound *tristesse* and exhibit a dissolution of form which recall the later Titian and Rembrandt. I cannot discern the same spirit in those lively and plastic costume drawings which continue the style of the drawings for the St Anne cartoon, but are earlier than those for the Trivulzio monument. I should not date any of the Windsor draw-ings 12573–77 later than 1507.

36

LEDA AND THE SWAN. Chatsworth, 717

A sketch in the Codex Atlanticus (289 recto), datable c. 1504, three small sketches at Windsor (12337), a drawing at Chatsworth, a drawing at Rotterdam (formerly at Weimar), an unpleasing painting once at Castle Neuwied (usually ascribed to Gianpetrino) – that is all that is left of Leonardo's composition of a kneeling Leda. The mother of Castor and Pollux, of Clytem-nestra and Helen, appears in this drawing sharply differentiated from the slender Venus of Botticelli, the tall figure of Eve as the Florentines drew her since Ghiberti, or even Raphael's Three Graces: it is a baroque type of a woman, fleshy, like a mare: fertility sym-bolized by heavy curves. This Leda is the re-born Bathing Venus of the Greek Baroque and the forerunner of the fat beauties of Rubens.

Morelli attributed this, and the drawing at Rotterdam, to Sodoma; Seidlitz thought that they were only copies after Leonardo. Kenneth Clark believes that the Chatsworth drawing may be a copy. But both drawings were accepted as genuine by Berenson, Suida, Giglioli, Heydenreich, and others, and are now almost generally regarded as autographs. They are certainly both from the same hand, and both not free from retouches.

13. In Luca Landucci's *Florentine Diary* there is a note under the 23rd May, 1507: 'The King of France entered Milan, and there were jousts and feasts'. Isabella d'Este was present. (Marie Herzfeld's edition of Landucci's diary, 1913, vol. II, p. 139 f.)

Leda. Pen and ink over black chalk, by Leonardo, about 1504. Windsor (12337 r., detail, enlarged).

Leda and the Swan. Pen and ink over black chalk, by Leonardo, about 1504, Rotterdam, Boymans Museum (Koenigs Collection).

In the present drawing the body of Leda was at first much thinner; parts were added from the armpits to the hips, and now both shoulders appear to be wrongly attached. The composition has a triangular shape, a pattern followed by Raphael in his Esterházy Madonna, which dates from the same time, about 1504. In the Rotterdam version (which, I believe, is earlier than the one at Chatsworth) the head of Leda is turned to look at the swan, and the swan is lowered and made heavier, appearing like a phallic symbol. The painted version formerly at Castle Neuwied is badly composed and has probably very little to do with any Leonardo design; but, of course, Gianpetrino was at all times *imitating* Leonardo. (The two very interesting Leda engravings by the 'Master I. B. with the Bird', on the other hand, produced probably in about 1500 or a few years later, are completely independent.)

A tiny sketch for the *Standing Leda* is stuck on the *verso* of the sheet 12642 at Windsor. Heydenreich, however, suggested tentatively that this sketch could be for a *Venus* by Leonardo, mentioned by Amoretti. (Seidlitz, 1935, p. 337; Heydenreich, 1954, p. 203.) A similar sketch for a *Standing Leda* is fol. 156 recto of the Codex Atlanticus. This figure has been used in a painting *Venus and Amor* by Beccafumi (Leonardo Exhibition at Los Angeles,

1949, No. 69), now in the Isaac Delgado Museum, New Orleans.

37

LEDA AND THE SWAN. Free copy of a lost Leonardo painting of about 1506. Rome, Collection of Contessa Gallotti Spiridon. (Formerly Coll. Comtesse de Rozière, Paris; Baronne de Ruble, Paris. – See Lionello Venturi, *Catalogo della Collezione Ludovico Spiridon*, Amsterdam, 1932.) Panel, 114×86 cm.

This composition is derived from the later version of the *Kneeling Leda* (plate 36): the heads of woman and bird are in the same direction. The right arm of Leda is stretched across her body, as in the sketch of the *Kneeling Leda* at Windsor (12337).

Raphael made a copy in pen and ink from Leonardo's cartoon (Windsor 12759), presumably during his stay in Florence (1504–08).[14]

---

14. This is far from being certain. Seidlitz (1935, p. 335), following Morelli, attributes this rather poor drawing to Sodoma and thinks that it was 'certainly' done by him in Milan after 1508. Gronau, Fischel, Kenneth Clark, Heydenreich, and Popham, on the other hand regard it as an authentic drawing by Raphael, datable 1505–08. Professor Amadore Porcella, who thinks that the Spiridon picture is an original work by Leonardo, painted in Rome (1514–16), assumes that Raphael copied it there and so late.

Leonardo's *Leda* is mentioned by the Anonimo Gad-diano, although in a doubtful way (see footnote 16 on p. 31). The reference is crossed out and replaced by a reference to the (now lost) cartoon of *Adam and Eve*. It may be that the *Leda* mentioned by the Anonimo in c. 1542, was a cartoon, in some ways resembling the *Adam and Eve* cartoon, not only because both contained a large number of plants but perhaps also alike in the movement of the female figure.

Lomazzo (1584 and 1590) gave some description of Leonardo's *Leda*: '*Facendo Leda tutta ignuda col cigno in grembo, che vergognosamente abassa gli occhi.*'[15]

According to Lomazzo this painting (or cartoon?) went to France and was in the possession of Francis I. The *Leda* which Cassiano del Pozzo saw in 1625 at the Palais de Fontainebleau was doubtless a painting; he describes it as a standing figure of Leda almost entirely naked, well finished but somewhat dry in style, con-sisting of three long panels which had broken apart, causing a certain loss of paint.

Père Dan, who in 1642 made a list of the pictures at Fontainebleau, does not mention Leonardo's *Leda*; but the name of the picture appears again, and for the last time, in a Fontainebleau Inventory of 1694.[16]

In 1722 a Leda cartoon was seen at Milan in the collec-tion of Marchese Casnedi by Edward Wright (*Some observations made in travelling through France and Italy in the years 1720 and 1722*, London, 1730, p. 471.) Accord-ing to Langton Douglas (pp. 37-41) the Casnedi collec-tion of cartoons, including a St Anne cartoon, can be traced back to Melzi's heritage, which means the drawings, cartoons, paintings and manuscripts left to Francesco Melzi by Leonardo in his Will. The St Anne cartoon from the Casnedi collection is now in the Royal Academy, London, the Leda cartoon is missing.

---

15. 'Entirely nude, with the swan in her lap, and her eyes bashfully cast down.' This description does not quite agree with the known copies of the *Standing Leda; in grembo* can hardly mean 'in her arms'. Adolf Rosenberg (*Leonardo*, Bielefeld, 1898, p. 125) has indeed understood that Lomazzo was describing a sitting Leda, similar to the one by Correggio (now Berlin, No. 218). Michelangelo's *Leda*, finished in 1530 and taken one year later to France, could certainly be described as '*col cigno in grembo*'. Michelangelo's *Leda*, as we know from Vasari, was also in Fontainebleau. My suspicion is that Lomazzo confused the two pictures. (Cf. Goldscheider, *Michelangelo Drawings*, London, 1966, plate 64, and p. 208, note on plate XI-a.) There is an old unwarrantable story that Leonardo's *Leda* was burnt in about 1700 at the instigation of Madame de Maintenon, when she had become old and pious, and Queen of France, and was indeed not in favour of lascivious paintings. According to another report Michelangelo's *Leda* was already burnt, in about 1640, under Louis XIII, by his minister Desnoyers.

16. It is uncertain whether this is the same picture, or only a copy, because the original might have been burned, together with Michelangelo's *Leda*, in about 1640. (See footnote 15.)

It remains doubtful, whether the painting of a *Standing Leda* at Fontainebleau was an original work of Leonardo, or a painted copy from his cartoon, perhaps by Melzi. All the versions which have come down to us are only free copies, most of them by Milanese painters, none of them from Leonardo's workshop, some even by Netherlanders who worked in Italy.[17]

38

DRAPERY STUDY FOR A KNEELING WOMAN. Windsor, 12521

Seidlitz and Popham connected the drawing with Verrocchio's Baptism of Christ (plate 43), Venturi with the Annunciation (plate 59), Sir Kenneth Clark with the Madonna of the Rocks in the National Gallery. I cannot see that Leonardo used this drapery study in any of his paintings; it was probably done for an Adoration of the Child (compare plate 70).

39

DRAPERY STUDY FOR A KNEELING WOMAN. Rome, Galleria Corsini. No. 125770.

Drawing of a figure with folded hands, either for an Adoration of the Child, or else for an Annunciation. Popp connected this drawing with the *Louvre Annuncia-tion* (plate I-c) pointing out that it was not used for the Madonna but for the angel, in a reversed way, as seen in a mirror. Baldass connected it with the drapery of the angel in plate 59, where it also would have been used in a reversed way.

40 and 41

DRAPERY STUDIES FOR THE MADONNA IN THE ST ANNE PAINTING. Windsor, 12532 and 12530. (Compare plate 68.) Both drawings are done with the brush in lamp black and white over black chalk; No. 40 is on red paper, and the hand in red chalk; No. 41, the drapery for a seated figure is on yellowish paper.

42

DRAPERY STUDY FOR THE RIGHT ARM OF ST PETER. Windsor, 12546. For *The Last Supper* (plate 73).

---

17. For a list of those copies see Seidlitz, p. 528; and Sirén, p. 187 f., with some illustrations. The best copy is the one reproduced here; others are in the possession of the Earl of Pembroke at Wilton House; in the Borghese Gallery, Rome; in the Collection of Mr. David Edge, London (formerly Doetsch and Richeton Collections; the twist of Leda's body in this copy is very similar to that in Raphael's pen and ink sketch). A very good version, but painted on canvas, is in the collection of Anthony Hyde, London.

For original Leonardo drawings of the *Head of Leda* see plates 10 and 11.

Zoan Andrea: The dancing muses, detail of an engraving after Mantegna's *Parnassus*, about 1497. (B. XIII, 305).

Domenico Ghirlandaio: Dancing Maidens, pen and ink drawing, about 1490. Stockholm, National Museum.

43

KNEELING ANGEL IN PROFILE. Detail from Verrocchio's *Baptism of Christ* (Florence, Uffizi), reproduced here in about one third of the original size.

Painted for the Church of the Monastery of San Salvi fuori la Porta alla Croce, at Florence. The inception of the picture by Verrocchio seems to date from about 1470 (according to Planiscig and Sandberg-Vavalà) or else from 1472 (Heydenreich). In its present state it is unfinished in parts, uneven in quality, and a work of several brushes or at least of several periods. Leonardo's share in this painting was first mentioned in 1510, by Francesco Albertini (*'uno angelo di Leonardo Vinci'*), and discussed, forty years later, by Vasari. In more recent times Bayersdorfer and Bode have tried to define Leonardo's contribution to the painting. The wooded cliffs on the right, and the lifeless palm on the left are obviously not by the same hand as the landscape above the two angels (plate 73) which is neither a decorative background nor a conventional rendering of stone, vegetation and water, but the portrait of an individual piece of nature.

Leonardo's share in this painting are the angel in profile on the left, the tuft of grass underneath him, and the landscape above him; nothing else. The head of the angel is damaged and much restored. The finest bit of what Leonardo added to Verrocchio's painting is the drapery of this angel.

If we compare Leonardo's first dated drawing of 1473 (plate 81) with the 'Baptism' landscape (plate 87), there remains little doubt that they both belong to the same period. (But dates between 1476 and 1495 have also been suggested.)

44

ST JOHN THE BAPTIST. Windsor, 12572
According to Valentiner, a sketch for a figure in the Pistoia altar-piece. See our note (p. 185) on plate I of the appendix and the illustration on p. 27. In 1478 Leonardo was in Pistoia; this drawing is of the same time, but it might have been done for the San Bernardino altar-piece, which certainly included a figure of St John. (See footnote 18 on p. 31.) Antonio Billi and the Anonimo Gaddiano mention an early *St John* by Leonardo.

45

DANCING MAIDENS. Venice, 233
The draperies of the maidens remind one of the angels in Botticelli's *Nativity*, dated 1500 (National Gallery, London), but still more of the dancing muses in Mantegna's *Parnassus*, about 1497 (Louvre, No. 1375), once in the studio of Isabella d'Este at Mantua. Was Leonardo influenced by Mantegna, or were he and the other painters inspired by a Hellenistic relief of the Horae? Of course, similar drawings, though not of the same quality, were produced in the workshops of Ghirlandaio and other Florentine artists.

The figure on the left in No. 45 is, curiously enough, dressed like a Fortuna (cf. the engraving by Nicoletto da Modena, or the much later painting by Rubens in the Prado). The characteristic part is the piece of garment, held over the head and used as a sail.

46

NEPTUNE. Windsor, 12570. 25.1×39.2 cm.
A study for the cartoon, which, according to Vasari, Leonardo did for his 'good friend Antonio Segni'. The

David. Detail of a pen and ink drawing, over black chalk, by
Leonardo, c. 1504, after Michelangelo's marble statue.
Windsor (12591 r).

definite drawing contained many more figures, as
Vasari mentions 'sprites, dolphins and winds, and
several most beautiful heads of sea gods'.

The motif was perhaps taken from the antique, as were
certainly a bronze plaquette in the Dreyfus Collection
(Molinier, No. 13), and a plaquette at Dijon (reproduced
in *Art Studies*, 1930, fig. 19). The horse at the right,
throwing his head sharply sideways, is exactly repeated
in Leone Leoni's Andrea Doria Plaquette (Victoria and
Albert Museum, No. A484–1910); but a very similar
sea-horse is already in an engraving by Mantegna, 'The
Combat of Tritons' (B.17), datable c. 1494, and this
composition might have inspired Leonardo.

At the top left of the drawing is a note in Leonardo's
handwriting: *a bassa i chavalli* (to lower the horses).
This, according to Popp and Kenneth Clark, was tried
out by Leonardo in the Windsor drawing, No. 12591,
of which a part is reproduced here. It is a free copy of
Michelangelo's *David*, with a slight sketch of sea-horses
under his feet. Only the figure of David is inked-in.[18]

---

18. In his *Life of Michelangelo* Vasari hints that the younger artist
received his commission for the *David* in competition with
Leonardo: 'Some of Michelangelo's friends wrote from Florence
urging him to return, as they did not want that block of marble in
the *opera* [the office of works for the Cathedral] to be spoiled which
Piero Soderini, then *gonfaloniere* for life in Florence, had repeatedly
proposed to give to Leonardo da Vinci.' Edmondo Solmi (*Rassegna
d'Arte*, 1912, p. 128 f.) argued that the Windsor drawing No. 12591
was an independent sketch by Leonardo (not a copy after Michelangelo's *David*, or a development of Windsor drawing No. 12570).

47

ALLEGORY OF FORTUNA. British Museum,
1895-9-15-482 (Catal. 1950, No. 104).

This is, I think, Leonardo's most beautiful allegorical
drawing, but I do not understand what is meant by it.
On the stump of a tree lies a shield, and against the trunk
leans a coat-of-arms with a lion rampant. (For a similar
escutcheon with lion and dragon, symbolizing strength
and prudence, see Richter § 692.) But what do the
curves under the shield represent? They can hardly be
fluttering ribbons, and are usually explained as flames.
Above the shield, touching it with just the toes of one
foot, hovers a winged figure, probably meaning Fama.
This figure is beautifully shaded in a rather baroque
way, and the movement is strongly expressed by the
streaming waves of hair and drapery. There is another
figure, running towards the tree, holding her garment
with one hand and touching the shield with the other
hand. This figure is Fortuna, recognizable by her fore-
lock. A part of the same figure, the head turned differently and the hair more elaborately drawn, is repeated
in the upper right-hand corner.

According to Popham, 'there seems to be no reason for
connecting the angel, or Victory, with the allegorical
composition underneath'. Seidlitz and Bodmer, however, take it for *one* consistent composition (and date it
to the earliest Milanese years, soon after 1483).

If Leonardo passed through Mantua on his way to Milan
in the autumn of 1481, he might have seen a chimney-
piece painting of *Fortuna* in the house of Marchese

Allegory of Fortuna ('Occasio'). Painting, probably after a design
by Mantegna, c. 1475. Milan.

Biondo (now in the Palazzo Ducale). The similarity consists, however, only in the subject and in the arrangement of the two main figures.

48

STUDY FOR THE ADORATION OF THE KINGS. Louvre (Gallichon Collection), R.F.1978 (cf. plate 49).

In March 1481 Leonardo made a contract with the monks of San Donato a Scopeto, a cloister outside Florence near the Porta Romana, to paint for them an altar-piece and to finish it in two years, or at most in two and a half years. The theme was 'The Adoration of the Kings'. The picture was never finished.[19]

A number of beautiful drawings are connected with this commission (see plates 32 and 58 and 102; but there are many more). No. 48 represents Leonardo's first idea for the painting. The scene is the courtyard of a ruined palace; at the left are two arcades, at the right five arcades and two flights of stairs, leading to a gallery, on which a man is sitting and blowing a trumpet. In the background are many figures, among them men on horseback, somewhat similar to the later sketches for the Anghiari battle. Most of the figures are drawn in the nude, in order to delineate the movements in a manner anatomically correct. The arms of the man who gives the goblet to the child are sketched in two different positions.

For a separate detailed drawing for the background see plate 58.

49–53

THE ADORATION OF THE KINGS. Uffizi, No. 1594. Wood, 258×243 cm.

The picture is just 'under-painted', a large drawing in umber brown over a sand-coloured priming. The most important figures – the Virgin and the Kings in the foreground – are the least-finished ones. The picture was begun in March 1481; when Leonardo left for Milan (probably in the autumn of 1482) the painting remained with Amerigo de' Benci, the father of Ginevra (see plate 23). Professor Simon Meller expressed the opinion that Leonardo resumed his work during his later stay in Florence, i.e. 1503, when he was working on the cartoon of the Anghiari battle; Strzygowski accepted this view, and thought that some of the horses

were added later. Although the whole picture looks as if it were done at one stroke, some of the drawings would seem to confirm this theory. This theory, of course, rests on slender foundations, but I mention it as being worthy of reconsideration.[20]

To understand how it was that Leonardo worked for so considerable a time at his 'Adoration of the Kings' and still left it 'unfinished', we may compare any one of Rembrandt's etchings, which, though of a different period and style, are nearest in artistic aim to Leonardo's Adoration. Let us take one of the best known, the Three Crosses (B. 78). Here, as in Leonardo's Adoration, stand some of the most important figures as white patches against the dark background or a dark group of figures. There exist several 'states' of this etching, comprising a greater or lesser number of figures and different shadings; here we can follow all the stages of work at which in Leonardo's painting we can only guess. Although Rembrandt must have worked for a very long time at this etching, it does not show the least degree of 'finish', not even as much as an average draughtsman could achieve in a few hours of work. We would not, however, call Rembrandt's Three Crosses unfinished; we can see quite well how the etching remained through all its states; and after all the laborious work done, the first creative idea was still in evidence like a brilliant improvisation. Leonardo's painting is no less finished than Rembrandt's etching.

This suggestion of 'sketchiness', indication instead of definition, last thoughts which look like first thoughts, is not altogether a modern idea. Vasari refers to it, in the Life of Luca della Robbia, whose highly finished Cantoria he compares with that of Donatello which is, as he thinks, but a sketch. 'Experience shows', says Vasari, 'that all works of art seen at a distance, whether paintings or sculptures, are bolder and more vigorous to the eye, if merely done in the rough, than if laboriously finished. . . . It often happens that these rapid sketches, which are thrown off suddenly in the first ardour of inspiration, express the idea perfectly in a few strokes; while too much care and labour, on the contrary, will often deprive the works of all force and character when the artist never knows when to take his hands off. . . . The artist who visualizes from the first what he is going to create, invariably proceeds on his

---

19. The commission was subsequently given to Filippino Lippi, who finished his Adoration of the Kings in March 1497 (1496, according to the Florentine calendar). The monastery of San Donato was destroyed during the siege of Florence in 1529; Filippino's 'Adoration, is now in the Uffizi, No. 1566.

20. In the Venice Academy there is a drawing by Cesare da Sesto, The Adoration of the Kings, in which the Madonna closely resembles Raphael's Madonna of Foligno; but the horses in the background are obviously taken from the 'Battle of Anghiari'. (Reprod. Morelli, Italian Painters, II, p. 91.)

A Leonardo drawing, acquired in 1953 by the British Museum, St George and the Dragon, is clearly based on the jousting horsemen in the upper right corner of No. 49; one horseman is directly copied, the other is transformed into a dragon (plates 103–104).

Outline copy of Leonardo's 'Uffizi Adoration', published by Müller-Walde, 1898. (This outline copy, omitting the uneven modulation of the original painting, gives a clear idea of the arrangement of the sixty or seventy figures of men and horses in the picture.)

way towards perfect realization with ease. . . . Nevertheless, there are some, though they are rare, who can only do well when they proceed slowly . . . as [among the poets] Bembo who expends months and even years in the production of a sonnet.'

Leonardo was a slow worker, and he never brought the Sforza monument beyond the stage of a model, nor some of his finest pictorial compositions beyond the stage of a 'cartoon'. If we are to credit Vasari, he left the *Last Supper* and the *Mona Lisa* 'unfinished', while we can see for ourselves that the *Ambrosiana Musician*, the *Lady with the Ermine*, and the *Adoration of the Kings* are all unfinished. But it is a moot point whether some works are capable of further elaboration without loss.

Leonardo's almost monochrome painting 'Adoration of the Kings' has a charm which no reproduction can communicate.

See also plates 32, 58 and 103.

54

CARTOON FOR THE VIRGIN AND CHILD WITH ST ANNE AND THE INFANT ST JOHN. London, National Gallery, No. 6337 (acquired from the Royal Academy, 1962). 141.5 × 104 cm.

There are at least three versions of Leonardo's St Anne composition.

(*a*) The first Milanese version, done shortly before Leonardo left the town, c. 1499 (Cartoon in the National Gallery, London). See plate 54.[21]

(*b*) The Florentine version, as described by Fra Pietro da

Novellara, 1501. (See Documents, No. XI, and plate 18.) This cartoon is lost.

(*c*) The second Milanese version, done during Leonardo's subsequent stay in the town, 1508–10. Painting in the Louvre; cartoon lost. (See plate 68.)

There are, besides, a number of tentative drawings, which in my opinion do not correspond with either of the three versions but suggest independent solutions.

Padre Sebastiano Resta (about 1696) saw the St Anne cartoon (plate 54) in Milan, in the collection of Conte Arconati. The cartoon came into the collection of Marchese Casnedi, where it remained until at least 1722; a few years later it was in the collection of Conte Sagredo at Venice, where it was bought by Robert Udny, the brother of the English Ambassador, in 1763. It became the property of the Royal Academy at a date prior to the 23rd March, 1791.

The witness who saw this cartoon in 1722 in the Casnedi collection at Milan is Edward Wright: 'A Holy Family, the same which is painted in S. Celsus.'[22] Langton Douglas (1944, p. 41) did not hesitate to identify this cartoon with the one now in the Royal Academy, London.

55

ST JOHN THE BAPTIST. Louvre, No. 1597. See Document XVI, p. 39. Panel, 69 × 57 cm.

Louis XIII of France gave the picture to Charles I, in exchange for a painting by Holbein and one by Titian. In 1649, when the King's collection was sold by auction, Leonardo's St John was bought by the banker Jabach on behalf of Cardinal Mazarin, from whom the picture passed to Louis XIV.

The picture is entirely by Leonardo's own hand, but damaged in parts and retouched.

56

MADONNA WITH THE FRUIT-PLATE. Louvre, No. 101. 33 × 25 cm.

57

ADORATION OF THE CHILD, WITH TWO ANGELS. Detroit, Institute of Arts (Cat. No. 1236; acquired 1957). Panel, 60 × 47 cm.

It is not known when Leonardo began his apprenticeship

21. This cartoon is not identical with the one described by Fra Pietro Novellara in 1501, which was done for an altar-piece in S. Annunziata after Filippino Lippi had resigned the commission in favour of Leonardo. The altar-piece has never been executed by Leonardo and the cartoon is lost.

22. Luini's *Holy Family* (now in the Ambrosiana; Suida, p. 130 and fig. 315) is a picture which is based on Leonardo's *St Anne cartoon*. – The church of S. Celso in Milan has been completely altered, and half of it was pulled down in 1826.

in Verrocchio's workshop, but a number of documented dates may help to form a conclusion. In 1468 the plague was raging in Florence, and only in October of that year Leonardo's father, Ser Piero, moved to the town and rented rooms for his legal office (as a notary to the Signoria of Florence). Leonardo remained apparently for another year in Vinci because in spring 1469 he is still mentioned in the taxation return of his family at Vinci. So it appears that he came to Florence, and into the workshop of Verrocchio, between the summer of 1469 and the spring of 1470.

At that time Verrocchio had some contracts for metal work, such as the copperball of the dome of Florence cathedral (finished in May 1471) and a richly decorated bell for the Monastery of Monte Scalari. In the same years, 1469–72, the Medici kept him busy with commissions for sculpture – the tomb of Piero and Giovanni in the old sacristy of San Lorenzo (completed in 1472) and a fountain with a bronze putto for the Medici villa at Careggi; and for the Medici, Verrocchio had even to organize the festivities when in 1471 Galeazzo Sforza came to Florence as a guest of Lorenzo Magnifico.

From 1470 onward, Verrocchio did no longer devote much of his time to painting; a great deal of the execution he had to leave to his pupils and assistants (Botticelli, Perugino and Leonardo amongst them; and, a few years later Lorenzo di Credi).

There are three pictures by Verrocchio which are said to have been painted with some help from Leonardo. The earliest of the three is the 'Adoration' now in Detroit (Plate 57), which was probably begun at the time when Leonardo joined the Verrocchio workshop and completed before he was admitted as a member of the Florentine Guild of Painters in 1472. The two angels, and part of the landscape, have been claimed to be his work. Left-handed brushstrokes, first noticed in this picture by Edgar P. Richardson (*The Adoration with two Angels*, Detroit 1957) are in favour of this hypothesis.

The two other paintings by Verrocchio of which Leonardo is believed to have painted some parts are 'The Baptism of Christ' (Plates 43 and 87) and 'The Madonna di Piazza' (ill. here on p. 27, and Plate I, p. 169).

The first to attach the name of Leonardo to the Detroit 'Adoration' (Plate 57) was Roberto Longhi. Stefano Bottari, Antonio Morassi and Sir Philip Hendy agreed with him.

58
STUDY FOR THE BACKGROUND OF THE ADORATION OF THE KINGS. Uffizi, I, 436.
See the notes on plates 48 and 49.
This is mainly a study of perspective; most of the lines are drawn with a ruler. All the figures are put in pen and ink on top of the linear construction.

59–62
THE ANNUNCIATION. Uffizi, No. 1618. Panel, 98×217 cm.
See also plates 86 and 98; and 39.

Painted for the Convent of Monte Oliveto near Florence; neither the name of the painter nor the date of the painting are documented.
Since 1867 in the Uffizi.

Maud Cruttwell ascribed the picture to Verrocchio. Morelli considered it to be the work of Ridolfo Ghirlandaio, Berenson thought it a joint work of Credi and Leonardo. Baron Liphart, who was the first to claim the Benois Madonna for Leonardo, was also the first to claim this painting for him. G. Passavant thinks it is an early work of Domenico Ghirlandaio, overpainted by Leonardo (*Mitteil. d. Kunsthist. Institutes in Florenz*, IX, 1960, pp. 71–98). By most other scholars considered to be an early work of Leonardo's.

At the age of twenty, in 1472, Leonardo was made a member of the Guild of Painters, which means he was allowed to accept independent commissions as a painter. The *Annunciation* might have been the first commission he ever received. At that time, however, and even four years later, he was still working as an assistant in Verrocchio's studio and staying in his house. Perugino became a member of the Painters' Guild in the same year as Leonardo and he also worked in Verrocchio's workshop. Lorenzo di Credi, who is recorded in the same workshop between 1480 and 1488, probably began there as an apprentice in about 1472. Botticelli became a member of the Guild of Painters in the same year as Perugino and Leonardo, 1472, and, I believe, was at that time also employed as an assistant in Verrocchio's workshop. There were several other assistants. Whether the commission for the *Annunciation* was given to Leonardo, or to his master Verrocchio, it was probably painted in Verrocchio's house and there one or the other of the assistants might have helped with it; but certainly not Lorenzo di Credi, who at that time was only a boy of fourteen. Heydenreich assumes that the Angel is from the hand of Leonardo, but not the Madonna.

Miss Cruttwell had already detected that the curious ornamentation of the reading-desk (plate 62) bore resemblance to Verrocchio's Medici Sarcophagus. The resemblance to the sarcophagus of Desiderio da Settignano's *Marsuppini monument* (ill. in Galassi's *La Scultura Fiorentina del Quattrocento*, 1949, plate 271), in which Verrocchio is said to have participated, is even stronger.

The two parts of the landscape, though painted in an orange evening light (plate 86), are rather in the spirit of Ghirlandaio; but 'the flowering carpet of plants' is highly original, based on direct observation of nature and technically related to much later work of Leonardo's (plate 98).

The picture is somewhat obscured by an old varnish which has turned yellow in parts. The tip of the angel's wing appears to be repainted.

In 1907 Sidney Colvin published the drawing for the right arm of the angel, which drawing is certainly by the young Leonardo.

Leonardo: Study for the right arm of the Angel of the *Annunciation* (plate 59). About 1472. Oxford, Christ Church.

63

MADONNA WITH THE CARNATION.
Munich, Ältere Pinakothek, No. 7779

Panel, 62×47 cm. Cut at the left side, of about 4 cm.

The picture is in a very poor condition, which can be seen even in the reproduction; the face of the Virgin, for instance, is nearly completely overpainted, forming a leathery *craquelure*. But, allowing for the bad preservation of the painting, a long list can be given connecting the Munich Madonna with the workshop of Verrocchio:

(1) Madonna by Credi, Munich 7820.
(2) The Pistoia Altar-piece (Detail, *Madonna*, plate I–b), illustr. p. 169.
(3) Madonna Dreyfus (plate I–a), illustr. p. 169.
(4) An altar-piece by Credi in Naples (Mackowsky, *Verrocchio*, fig. 77).
(5) A silver-point drawing by Verrocchio (sometimes ascribed to Credi) in Dresden (B.B. 672, fig. 139).
(6) A Head of the Madonna in the Louvre, drawing (Suida, fig. 4: attributed to Leonardo).
(7) A Head by Verrocchio in the British Museum (Cat. 1950, No. 258 r.).

Comparing the black chalk drawing in the British Museum with the head of the Madonna in the Munich picture (plate 63), we certainly find the same eyes, mouth and hair-dress, and we can even assume that the same model was used. A comparison with the other paintings mentioned in the list (which could be extended) would give a similar result; the brooch and the long fold underneath are significant.

The Munich picture was certainly executed in Verrocchio's workshop; the landscape, the draperies, and the vase of flowers, all favour an attribution to Leonardo. But still it is an unpleasant picture.

Berenson, Kenneth Clark, and Heydenreich think that Leonardo collaborated in this work to some extent; Baldass thinks Leonardo had probably no share in it; he emphasizes that even the *composition* of the picture cannot be by him;[23] Fabriczy thought the picture was composed by Leonardo but finished by Credi; Hildebrandt had a similar opinion; according to Bode, Suida, Venturi, and Valentiner, it is an early work of Leonardo's; some other writers suggested that it was an early work of Credi's; Bodmer assumed that it was either a replica or a free version of a lost Madonna painting by Leonardo.

The pedigree of the picture does not go back beyond 1889 when it was bought, from a private collection in Bavaria, by Bayersdorfer for the Munich Gallery and exhibited there as a Leonardo.

64

MADONNA OF THE ROCKS.
Louvre, No. 1599. Painted on wood (transferred to canvas), 197× 119.5 cm.

On April 25th, 1483, Leonardo and the brothers Evangelista and Ambrogio de Predis received the commission for this altar-piece from the Confraternity of the Immaculate Conception, Milan. This picture was finished in 1485, or perhaps a little later; this is the first version of the *Madonna of the Rocks*, now in the *Louvre*. Adolfo Venturi contended that King Louis XII took this painting to France, which is credible enough, as that King even attempted to have Leonardo's *Last Supper* cut from the wall. If Venturi is right, the *Madonna of the Rocks* had already been in France for some time when Leonardo arrived there; however, we cannot be certain about this, as no mention is made of the picture being in France until 1625, when it was at Château de Fontainebleau.

Heydenreich (1954, p. 435 f.) suggested that the picture might have been taken already by Ludovico Sforza from

23. Ludwig Baldass, in *Zeitschrift für Kunstwissenschaft*, VII, 1953, p. 175, n. 25.

the chapel of the Confraternity. This does not contradict Venturi's theory; Louis XII could have carried the picture away from the Duke's castle.

According to Heydenreich, the second version of the *Madonna of the Rocks* was begun by Leonardo and Ambrogio de Predis in about 1495. Then a lawsuit followed, which lasted for over ten years, as Predis insisted on supplementary payment. In April 1506 the Confraternity agreed to an additional payment. Leonardo came to Milan in May 1506, received 100 lire in 1507, went back to Florence, came again in July 1508, and received again 100 lire. Soon afterwards the *Madonna of the Rocks* was placed in the Chapel of the Confraternity in the Church of San Francesco, where it remained until 1781. It was sold, and in 1785 it was brought to England; at one time it belonged to Lord Suffolk, and in 1880 it was bought by the National Gallery. (About this second version of the altar-piece see also note on plate 65.)

The Louvre version suffered when it was transferred from panel to canvas (which was done about 1800); it has been retouched in many places, especially in the drapery of the Virgin, and the lower part of the background. The varnish has turned yellow and is falsifying the colours. See also plates 78, 90 and 99.

65

MADONNA OF THE ROCKS. National Gallery, London, No. 1093. Painted on wood, 189.5 × 120 cm. See the note on No. 64; and for the whole very complicated problem, Martin Davies, *The Virgin of the Rocks*, 1947; also the same author's National Gallery Catalogue, London, 1951, 'The Earlier Italian Schools', pp. 204–219. (Against Davies's early dating of the Louvre version, see Valentiner in the Catalogue of the Leonardo exhibition at the Los Angeles County Museum, 1949, p. 61; and against Davies's interpretation of the sources, see Heydenreich, 1954, p. 436, footnote.) Most writers assume that Predis and other assistants had an important share in the painting of this second version; only Bode (*Studien über Leonardo da Vinci*, 1921, p. 82) decided: 'The *Madonna of the Rocks* in London, from the church of S. Francesco in Milan, is doubtless an original by Leonardo, and not a replica painted by Predis; if he took any share in it at all, it can only have been in some unimportant details.' According to Suida, most of the paint was put on by Leonardo (*Leonardo und sein Kreis*, 1929, p. 49 f.); both children, the head of the angel, the hand of the Virgin, the draperies and all the flowers are, according to Suida, painted by the master himself. Kenneth Clark (1958, p. 128 f.) is of a similar opinion, praising particularly the angel's head;

but he does not deny that it is a workshop production. The two wings of the altar-piece (National Gallery, London, Nos. 1661 and 1662) are not by Leonardo. The left wing, an angel in green, was probably executed in the Predis workshop; the right wing, an angel in red, has tentatively been ascribed by Kenneth Clark to Ferrando de Llanos (p. 53 and p. 129).

The central panel of the altar-piece was cleaned in 1949. See also plate 95.

66

STUDY FOR THE HEAD OF THE 'MADONNA LITTA'. Louvre, No. 2376
According to Berenson (*Florentine Drawings*, second edition, No. 1067C, and p. 562), one of the earliest drawings by Leonardo. Seidlitz was of the same opinion. Demonts and Bodmer date it about 1490–94, Kenneth Clark about 1480. For the dating of this drawing compare No. 20, which is related in style.

Seidlitz thought that Ambrogio de Predis strengthened the outlines of the profile when he pressed them through with a stylus on to the panel on which he painted the 'Madonna Litta' (plate 67).

67

MADONNA LITTA. Hermitage, Leningrad, No. 249 (Cat. 1891 and 1916, No. 13a). Painted on wood, transferred to canvas, 42 × 33 cm.

The picture is named after Conte Litta, Milan, in whose collection it was before it came to the Hermitage, in 1865. The Hermitage Catalogue tries to identify it with a picture which was in 1543 in the Contarini collection at Venice.

The painting is in a bad state of preservation and completely retouched. It is usually ascribed to Boltraffio, or to Ambrogio de Predis. There is no doubt that it is based on drawings by Leonardo (see plate 66).

Morelli attributed it to Bernardino de' Conti, but there is a replica by this painter in the Museo Poldi-Pezzoli in Milan (No. 639), very different in quality from the Hermitage painting. Several other replicas of the Madonna Litta are known.

According to Marie Herzfeld, the *Madonna Litta* is by the same painter as the *Resurrection of Christ with S. Lucia and S. Lionardo* (Berlin Museum, No. 90B). This very uneven picture, of which small parts are remarkably fine, seems to me to be painted by Ambrogio de Predis at a time when he helped Leonardo with the *Madonna of the Rocks*, and when Leonardo was always around to help him; and did so indeed by designing the two saints in the *Resurrection of Christ*.

68–69

VIRGIN AND CHILD WITH ST ANNE
AND THE INFANT ST JOHN. Louvre, No. 1598.
Wood, 170×129 cm.
See note on plate 54; and plate 79.
Painted with the help of an assistant; only the landscape,
the figure of St Anne and the head and the right arm of
the Virgin are outstanding. It might be thought that the
assistant was Melzi, but in this case it is inexplicable why
Melzi did not finish the picture, as he took it with him
to Italy, after Leonardo's death.

The picture is not in a good condition. The outlines
have been strengthened by a restorer; a dark, yellow
varnish has obscured the colours. In the detail photograph, plate 69, we have tried, by means of a long
exposure, to penetrate through the yellow varnish. A
few blue patches in the sky show the original colour;
the cloak of the Madonna was originally also of a purer
blue, the flesh less red.

In 1517, Cardinal Luigi d'Aragona saw a *St Anne* in
Leonardo's studio (cf. Document No. XVI, on p. 39).
Paolo Giovio, in about 1527, stated that Francis I owned
Leonardo's *St Anne* painting; but Giovio was never in
France and he probably meant a cartoon. When Melzi
returned to Italy, he took the drawings and pictures,
left to him by Leonardo in his Will, to Italy; amongst
them the *St Anne* painting. When Cardinal Richelieu
crossed into Italy, in 1629, to settle the Mantuan succession question by war, he found the picture in Casale,
a town on the river Po, bought it, brought it to Paris
and presented it to the King. Since 1801 it has been in
the Louvre. (See also note 51 on p. 22.)

70

STUDIES FOR THE ADORATION OF THE
CHILD. Metropolitan Museum, New York
Here an idea is developed which first appeared in the
sketches for 'The Adoration of the Shepherds'. The
drawing is still closer to the 'Adoration' than to the
'Madonna of the Rocks'.

A passage in the Vasari biography refers to a *natività*
painting by Leonardo: 'Ludovico Sforza begged
Leonardo to paint an altar-piece of the Nativity, which
was sent by the Duke to the Emperor'.[24] As this paint-

---

24. According to Vasari, this painting, now lost, was done soon
after Leonardo's arrival in Milan. The Anonimo Gaddiano (ed. Frey,
p. 112) mentions the picture as being in the possession of Maximilian I, and Carducho (*Dialogos*, p. 20) as in the Collection of
Charles V. (Professor H. Siebenhüner, in a footnote to his Vasari
edition, 1940, p. 297, suggests that this *Nativity* was nothing but the
Louvre version of the *Madonna of the Rocks*. This is an ingenious,
though not easily acceptable idea.)

Adoration of the Child. Silver-point drawing by Leonardo,
Windsor, No. 12560 (detail)

Kneeling Madonna. Pen and ink drawing by Leonardo,
Milan, Ambrosiana (Cod. Atl. 358 r., detail).

ing is lost we cannot with any certainty connect the
drawing with it.

A small sketch at Windsor (No. 12560), and another,
very slight one, in the Codice Atlantico are for the same
composition as plate 70. Several versions of a painting,
The Madonna with the playing children, can be connected
with these drawings. (Bodmer 78, 79; another version
in the Budapest Museum; and the best one in the
Ashmolean Museum, Oxford, from the collection of
Henry Harris.) All those paintings are probably based
on a (lost) cartoon by Leonardo.

PLATE I. *Paintings by Lorenzo di Credi.* (a) *The Dreyfus Madonna* (attributed to Leonardo by Suida, Langton Douglas, Degenhart, a.o.) Washington, Kress Collection. – (b) *Madonna and Child.* Detail from the Altar-piece in Pistoia Cathedral, painted 1475–85. – (c) *Annunciation.* Detail from a predella panel of the Pistoia Altar-piece (painted with the help of Leonardo?). Paris, Louvre. – (d) *San Donato and the Tax Collector.* Part of the same predella (attributed to Leonardo by Bayersdorfer, Valentiner, Suida, and Langton Douglas). Worcester, U.S.A., Art Museum.

PLATE II. Leonardo: *Portraits of Duke Ludovico Sforza and Duchess Beatrice, with their children,* 1497. (Details from Montorfano's *Crucifixion*.) Milan, S. Maria delle Grazie.

(b) School of Leonardo: *Portrait of a young Lady* (attributed here to Bernardino de' Conti).
About 1506. Washington, Kress Collection.

PLATE III. (a) Leonardo Workshop (attributed here to Francesco Melzi): "*La Belle Ferronnière*".
(Detail.) About 1517. Paris, Louvre.

PLATE IV. (a) Leonardo: *Rough Sketch for the 'Last Supper'*. About 1495. Windsor Castle (No. 12542).
(b) Leonardo: *The Last Supper*. Engraving by Raffaello Morghen after a drawing by Teodoro Matteini (published in 1800).

71–72

SKETCH FOR THE LAST SUPPER. Venice, 254.
26×39 cm.
This is a very important drawing as far as the composition is concerned. In my opinion, it is a copy, by a pupil, after Leonardo's first cartoon (or large drawing) for the *Last Supper*; the names of the Apostles are added in Leonardo's handwriting. No. 72 shows how the cartoon must have looked originally; the sheet used by the copyist for the Venice Academy drawing was too short to take all the figures, the four Apostles who should be at the left are placed underneath, but the shoulder and arm of one of them are given twice, with all the accidental features of the sketch exactly repeated. Otherwise the copy is rather weak, the hands especially being awkwardly drawn; but the copyist followed the original very closely as he even imitated the shading from left to right. (Cf. Beltrami, in *Boll. della Racc. Vinc.* 1910.) Berenson and Bodmer accept this drawing as genuine; and so does Popham (p. 118) who thinks that Leonardo himself copied here one of his earlier drawings. Kenneth Clark (1958, p. 94) accepts it too, although apparently with some doubts. Another sketch for the *Last Supper* (plate IV–a), which must date from the same time, is very different in character. Giglioli (*Leonardo*, 1944, p. 116) thinks that the drawing No. 71 is by Leonardo, but of the handwriting only three words.
In these first sketches Leonardo followed the Florentine tradition in placing Judas isolated on one side of the table and figuring St John sleeping with his head on his arms; we find the same arrangement of figures in Castagno's 'Cenacolo' at Florence; or also in Ghirlandaio's; or Francesco Botticini's at Empoli.

73–75

THE LAST SUPPER. Santa Maria delle Grazie, Milan. Wall-painting, 420×910 cm.
See Documents, Nos. VII and VIII.
Painted at the instance of Duke Ludovico Moro for the dining-room of the Cloister of the Dominican monks of Santa Maria delle Grazie. The building is no longer used as a monastery, but Leonardo's painting is still there, or at least the ruins of it. A door, leading to the kitchen, was cut through the middle of the lower part of the painting. Already Leonardo's contemporaries were complaining about the poor state of preservation of the Last Supper. What we can see of it at the present time is the original grand composition which could not be obliterated, patches of the old paint here and there, and the work of generations of restorers. The first restoration took place in 1726, the next in 1770; during the French occupation, 1796–1815, the painting was exposed to

much damage; in 1800 the Refectory was used as a forage-room by the soldiers; afterwards, between 1820 and 1908, it was thoroughly restored three times.[25] And yet this painting, the greatest before Michelangelo's and Raphael's Vatican Frescoes, still radiates vitality, just as a tragedy of Sophocles speaks to us again even in the poorest translation, or the Parthenon frieze through mutilated and broken fragments.
Some beautiful drawings were left finished by Leonardo in preparation for his wall-painting – see Nos. 9, 14–17. The three lunettes above the *Last Supper*, with the Sforza coat-of-arms surrounded by garlands of fruit, are also from the hand of Leonardo; they had been whitewashed, probably in the 18th century, and were uncovered in 1854, when the whole painting was restored (mainly by fixing the flaking paint with wax to the wall). There is very little left now of those lunette paintings (plates 73 and 89).

76–77

ST JEROME. Pinacoteca Vaticana, No. 337 (151). Panel, 103×75 cm.
The authenticity of this painting has never been doubted, though there is no literary documentation to it and it is not mentioned in any of the old Leonardo biographies. Poggi and Rinaldis assume that it was painted immediately before Leonardo left for Milan,[26] i.e. about 1481–82. (Cf. the head at the right of plate 52, which is of the same period.)
The painting was found by Cardinal Fesch (c. 1820) in a second-hand shop in Rome; it was being used as the door of a small wardrobe, the head of the Saint being cut out. The Cardinal, an uncle of Napoleon, was lucky enough to find the missing part of the panel a few years later – in the workshop of a cobbler, who was using the board as a table-top. In 1845, six years after the Cardinal's death, Pius IX bought the restored painting.

---

25. The reproductions in the present volume are based on photographs taken after the restoration in 1955 (carried out by Commendatore Mauro Pelliccioli, Milan). Raffaello Morghen's engraving, made before the *Last Supper* had suffered its worst damages, has now almost documentary value, though it contains some minor inaccuracies (plate IV–b).

26. Was this picture done in competition with Perugino? Vasari states that Perugino, while he studied in Florence under Verrocchio, painted a *St Jerome in Penitence* on a wall in the cloister of Camaldoli, and that this mural was 'much valued by the Florentines and greatly praised because he had made the saint old, lean and shrivelled, and wasted to a skeleton.' Leonardo's *St Jerome* belongs to his early Milanese period; for the landscape compare plate 64, for the single figure in a large space compare plate 70, and the illustrations on p. 168. (Perugino is mentioned by Leonardo in the *Codex Atlanticus*: 'A naked figure by Perugino.')

78

CAVE. Detail from the *Madonna of the Rocks*, Louvre, plate 64.

79

A LANDSCAPE OF NAKED MOUNTAINS. Detail from the *St Anne*, Louvre, plate 68.

80

A RAVINE WITH WATER BIRDS. Windsor, 12395
This drawing does not make the same impression of spontaneity as the earlier No. 81, and at least parts of it seem to be drawn from memory. Compare also the monumental landscape from *St Jerome*, which is about three years later (plate 77).

81

ARNO LANDSCAPE. Florence, Uffizi, No. 8P.
Dated by the inscription '*dì di santa Maria della neve addi 5 daghossto* 1473' (the day of the Holy Virgin of the Snows, August the 5th, 1473). According to Seidlitz, this day was celebrated by the Church as the 'day of temptation'; according to Ravaisson-Mollien, the 5th of August was still celebrated in some way by the end of the 19th century on the Rigi in Switzerland as 'the day of Maria in the Snow'.
The writing on the *recto* is from right to left. The *verso* contains a sketch in black chalk, gone over with pen, of a mountainous landscape, with a bridge, the pen-and-ink sketch of a naked running man, and a head; also the note, 'Io morando danto sono chontento'. This is written in the normal way, from left to right, not inverted.

82

HURRICANE (also called 'Apocalyptic Storm', or 'The Deluge'). Windsor, 12376. 27×40.8 cm.
Earlier than the ten drawings of the 'Deluge series', Windsor Nos. 12377–86, of which one is reproduced here as No. 85.
This drawing shows: horsemen thrown to the ground by a hurricane, and an uprooted tree in the lower right corner. In the distance are seen the whirling waves of the sea, clouds, and Storm Gods blowing through pipes or trumpets. The group of six Wind Gods at the left recalls the trumpet-blowing angels in Michelangelo's 'Last Judgement', painted twenty years later.
Popp calls this drawing *Diluvio*, with reference to fol. 6 *verso* in Manuscript G. (Richter, §§ 607–609) and Windsor No. 12665: '. . . inundated valleys, in the

depths of which were seen the bending tree-tops . . . Let Aeolus with the Winds be shown entangling the trees floating uprooted, and whirling in the huge waves . . .'

83

STORM IN THE ALPS. Windsor, 12409
I am dating this 'about 1500' in concordance with Popp, Popham and Clark, who are dating it 1499–1500. But it might be a little later. I imagine that these bird's-eye view landscapes were drawn at the time when Leonardo was most interested in the problems of aviation. There is a note in the Leicester Manuscript (Richter § 1060), datable c. 1504–1505, about the weather in the Alps, which reads like a text to this illustration.

84

A BIRD'S-EYE VIEW OF A RIVER LANDSCAPE, WITH A FERRY BOAT. Windsor, 12400
This drawing is probably not much earlier than the Codex 'About the Flight of Birds', 1505, at the Royal Library, Turin. Similar sketches, e.g., in Manuscript K, are somewhat later.

85

THE DELUGE. Windsor, 12379
The first of the ten drawings at Windsor Castle, which form a series; certainly of a late period, when Leonardo studied intensively the movement of water.
These drawings, despite their almost abstract pattern, convey the reality of a vision.
One of the drawings forming the Deluge series (No. 12381), is only preserved in a copy from a pupil's hand (possibly by Melzi, according to Kenneth Clark).

86

LANDSCAPE. Detail from the *Uffizi Annunciation*. See note on plate 59.

87

LANDSCAPE. Detail from the *Baptism of Christ*. See note on plate 43.

88

PLANT ORNAMENT. Panel, 42×37 cm.
On the reverse of the 'Ginevra de' Benci' portrait. Cut at the lower end by about 20 cm. See note on plate 23.

Reconstruction of the painting on the back of the Ginevra panel before cutting. (After Dr. Jens Thiis, 1909.)
Compare plate 88.

89

FRUIT GARLANDS. Detail from a lunette over the *Last Supper*. See note on plate 73.

90

PLANTS. From the Louvre version of the *Madonna of the Rocks* (plate 64)
Plant life in the shadow of the woods is depicted here in a deep *sfumato*. The brush, loaded with a yellowish pigment, went rapidly over the dark ground, producing a kind of clair–obscure (which points forward to the technique Rembrandt sometimes used in painting backgrounds and garments). But Leonardo knew the individual shapes of the plants by heart, and his brush-strokes, in all their speed, reproduced them conscientiously.

91

FLOWERING PLANTS. Windsor, 12424. 19.8× 16 cm.
The large flower is a Star of Bethlehem; the others are a Wood anemone, a stalk of Crowsfoot, etc.
Leonardo was interested in all the organic forms which life is taking, and he drew plants in the same way as portraits, animals, or anatomical details. In a little note-book which he used (between 1490 and 1493) he put down 'Maestro da Marliano has a fine herbal. He lives opposite Strami the carpenters'. Leonardo invented also

a method of 'natural impression', which consists in covering a dried leaf or plant with a thin layer of oil paint and printing it off on paper, either white on black or black on white. Leonardo's botanical drawings were probably all done as scientific illustrations; but he used these studies in his cartoons and paintings whenever there was need for them. Even in his earliest works there is some botanical detail which is very well observed and reproduced, e.g. the tuft of grass underneath the Angel he added to Verrocchio's picture (plate 43), or the carpet of flowers in the Uffizi Annunciation (plate 98). He put plants into his (lost) Adam and Eve cartoon, his Madonna with a Vase of Flowers, his Madonna of the Rocks, into the three lunettes above the 'Last Supper', the Leda cartoons and paintings, into the designs he gave to his pupils Melzi and Gianpetrino for their *Colombine, Flora,* and *Pomona.* For all those compositions Leonardo used, I should think, studies of plants which he had drawn at *various* dates. The 'wall decoration in the shape of interlaced branches' which Leonardo painted in 1498 on the ceiling of the Sala delle Asse in the Castello Sforzesco at Milan, must once have been very beautiful; what we can see there now is too much restored to be called Leonardo's work; it only

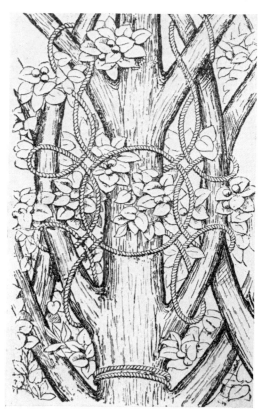

A detail of the original decoration by Leonardo in the Sala delle Asse in the Castello Sforzesco. Copied by Luca Beltrami (*Leonardo da Vinci e la Sala delle Asse*, Milan, 1902).

The central design of this decoration is related to the abstract ornament of the 'Knots' (see the illustration on p. 12.)

shows his invention – a geometrical pattern of plant life formed in a naturalistic way. The restoration of this ceiling painting was prepared by Luca Beltrami in 1884, and he also copied carefully in pen and ink whatever traces he could find of the original work. Those copies he published in 1902, a year after the Milanese painter Ernesto Rusca had ruined Leonardo's work by complete overpainting (of which only a part has been removed since).

92

ANEMONES. Windsor, 12423

93

STUDIES OF FLOWERS. Venice, Academy, 237

94

LILY. Windsor, 12418. 31.4×17.7 cm.
The earliest of Leonardo's botanical studies, done in a style different from the later drawings; the technique resembles that of the early drapery studies.
I thought for some time it might have been a preparatory study for an altar-piece for San Francesco in Brescia; Leonardo received the commission for it in 1497, but never executed the painting. There is a note in Manuscript I–2, 107a (Richter, § 679), 'Anthony, a lily and a book'. 1497, though, seems too late as a date for Leonardo's drawing, which is of the same period as the *St John*, plate 44. It is probable that Leonardo also designed a 'Madonna of the Lily', of which only copies are extant, one of them at Highnam Court in Gloucester. (Cf. Suida, p. 52.)

95

UNDERGROWTH. Detail from the London version of the *Madonna of the Rocks* (plate 65)

96

FLOWERING RUSHES. Windsor, 12430 *recto*
According to Kenneth Clark, 'done in connection with the *Kneeling Leda*' (cf. plate 36, and illustration on p. 159). The front of the sheet has a pink preparation; the back is white and contains a study of a bulrush with one seed-vessel.

97

OAK-LEAVES WITH ACORNS, etc. Windsor, 12422
Done, according to Malaguzzi Valeri, in connection

with the painting of the garlands above the *Last Supper*; but, in their present state, those garlands contain nothing very similar; Bodmer points to the decorations in the Sala della Asse, without believing that the present drawing was actually done for it. Whereas Leonardo's other studies of plants are as flat as they appear in far-eastern painting, this branch of oak-leaves makes a pronounced sculpturesque impression.
Compare the wreath of oak-leaves in plate 2.

98

FLOWERING MEADOW. Detail from the *Uffizi Annunciation*. See note on plate 59.

99

IRISES AND WOOD ANEMONES. Detail from the Louvre version of the *Madonna of the Rocks* (plate 64)

100

A DOG. Windsor, 12361
This drawing is shaded from left to right, and it is certainly genuine. Accepted as an original drawing of Leonardo's by Adolfo Venturi (Comm. Vinc. 130) and Popham (No. 82). Kenneth Clark regarded it as a copy and ascribed it tentatively to Melzi.

101

STUDY OF A BEAR, New York, Lehman Collection.
The bear, and the study of a paw, are drawn in silverpoint over the sketch of a Madonna. This drawing, according to its technique, must be early; it is in fact of the same date as the two similar drawings, the study of *Ox and Ass* at Windsor (plate 102), and the study of *Crabs* in the Cologne Museum.

102

ASS AND OX. Windsor, 12362
Probably a sketch for animals in an *Adoration of the Shepherds*, or *Adoration of the Kings*.

103

FIGHTING HORSEMEN. Detail from the background of the *Adoration of the Kings* (plate 49)
This motive was developed into a *Dragon-Fight* (plate 104); and, twenty years later, to the central group in the *Battle of Anghiari* (plate 108).

104

DRAGON-FIGHT. London, British Museum (1952-10-11-2). Pen and brown ink, with brown wash, over a sketch drawn with the stylus. 13.9×19 cm.
From the collection of George Henry Haydon, who died in 1891; the drawing formed part of a small album belonging to his grand-daughter, Mrs. Winifred Reavell.

105

STUDIES OF A DRAGON-FIGHT. Windsor, 12331. 29.8×21.2 cm.
Other studies for horsemen fighting a dragon are at the Louvre (bequest of Baron Edmond de Rothschild; reprod. Richter I, plate XXXIIIA) and in the Ashmolean Museum, Oxford (reprod. by Colvin); a studio copy of a small drawing at the Ambrosiana, Milan (reprod. Rosenberg, fig. 33; Photo Braun, No. 75043), and the original drawing, now in the British Museum. A note of 1492 by Leonardo, how to draw an imaginary animal (a dragon) so that it should appear natural, is transliterated in Richter, § 585.

The date of this drawing is controversial; it has been dated by various scholars between 1480 and 1514. Bodmer connects it rightly with sketches for the *Battle of Anghiari*, dating the drawing 1505–08 (cf. e.g. BB. 1098).
This drawing, and No. 104, were probably intended for a painting of St George. One of the earliest pictures Raphael painted during his stay in Florence was a St George (which, a few years later, was brought to the King of England by Baldassare Castiglione; now in the Hermitage, Leningrad). It seems probable that Leonardo saw Raphael's composition and felt incited to compose his own, much wilder version.

106

STUDY FOR THE SFORZA MONUMENT. Windsor, 12358 *recto*.
See Document I, on p. 33. In this letter, datable 1482, to Ludovico Sforza of Milan, Leonardo says: 'Again, the bronze horse could be taken up.' From 1479 onward – in the same year Verrocchio received his commission for the Colleoni monument – Ludovico Sforza had

School of Leonardo: Engraving after small-scale models for the Sforza monument. London, British Museum.

Antonio Pollaiuolo: Drawing for the Sforza monument, about 1480–82. Munich, Print room.

Medicean Gem. Etching in Leonardo Agostini's *Le Gemme Antiche Figurate*, vol. II, 1669,

carried on negotiations in order to find the right
artist who could design and cast in bronze a large
equestrian monument for Francesco Sforza, his father.
In the 'Life of Antonio Pollaiuolo', Vasari says: 'After
his death a drawing and a model were discovered for
an equestrian monument of Francesco Sforza, Duke of
Milan, which he made for Ludovico Sforza'.
Of Pollaiuolo's design two copies are extant, one in the
Munich Print room, and one in the Lehman collection,
New York.
Pollaiuolo's sketches for an equestrian monument were,
according to Kenneth Clark, perhaps imitated by
Leonardo; unless both artists based their designs on
'some classical relief'.
The *motif* of the galloping rider trampling down an
enemy is known from Roman coins – e.g. one of Lucius
Verus, and from antique gems – e.g. Furtwängler,
XXV, 52. But a cameo, once in the Medici Collection,
shows the foe defending himself with his shield in a
very similar position to that in some of Leonardo's
drawings, especially when he reverted to the same idea
for the Trivulzio monument (see plate 111).
No. 106 belongs to Leonardo's latest and finest silverpoint drawings; he did not use that technique after 1490.
The arms of the rider are tentatively sketched in
different directions: the left arm, holding the reins, once
near the mane, and once drawn back; the right arm
with the baton once stretched forward and once back-
ward. The prostrate foe holds a shield over his head.
A drawing at Windsor (12357), and an engraving at the
British Museum (reproduced here) contain traces of
small-scale models for the Sforza monument.
See also footnote 28 on p. 18; and plate VIII.

107

STUDIES OF HORSES' LEGS. Turin, Royal
Library, No. 15580

108

THE FIGHT FOR THE STANDARD. Copy of
the central part of Leonardo's cartoon, The Battle of
Anghiari. Drawing by Rubens; black chalk, pen
and brush; 43.5×56.5 cm. The Hague, Her Royal
Highness, Princess Wilhelmina of Holland.
See footnotes 43–46 on pp. 20–21.
A large wall in the Sala del Gran Consiglio of the
Palazzo Vecchio in Florence, was to be decorated with
two patriotic paintings. In October 1503 Leonardo
received a commission for one of those paintings. The
section to cover measured about 24 by 60 feet. Leonardo
chose as his theme an incident from the war between
the Florentines and the Milanese. About ten months

Michelangelo: Copy of a part of Leonardo's *Battle of Anghiari*
cartoon. Pen and ink drawing, c. 1504. British Museum.

later Michelangelo was given a commission for the other
painting. The section on the wall he agreed to paint had
the same measurements as that of Leonardo's painting.
He chose a scene from the war against Pisa, the *Battle
of Cascina.*
Leonardo finished his cartoon in the spring of 1505 and
began to paint the centre group on the wall. He never
finished his work; on May 30th, 1506, he returned on
short leave to Milan; but after that he did not take up
this work again.
No complete copy of the lost Anghiari cartoon is preserved – only a few original sketches, many more studies
of horses, and a much retouched Head of a Warrior at
Oxford (probably only a copy, but apparently in the
original size of the cartoon, namely larger than life).
There are many copies of the centre scene, the *Fight for
the Standard,* including one drawing in the Louvre,
attributed to Rubens. Michelangelo and Raphael copied
some other parts of Leonardo's cartoon, as has been
repeatedly pointed out.

Raphael: Copy of a part of Leonardo's *Battle of Anghiari* cartoon.
Silver-point, c. 1505. Oxford, Ashmolean Museum.

According to Cellini, Leonardo's cartoon was in his
time still to be seen in the Sala del Papa of the Monastery
S. Maria Novella. But according to the Anonimo
Gaddiano (see p. 30) Leonardo had taken parts of the

The Fight for the Standard. Engraving from J. B. Séroux
d'Agincourt's *Histoire de l'Art par les monuments*
(Paris, 1811–23, plate 173-3).

The Calvacade. Black chalk drawing by Leonardo. Windsor, 12339 r.
(According to Geymüller, 1886, for the group at
the extreme right of the cartoon.)

cartoon with him to France. (Goethe, too, assumed that
the cartoon was lost in France.) The original cartoon
was of an enormous size (c. 8×20 m.), and had to be
left behind in Florence. But Leonardo had certainly
made also a *modello* in a smaller size; and perhaps full-
size copies in outline (at least of the part he transferred
to the wall) in order that there should be no need to cut
up the original. We do not know what exactly
Leonardo took to France; but those parts of the cartoon
may still have existed in France when Rubens arrived
there. (Leonardo's wall-painting in Florence did not
exist any longer in Rubens's time.)

There is no agreement amongst scholars about the
reconstruction of the cartoon. It is, however, now
generally agreed that the composition consisted of three
parts. Some students believe that if one puts next to the
sketches of Michelangelo and Raphael, towards the
right, Leonardo's drawing, Windsor, No. 12339 *recto*,
(see illustration), it completes the composition. Other
students suggested: on the left a part of our plate 109
(the group in the lower left corner, the fighting horsemen towards the left of a bridge), in the centre plate
108, and on the right Windsor drawing No. 12339
recto. Neither reconstruction is quite convincing.[27]

Between 1558 and 1565 Vasari destroyed Leonardo's
wall-painting *The Fight for the Standard* by overpainting
it with one of his frescoes. Several copies of this battle
scene are extant, the best of them in the Uffizi. This copy
is not quite complete; it does not show the crouching
man in the lower left corner, and also not the lower end

of the painting. This part was probably covered by
panelling, or by benches, at the time when the copyist
did his work. The engraving in the publication by
Séroux d'Agincourt is made from a (now missing) copy,
which also Rubens may have known.

109-110

STUDIES FOR THE BATTLE OF ANGH-
IARI. Venice, Academy, 215A and 215; 16.1×15.3
cm.; and 14.5×15.2 cm.

A part of the blank paper is not reproduced here. The
upper sketch in No. 110 is for the centre part of the
cartoon. The lower sketch in No. 109 shows, on the
right, an idea for the same part; continued, towards the
left, with another scene, *The Fight near the Bridge*.
See note on plate 108.

111

STUDY FOR THE TRIVULZIO MONU-
MENT. Windsor, 12355

Leonardo made preparatory studies for two equestrian
monuments: that of Francesco Sforza, from 1483 to
1496, and that of Marshal Giacomo Trivulzio probably
1508 to 1512. The first monument certainly reached the
model stage (see Documents, I, item 10; and II–VI).
Leonardo intended to adorn the monument with 'six
harpies with candelabra'. The horse was to be life-size,
so the complete monument – as given in this sketch –
would have been about 21 feet high.

The most interesting part of plate 111 are the designs of
the elaborate base[28] on which horse and rider were to

27. See also G. Neufeld, *Leonardo da Vinci's Battle of Anghiari:
a genetic reconstruction*, in *The Art Bulletin*, XXXI, 1949, p. 170f.;
and J. Wilde, *Michelangelo and Leonardo*, in *Burlington Magazine*,
1953, pp. 70–77.

28. A. Venturi, in *L'Arte XVII*, 1914, p. 153 f.

be placed. Neither Donatello's *Gattamelata* nor Verrocchio's *Colleoni* stand on such a great triumphal arch; Baroncelli's equestrian monument of 1454 at Ferrara was the only possible model, as Leon Battista Alberti had designed for it a base with arches. Unfortunately this monument was destroyed during the French Revolution.

112–113

STUDIES OF HORSES. Windsor, 12290 and 12321

Kenneth Clark (1954) dates the first of the two drawings correctly 'about 1490–1'. The other drawing is of the same period, and both, according to this date, must be studies for the Sforza monument.

114

HORSE AND RIDER. Budapest Museum. Bronze statuette, 24 cm. high. (The socle is modern.)

The style of this bronze has been compared to the drawings for *The Fight for the Standard* (plate 108), and with the style of the designs for the Trivulzio monument (plate 111). It is clearly the most Leonardesque of all bronzes attributed to the master.

The rider is cast separately. In his left hand he is holding a shield (not visible in our reproduction); the right hand was holding a sword, which is now lost.

Compare plate VI.

There is a drawing at Windsor (12328), with a note by Leonardo that he should not forget to make small models in wax of the horses and men drawn (plate VIII–a). This note can be connected with the horseman in Budapest (plate 114) and similar bronzes.

A small bronze figure of a man, covering himself with his shield, in the Collection of Principe Trivulzio in Milan, belonged originally either to this or to a similar bronze group. There are other fine bronzes of rearing and of pacing horses: in the Metropolitan Museum, the Frick Collection, the Rijksmuseum, the Berlin Museum, the Paget Collection, London, the Bargello, the Castello Sforzesco, the Wallace Collection, the British Museum, the Jeannerat Collection, London, and in the Collection of Duchessa dell'Arenella, Naples.

Gian Francesco Rustici (with the help of Leonardo): The Baptist between a
Pharisee and a Levite, 1506–11. Bronze group over the north door of
the Florentine Baptistery.

PLATE V. Gian Francesco Rustici (with the help of Leonardo): *Pharisee and Levite,* from the bronze group *St. John preaching,* 1506–11. Florence, Baptistery (above Ghiberti's first door).

PLATE VI. Gian Francesco Rustici (with the help of Leonardo?): *Battle scene*. Terracotta. About 1508. Florence, Bargello.

PLATE VII. Attributed (by Valentiner) to Leonardo: *Head*, detail of Verrocchio's terracotta relief *Resurrection of Christ*. About 1478. Florence, Bargello.

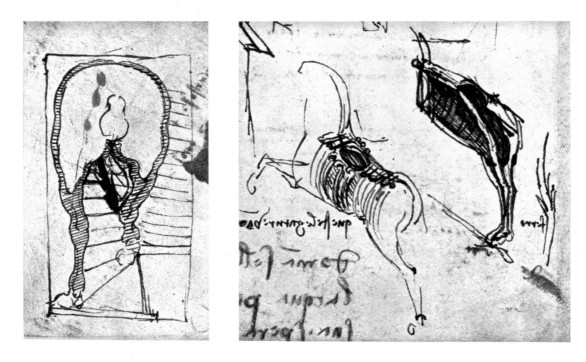

PLATE VIII. (a) Leonardo: *Sketches of men and horses*, with the inscription *"fanne un picholo di cera lūgho un dito"* (make a little wax model after it, one finger long). Detail of a drawing, about 1506. Windsor Castle (No. 12328 r.). – (b) and (c) *Sketches in preparation of casting the Bronze Horse for the Sforza Monument.* 1491–93. Details of two drawings at Windsor Castle. (b) *The Horse within a mould.* – (c) *Two sketches of moulds for casting a prancing horse.*

NOTES ON THE SUPPLEMENTARY PLATES

Plate I. *Paintings by Lorenzo di Credi, supposed to have been painted with the help of Leonardo, or sometimes even attributed to Leonardo himself.* – (a) Madonna and Child with Pomegranate (known as the 'Dreyfus Madonna'). Panel, 16×12.6 cm. Berenson lists this picture as by Lorenzo di Credi; the attribution to Leonardo is mainly due to Langton Douglas and Valentiner. The drawing in the Dresden Print Room, considered a preparatory study for this Madonna, is according to Berenson (No. 672) by Credi; according to Langton Douglas by Verrocchio; according to Valentiner by Verrocchio, overdrawn by Lorenzo di Credi. Heydenreich connects the Dreyfus Madonna with the Munich Madonna (plate 63) and contends that the latter was painted in Verrocchio's workshop with the help of Leonardo, the former only under his influence. The description: 'Painted in Verrocchio's studio by Lorenzo di Credi, perhaps assisted by young Leonardo; from the same period as the Pistoia Altarpiece', comes probably very near to the full truth. – (b) A detail from the Pistoia Altar-piece (called 'Madonna di Piazza'). This altarpiece was commissioned from Verrocchio in 1474; in 1478 it was nearly finished; in 1486 it was completed by Lorenzo di Credi. Langton Douglas and Valentiner assumed that Leonardo collaborated in this painting between 1475 and 1478, not only by helping in the painting of the predella but also of the central panel. (See illustration on p. 27. The detail, reproduced as plate I-a, measures in the original 52×36 cm.) – (c) and (d) Parts of the Predella of the Pistoia Altarpiece. Panels, about 14 cm. deep. One cannot improve on Berenson's conclusion, who calls the panel in the Louvre 'Lorenzo di Credi, retouched by Leonardo', and the panel in Worcester simply 'by Lorenzo di Credi'.

Plate II. The Sforza portraits in Montorfano's 'Crucifixion'. This attribution rests on Vasari's statement (see p. 17). The figures of the donors Ludovico Moro and his wife, Beatrice d'Este, with their sons Massimiliano and Francesco, in the 'Pala Sforzesca' (Brera; Suida, fig. 15) are rather similar. (See also Document VII, p. 34.) Whereas Montorfano's work is well preserved, the Sforza portraits (plate II) have completely flaked off, showing the naked wall and an outline drawing of the figures; they were not painted on top of Montorfano's finished fresco but directly on the wall, which means that a space had been reserved for the portraits. These portraits are probably based on two cartoons, or large drawings, by Leonardo, who apparently had no share in the execution of the painting of the figures (1497–98).

Plate III-a. 'LA BELLE FERRONNIÈRE'. Louvre, No. 1600. Panel; size of this detail, 45×34 cm.
The lady wears a small *scuffa*, or cap, on the back of her head, and a *ferronnière* round her brow. (A *ferronnière* is a head-band which originally formed the velvet rim of a hair net, but was later made of gold and ornamented with jewels.) This was a common Lombard fashion.
Claiming it in 1839 as a portrait of Lucrezia Crivelli, Waagen was the first to attribute it to Leonardo. In 1894 Frizzoni was the first to attribute it to Boltraffio. In our time some of the best authorities – including A. Venturi, Berenson, Sir Charles Holmes, Kenneth Clark, and Beltrami – have reverted to the belief in Leonardo's authorship.
We recall a letter, written by Pietro da Novellara in 1501 (Documents, XI) in which he says: 'Leonardo has done nothing else, except that he now and then lends a hand to one or another of the portraits which his two assistants are painting'. Giovanni Antonio Boltraffio, born in 1467, joined Leonardo's studio not later than 1490. But X-ray photographs of the Belle Ferronnière, exhibited side by side with other X-ray photographs of paintings undoubtedly by Boltraffio (Vienna Academy, 1953, Catal. L. Münz, p. 10) proved clearly that not a single brush-stroke in this painting could be from the hand of Boltraffio; nor is anything in it by Leonardo himself. Plate III-a shows the portrait to its best advantage: without the stone breastwork and with a little less of the vast dead background. There is a possibility that the Leonardo pupil who painted this prosaic portrait had the use of a drawing by his master, perhaps similar to plate 25, and less sketchy than plate 5. The indifferent colouring but sensitive shading of the figure is in the manner of Melzi, best known from the sweet heads of his 'Colombine' and 'Pomona' (Bodmer, figs. 89 and 90; Suida, 299 and 302).

Plate III-b. PORTRAIT OF A LADY. Washington, National Gallery, Kress Collection. Panel, 48×34.5 cm.
The painting was first attributed to Leonardo by Suida (1940) and identified as a portrait of Beatrice d'Este; but the portrait of Beatrice d'Este in the Castello Sforzesco shows a different profile. A variant of the portrait (in the Musée Jacquemart-André, Paris) including both hands, has been identified by Emil Schaeffer (verbally) as a likeness of Beatrice of Portugal, Duchess of Savoy, the sister-in-law of Charles V. The fashion worn by this lady indicates a date of about 1506 (cf. O. Fischel, *Raphael*, London, 1946, plate 49).

Plate IV. The Last Supper. See note on plates 71–73.

Plate V. Rustici: *The Baptist between a Pharisee and a Levite*. Florence, Baptistery. (See the illustration on p. 180.) Rustici received the commission for this bronze group towards the end of 1506 and worked on it till September 1509, when he began, with the help of Bernardino da Milano, the casting in bronze. Leonardo stayed in Florence from September 1507 to June 1508, living in Piero di Braccio Martelli's house, in which was also Rustici's studio. In the Life of Baccio Bandinelli, Vasari gives some further information: 'Baccio's father, perceiving his son's bent . . . put the boy in charge of Giovan Francesco Rustici, one of the best sculptors of the city, where Leonardo continually practised. . . . Encouraged by Leonardo's advice, Baccio began to copy an ancient marble head of a woman which he had modelled from one in the Medici palace'. In the Life of Rustici we read: 'Rustici learned much from Leonardo, especially in making horses, of which he was very fond, producing them in clay, in wax, in full and in bas-relief, and every imaginable way. . . . As he lived awhile in the via de' Martelli, he was very friendly with the family'. In the same chapter, Vasari supplies more information about Leonardo's help with Rustici's bronze group over the door of the Florence baptistery: 'While engaged upon this work Rustici would allow no one near save Leonardo da Vinci, who never left him while he was moulding and casting until the work was finished. Many therefore believe, though nothing definite is known, that Leonardo worked at them himself, or at least helped Rustici with his advice and judgement.' I do not believe that Leonardo had anything to do with the central figure, the short-legged, long-armed St John whose drapery is badly designed and modelled; though Rustici might have used Leonardo's drawing of the *Angel of the Annunciation* for the upward pointing right arm. But the Pharisee and the Levite are of a much higher quality than that of anything ever attributed to Rustici (by Charles Loeser, Kennedy, Middeldorf, and Valentiner).

Plate VI. Rustici: *Battle Scene*. Florence, Museo Nazionale del Bargello. Terracotta, 45.5 cm. high.
There are similar terracotta groups by Rustici in the Palazzo Vecchio, and in two private collections in Florence, and in the Camondo Collection of the Louvre. Most of them have been discussed in full by R. Stites (in *Art Studies*, 1926–1931). A similar sculpture is described in a *novella* by Antonfrancesco Grazzini (about 1550): 'In the shop of a terracotta dealer behind San Giovanni, or also in the *bottega* of Verrocchio in the Via del Garbo, a relief is to be seen of a rider on a horse, which kicks and bites four or five men crouching

underneath, while the rider himself wounds one and crushes another. They, however, assail both horse and rider with swords and hatchets, nails and teeth, in the strangest attitudes and wildest contortions.' After Verrocchio's death his *bottega* was carried on and, according to Vasari, Rustici worked there at one time.

Plate VII. *Verrocchio's 'Resurrection of Christ'*, terracotta relief from the Villa Careggi. Florence, Bargello.
Valentiner, and others, assume that Leonardo collaborated in this work (see Valentiner, *Studies of Italian Renaissance Sculpture*, London, 1950, p. 166 f.). The detail shown in plate VII should be compared with the 'Head of a Warrior', plate 13.
About the *Rattier relief* from Verrocchio's workshop, attributed to Leonardo, see note on plate 3. The marble bust of a *Lady holding Primulas*, usually regarded as a work of Verrocchio, though attributed to Leonardo by Mackowsky, Suida and others, is illustrated on p. 25. A beautiful relief of a *Madonna and Child* (formerly in the Dibblee collection, Oxford; illustrated here), also

Workshop of Verrocchio (attributed to Leonardo by Mackowsky and A. Venturi): *Madonna and Child*, stucco relief, about 1476. Formerly London, Mrs. Raymond Johnes. (Sold at Christie's in 1964.)

comes from the Verrocchio bottega. There is another specimen known, of exactly the same size, in the collection of Professor Piero Tozzi, New York (ill. Valentiner, *Studies of Italian Renaissance Sculpture*, fig. 187). Both *stucchi* are obviously taken from the same (lost) marble relief, but the Tozzi relief has been worked over with the knife by some pupil. These stucco versions are, as always has been admitted, based on Verrocchio's *Madonna with the standing Child*, a terracotta relief dating from about 1472–76 (Florence, Bargello). There are great differences between Verrocchio's terracotta relief and the stucco. In the stucco we find a flow of line similar to the *Rattier relief;* the child with his large head and his short legs is rendered in a naturalistic spirit; the heads, and arms, and hands in the stucco version are

dropping in an almost Botticellesque manner, indeed different from Verrocchio's vigorous conception. (See T. Cook, *The Signa Madonna*, London 1919, and A. Venturi in *L'Arte*, 1922.)

Leonardo lived for at least ten years in Verrocchio's house (1469–79); we know from Vasari and Albertini that he painted one angel in his master's *Baptism of Christ*; but we do not know which sculptures from the Verrocchio workshop are partly or completely the work of Leonardo.

Plate VIII. See note on plates 106 and 114.

NOTES ON THE PLATES IN THE TEXT

p. 25. Verrocchio: *Lady with Primroses*. About 1475–78. Marble, 61 cm. high. (About the attributions to Leonardo see Emil Möller, *La Gentildonna dalle Belle Mani di Leonardo da Vinci*, Bologna 1954.)

p. 26. Leonardo: *Madonna Benois*. Hermitage, Leningrad. No. 2773 (Cat. 1916, No. 1981). Painted on wood, transferred to canvas, 48×31.5 cm.

Since 1914 in the Hermitage, formerly in the Collection of Madame Léon Benois (after whom the picture is named; her grandfather had bought it in Astrakhan, from an Italian, in 1824). One of Leonardo's earliest paintings, and one which was endlessly repeated, not only by Italian painters but also by the Flemish school. The best of these replicas is in the Galleria Colonna at Rome, ascribed to Filippino Lippi or sometimes to Lorenzo di Credi (Photo Alinari 7342). Other copies are in the collection of the Earl Spencer, at Althorp, and in the Magdeburg Museum (with the figure of St Joseph added); another copy, rather in the style of Botticini, was in the Toscanelli sale, Florence 1883 (repr. Reinach, *Répertoire*, I, 109). The Madonna alone was copied by Raphael, in his 'Virgin with the Carnation' (of which the original is lost, but several copies are known; cf. Crowe and Cavalcaselle, I, p. 273). The Child alone was often copied, for instance, by Lorenzo di Credi in a Madonna painting in the Turin Gallery, No. 115 (Photo Alinari 14814).

The numerous repetitions of this little painting prove indeed that it cannot have been by a second-rate painter.

The picture is not too well preserved; it suffered when it was transferred from panel to canvas; there are retouchings in the drapery, mouth, neck and hands of the Madonna, left knee and right hand of the child, most of the background, etc. Before restoration, the window probably contained a landscape, as the copy in the Galleria Colonna does.

Bodmer, and others, assumed that this little picture was painted, in about 1478, by young Leonardo 'with the help of pupils'. Thiis ascribed it to Sogliani. Heydenreich calls it 'unfinished'; he believes it to be a workshop production, on which Leonardo worked again after 1500 (cf., for the lower part of the drapery, plate 41). It seems to me that all this criticism is caused only by the poor preservation of this genuine early painting.

A sketch in the British Museum (Cat. No. 100 verso), a Madonna and Child, corresponds with the picture.

p. 35. Leonardo (also attributed to Antonio Rossellino): *Madonna with the Laughing Child*. About 1472–78. Terracotta, 48.5 cm. high. London, Victoria and Albert Museum. (See John Goldsmith Phillips, *The Virgin with the Laughing Child*, in 'Studies in the History of Art, dedicated to William E. Suida', London 1959, pp. 146–153.)

p. 36. *Leonardo's Madonna with the Yarn-Winder*. Canvas, 49×37 cm. Drumlanrig Castle, The Duke of Buccleuch. (Attributed to Leonardo by Emil Möller in the Burlington Magazine, 1926, pp. 61–68.)

SHORT BIBLIOGRAPHY

THIS LIST CONTAINS ONLY BOOKS ON LEONARDO AS AN ARTIST

The books and articles are arranged in chronological order

BIBLIOGRAPHY

(1) *Raccolta Vinciana presso l'Archivio Storico del Commune di Milano*, ed. Ettore Verga, since 1905.

(2) Ettore Verga, *Bibliografia Vinciana, 1493–1930.* Bologna 1931 (2 vols.).

(3) *Leonardo Bibliography* in *Raccolta Vinciana* XIV–XVI, Milan 1930–39. (Continuing No. 2.)

(4) *Leonardo Bibliography 1939–1952*, by L. H. Heydenreich, in *Zeitschrift für Kunstwissenschaft*, vol. XV, 1952, pp. 195–200. (Continuing No. 3.)

THE MANUSCRIPTS

A list of all publications of Leonardo's MSS. in Richter, II, pp. 419–42; also Kate T. Steinitz, *The Manuscripts of Leonardo da Vinci* (The Elmer Belt Library of Vinciana), Los Angeles 1948. See also Augusto Mariani, *Leonardo da Vinci, Tutti gli scritti* (I: *scritti letterari*), Milan 1952; and *I manoscritti di Leonardo da Vinci* (in *Saggi e ricerche*, Rome 1954).

(5) E. Solmi, *Le fonti dei manoscritti di Leonardo da Vinci.* Turin 1908.

(6) Gerolamo Calvi, *I Manoscritti di Leonardo da Vinci dal punto di vista cronologico, storico e biografico.* Bologna 1925.

(7) Edward McCurdy, *Leonardo da Vinci's Note-Books.* London 1906. (New edition, in 2 vols., London 1938.)

(8) *The Literary Works of Leonardo da Vinci.* Compiled and edited from the original manuscripts by Jean Paul Richter. Second edition enlarged and revised. 2 vols. Oxford University Press, London and New York 1939.

LEONARDO'S TREATISE ON PAINTING

(9) *Il Trattato della Pittura:* Bibliography 1651–1913, by Aldo Mieli, in *Archivo di storia della scienza* I, 1919–20, p. 177 f.

(10) *Trattato della Pittura di Leonardo da Vinci*, Prefazione di Angelo Borzelli. Lanciano 1914. (The first edition of Leonardo's Trattato was issued in Paris, 1651.)

(11) *Trattato della Pittura*, Italian edition of the Cod. Urbinas Lat. 1270 in the Vatican, with German translation in *Quellenschriften für Kunstgeschichte*, ed. Heinrich Ludwig, 3 vols. Vienna 1882. (Second edition, in German, by Marie Herzfeld, Jena 1909.) Additions: *Das Buch von der Malerei, Neues Material*, ed. H. Ludwig. Stuttgart 1885.

(12) *Treatise on Painting* (Cod. Urbinas Lat. 1270) by Leonardo da Vinci, translated and annotated by A. Philip McMahon, 2 vols. Princeton 1956.

(13) Lionello Venturi, *La Critica e l'Arte di Leonardo da Vinci.* Bologna 1919.

THE DOCUMENTS

(14) Carlo Amoretti, *Memorie storiche sulla vita . . . de Leonardo da Vinci.* Milan 1804.

(15) G. Campori, *Nuovi documenti per la vita di Leonardo da Vinci.* Modena 1865.

(16) G. Milanesi, *Documenti inediti riguardanti Leonardo da Vinci.* Florence 1872.

(17) G. Uzielli, *Ricerche intorno a Leonardo da Vinci:* vol. I, Florence 1872 (second edition, Turin 1896). vol. II, Rome 1884.

(18) N. Smiraglia Scognamiglio, *Ricerche e documenti sulla giovinezza di Leonardo da Vinci.* Naples 1900.

(19) C. Brun, *Die Quellen zur Biographie Leonardos*, in *Festgabe für Hugo Blümmer*, Zürich 1914.

(20) G. Calvi, *Contributi alla Biografia di Leonardo da Vinci*, in *Archivio Storico Lombardo*, 1916, XLIII.

(21) Luca Beltrami, *Documenti e Memorie riguardanti la vita e le opere di Leonardo da Vinci.* Milan 1919.

(22) Aldo de Rinaldis, *Storia dell' opera pittorica di Leonardo da Vinci.* Bologna 1926.

Many documents are quoted in the notes to the Vasari editions by Milanesi, Horne and Poggi (Nos. 26–28). A useful survey, by W. v. Seidlitz, *Regesten zum Leben Leonardos da Vinci*, in *Repertorium f. Kunstwissenschaft* XXXIV, 1911, pp. 448–458.

THE EARLY BIOGRAPHIES

(23) *Libro di Antonio Billi*, ed. Carl Frey, Berlin, 1892. (The earliest life among the Florentine art annalists, named after the merchant who was either the author or the possessor of the book, written about 1518.)

(24) Paolo Giovio, *The Life of Leonardo da Vinci*, in Richter, I, pp. 2–3, Oxford 1939. (Written c. 1527.)

(25) *Anonimo Magliabecchiano (or Gaddiano)*, ed. Carl Frey, Berlin 1892. (Written between 1540–48, derived information from Billi's book and served as a source for Vasari.)

(26) Giorgio Vasari, *Le Vite de' più eccellenti Pittori, Scultori ed Architettori, con nuove annotazioni e commenti di Gaetano Milanesi.* Vol. IV, Florence 1879. (First edition of Vasari's book 1550, second edition 1568.)

(27) *The Life of Leonardo da Vinci by Giorgio Vasari*, done into English with a commentary by Herbert Horne. London 1903.

(28) Giovanni Poggi, *Leonardo da Vinci, La Vita di Giorgio Vasari nuovamente commentata e illustrata.* Florence 1919 (with 200 plates).

(29) Antonio de Beatis, *Die Reise des Kardinals Luigi d'Aragona*, ed. L. Pastor, Freiburg 1905. (The Cardinal visited Leonardo at Amboise, in October 1517.)

(30) G. Paolo Lomazzo, *Trattato dell' Arte della pittura.* Milan 1584 (English translation, Oxford 1598).

(31) G. Paolo Lomazzo, *Idea del tempio della pittura.* Milan 1590. (Lomazzo had direct information about Leonardo from Francesco Melzi.)

The Leonardo biographies from Nos. 24, 25 and 26, translated into English, are printed in the present volume; the short note on Leonardo in the Libro di Antonio Billi is analysed on p. 28.

LEONARDO'S APPEARANCE

(32) Luca Beltrami, *Il volto di Leonardo da Vinci.* (Istituto di Studi Vinciani), Rome 1919. (Also in *Emporium*, Bergamo 1919, pp. 3–17.)

(33) Emil Möller, *Wie sah Leonardo aus?* in *Belvedere*, IX, Vienna 1926, pp. 29–46.

(34) L. Planiscig, *Leonardos Porträte und Aristoteles*, in *Festschrift für Julius Schlosser.* Vienna 1927.

(35) Giorgio Nicodemi, *Il volto di Leonardo da Vinci*, in *Leonardo da Vinci* (Mostra, Milan 1939) ed. Istituto Geografico de Agostini, Novara (1939).

BOOKS AND ESSAYS ON LEONARDO'S ART

(36) Carlo Giuseppi Gerli, *Disegni di Leonardo da Vinci incisi e publ.* Milan 1734.

(37) Gabriel Séailles, *Léonard de Vinci, l'artiste et le savant.* Paris 1892. (New edition, Paris 1912.)

(38) Walter Pater, *The Renaissance.* London 1893 (pp. 103–135: Essay on Leonardo).

(39) Paul Müller-Walde, *Leonardo da Vinci: Lebensskizze und Forschungen.* München 1889–90 (unfinished).

(40) Paul Müller-Walde, *Beiträge zur Kenntnis des Leonardo da Vinci*, in *Jahrbuch der preussischen Kunstsammlungen*, Berlin 1897–99. (I. Ein neues Dokument zur Geschichte des Reiterdenkmals für Francesco Sforza. – II. Eine Skizze zur Leda. – III–IV. Vorbereitungen zum hl. Johannes des Louvre. – Eine frühe Redaktion von Leonardo's Komposition der Madonna mit der hl. Anna und dem Lamm. – VII–VIII. Leonardo und die antike Reiterstatue des Regisole. Entwürfe zum Reiterdenkmal für Trivulzio. Plaketten nach Studien Leonardos zu Reiterdenkmälern und zur Reiterschlacht von Anghiari.)

(41) Edmondo Solmi, *Leonardo.* Florence 1900.

(42) W. v. Seidlitz, *Leonardo da Vinci, der Wendepunkt der Renaissance*, 2 vols. Berlin 1909. (The second edition, very different from the first, Vienna 1935.)

(43) Bernard Berenson, *The Study and Criticism of Italian Art*, III. London 1916 (pp. 1–37: Leonardo da Vinci, an attempt at revaluation).

(44) Osvald Sirén, *Leonardo da Vinci, The Artist and the Man.* New Haven 1916. (Revised French edition, 3 vols., Paris and Brussels 1928. See the review by Sir Eric Maclagan, in *Burlington Magazine*, LIV, 1929, p. 277.)

(45) Giulio Carotti, *Leonardo da Vinci.* Turin 1921.

(46) Wilhelm von Bode, *Studien über Leonardo da Vinci.* Berlin 1921.

(47) A. Schiaparelli, *Leonardo ritrattista.* Milan 1921.

(48) Ettore Verga, *Gli studi intorno a Leonardo da Vinci.* Rome 1923.

(49) Max Dvořák, *Geschichte der italienischen Kunst im Zeitalter der Renaissance: Akademische Vorlesungen* (Vienna, 1918–20). Munich, 1927 (vol. I, pp. 143–194: Leonardo.)

(50) Edmund Hildebrandt, *Leonardo da Vinci.* Berlin 1927.

(51) Edward McCurdy, *The mind of Leonardo da Vinci.* London 1928.

(52) Anny A. Popp, *Leonardo da Vinci: Zeichnungen.* München 1928.

(53) *I disegni di Leonardo da Vinci.* Published in facsimile by the R. Commissione Vinciana (A. Venturi). Part I–VII. Rome 1928–52 (252 plates).

(54) Wilhelm Suida, *Leonardo und sein Kreis.* München 1929.

(55) Sir Kenneth Clark, *Leonardo da Vinci: An Account of his development as an artist.* Cambridge 1929. (Revised edition, Penguin books No. A430, London 1958.)

(56) Heinrich Bodmer, *Leonardo: des Meisters Gemälde und Zeichnungen.* Klassiker der Kunst, vol. 37. Stuttgart 1931. (With 360 illustrations.)

(57) Edward McCurdy, *Leonardo da Vinci: The Artist.* London 1933.

(58) Girolamo Calvi, *Vita di Leonardo da Vinci.* Brescia 1936 (second edition, 1949).

(59) Bernard Berenson, *The Drawings of the Florentine Painters*, Amplified Edition, 3 vols. Chicago 1938. (A Catalogue of Leonardo Drawings, vol. II, pp. 109–138; and 99 illustrations in vol. III.)

(60) H. Bodmer, *Disegni di Leonardo* (100 illustrations). Florence 1939 (second edition, 1943).

(61) Odoardo H. Giglioli, *Leonardo. Iniziazione alla connoscenza di Lui e delle questioni Vinciane.* Florence 1944.

(62) R. Langton Douglas, *Leonardo da Vinci.* Chicago 1944.

(63) *The Drawings of Leonardo da Vinci*, with an Introduction and Notes by A. E. Popham. London 1946.

(64) Giorgio Castelfranco: *Leonardo da Vinci.* Milan 1952.

(65) Ludwig Heinrich Heydenreich, *Leonardo da Vinci*, second edition, 2 vols., Basel 1954. (English edition, 1 vol., London 1954.)

LEONARDO'S EARLIEST PERIOD

(66) Sigmund Freud, *Eine Kindheitserinnerung des Leonardo da Vinci.* Vienna 1910. (Also an English translation, by Prof. A. A. Brill.)

(67) Jens Thiis, *Leonardo da Vinci: The Florentine years of Leonardo and Verrocchio.* London (1913). (Swedish edition 1909; revised French edition 1928.)

(68) Sir Charles Holmes, in *Burlington Magazine*, February 1914, *review of Thiis's book on Leonardo.* (About Leonardo's activities in Verrocchio's workshop.)

(69) W. R. Valentiner, *Leonardo as Verrocchio's co-worker*, in

The Art Bulletin (XII, 1), University of Chicago, March 1930, pp. 43–89.

(70) W. R. Valentiner, *Leonardo und Desiderio*, in *Jahrb. d. preuss. Kunstsamml.* LXI, 1932, p. 53 f.

(71) Emil Möller, *Leonardo e il Verrocchio* in *Raccolta Vinciana* XIV, Milan 1930–4.

(72) Bernard Berenson, *Verrocchio e Leonardo – Leonardo e Credi*, in *Bollettino d'Arte*, 1933–34 (pp. 241–264; 193–213).

(73) Adolfo Venturi, *Leonardo scultore nella bottega del Verrocchio* in *Nuova Antologia*, 1934, March, pp. 34–39; *L'Arte* 1936, pp. 243–265.

(74) W. R. Valentiner, *Über zwei Kompositionen Leonardos*, in *Jahrb. d. preuss. Kunstsamml.*, vol. 56, 1935, p. 213 f.

(75) W. R. Valentiner, *Leonardo's Early Life*, in the 'Catalogue of the Leonardo Exhibition', Los Angeles County Museum, 1949, pp. 43–60.

(76) W. R. Valentiner, *Studies of Italian Renaissance Sculpture*, London 1950 (*On Leonardo's Relation to Verrocchio*, pp. 113–177. *Two Terracotta Reliefs by Leonardo*, pp. 178–192.)

(77) Ludwig Baldass, *Zu den Gemälden der ersten Periode des Leonardo da Vinci*, in *Zeitschrift für Kunstwissenschaft*, vol. VII, 3–4, Berlin 1953, pp. 165–182.

LEONARDO THE SCULPTOR

(78) L. Courajod, *Léonard de Vinci et la statue équestre de Francesco Sforza*. Paris 1879.

(79) Fr. Haak, *Zur Entwicklung des italienischen Reiterdenkmals*, in *Zeitschr. f. bild. Kunst*, N.F. VII, 1896, p. 273 f.

(80) Simon Meller, *Die Reiterdarstellungen Leonardos und die Budapester Bronzestatuette*, in *Jahrb. d. preuss. Kunstsamml.*, Berlin 1916, pp. 113–140.

(81) A. Cook, *Leonardo da Vinci, Sculptor*. London 1923. (See the review by Sir Eric Maclagan, in Burlington Magazine, XLIII, 1923, II, p. 68 f.)

(82) Francesco Malaguzzi Valeri, *Leonardo da Vinci e la scultura*. Bologna 1922.

(83) Raymond S. Stites, *Leonardo da Vinci, Sculptor*, in *Art Studies*, 1926 (p. 103 f.), 1930 (p. 254 f.), 1931 (p. 289 f.). Cambridge, U.S.A.

(84) Adolfo Venturi, in his *Storia dell'Arte Italiana*, vol. X, 1. Milan 1935.

(85) John Goldsmith Phillips, *The Virgin with the Laughing Child*. (A terracotta statuette in the Victoria and Albert Museum, attributed to Leonardo.) In 'Studies in the History of Art, dedicated to William E. Suida', London 1959, pp. 146–153.
See also Nos. 65, 73 and 76.

SINGLE LEONARDO PAINTINGS

(86) 'The Last Supper'. Giuseppe Bossi, *Del 'Cenacolo' di Leonardo da Vinci*. Milan 1810.

(87) Goethe, *Über Leonards da Vinci Abendmahl zu Mailand*, in *Kunst und Alterthum*, III, 1817. (A review of Bossi's book.)

(88) J. Strzygowski, *Leonardos Abendmahl und Goethes Deutung*, in *Goethe-Jahrbuch* 1896, p. 138 f.

(89) Otto Hoerth, *Das Abendmahl des Leonardo da Vinci*. Leipzig 1907.

(90) Luca Beltrami, *Il Cenacolo di Leonardo*. Milan 1908.

(91) Heinrich Wölfflin, *Die Klassische Kunst*; 1898, 6th ed. Munich 1914 (pp. 23–42: analysis of the composition of four Leonardo paintings – Last Supper, Mona Lisa, St Anne, Battle of Anghiari). English edition, Phaidon Press, 1955.

(92) Salomon Reinach, *La Tristesse de Mona Lisa*, in *Bulletin des Musées de France*. Paris 1909.

(93) Luca Beltrami, *Leonardo da Vinci e la Sala delle Asse*. Milan 1902.

(94) M. Lessing, *Die Anghiarischlacht des Leonardo da Vinci*. Bonn 1935.

(95) K. F. Suter, *Leonardos Schlachtenbild*, Strasburg 1937.

(96) Emil Möller, *Das Abendmahl des Lionardo da Vinci*. Baden-Baden 1952.

DRAWINGS IN INDIVIDUAL COLLECTIONS

Florence, Uffizi.

(97) Pasquale Nerino Ferri, *Catalogo riassuntivo della raccolta di disegni antichi e moderni della R. Galleria degli Uffizi di Firenze*. Rome 1890.

(98) Giovanni Poggi, *Drawings by Leonardo da Vinci*. (The drawings of the Royal Gallery of the Uffizi in Florence, published by Leo S. Olschki, fifth series, third portfolio; 20 plates.) Florence 1922.

London, British Museum.

(99) *I manoscritti e i disegni di Leonardo da Vinci*, *Il Codice Arundel* 263; ed. R. Commissione Vinciana, Rome 1923–30. (Four parts.)

(100) *Italian Drawings, The fourteenth and fifteenth centuries* (Catalogue) by A. E. Popham and Philip Pouncey, 2 vols. London 1950.

Milan, Ambrosiana.

(101) S. Dozio, *Degli scritti e disegni di Leonardo da Vinci all'Ambrosiana*. Milan 1871.

(102) Giovanni Piumati, *Il Codice Atlantico di Leonardo da Vinci nella Biblioteca Ambrosiana*. Milan 1894–1904.

(103) L. Beltrami, *Disegni di Leonardo e della sua scuola alla Biblioteca Ambrosiana*. Milan 1904.

(104) Carlo Pedretti, *Studi Vinciani*, Geneva 1957.

(105) Carlo Pedretti, *Leonardo da Vinci: Fragments . . . from the Codex Atlanticus*. London 1957.

Milan, Brera.

(106) Francesco Malaguzzi Valeri, *I disegni della R. Pinacoteca di Brera*. Milan 1906.

Milan 1939, Leonardo Exhibition.

(107) *Catalogo della Mostra di Leonardo da Vinci*. Milan 1939.

(108) Leonardo da Vinci, *Pubblicazione promossa dalla mostra di Leonardo da Vinci, Milano*. Novara 1939. (English edition, London 1957.)

Paris, Louvre.

(109) L. Demonts, *Les dessins de Leonardo da Vinci au Musée du Louvre*. Paris 1922.

Oxford.

(110) Sidney Colvin, *Drawings of the old Masters in the University Galleries and in the Library of Christ Church, Oxford,* 3 vols. Oxford 1907.

(111) *Catalogue of the Collection of Drawings in the Ashmolean Museum* (vol. II: Italian Schools) by K. T. Parker. Oxford 1956.

Turin, Library.

(112) Pietro Carlevaris, *I disegni di Leonardo da Vinci della Biblioteca di S. M. di Torino.* Turin 1888.

Venice, Accademia.

(113) Gino Fogolari, *I disegni della R. Galleria dell' Accademia di Venezia.* Milan 1913.

Windsor Castle.

(114) Sir Kenneth Clark, *A Catalogue of the drawings of Leonardo da Vinci . . . at Windsor Castle.* Cambridge 1935, 2 vols.

MISCELLANEA

(115) Victor Mortet, *La mésure de la figure humaine et le canon des proportions d'après les dessins de Villard de Honnecourt, d'Albert Dürer et de Léonard de Vinci.* 'Melanges Chatelain', Paris 1910.

(116) O. Münsterberg, *Leonardo und die chinesische Landschafts-malerei,* in *Orientalisches Archiv,* 1911.

(117) Francesco Malaguzzi Valeri, *La Corte di Ludovico il Moro.* Milan 1915 (vol. II, Bramante e Leonardo).

(118) Luca Beltrami, *La destra mano di Leonardo da Vinci.* Milan 1919.

(119) Giambattista de Toni, *Le piante e gli animali in Leonardo da Vinci.* Bologna (1922).

(120) Emil Möller, *Salai und Leonardo da Vinci* in *Jahrbuch d. Kunsthist. Samml. in Wien.* Vienna 1928, pp. 139–161.

(121) A. Baldacci, *Le piante e la pittura di Leonardo da Vinci.* Bologna 1930.

(122) A. Blum, *Léonard de Vinci, Graveur,* in *Gazette des Beaux-Arts,* 1932, p. 88 f. (with bibliography).

(123) Paul Valéry, *Introduction to the method of Leonardo da Vinci,* translated from the French by Thomas McCreevy. London 1929.

(124) Paul Valéry, *Les divers essais sur Léonard de Vinci, commentés et annotés par lui-même.* Paris 1931.

(125) Giuseppina Fumagalli, *Eros di Leonardo.* Milan 1952.

(126) G. Castelfranco, *Il concetto di forza di Leonardo,* in Proporzioni III, 1950, p. 117 f.

(127) Ludwig Goldscheider, *Leonardo da Vinci: Landscapes and Plants.* London 1952.

(128) Joseph Gantner, *Leonardos Visionen von der Sintflut und vom Untergang der Welt.* Bern 1958.

(129) K. R. Eissler, *Leonardo da Vinci. Psycho-analytical notes on the enigma.* London 1962.

INDEX TO BIBLIOGRAPHY

INDEX OF COLLECTIONS

Chapter 8
**China and
the Himalaya**

Chapter 9
**Western and
Central Asia**

Chapter 10
Africa

County Council

Libraries, books and more . . .

8.5.13

WITHDRAWN

LPINES

n Mountain to Garden

Please return/renew this item by the last due date.
Library items may be renewed by phone on
030 33 33 1234 (24 hours) or via our website

www.cumbria.gov.uk/libraries

Cumbria Libraries
CLIC
Interactive Catalogue

Ask for a CLIC password

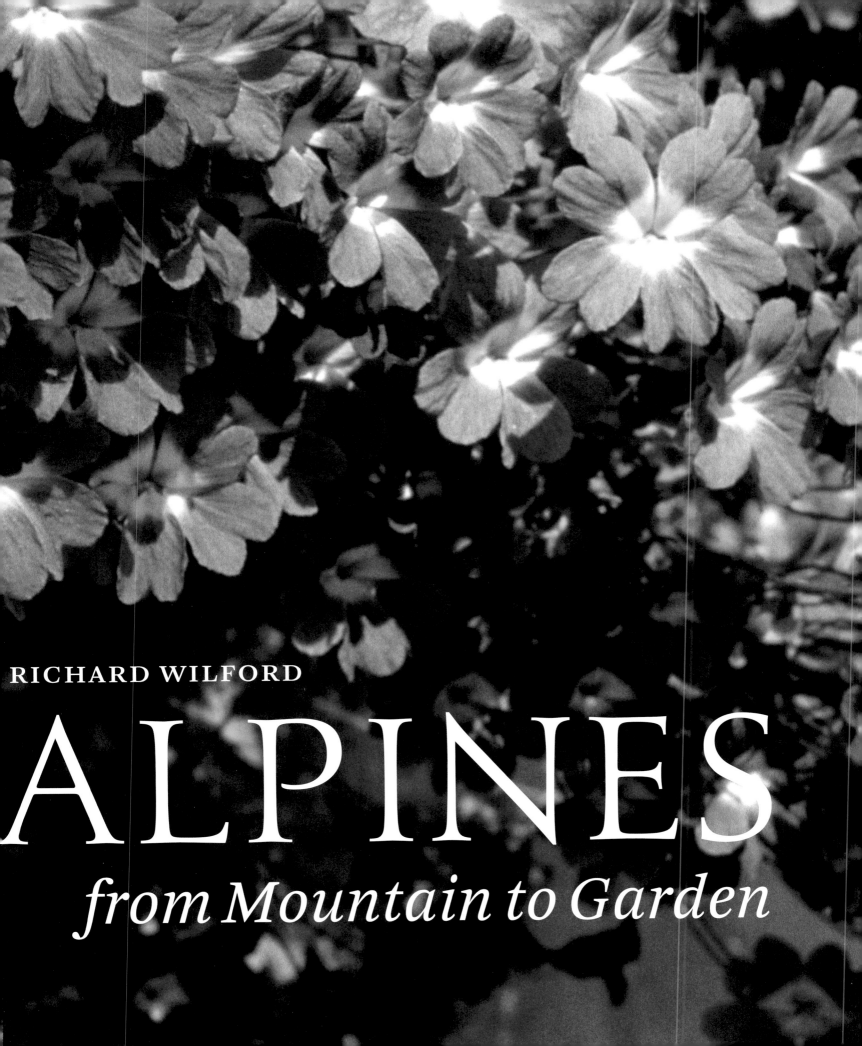

RICHARD WILFORD

ALPINES
from Mountain to Garden

First published in 2010 by
Royal Botanic Gardens, Kew,
Richmond, Surrey, TW9 3AB, UK
www.kew.org

ISBN 978-1-84246-172-3

British Library Cataloguing in Publication Data
A catalogue record for this book is available from the British Library

Production editor: Ruth Linklater
Typesetting and page layout: Christine Beard
Publishing, Design & Photography, Royal Botanic Gardens, Kew

Cover and page design: Lyn Davies Design
Maps: Pat Davies and John Stone

Printed and bound by
Firmengruppe APPL, aprinta druck,
Wemding, Germany

Mixed Sources
Product group from well-managed
forests, controlled sources and
recycled wood or fibre
www.fsc.org   Cert no. SGS-COC-004238
© 1996 Forest Stewardship Council
FSC

For information or to purchase all Kew titles please visit
www.kewbooks.com or email publishing@kew.org

Kew's mission is to inspire and deliver science-based plant conservation worldwide, enhancing the quality of life.
All proceeds go to support Kew's work in saving the world's plants for life.

Contents

Foreword

by Martyn Rix

Alpine plants appeal to gardeners because of their small size, neat habit and relatively large flowers. Add to this the romance of their mountain homes — close-cropped alpine meadows, gravelly screes and hot or cold cliffs, and both interest and attractiveness are heightened. Rarity in the wild and difficulty in cultivation often add to this heady mix, and sometimes even the name recalls someone who has died far from home, bringing these romantic plants into cultivation. Who can resist the charm of the ice-blue *Gentiana farreri*, or rose-pink *Fritillaria alburyana*? True alpine plants have to attract pollinators in often sparsely vegetated habitats, and at the same time resist exposure: wind, intense winter cold and intense summer sunlight. To survive, they have evolved their neat habit and large flowers. The actual species in the alpine zone reflect the flora in the surrounding area; there are numerous

alpine primulas in Europe and the Himalaya, but few in the Rockies. In the Andes are found alpine petunias, alstroemerias and tropaeolums, in New Zealand, celmisias. Climatic conditions impose numerous similarities in plant habit: cushions of *Raoulia* from New Zealand look like *Arenaria tetraquetra* in the Sierra Nevada and *Gypsophila aretioides* in the Elburz in Iran. In some mountain ranges different genera have diversified, such as saxifrages in the Alps, *Dionysia* in the Zagros or rosulate violets in the Andes.

Richard Wilford is well-placed to explain these interesting similarities and differences, with fascinating examples. He has travelled widely in the mountains himself, and for 21 years has looked after a range of hardy collections at Kew, growing and propagating an unrivalled variety of alpines, dwarf bulbs and woodland plants. The Davies Alpine House, the Rock Garden and the Woodland Garden are filled with rare and beautiful plants from around the world. These plants are not only used for display to the public, but are studied by scientists in the Jodrell Laboratory, who read their DNA sequences, and taxonomists in the herbarium who classify them. Richard has contributed many writings to *Kew* magazine, and to *Curtis's Botanical Magazine*, in which the paintings in this book were first published. Alpine plants have been grown avidly in England ever since the time of William Curtis, who started the magazine at Chelsea in 1787, with a painting of *Iris persica*, still considered rare and difficult to grow.

Anyone who visits Kew will be fascinated by the wide range of alpines grown successfully there, and this book will not only increase this interest but inspire others to try to grow them as well.

OPPOSITE
Cyclamen coum subsp. *caucasicum* carpeting a woodland floor near Tbilisi, Georgia.

BELOW LEFT
Campanula fragilis subsp. *cavolinii*, from the Apennines of Italy. The compact growth habit and large flowers are typical of many alpine plants.

Preface

From the very beginning I wanted this book on alpines to look at the geography, history and cultivation of these beautiful plants. That beginning was several years ago now and the scope of this book has changed over the intervening period but it has always been arranged so that each chapter focused on a different region. By approaching the subject in this way I hope to give an insight into the world of alpine plants, where they come from and how they arrived in our gardens.

The alpine flora is one of the few that can be found worldwide, from tropical mountain peaks to tundra. In the chapters that follow, the mountains and their associated climates are discussed, and a selection of the plants that grow there are looked at in detail. How these plants ended up in our gardens is down to the plant hunters who searched for and collected them. Their stories are fascinating, particularly when they were among the first to explore a region, and those who collected alpines often had the hardest job of all, contending with harsh weather and challenging terrain.

The inspiration for this book was *Curtis's Botanical Magazine*, a journal that has been published continually since 1787, describing and illustrating plants new to cultivation. Over thirty botanical paintings from this magazine are reproduced here and they have been chosen to illustrate the story of alpine plant introductions over the past two centuries and more. I would like to thank Brian Mathew, who was editor when he suggested a book on alpine plants that have appeared in the magazine, for encouraging me to write it and for looking through the early manuscripts. I must also thank Martyn Rix, not only for kindly writing the foreword, but also for his support when he took over the role of editor from Brian.

Alpine grower and prolific writer Robert Rolfe edited an early version of this book and his comments and guidance at that time were extremely valuable. I hope he approves of the final version. I would also like to thank Gina Fullerlove, Head of Kew Publishing, and her team, including John Harris, Lloyd Kirton, Christine Beard and Ruth Linklater, for their patience as I struggled to find the time to finish this book and for allowing several last minute changes. I am also grateful to Pat Davies, who painted the wonderful maps for each chapter.

The Library at Kew has been a great resource and each chapter ends with a bibliography of references and further reading. The living collections at Kew have also been invaluable and some of the horticulturists responsible for their care have helped by lending photographs and reading some of the chapters for me. In particular I would like to thank Joanne Everson, Katie Price, Kit Strange and Christopher Ryan. Lastly, I want to thank my wife Kate and sons Tom and Matthew, for giving me the time and space I needed to complete this book.

I hope this book inspires you to find out more about alpines and have a go at growing some yourself, if you are not already. You may even make your own journey, to seek out some of these plants growing in the beautiful mountains they call home.

OPPOSITE
The Rock Garden at The Royal Botanic Gardens, Kew.

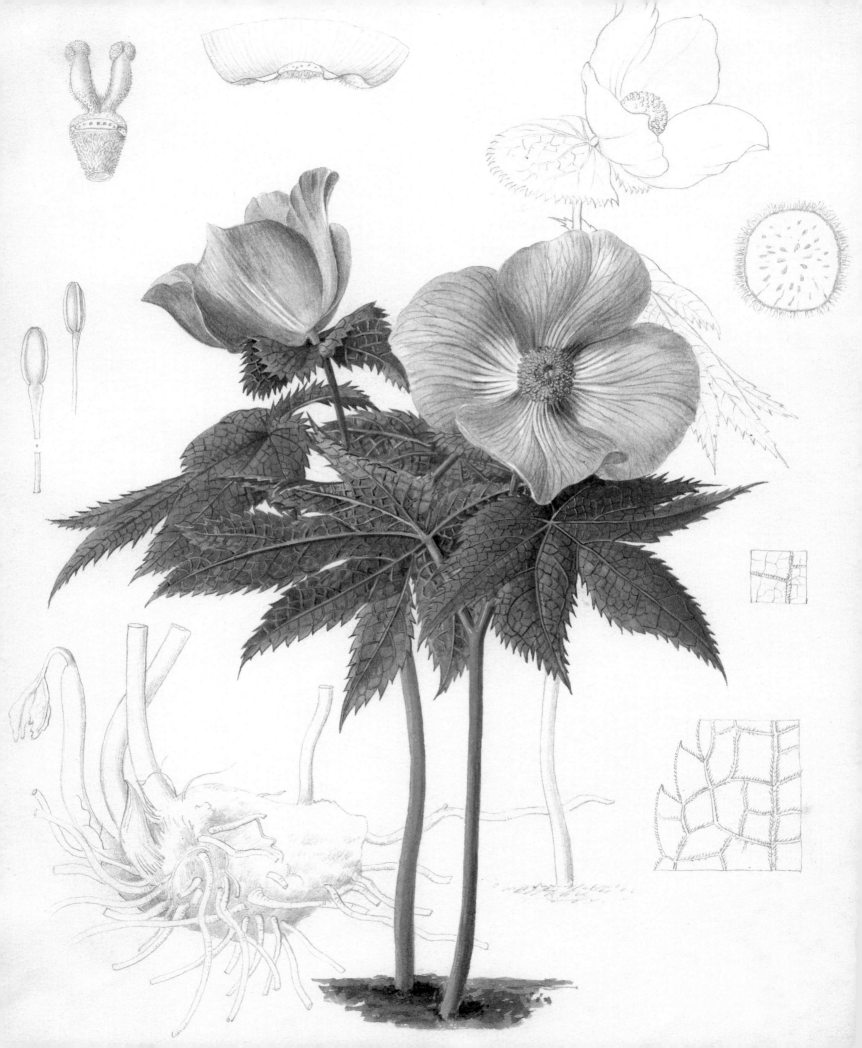

List of paintings
reproduced from *Curtis's Botanical Magazine*

Chapter 1 **Introduction**

It can be hard to explain the lure of the mountains. It is not only rock climbers who are drawn to the peaks, cliffs and ridges of the world's mountain ranges, gardeners and botanists go there too, in search of alpine plants. There is a feeling of exhilaration as you ascend a mountain range to look for alpines, and the excitement increases the higher you go. The twisting roads, sheer cliffs and glistening snow on the distant peaks all contribute to the sense of anticipation. Around every hairpin bend you stare out of the car window, straining your eyes to spot a splash of colour on the rocky slopes, but it is only when you start walking that these jewels of the hills really reveal themselves.

There are plants all around us, but those that shelter in cracks and crevices, cling to rocky ledges or carpet the lofty meadows with colour have a special appeal. Maybe it's the fact that they live in such hostile conditions, and yet manage to burst into life as spring reaches their high altitude home, that makes them so mesmerising. Maybe it's the abundance or size of the flowers produced by such compact plants that makes them so appealing. Whatever the reason, some people go to great lengths to grow alpine plants. Most remarkably, many alpines need little special treatment to survive and even thrive in our gardens, an environment very different to their mountain home. You might even have some in your own garden without realising their origins. The aubrieta hanging down a stone wall, the houseleeks clinging to a roof or the crocus pushing through the lawn are all plants of the mountains. How they got there and where they came from is what this book is about.

If you are drawn to the mountains and the plants that live there, you are not alone. Over the centuries, some of the most famous names in botanical exploration, including Sir Joseph Hooker, Robert Fortune, David Douglas, George Forrest and Frank Kingdon-Ward, have made for the hills when exploring new regions. They were often among the first Europeans to study the flora of a continent or mountain range, and it is hard to imagine how they must have felt when confronted with plants that were completely new to them. The first explorers were often members of scientific expeditions sent out to investigate newly acquired territories or recently discovered continents, but they were soon followed by commercial plant hunters, paid by nurseries in Europe to send back plants and seeds for the horticultural industry.

New plant introductions often caused much excitement when they flowered for the first time in cultivation. The golden rayed lily (*Lilium auratum*) in the 1860s, the Himalayan blue poppy (*Meconopsis baileyi*) in the 1920s and more recently the Chinese *Helleborus thibetanus* are just some of the species praised in the horticultural press and admired at flower shows across Europe and America.

A few alpine plants were already well-known in gardens in the eighteenth century, but during the nineteenth century, as more were collected and their cultivation requirements became better understood, they became more widely grown. This interest continued to grow in the twentieth century, and in 1929, the Alpine Garden Society (AGS) of England and Wales was formed with the aim of 'promoting an interest in all aspects of alpine plants [and] their cultivation in rock gardens'.

How alpines arrived from the world's mountains is a fascinating story, involving many tales of exploration, adventure and perseverance. It is easy to forget where a plant lives in the wild when it seems so happy in a garden setting, but the plant hunters who sought them out and brought them to our gardens may have undertaken incredibly long journeys, often in little-known, sometimes hostile countries. Just as important to the success of these new plant introductions were the nurserymen and gardeners who cherished and nurtured the treasures sent back from the hills, learning how to grow them to perfection and passing on their skills. Then there are the botanists who identified, named and classified these plants, and continue to do so as the complex relationships between species are gradually becoming better understood. Long before colour photography, many of the new discoveries were painted by botanical artists to illustrate floras and journals, creating an invaluable record of new plant introductions over the centuries.

In the late eighteenth and early nineteenth centuries, several botanical journals appeared that illustrated the new plant introductions arriving in Britain from around the world. They included the *Botanical Cabinet*, the *Botanical Register* and the longest-running of them all, the *Botanical Magazine*. The *Botanical Magazine* is the oldest botanical periodical still being published and is thought to be the world's longest surviving magazine in colour. Founded by William Curtis (1746–1799), the first part of the *Botanical Magazine* came out on 1 February 1787 and it has continued in an unbroken series ever since. It was an instant success, with a reported 3000 copies sold of the early issues. After Curtis's death, the magazine was renamed *Curtis's Botanical Magazine* and its fortunes have varied throughout its long life. Early on, it survived competition from similar publications, but in the nineteenth century, rising costs and dwindling subscriber numbers were constant threats. Nevertheless, publication continued into the twentieth century, largely due to the faith and determination shown by two of its editors, Sir William Jackson Hooker, who was editor from 1826 to 1865, and his son, Sir Joseph Dalton Hooker, editor from 1865 to 1904. Both also became Directors of the Royal Botanic Gardens, Kew. Today, over 220 years since it was founded, *Curtis's Botanical Magazine* is still publishing the work of the finest contemporary botanical artists.

Botanical paintings can be important when it comes to naming and classifying plants. They often accompany the descriptions of new species and so provide a valuable record of the appearance of a plant. For example, Curtis described the silver-edged primula (*Primula marginata*)

in his *Botanical Magazine* in 1792. This species was introduced from the Alps in 1777 and Curtis grew it in his garden. The painting shows the flower colour, leaf characteristics and habit of the plant, including the roots, and so adds useful information that may not be shown in a pressed herbarium specimen.

Throughout this book, paintings from *Curtis's Botanical Magazine* have been reproduced to illustrate the history of alpine plant introductions from the world's mountains. The species have been chosen to show the broad range of plants that come under the general term 'alpine'. However, 'alpine' has a number of definitions.

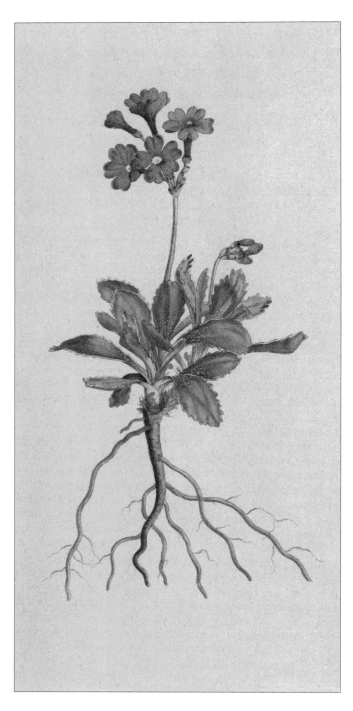

Primula marginata,
Curtis's Botanical Magazine,
plate 191 (1792).
Artist: Francis Sansom.

ABOVE
The mountains of North
Norway, where the tree
line is only just above
sea level.

What is an alpine?

Strictly speaking, alpine plants are found only above the tree line in mountainous regions. The tree line occurs at the altitude at which it is no longer possible for a plant to both produce enough energy to create woody tissue in the form of a trunk and carry out the essential processes of respiration and renewal of foliage. Various factors will influence the ability of a plant to form and maintain a woody trunk, such as duration of snow cover, light levels, day length in the growing season and the effect of repeated damage caused by ice, snow and wind, but the greatest influence is temperature. Temperature decreases with altitude and the tree line is said to occur at the point at which the average temperature of the warmest month is 10°C. Latitude has an effect on day length and temperature, and the altitude at which the tree line occurs comes closer to sea level towards the north and south poles.

Above the tree line is the alpine zone, where 'true' alpines are found. Habitats in the alpine zone vary enormously. Rocky slopes and cliffs may not have much soil, and the alpines that grow there usually have long taproots that delve deep down to search for moisture and nutrients. Valleys eroded by glaciers

will often have only very thin soils with plenty of exposed rock and debris left by the retreating ice. Erosion of mountain peaks and ridges, particularly by repeated freezing and thawing of water in cracks in the rock, creates steep piles of rubble called scree slopes. Plants that grow on scree slopes have to cope with loose, shifting rocks and stones. Rain will quickly drain through a scree slope, so long searching roots are needed to find water, which sometimes occurs as underground streams running beneath the scree.

As a scree slope becomes stable, it can be colonised by more plants and can eventually become a meadow, where soil can collect and the rocks are stabilised by the roots of plants. The scree plants that previously occupied the slope cannot compete with this relatively abundant vegetation and die out, being replaced by grasses and herbaceous perennials that form a rich and diverse tapestry of species.

All the plants that grow in these habitats above the tree line can rightly be called alpines. However, many of these habitats also occur below the tree line, in the subalpine zone, and the plants that grow in them are like alpines in every respect except their elevation on the mountain slope. This is where the common definition of alpine becomes unclear. A

steep-sided gorge or a scree slope below the tree line will support a range of plants that are just like the true alpines higher up the mountain, and they are equally suitable for growing in a rock garden or an alpine house. Although a tree is unlikely to be called an alpine, there are many plants that grow in subalpine woods and along streams that are perfect for an alpine plant collection. This means that, in horticultural terms, an alpine is classed as any hardy plant that is a suitable size for growing on a rock garden, alpine trough garden or raised bed. This vague definition covers an assortment of plants, including bulbs, cushion plants, meadow flowers, small shrubs and woodland perennials.

Rock gardens themselves provide a variety of different habitats, from free-draining, stony scree beds to shady gullies with more moisture-retentive soil. To simulate meltwater rushing down a mountainside, waterfalls, ponds and streams are often built into rock gardens, and moisture-loving species and aquatic plants can be grown here. The size of a rock garden will also influence the plants chosen. Some of the largest rock gardens are planted with small trees and shrubs and, if appropriate, species are chosen that can give a 'feel' of the mountains.

In the March 1937 issue of the *Quarterly Bulletin of the Alpine Garden Society*, Fred Stoker contributed 11 pages of discussion about the meaning of 'alpine'. He describes how an 'argument raged' about the subject at an Alpine Garden Society Annual Dinner and goes on to discuss the various environmental conditions that alpine plants are adapted to. He writes that the term alpine "refers to a manner of life and to the taking of a form necessary to live that life" but does not come up with a simple definition. Prof. John Richards took a light-hearted look at the meaning of 'alpine' in the *Bulletin* of March 2000, writing that members of the AGS know what they want to grow and what is and what isn't an alpine plant "but there isn't a word for it".

To complicate matters further, the conditions required to grow alpines also suit some plants from the Mediterranean region. Plants growing near sea level around the Mediterranean may not be frost hardy but a short distance inland, in the nearby hills and mountains, are habitats that support an intriguing range of species that can be grown outside, in free-draining soil and a sunny position. Alpine plants generally need a well-drained soil so that excess water drains away in winter, when they are

ABOVE
Scree slopes form at the
base of eroded ridges,
here along the Langma
La, in the Everest region
of the Himalaya.
Photo: Joanne Everson.

normally dormant. Mediterranean plants need the same soil-type because they are adapted to long, dry summers. They do most of their growing in the mild, wet winters. They may not be called 'alpine' but many are undoubtedly suitable for the rock garden.

Alpines have adapted to their harsh natural environment in various ways. Forming a low cushion or spreading mat is one of the most common ways to resist high winds and desiccation. Annuals are rare in the alpine zone as there is not enough time to germinate, grow, flower and set seed in the short growing season, but biennials are more common, taking two years to complete their life cycle. Most alpines are low growing, with compressed or prostrate stems, which allows them to survive being buried by deep snow without damage. During the long winter, a layer of snow will give some protection from extremely low temperatures, acting like a blanket. Under the snow, with all water frozen, the alpine will also be kept dry and dormant until the spring, when the thaw will provide plenty of water. All this presents a challenge to the gardener at or near sea level. A relatively mild, damp winter can readily cause alpine plants to rot. They do not become completely dormant, they are

not kept dry and the poor winter light levels lead to etiolation, when the plant tries to grow towards the light and the stem becomes weak and straggly. Growing alpines successfully requires a combination of high light levels, good air movement, cool summer temperatures and well-drained soil or some protection from winter rain.

Plant hunting today

One thing that strikes you when reading accounts of plant hunting in the past is the length of time expeditions took. David Douglas set off for western North America in 1824 and returned to London in 1827. Ernest Wilson left for China on a trip for the nursery of Veitch and Sons in 1899 and didn't return until 1902. The sea voyage to their destination could take months, and once there, plant hunters had to travel without maps, with little or no knowledge of the local people and customs, and often with only just enough money for basic essentials. Nurseries that sponsored or employed plant hunters were very competitive and great efforts were made to be the first to introduce a new species. Not only did these plant hunters have to

collection of threatened species to ensure it is carried out in a sustainable manner. The species covered are listed in three appendices to the CITES legislation. Trade is prohibited for wild species listed in Appendix I, but trade in artificially propagated specimens is allowed subject to the granting of a permit. These are species threatened with extinction and their populations are affected by trade. Species listed in Appendix II are not threatened with extinction but they could be if trade is not regulated. Trade in wild and artificially propagated specimens of the species listed on Appendix II is allowed subject to permit, and quotas are often set to regulate this trade. Trade in species listed in Appendix III is monitored, and they may move to Appendix II if thought necessary to protect wild populations. Plants listed on the CITES appendices that may be of interest to alpine gardeners include all orchids (in Appendix I) and all species of *Galanthus* and *Cyclamen* (in Appendix II).

The Convention on Biological Diversity (CBD) was established in 1992 and is an international treaty aimed at sustaining the rich diversity of life on Earth. It establishes three main goals: the conservation of biological diversity, the sustainable use of its components, and the fair and equitable sharing of benefits from the use of genetic resources. It also reaffirms that countries have sovereign rights over their own biological resources. Countries have drafted national legislation that will affect the way their biological resources can be acquired, used and supplied to others, so plant collectors have to abide by the law of the country in which they are collecting. Permission to collect may be granted with certain conditions, such as the sharing of any profits made from trading in a species, or restrictions may be imposed on the use of the material, such as allowing only scientific research and not commercial use. Botanic gardens and other scientific institutions are often allowed to collect seeds in a country on condition that the seed and any plants raised from that seed are not passed on to a third party. To someone trying to get hold of a certain plant, it can seem like the botanic gardens are trying to keep all the best material for themselves, but the reality is that if they do not abide by the conditions under which they were allowed to collect, they will not be allowed to collect in that location again, and they would be breaking the law. To put it simply, you cannot visit a country and dig up plants or collect seed without the permission of that country, in just the same way you shouldn't (and I hope, wouldn't) go into someone else's garden and take plants for your own garden without the agreement of the owner. This is probably the only aspect of plant hunting that was a lot more simple in the past. Digging up plants and sending them home, even if only a small percentage survived, was commonplace but today's legislation aims to prevent this. After all, it is the plants that

survive in distant, unknown regions of the world but they were under pressure to produce results that justified the nursery's expense in sending them out there.

Things are very different today, and successful collecting expeditions last only a few weeks. Today, it is unacceptable to remove plants from the wild without the permission of the landowner or country; collecting is usually closely monitored by the regional authorities and must be carried out in accordance with local and international law. The Convention on International Trade in Endangered Species of Wild Fauna and Flora (CITES) regulates and monitors the trade in threatened plants and animals. The aim of CITES is to protect wild populations by encouraging artificial propagation for trade and monitoring wild

need protection, not the plant hunters. Nevertheless, done properly, sustainably, with the right permissions granted and with respect for natural habitats and wild populations, plant hunting continues to reward botanists and horticulturists with new plants and furthers our understanding of the world's flora.

Plant naming

Plant names follow the binomial system invented in the eighteenth century by Swedish naturalist Carl (or Carolus) Linnaeus. Each name is in two parts, the name of the genus and that specific to the species. In 1753, Linnaeus published *Species Plantarum*, in which he described all the plants known to him and named them using a genus and species. Before this, plant species often had long descriptive names in Latin, usually consisting of several words. Linnaeus simplified matters by bringing similar plants together under one genus name and by giving each one an individual species name.

Nowadays, a species name is only valid if it is published in a recognised publication together with a Latin description of the species. An herbarium specimen must be taken and this is called the type specimen. The location where the type specimen was growing in the wild is called the type locality.

Even if a name is validly published, it may not be accepted by the scientific community. Joseph Hooker described the Spanish *Draba mawii* in 1875, but subsequent publications treated this plant as a variety or subspecies of *D. dedeana*, a plant previously described by Boissier and Reuter in 1845. More recently, *D. mawii* has been reduced to a mere synonym of *D. dedeana*. In the following chapters, there are plenty of examples of plant species that have had two or more names since they were first described. As we increase our understanding of how plants have evolved, how they vary across their natural range and how different plants are related to each other, in particular by studying their DNA, name changes are inevitable and necessary.

Chapter 2 **Growing alpines**

There are many different ways to grow an alpine plant. Much will depend on the habitat and climate of a particular species' natural home, but the main factors to consider when growing plants from high altitudes in lowland conditions are drainage, ventilation, light levels, temperature and when and how much to water. The last of these is probably the most important as watering has to be done regularly and it is the easiest thing to get wrong. Having said that, there are many alpine plants that will do perfectly well in the open garden with very little attention, as long as they are kept out of waterlogged soil and have enough light. Planting in the open is the best way to provide adequate ventilation. When alpines are housed in a glasshouse or cold frame, air movement can become too restricted and temperatures in summer can begin to rise. Good ventilation is important because moving air helps keep temperatures down and drives away dampness. Soil drainage is also important because alpine plants are used to being dry in winter in their natural environment. It is only when spring arrives and temperatures rise that the snow and ice melts and alpine plants are deluged with a plentiful supply of moisture as water cascades down the mountainsides, flooding the meadows and valleys below. Keeping away excess rainfall in winter is key to the successful cultivation of alpine plants, and this can be achieved by covering them with glass or planting them in a situation where excess water quickly drains away. The basic function of a rock garden is to raise the planting area above ground level and so provide good soil drainage. The soil may have extra grit or sand added to further improve

drainage and the structure of the rock garden creates an array of nooks and crannies for planting alpines that will fill a crevice or hang down from a ledge. The rocks will also provide different aspects. A north facing slope (in the northern hemisphere) will be more shaded and suit plants that need a cooler summer. South facing slopes have the best light but can be hot on a sunny day. Planting next to or near rocks, will give the roots some protection from the sun, and moisture usually remains for longer periods under the rocks, which can be vitally important for the survival of an alpine in

OPPOSITE
An alpine trough garden.

BELOW
A display of pot-grown alpine bulbs.

a hot, lowland summer. The most useful characteristic of a rock garden is the variety of habitats it provides, from narrow gullies to open screes, vertical crevices and shaded corners. An imaginatively built rock garden can provide locations for the broadest range of alpines.

Narrow planting pockets and cracks and crevices can be built into vertical walls on a rock garden and these provide perfect drainage for plants that are more sensitive to winter wet. These include saxifrages, androsaces, drabas and other rosette- and cushion-forming plants. Trailing and spreading plants will also enjoy the freedom to sprawl over the rocks and over time these species will naturally find their favoured location, filling the gaps between rocks and giving a natural look to the garden. To keep the foliage of alpine plants away from the wet soil, a thick mulch of grit is usually applied to the beds. This mulch also helps to keep weeds under control.

The largest rock gardens will have pools, streams and waterfalls. These simulate the water gushing down a mountainside as the snow melts at higher altitudes. Plants that grow along these water courses will grow in moist soil but still receive plenty of sunlight. In more shaded areas, beneath a cliff or in a subalpine woodland, there are plants that are adapted to living in shade. A rock garden can provide an assortment of locations that offer different conditions in which to grow the whole range of species that come under the general description of alpine plants.

Not all gardens have room for a rock garden or the design may not lend itself to the inclusion of a such a naturalistic feature. In these situations, there are alternative ways to provide similar conditions. A raised bed or retaining wall can be constructed to offer the same advantages of a well-drained planting bed but in a more formal guise. Dry stone walls, railway sleepers and bricks can all be used to raise the

soil level and can also provide vertical planting areas similar to those found in a rock garden. Alpine trough gardens provide an opportunity to grow alpine plants on a smaller scale. These are traditionally made from old stone sinks but any container can be used if filled with free-draining, gritty soil. Rocks and stones can be placed in the trough to create a miniature landscape space and the soil mix can be tailored to the plants' needs.

Tufa is also sometimes used to grow alpines that need very good drainage. This is a rock formed from lime deposits. It has an open texture and can absorb water. If planted directly into holes made into the tufa, a plant's roots can penetrate the soft rock and extract the moisture and nutrients they need. Foliage growing over the tufa is

kept dry because any surface water is quickly absorbed by the rock. By planting in tufa, many cushion plants can be successfully cultivated in the open.

A woodland garden may not be an immediately obvious place to grow alpines, but a huge range of beautiful mountain plants are found in locations with summer shade and relatively moist soils. Mountain ranges such as the Appalachians in North America and the Japanese Alps are heavily forested, with only small areas of alpine-zone vegetation. The plants that grow under the trees in these forests are ideally suited to a woodland garden. Deciduous trees draw excess moisture out of the soil in summer but in the winter and spring, when the branches are bare, plenty of light falls on the woodland floor and water is freely available to the ground cover plants. Spring is the most colourful time in a woodland garden as this is when many woodland bulbs flower, before they die down for the summer. Anemones, fritillaries, dog's tooth violets and trilliums are among the wonderful range of woodland plants in cultivation. In areas with a monsoon climate, such as the Himalayan Mountains of northern India and Nepal, the plants are used to high rainfall in the summer months.

For gardeners wishing to grow a wider range of alpine plants, more specialised conditions will need to be provided. This usually means growing plants under glass. A cold frame is the simplest structure that can be used to protect plants from rain, whether summer dormant bulbs or winter dormant alpines. These are plants that will not put up with getting wet at the wrong time of year. The structure will also protect delicate flowers from wind and rain early in the growing season. The frame itself can be a simple glass box with a lid that can be propped open. Larger cold frames may consist of a brick-built raised bed with a wooden structure over the top to hold the hinged, glazed covers, called frame lights. Either way, the main function is to keep the rain off. Cold frames should generally be sited in a sunny position so that the plants receive the maximum possible light, but on hot sunny days they may need some shading to prevent the plants from overheating.

Plants grown in frames are usually kept in pots so that they can be easily moved around, maybe to put on a display in other parts of the garden when in flower. Once flowering is over, they are safely returned to the frame for the winter. The frame lights are best removed in summer to increase air movement at a time when temperatures are rising and there is no need to protect the plants from rain because they are in full growth.

Although cold frames are, in many ways, the ideal home for alpines that need to be grown under glass, they are not always the most attractive structures. Alpine houses can be

LEFT
An alpine trough garden is a smaller alternative to a rock garden or raised bed.

BELOW
Campanula elatines, from the Italian Alps, growing on a tufa block.

RIGHT
A woodland garden
provides cool shade
and humus-rich soil
for plants from
subalpine forests.

FAR RIGHT
In spring, before the
leaves have unfurled on
the trees, a range of
bulbs will flower on a
woodland garden floor.

RIGHT
Raised beds in the
Alpine Nursery at Kew
are used to grow bulbs
in pots, which are
plunged into sand to
protect from freezing
temperatures and to aid
watering. These beds
are under glass to
ensure that the bulbs
have a dry summer rest.

a feature in a garden and are suitable for growing alpines
as long as they are adequately ventilated and shaded. They
also provide a more comfortable environment in which to
study and cultivate alpine plants. An alpine house should
ideally have vents in the sides as well as in the roof to
ensure air moves over and around the plants. Fans, either
hanging from the roof or built into each end of the
glasshouse, can be installed to improve ventilation even
further and lower the temperature, which can soar on a
warm summer's day. The house will also need shading to
help keep temperatures down.

To increase the range of plants that can be grown in an
alpine house, it can be moderately heated to protect the
plants in very cold weather. Although many alpines come
from the coldest parts of the world, a layer of snow often
insulates them from extreme conditions. In cultivation, if
there is no snow cover, they may be subjected to temperatures
much lower than they would normally experience in the wild,
so a little heating may be beneficial in harsh winters.

LEFT
The Davies Alpine
House at Kew, where
temperatures and
ventilation are
controlled to provide the
best possible conditions
for alpine plants.

LEFT
Plants on a cliff inside
the Davies Alpine
House, including the
silver-leaved *Centaurea
clementei* from southern
Spain and Morocco, and
the yellow-flowered
Corydalis tomentella
from China.

Growing alpines 13

Moderate heating will also allow the cultivation of slightly tender species from regions with a Mediterranean climate. However, the most important function of an alpine house, like a cold frame, is to keep off excess rain.

In a glasshouse or cold frame, alpines are often grown in pots. This allows them to be moved around easily and permits the use of different soil mixes for different plants, satisfying their individual needs. A loam-based soil mix is recommended for the majority of alpines. Grit or stone chippings can be added to this soil to improve the drainage. For plants that require particularly sharp drainage, up to three-quarters of the soil mix may consist of grit, but about a half to a third is the standard proportion. To create a well-drained but moisture-retentive soil mix, i.e. a mix that holds some moisture but allows excess water to drain away freely, some leaf mould, coir (coconut fibre), well-rotted garden compost or composted bark can also be added.

Some feeding, usually with a dilute, low-nitrogen feed to avoid causing excessive leaf growth, will supply extra nutrients but regular potting on is recommended to provide fresh soil and also give the roots more space. In

general, plants are potted on when they root down into the bench sand through the pot's drainage hole. In the wild, alpines may live in very poor soils but their long root systems reach deep down to find the moisture and nutrients they need and to provide anchorage.

Traditionally, clay pots are used for growing alpines as they dry out more quickly than plastic pots and so allow greater control over the amount of water a plant receives. An over-watered plastic pot can take a long time to dry out in winter, but plastic pots are still often used and are perfectly acceptable as long as due attention is paid to moisture levels in the soil.

The disadvantages of using pots are that the soil can dry out quickly, the plants can become pot-bound and, in winter, there is a danger of the soil freezing solid, damaging or killing the roots. Plunging the pots in sand, to just below their rim, can help prevent the soil from freezing, keep it cool in summer and can also help with watering. If you use clay pots, the moisture in the plunge sand can pass through the side of the pot and reach the soil. In this way, a small amount of moisture can be given to the plant without having to water the soil directly. This is especially useful at the beginning and end of the growing season, when you may only need to provide a little water. Even in winter, the plunge sand can be kept just moist for those plants that do not need to be kept completely dry. Pots that are plunged in moist sand also dry out much more slowly, so you do not have to water so often.

Seeds of alpine plants will generally need a period of cold before they germinate. If they are sown as soon as they are harvested, they may germinate quickly but you will then have to overwinter the seedlings in poor light conditions and freezing temperatures. Seedlings that germinate between September and January are most at risk. For this reason, unless germination is known to be very slow or seed viability is short-lived, sow the seed in mid- to late winter so that germination takes place in spring, as temperatures and light levels are rising. The seedlings then have a whole growing season to establish themselves before the next winter. Seed pots can be left in an open frame, exposed to the cold and rain, but once the seedlings appear bring them into the more protected environment of a covered frame or alpine house. Seeds of slightly tender species should be sown into pots kept in a cold frame or alpine house to protect them from freezing.

Cuttings can also be taken of many alpine plants and this is best done after flowering, usually in late spring or early summer. However, it is always worth experimenting by trying cuttings at different times of year to find the best method for different species. Cuttings should be kept in a cool, shaded location and misting is not recommended for most alpines, as the dampness can cause them to rot.

It is difficult to give general advice on propagation because the cuttings and seeds of different plants will need slightly different conditions to grow. The same can be said of any cultivation advice. Alpines grow in a vast range of environments, as is clear from the chapters that follow. Precipitation can vary enormously across a mountain range, with some slopes having a metre or more of rain in a year, while on the other side of the range, in the rain shadow, precipitation can be much lower. Cultivation notes are provided for many of the plants that are included in the following chapters, and details of each region's climate are given to help you understand the requirements of various species. The general remarks in this chapter will at least give you a good start and allow you to enjoy the richness and beauty of the world's alpine flora.

BELOW
The Rock Garden at Kew is constructed with Wealden Sussex sandstone. The rocks provide a variety of habitats in which to grow a wide range of alpine plants.

Adonis vernalis *Gentiana occidentalis* *Leontopodium alpinum* *Pulsatilla halleri* *Saxifraga cebennensis*

ICELAND

Scandinavia

• Oslo

Stockholm •

• Moscow

Scottish
Highlands

Gothenburg •

• Edinburgh

Copenhagen •

Baltic

North
Sea

The
Burren

Dublin •

• Berlin

London •

Amsterdam •

Carpathians

Gerlach

• Paris

Transylvanian
Alps

Bay of
Biscay

The Alps

Geneva •   Eiger
Mont   Matterhorn
Blanc   Julien
                                        Alps

Black
Sea

Cantabrian
Mountains

Alpes
Maritimes

Dolomites

Pyrenees
Pico
d'Aneto

Montpellier •

Apennines

Adriatic Sea

Balkans

Istanbul •

Corsica

Mount
Olympus

Lisbon •

Madrid •

Balearic
Islands

Sardinia

Rome •

TURKEY

Iberian
Peninsula

Sierra
Nevada

Ionian
Sea

Athens •

Sicily

Peloponnese

Crete

Mediterranean Sea

N

Chapter 3 **Europe**

From the sierras of the Iberian Peninsula to the Caucasus Mountains on the edge of Asia, and from the Scandinavian Arctic to the Mediterranean islands, Europe is home to a wide range of alpine habitats. Alpine plants can be found on Europe's major mountain ranges, the Alps, Pyrenees and Carpathians, as well as on smaller ranges, such as Spain's Sierra Nevada, the Apennines of Italy and the Dinaric Alps in the Balkans. In southern Europe, the varied and distinct flora of the Mediterranean region includes many species suitable for growing on a rock garden.

The Alps, Europe's best known and highest mountains, stretch over 965 km (600 miles) from south-east France, through Switzerland, northern Italy, southern Germany and Austria, to Slovenia. They are composed of a number of ranges, including the Alpes Maritimes near the Mediterranean coast of France, the Dolomites of northern Italy, the dramatic Bernese Alps in Switzerland and the Julien Alps, Steiner Alps and Karawanken, along the border of Austria and Slovenia. Many peaks are permanently covered with snow, and the highest is Mont Blanc at 4,808 m (15,774 feet) on the border of France and Italy.

Compared to many of the world's mountain ranges, the Alps are heavily populated. The development of ski resorts has damaged some habitats but the associated chair lifts, cable cars and cog railways that snake along the valleys and up the slopes and cliffs make the alpine meadows, ridges and lower peaks surprisingly accessible. Modern-day plant hunters, armed with no more than a camera, a notebook and a stout pair of walking boots, can reach these habitats and see many 'classic' alpine plants,

such as gentians, saxifrages and campanulas. With a little more effort, cushion-forming androsaces can be seen sheltering in cracks and crevices. At high altitudes, the 'king of the Alps', *Eritrichium nanum*, may be found producing its stunning blue flowers as the snow and ice melts around it.

Another mountain range popular with both skiers and plant enthusiasts is the Pyrenees, which form a physical border between France and Spain, stretching from the Bay of Biscay to the Mediterranean, a distance of nearly 435 km (270 miles). The highest peak is the Pico d'Aneto at

BELOW
The Eiger and Jungfrau in the Swiss Alps.

3,404 m (11,168 feet). Many alpine plants are found naturally in both this range and the Alps, but others, such as *Gentiana occidentalis* and the cushion-forming *Androsace cylindrica*, are found only in the Pyrenees.

On the Spanish side, the Pyrenees drop less steeply than on the French side, descending gradually into a series of shorter ranges in the Iberian Peninsula. The numerous mountain ridges in this region are often separated by deep valleys or wide, flat plains. They include the Picos de Europa in the Cantabrian Mountains of northern Spain and the Sierra Nevada in southern Spain, which reach 3,482 m (11,424 feet) at the peak of Mulhacen, the highest mountain in the Iberian Peninsula. Many of these isolated ranges are home to species found nowhere else, plants like the small, yellow-flowered snapdragon *Antirrhinum grosii*, which occurs naturally only on steep rocky slopes and in crevices in the Sierra de Gredos and Sierra de Candelario, west of Madrid in central Spain.

The highest point in mainland Greece, in south-east Europe, is Mt Olympus at 2,917 m (9,570 feet). Other significant peaks on the Balkan Peninsula include Smolikas at 2,637 m (8,652 feet) and Parnassos at 2,457 m (8,061 feet). The rich and varied flora of Greece includes many desirable alpine and Mediterranean plants, such as the deep pink *Dianthus haematocalyx*, the tuberous-rooted *Anemone blanda*, which comes in various shades of blue, and the early-spring-flowering *Crocus sieberi*.

Much of western Europe has a maritime climate that is influenced by the Gulf Stream, which crosses the Atlantic from the Gulf of Mexico and bathes the west coast of Europe with warm waters. This has the effect of moderating temperatures so that winters tend to be fairly mild and summers only moderately warm. Moisture-laden air coming off the sea ensures that rainfall can occur at any time of year. Further east, away from the effect of the sea,

the climate is more continental and Eastern Europe can experience very cold winters and hot summers.

The major mountain range in Eastern Europe is the Carpathians, whose highest peak at 2,655 m (8,711 feet) is Gerlach in the Tatransky National Park in northern Slovakia. Although not as high as the Alps or the Pyrenees, the Carpathians extend nearly 1,450 km (900 miles) in an arc from western Slovakia, through the Tatra Mountains of southern Poland and northern Slovakia, then south and east through Ukraine, as far as the Transylvanian Alps of Romania.

The earliest alpine plants introduced to Britain came from Europe, and several plants that grow in the Alps had found their way into gardens long before the nineteenth century. The popular trumpet gentian, *Gentiana acaulis*, was introduced sometime in the eighteenth century, the

ABOVE
The view from Mt Parnes, near Athens, Greece.

BELOW LEFT
Adonis vernalis was cultivated in the sixteenth century.

BELOW RIGHT
Anemone blanda growing in the mountains near Athens

golden-flowered *Adonis vernalis*, which is found from Spain to south-east Sweden and Russia's Ural Mountains, is known to have been in cultivation in the sixteenth century and the tall, yellow-flowered *Gentiana lutea*, which grows in the mountains of central and southern Europe, was introduced into gardens around 1500.

The detailed cataloguing of European alpines began in the eighteenth century, and several are included in Philip Miller's *Gardeners Dictionary* of 1731. In the late eighteenth century, *Flore Français* was published by the French botanist Jean Baptiste Lamarck and included plants from the French Alps. The third edition of this flora, published in 1805, was almost entirely rewritten by the famous Swiss-born botanist, naturalist and doctor of medicine, Augustin Pyramus de Candolle. Nicolaus Host wrote *Synopsis Plantarum* in Austria in 1797, and followed it with two volumes of *Flora Austriaca* between 1827 and 1831. The French naturalist Philippe Picot de Lapeyrouse published *Figures de la Flore des Pyrénées* in 1801. Examples of nineteenth century floras that include plants from the Alps are *Flora Helvetica* by the Swiss botanist Jean-François Gaudin, published in seven volumes between 1828 and 1833, and *Synopsis Florae Germanicae et Helveticae* by the German botanist Wilhelm Koch, published in 1837.

Another Swiss botanist, Edmond Boissier (1810–1885), had a particular interest in alpine plants and made trips to the Alps, the Eastern Mediterranean and the Near East in the nineteenth century. Spain was little known botanically when he travelled through the south of the country in 1837. He wrote an account of this journey, *Voyage Botanique dans le Midi de L'Espagne*, which appeared in two volumes between 1839 and 1845, and which provide an early insight into the flora of the Iberian Peninsula. Between 1842 and 1859, Boissier published *Diagnoses Plantarum Orientalium Novarum* and this was followed by the monumental *Flora Orientalis*, which appeared between 1867 and 1884. *Flora Orientalis* covers a region that extends as far east as Afghanistan and Turkestan but includes European countries at the eastern end of the Mediterranean, such as Greece, Cyprus and Turkey-in-Europe.

These heavyweight floras and surveys were beyond the reach of most amateur gardeners, both in terms of their availability and the impenetrable language and style they adopted. By the late nineteenth century, however, various pocket books and illustrated guides to the flowers of the Alps were appearing. French gardener Henry Correvon produced *Les Plantes des Alpes* in 1885 and then a pocket guide to the mountain plants of Europe in 1894. The English botanist and publisher Alfred Bennett wrote *The Flora of the Alps* in 1897, in which plants from Switzerland and neighbouring mountain regions and from the Pyrenees, were described and illustrated. Inevitably,

books began to be written about growing these mountain plants in the garden. Probably the first such book was published in 1870 by the famous Victorian gardener William Robinson and was called *Alpine Flowers for English Gardens*.

This longstanding interest in the mountain plants of Europe has meant that many of the more commonly grown European species, including gentians, saxifrages, houseleeks, bellflowers and edelweiss, have become synonymous with the word alpine. These 'classic' alpines are well worth looking at more closely because you will often come across them in gardens, even if the owner has no particular interest in alpines. Some have been in cultivation for a long time and they often form the basis of an alpine plant collection.

BELOW
Leontopodium alpinum, better known as edelweiss.

Gentiana acaulis
Family: Gentianaceae

The spring-flowering *Gentiana acaulis* was the first gentian to be featured in the *Botanical Magazine*, appearing in the second volume in 1788. This species is found in the Balkans and the mountains of southern and central Europe, including the Alps, Pyrenees and Carpathians. Its habitats include rocky meadows, screes and alpine and subalpine coniferous forests at altitudes of 1,700–3,000 m (5,577–9,843 feet).

 Gentiana acaulis is likely to have been introduced into cultivation in the eighteenth century. Its large, trumpet-shaped flowers are held close to the mat of lanceolate or elliptic leaves on a short stem, which elongates when the plant is in fruit. These glorious, deep blue flowers can reach up to 7 cm long and have green spots in the throat. The five-pointed corolla lobes are 6–9 mm long and are separated by small triangular lobe-like plicae.

 This is one of the 'Acaulis group' of gentians, which comprises species with very short stems, so the flowers appear to sit directly on the mat of leaves. The other species in this group differ from *Gentiana acaulis* in the shape of the leaves, the shape of the sepals and their size relative to the corolla, and the markings on the inside of the flower. *Gentiana kochiana* and *G. excisa* have been included in the 'Acaulis group' but are more often treated as synonyms of *G. acaulis*.

Gentiana acaulis is best grown in an exposed position in full sun, firmly planted in soil that doesn't completely dry out. Additional watering may be necessary during dry periods. In less exposed situations, the mat of leaves can become loose and the stems may elongate. The stem of *G. acaulis* is very short at first, but by the time the seeds are ripe it can be 15 cm long.

 It is often stated that *Gentiana acaulis* can be shy to flower. Where this proves the case, planting in different locations is worth a try in order to find a place where the plant is happy. Alternatively, it may be that the grower possesses a clone that rarely or never blooms, so new material should be sought. Over the years, many authors have suggested feeding to encourage blooming, and a high potash liquid fertiliser, applied in midsummer and again in early spring, is well worth trying. The normal flowering period is from March to May but the odd flower can appear throughout the summer and well into autumn. Established plants will form a dense carpet of leaves and regular division may be needed to keep them flowering. *Gentiana acaulis* and the rarely cultivated *G. alpina* grow naturally in acidic soils but they will tolerate mildly alkaline conditions. Other allied species, such as *G. clusii* and *G. occidentalis*, are lime-lovers.

The tendency for *Gentiana acaulis* to produce stolons and runners ensures a good supply of material for cuttings. From midsummer onwards, remove rosettes of leaves with a short portion of stem and pot them into a free-draining cuttings mix. Propagation from seed sown in autumn is also straightforward, as long as the seed is fresh.

Curtis's Botanical Magazine, plate 52 (1788). Artist: James Sowerby.

The classic alpines of Europe

The European mountains have been extensively explored over a long period of time, so it is not surprising that most of the tried and tested alpine plants, those that can be termed 'classic alpines', come from Europe. Gentians and saxifrages are well known alpines, but surely the best-known alpine, at least by name, is edelweiss.

Edelweiss, *Leontopodium alpinum*, is found on grassy and rocky slopes in mountains throughout Europe, but altogether, around thirty species of *Leontopodium* are distributed across Europe and Asia. Growing to around 20 or 30 cm tall, *L. alpinum* has narrow, grey, densely felted leaves that reach up to 4 cm long. At the end of the stem is the inflorescence, consisting of a cluster of flower heads (capitula) surrounded by pointed oblanceolate bracts that are densely felted like the leaves. The tiny florets are yellowish white and the whole inflorescence can reach 5 cm across.

Visitors often search out edelweiss when they find themselves in a public alpine house such as the Davies Alpine House at the Royal Botanic Gardens, Kew, because it is the one plant many people associate with mountains, even though edelweiss is far from being the most attractive European alpine. Edelweiss can hardly compare to an electrifying blue gentian or a sumptuous, velvety pasque flower. It is also not as widely grown as some of the plants mentioned below. A look at classic European alpines should really begin with that symbol of the alpine flora, the gentian.

GENTIANA

Although gentians form a large genus, the deep blue flowers of one species, the trumpet gentian, *Gentiana acaulis*, typify these plants in many people's minds. In fact, *G. acaulis* has been adopted as the logo of the Alpine Garden Society of England and Wales. The majority of gentians do have blue flowers but they also come in other colours, ranging from yellow to reddish-purple and white.

The genus *Gentiana* is centred in Asia, where more than half the species originate, but has a worldwide distribution. The species vary greatly in both size and flower colour. The tallest is the yellow-flowered *G. lutea*, which grows (often in large colonies) in the mountains of central and southern Europe and was probably the first gentian to be introduced into cultivation. It can reach 2 m tall and has broad, ribbed leaves of up to 30 cm in length.

The name of the genus is derived from King Gentius of Illyria, who reputedly prepared a remedy for plague from the leaves and roots of a gentian (probably *Gentiana lutea*). The many species have been subjected to a number of classifications. The Czech botanist Josef Halda (1996), for example, divides the genus into 16 subgenera and recognises around 450 species.

LEFT
Gentiana acaulis.

BELOW
Gentiana lutea.

The typical gentian flower is composed of five petals that are fused to form a funnel or bell-shaped tube. This tube splits into lobes (corolla lobes) towards the tip, although in some species, such as *Gentiana lutea*, the petals are split almost to their base. Some have lobe-like structures called plicae between the corolla lobes. These vary greatly in size, sometimes reaching the same length as the corolla lobes; in other examples, the plicae are finely dissected (fimbriate).

In *Flora Europaea* (Tutin, 1972) the European species of *Gentiana* are placed into seven sections. *Gentiana acaulis* comes under section *Megalanthe* along with six other spring-flowering species, including *G. clusii* from central and southern Europe, *G. occidentalis*, which is only found in the Pyrenees, and *G. alpina* from the Alps, Pyrenees and Sierra Nevada of southern Spain. Halda places the same species in his subgenus *Ciminalis*. Either way, these species

are commonly referred to as the 'Acaulis group' and are very similar to each other in appearance. They are rosette-forming perennials that produce stolons and runners, have leaves crowded towards the base of the stem and display solitary flowers.

Other commonly grown European gentians include *Gentiana verna*, the 'spring gentian', which has a wide range, extending from the mountains of central and southern Europe to Arctic Russia, taking in the west of Ireland. Notably, they grow on the limestone outcrop of the Burren and in the upper valley of the River Tees in northern England. This gentian is also found further east in Turkey, Iran and Central Asia. Halda recognises five subspecies of *G. verna*. The typical form, subsp. *verna*, is mainly a plant of the European mountains. It forms a loose mat of leaf rosettes from which the short, erect leafy stems arise, each with a single deep blue flower. The corolla has a narrow tube, 3 or 4 cm long, and wide spreading lobes. In the centre is a disk-like stigma forming a white 'eye'. This beautiful little plant is not easy to grow, resenting disturbance and needing moist but free-draining soil and a sunny position but without too much heat in summer. It is usually grown in a scree or trough garden but often still only lives for two or three years. It can be propagated by cuttings after flowering, in the same way as *G. acaulis*.

The other four subspecies of *G. verna* differ mainly in the shape of their leaves. *Gentiana verna* subsp. *tergestina* comes from central and south-east Europe and has narrow

lanceolate, pointed leaves. Subspecies *balcanica* is also from south-east Europe but has broadly ovate leaves, and subsp. *pontica*, from south-east Europe eastwards through Turkey and the Caucasus to Iran and Iraq, has broadly ovate leaves only twice as long as they are wide. The most distinct form is the yellow-flowered subsp. *oschtenica* (syn. *G. oschtenica*), from the western Caucasus.

In contrast to these low-growing, spring-flowering gentians, the willow gentian, *Gentiana asclepiadea*, can have stems up to one metre long, decked with flowers in mid- to late summer. This species has been grown in gardens since the beginning of the seventeenth century, if not earlier, and was mentioned by John Parkinson in *Paradisi in sole Paradisus Terrestris*, published in 1629. In the wild, its range extends from the mountains of Europe to Turkey and the Caucasus. It grows in open woodland and subalpine meadows, and in the garden prefers a humus-rich soil and partial shade. The densely leafy stems begin erect but then arch over under the weight of deep blue flowers, 3–5 cm long, held in the axils of the pointed, ovate leaves. Pale blue- and white-flowered forms also exist.

Gentiana asclepiadea is in subgenus *Pneumonanthe*, which includes species distributed across the Northern Hemisphere from British Columbia to Japan. The species that gives this section its name, the European *G. pneumonanthe*, was named by Linnaeus in 1753. It flowers in mid-summer and is smaller than *G. asclepiadea*, with spindly stems that reach around 40 cm in length. The blue flowers are held at the end of the stems and in the leaf axils. This species prefers neutral to acid, humus-rich soil that retains some moisture in the summer months.

Hardly European but worth mentioning here because it is also in subgenus *Pneumonanthe*, is one of the best summer-flowering gentians for the rock garden. The range of *Gentiana septemfida* extends from the Caucasus Mountains at the edge of Europe, through eastern Turkey to Iran and Iraq. It grows in meadows and woodland margins up to 3,400 m (11,155 feet) altitude and has several densely leafy, prostrate or ascending stems, up to 40 cm in length. The dark blue, trumpet-like flowers reach 5 cm long and have conspicuous fimbriate plicae between the corolla lobes. They are held in clusters at the tip of the stems and also in the upper leaf axils. This floriferous, easy species is a good value rock garden plant, producing its colourful blooms for several weeks from late July to September.

BELOW LEFT
Gentiana pneumonanthe.

BELOW RIGHT
Gentiana septemfida in cultivation, growing with *Euphorbia myrsinites.*

THE SILVER SAXIFRAGES

The 'silver' or 'encrusted' saxifrages belong to section *Ligulatae*, which contains eight species. This section was established in 1803 by an English gardener, Adrian Haworth. Linnaeus described *Saxifraga* in 1737 and recognised 37 species, but Haworth made the first attempt to subdivide the genus. In his *Miscellanea naturalia*, he divided 49 species between six sections.

The silver saxifrages possess lime-secreting pores, called hydathodes, either along the leaf margins or on their upper surface. The calcareous deposits give the leaves a silvery bloom, sometimes with marked encrustations along the margins. This effect is more pronounced in dry weather when humidity is low. Silver saxifrages have thick, leathery leaves without a distinct petiole and they form evergreen rosettes.

All of the species produce a panicle of flowers and their colour is usually white, often with red spots. *Saxifraga paniculata* occasionally has red or pink flowers and is the most widespread species, occurring in the mountains of Europe and also in Turkey, the Caucasus and Iran, and to the west in Iceland and even North America. Many hybrids of silver saxifrages have been raised in cultivation. They make impressive plants when in flower but the foliage is also attractive as the lime-encrusted leaves are arranged in neat rosettes.

One of the species in section *Ligulatae* forms solitary rosettes and generally dies after flowering. This is the wonderful *Saxifraga longifolia*, which produces tall, branched flower spikes that can carry up to 800 flowers. It grows on steep limestone cliffs in the Pyrenees, as well as in the Atlas Mountains of Morocco, in eastern Spain and very locally in south-east Spain, in the mountains above Alicante. The French naturalist Philippe Picot de Lapeyrouse described it from a Pyrenean plant in 1801, in his *Figures de la Flore des Pyrénées*.

The other seven silver saxifrages, which include well-known species such as *Saxifraga cochlearis*, *S. callosa* and *S. cotyledon*, produce several rosettes that form a mat or cushion of foliage. When the flowering rosette dies, the smaller rosettes grow on. They are fantastic rock garden plants, forming clusters of leaf rosettes in nooks and crannies, and then producing sprays of flowers in late spring.

Planted in the right spot on a rock garden, most species will do well with little attention. They need plenty of moisture during the spring and summer but don't want to be too wet in winter, so good drainage is important. Some growers keep them in pots, for displaying in an alpine house or exhibiting at shows, and these should be plunged in sand to prevent the soil drying too quickly. If housed in a cold frame, the frame lights should be closed in wet winter weather, and in summer, the pots will need shading on hot, sunny days.

TOP
Saxifraga cotyledon.

ABOVE
Saxifraga cochlearis.

LEFT
The leaf rosette of *Saxifraga callosa* subsp. *catalaunica.*

The genus *Saxifraga* is another mainstay of the alpine garden. The species come in a myriad of sizes and forms, with attractive foliage and flowers in a range of colours. These flowers have five sepals, five petals and ten stamens arranged in two whorls of five but much more variation is found in the foliage, and it is the characteristics of the foliage that have been used to split the genus into groups. One of the most significant revisions of *Saxifraga* was undertaken by the German botanist Adolf Engler. His work culminated in the publication, in collaboration with Edgar Irmscher, of a monograph of the genus in *Das Pflanzenreich*, which appeared in two parts, in 1916 and 1919. This is a very detailed study and most later treatments are based on this work. The classification most commonly followed in recent years is by Richard Gornall (1987), who divided *Saxifraga* into 15 sections. Nowadays, as a result of molecular studies, the original genus has been split into *Saxifraga* and *Micranthes*. However, most of the widely grown species are still in *Saxifraga*, which is further divided into twelve sections (McGregor, 2008).

Three of these sections are particularly important when looking at the European saxifrages that have made a significant impact in the horticultural world: section *Ligulatae*, section *Saxifraga* and section *Porphyrion*. The first of these contains the eight species of silver saxifrages, which have wonderful rosettes of silvery-grey leaves with lime-encrusted margins. Many of these are widely grown and include the well-known species *Saxifraga cochlearis* and *S. longifolia*.

Section *Saxifraga* contains the mossy saxifrages. The common name for these plants comes from the bright green leaves that are often divided into narrow lobes and create a mound of foliage, the whole plant looking something like a large moss. They are also sometimes called the dactyloid saxifrages in reference to the old section *Dactyloides*, in which these species were classified before Gornall included them within section *Saxifraga*.

There are around 70 species in section *Saxifraga*, classified in four subsections by Gornall, although this system is likely to be revised in the future as more research is carried out (McGregor, 2008). Most of the commonly grown species are in subsection *Triplinervium*, which itself contains around 50 species divided into seven series. They include the cushion forming *S. cebennensis*, in series *Cespitosae*, from the limestone plateau and deep gorges

FAR LEFT
Saxifraga cebennensis.

LEFT
Frosted leaves of
Saxifraga rosacea.

north of Montpellier in southern France. In cultivation, this saxifrage can be grown in the open but the tight, domed cushions often do better when protected from winter rain in an alpine house or cold frame. The flower stems reach 5–8 cm long and hold two or three white flowers in late spring.

Also in this series is *Saxifraga rosacea*, a species that does well on a rock garden. The species name, meaning rose-like, refers to the shape of the tightly packed leaf rosettes rather than the flowers. This species is found in Iceland, the Faeroe Islands and Ireland, as well as in central Europe, from eastern France, through southern Germany, to the Czech Republic, south-west Poland and Austria. In cultivation, given room, it will gradually spread to form an extensive mat of pale to mid-green leaf rosettes that give rise to white flowers held on stems up to 25 cm tall.

The species in series *Ceratophyllae* come from northern Spain and Madeira. They tend to have stiff, leathery leaves and the stems become woody at their base. After three or four years growing in a pot, these plants will form huge globes of bright green leaves that produce masses of white flowers in May, held on stems that can reach up to 30 cm long in the Spanish *Saxifraga trifurcata*. Any older than this and they become difficult to sustain in a container, being virtually impossible to pot on without causing irreparable damage. Regular propagation from cuttings ensures a continual supply of young stock to replace these older plants. On a rock garden, many of these species will gradually spread along cracks and between rocks to form mounds of foliage, producing their characteristic cymes of white flowers in late spring. The Madeiran species are *Saxifraga maderensis*, *S. pickeringii* and *S. portosanctana*. They are less hardy than the Spanish species but can still be grown outside in sheltered positions in milder regions.

The attractive *Saxifraga pedemontana* belongs to series *Pentadactyles* and was described, from plants growing in the Maritime Alps, by Carlo Allioni in 1785. Five subspecies are now recognised, differing mainly in the size, shape and texture of their leaves, and each one is found in a distinct geographical area. Subspecies *demnatensis* grows in Morocco but the others are all European. Subspecies *pedemontana* is the form found in the Maritime Alps and is the largest and most robust, with flowering stems to 18 cm long. Subspecies *prostii* is from the Cévennes in southern France and does well when grown in the open on a rock garden. Subspecies *cervicornis* grows on the Mediterranean islands of Corsica and Sardinia, and subspecies *cymosa* is from the Carpathians and the northern Balkan Peninsula.

Also in series *Pentadactyles* is *Saxifraga canaliculata*, a showy species when in flower that comes from northern Spain, particularly the Picos de Europa. The leaves of this plant are especially sticky and deeply divided into linear

ABOVE
Mossy saxifrages grown in pots in the Alpine Nursery at Kew.

LEFT
Saxifraga pedemontana subsp. *prostii* on Kew's rock garden.

lobes. The white flowers have wide petals and are held in a compact cyme on a stem up to 15 cm in length. It too is easily grown on a rock garden.

A general requirement of the mossy saxifrages in cultivation is a little more moisture and shade than is needed by other saxifrage species. The green cushions can be scorched by hot sun if planted in a very exposed position and they need plenty of moisture in spring and summer but must not be waterlogged in winter. On a rock garden, a north-facing pocket or crevice is ideal.

Mossy saxifrages have been in cultivation for many years. For example, *Saxifraga trifurcata* was introduced into Britain in 1804 and was featured in *Curtis's Botanical Magazine* (as *S. ceratophylla*) in 1814, when it was already being stocked by nurseries (Sims, 1814). Flower colour in the mossy saxifrages is white, cream or occasionally greenish but there are a large number of hybrids in this group that have flowers in shades of pink, carmine, scarlet and yellow. The hybrids are far more widely cultivated than the species and have also been grown in gardens for many years. In fact, they have been more popular in the past than they are today.

The most popular section in *Saxifraga* is section *Porphyrion*, which contains over 100 species divided into five subsections. Subsection *Porophyllum* comprises series *Kabschia*, series *Engleria* and series *Tetrameridium*. The other subsections are *Oppositifoliae*, *Xanthizoon*, *Squarrosae* and *Florulentae*. The last of these contains the endangered *Saxifraga florulenta*, from the Maritime Alps, previously classified in Section *Ligulatae*.

The species of section *Porphyrion* mostly have hard, pointed, needle-like or sometimes almost circular leaves, usually without a distinct petiole and, like saxifrages in section *Ligulatae*, possessing lime-secreting hydathodes. The flowers are generally either solitary or held in cymes. After flowering, the leaves at the base of the flower stem persist and the rosettes divide.

In series *Engleria*, which is named after Adolf Engler, there are around eight species, including *Saxifraga stribrnyi*, *S. sempervivum* and *S. media*. They are found mainly in the Balkan Peninsula but also in the Pyrenees, Carpathians, Turkey and as far east as the Himalaya. The species in series *Engleria* are attractive plants, with their lime-encrusted leaves often held in neat rosettes. The alternate leaves are linear-oblong to spathulate with many lime-secreting hydathodes. The rosettes often form attractive mounds of glaucous foliage from which the red, pink or purple-tinged flowering stems arise, reaching 20 cm tall in some species, such as *S. sempervivum*. The flowers are held in a spike-like inflorescence but individually they are quite insignificant, with the petals similar in length to the sepals. These species look their best as these densely

ABOVE
Saxifraga canaliculata.

LEFT
Saxifraga stribrnyi, in series *Engleria*.

Saxifraga burseriana
Family: Saxifragaceae

Saxifraga burseriana (sometimes spelt *S. burserana*) belongs to a popular group of species known as the 'kabschia' saxifrages. *Kabschia* was one of the sections of *Saxifraga* described by Engler in 1867, but it is now treated as a series in subsection *Porophyllum* of section *Porphyrion*. The name commemorates a German botanist, Wilhelm Kabsch (1835–64), who was unfortunately killed when he tumbled off a cliff while studying phytogeography in the Alps (Harding, 1970). *Saxifraga burseriana* was described by Linnaeus in 1753 and is named after Joachim Burser (1583–1649), a German physician and botanist whose herbarium was studied by Linnaeus (Stearn, 1992). It displays solitary (occasionally twinned) white flowers, held on reddish stems above a compact mound of narrow, fleshy, glaucous leaves.

Saxifraga burseriana is found on calcareous rocks, sometimes in crevices but usually on screes or disintegrating rocky surfaces, in the Eastern Alps. Its range is split in two: in the north it occurs in Austria and the Bavarian Alps and to the south in northern Italy, southern Austria and Slovenia (Webb & Gornall, 1989). It usually grows at altitudes of 1,500–2,200 m (4,921–7,218 feet) but can be found as low as 230 m (756 feet) in the valley of the Adige and has been recorded as high as 2,500 m (8,202 feet). The plant painted for *Curtis's Botanical Magazine* was collected at 1,500 m (4,921 feet) in the Julian Alps by Brian Mathew in June 1975.

The leaves of this species are around 1 cm long, narrowly lanceolate, tapering to a stiff pointed tip and with 5–7 hydathodes on their upper surface. The minutely hairy, red flower stems can reach 5 cm tall and have a few stem leaves. This is one of the most beautiful kabschia saxifrages and, in *Curtis's Botanical Magazine*, David Webb writes: "Within this section there are few species that can challenge and none that clearly surpass *S. burseriana* in beauty. The neat blue-grey foliage, the bright red peduncles and the large, snowy-white flowers combine to form a colour scheme that is very striking, and yet with a touch of puritan restraint" (Webb, 1977).

Like the other kabschia saxifrages, *Saxifraga burseriana* likes plenty of moisture from early spring to summer, when in full growth. In cultivation, it can flower very early in the year, in February and March, and the period after flowering is when most growth takes place. In the winter, little water is needed but the plants should not be allowed to dry out completely. On a rock garden, this species can be grown in a free-draining scree but will almost certainly require some watering in summer.

Whether grown in a pot, a trough or out in the open garden, kabschia saxifrages require the maximum possible light in winter, but in summer they need some shade. Too much hot summer sun will lead to scorching of the leaves, causing portions of the cushion to die away. Conversely, too much shade may result in poor flowering.

Saxifraga burseriana is not a variable species and cultivars, such as 'Gloria' and 'Brookside', are described mainly on the basis of variation in flower size and petal shape. No natural hybrids are known, but there are numerous artificial hybrids formed by crossing this species with others in section *Porphyrion*.

Curtis's Botanical Magazine,
plate 747 (1977)
Artist: Margaret Stones.

glandular-hairy, leafy inflorescences unfurl. The petals are sometimes white, greenish or yellow, as in *S. corymbosa*, from Greece and Turkey, which has yellow flowers.

The species of series *Kabschia* are the most popular saxifrages in cultivation and many artificial hybrids have been raised. These hybrids may be very attractive but unfortunately they have often eclipsed the parent species. The 70 or so species in this series are found in the mountains of southern and central Europe, the Caucasus, Iran and the Himalaya. They have stiff, alternate leaves in crowded shoots that form dense cushions. Unlike those in series *Engleria*, the *Kabschia* species have flowers whose petals are longer than the sepals and may be white, pink, purple or yellow. One of the most beautiful species is *Saxifraga burseriana*, from the eastern Alps, but any decent alpine nursery will have a large range of kabschia saxifrages to choose from. Given plenty of moisture in spring and summer, and some protection from hot summer sun, they should do well on a rock garden or in an alpine trough garden.

Subsection *Oppositifoliae* contains four species, including the purple saxifrage, *Saxifraga oppositifolia*, and *S. retusa*. The latter is found in various distinct and widely separated locations in the mountains of central and southern Europe. By contrast, *S. oppositifolia* is the most widely distributed saxifrage and is found from Alaska and Canada, through Greenland and Europe, to arctic Russia, Kamchatka, the western Himalaya, the Tien Shan and the Altai mountains. In Europe, *S. oppositifolia* occurs in Iceland, Scandinavia and parts of Britain and Ireland, as well as further south and east, including locations in the Pyrenees and the Alps, the Sierra Nevada and Picos de Europa of Spain, the Apennines, Carpathians and the mountains of the Balkan Peninsula.

Saxifraga oppositifolia is a distinctive species that takes its name from the tiny opposite leaves on the branched, prostrate stems. It forms a dense to loose mat with pink to dark purple, occasionally white, solitary flowers held on leafy, 1–2 cm long stems. The petals are normally between 5 and 12 mm long. The flowering time varies according to latitude and altitude. In cultivation in Britain, *S. oppositifolia* can flower in March, but above the Arctic Circle, it may not flower until July or August. Not surprisingly, given the vast natural range of *S. oppositifolia*, there is some variation in this species, with one Pyrenean form, named subsp. *paradoxa* by David Webb in 1987, having alternate instead of opposite leaves.

SEMPERVIVUM

Saxifraga sempervivum is so-called because of the similarity of its leaf rosettes to those of another group of well-known alpines, the sempervivums or houseleeks. These are amongst the easiest alpine plants to grow in gardens, producing neat rosettes of succulent leaves that can survive in the most unlikely places, including walls, roofs and cracks in paving, although they weren't always thought of in this way. In Curtis's account of *Sempervivum arachnoideum* that appeared in the *Botanical Magazine* in 1788 (plate 68),

Closely related to *Sempervivum* is *Jovibarba*. Both are genera of stemless or short-stemmed, succulent, perennial plants whose rosettes are monocarpic but increase vegetatively by axillary stolons (Mitchell, 1973). These two genera differ in the number of petals per flower, with *Sempervivum* having 8–16 petals and *Jovibarba* having 6–7. Also, in *Jovibarba* the petals are erect rather than spreading, and fringed with glandular hairs. Species in both genera can have whitish or yellow flowers but some species of *Sempervivum* have red or purple flowers.

Sempervivum arachnoideum, the cobweb houseleek, is one of the six species of *Sempervivum* originally described by Linnaeus in 1753. It has a wide distribution in Europe, occurring in the Alps, Pyrenees, Apennines and Carpathians. This species is unique in the genus in having hairs stretching from leaf-tip to leaf-tip.

Although sempervivums can survive long periods of drought, they do best if provided with adequate moisture during their growing season. Good drainage is necessary to prevent damping off, particularly for 'hairy' species such as *Sempervivum arachnoideum*. They can be grown in pots and look particularly effective when allowed to increase by their stolons to fill and spill over the edge of a shallow pan.

LEFT
Sempervivum arachnoideum 'Robin'.

ABOVE
Sempervivum tectorum, from the mountains of Europe.

he mentions that it was not uncommon for these succulents to be treated as if they came from a warm climate and 'nursed up in stoves'. This suggests that, in the late eighteenth century, growing these plants in the open garden, on walls or rockwork, was a fairly new idea. They are of course perfectly hardy, and left to their own devices, the fleshy-leaved rosettes of sempervivums gradually spread by producing stolons, forming a compact mound of often attractively coloured foliage that will persist for many years; in fact, *Sempervivum* means 'always alive'.

R. Lloyd Praeger wrote a monograph of the genus *Sempervivum* that was published in 1932, in which he recognised 23 species. Today, there are thought to be around double that number. The genus is distributed across the mountainous areas of Europe and into Turkey, the Caucasus, Iran and the Atlas Mountains of Morocco.

CAMPANULA

The genus *Campanula*, the bellflowers, includes a wide variety of plants, many too large for a rock garden and numerous smaller, more compact species. The first monograph on this genus, written in Geneva by Alphonse de Candolle in 1830, included 137 species and many subspecies and forms. By the time H. Clifford Crook wrote *Campanulas, Their Cultivation and Classification* in 1951, around 300 species were known. They are found across the Northern Hemisphere but their centre of distribution is in the Caucasus Mountains. There is also a high concentration of these species in the Mediterranean region, particularly Greece, Turkey and the Balkans. Many of the smaller campanulas make fine rock garden or alpine house plants. In his recent book, *Dwarf Campanulas*, Graham Nicholls (2007) gives a thorough account of these plants, with plenty of cultivation information.

Campanulas have flowers consisting of five petals that are fused at their base. The flowers are generally bell-shaped but in some species can be more star-shaped or fused for much of their length to form a narrow tube. The seed capsules split from pores, which may be towards the base or the apex. The shape of the calyx lobes and the presence or absence of appendages between these lobes are also important diagnostic features.

One of the most widespread species is *Campanula rotundifolia*, which occurs over much of northern and central Europe, in North America and in Asia. It is known as bluebell in Scotland. The dainty bell-shaped flowers are around 2 cm long and held on stems that can grow to 50 cm tall or more. Its name comes from the rounded basal leaves, which can die back by flowering time, leaving just the linear to lanceolate stem leaves.

Closely related to *Campanula rotundifolia* is *C. cochlearifolia*, one of the most popular and easy dwarf species in cultivation. In the wild it grows in the European mountains, from the Carpathians in the east to the Pyrenees and northern Spain in the west. It spreads to form low mats of shiny green leaves topped by delicate blue bells on stems up to 10 cm tall. White forms are also known.

One of the most distinctive species of *Campanula* is *C. zoysii*. This plant is found in scattered locations in the Alps of Slovenia, Austria and Italy, chiefly in the Julian and

TOP RIGHT
Campanula cochlearifolia in an alpine trough garden.

RIGHT
Campanula fragilis, a beautiful species from central and southern Italy.

Steiner Alps and the Karawanken. It grows in cracks and crevices, on steep limestone cliffs, at altitudes of 1,700–2,300 m (5,577–7,546 feet), although seeds can be brought down to lower elevations by meltwater. The name commemorates Karel Zois, who discovered this plant in Slovenia and sent material to the Austrian botanist Franz Xavier von Wulfen, who described it in 1789. It was introduced to cultivation in 1813.

This is a tufted perennial with small, rounded, shiny leaves, but it is the unusual flowers that distinguish this species. The flower stems reach 5–10 cm tall and can carry up to six blue flowers, each about 1.5–2 cm long and with a characteristic crimped constriction at the mouth. Beyond this constriction, the corolla lobes don't open out but are bent inwards, with their edges and tips touching to form a 5-sided pyramid. In the wild, *C. zoysii* shows variation in flower shape and colour. Some forms have inflated, almost spherical flowers, whereas others have slim, elongated flowers with nearly parallel sides. Colour varies from pure white to pale blue or rich violet. Very rarely, plants with bi-coloured flowers have also been found. In these forms, the mouth and upper half of the corolla is white and the lower half is rich china-blue (Doncaster, 1943). Another oddity, with cream variegated leaves, is also known.

Campanula zoysii is not easy to keep going. It does best grown in a sunny position in tufa, a trough garden, or a rock garden crevice or scree. Good drainage is important to keep the plant fairly dry in the winter but this species needs plenty of moisture throughout the summer. In a frame or alpine house, the amount of water the plant receives can be controlled. Most accounts of this species in cultivation refer to its susceptibility to slug damage. Another common problem is its tendency to flower so well that it has no strength to make new growth for the next year. Specimens over five years old are rarely encountered in cultivation so regular propagation is necessary. The species can be propagated from seed or from cuttings taken in early spring before flowering or late in summer.

The genus *Pulsatilla* provides some of the most beautiful, large-flowered rock garden plants. The 30 or so species vary considerably across their range, particularly in hairiness (pubescence), dissection of leaves and the size and colour of the petals (perianth segments) (Tutin, 1964). These characteristics have been used to distinguish species, but the variation exhibited has led to difficulties with their classification. They are found from North America to Europe and Asia.

The French botanist Joseph Pitton de Tournefort used the name *Pulsatilla* in *Institutiones Rei Herbariae* in 1700, but in 1753, Linnaeus included the species under the genus *Anemone*. The name *Pulsatilla* was still used, for example by Philip Miller in the 1768 edition of his *Gardeners' Dictionary*, but the classification adopted by Linnaeus was accepted well into the twentieth century and some authorities still regard the species of *Pulsatilla* as members of the genus *Anemone*. The two genera are closely related and share several characteristics but pulsatillas differ in the presence of nectar-producing staminodes and the long feathery styles attached to each seed.

The best known and most widely grown species is *Pulsatilla vulgaris*, the pasque flower. The nodding, purple flowers of this species are held above dissected, ferny leaves in spring. By the summer, the flower stems have elongated and hold the characteristic ornamental seed heads. The common name comes from the French word *Pâques*,

ABOVE
Pulsatilla vulgaris subsp. *grandis*.

meaning Easter, because the flowers appear around Easter time. It is widespread in central and eastern Europe, but in England it is a rare wildflower that only grows naturally on undisturbed chalk or limestone grassland, in scattered sites from Gloucestershire to Lincolnshire. Red- and white-flowered forms are also commonly grown in gardens.

One of the finest forms of the pasque flower is *Pulsatilla vulgaris* subsp. *grandis*. Sometimes classified as a separate species (*P. grandis*) or as a subspecies of *P. halleri*, this robust

FAR LEFT
Pulsatilla halleri var. *segusiana*, from the Italian Alps.

LEFT
Pulsatilla vernalis.

plant has particularly large, upright flowers, up to 9 cm or more across, backed with silvery or golden brown hairs. These magnificent, bright purple blooms open wide before the leaves have fully developed, creating a mound of colour in March or April. The whole plant can reach 50 cm across.

Pulsatilla halleri has leaves that are coarsely dissected in comparison to those of *P. vulgaris*, and the whole plant is more hairy. As the buds of *P. halleri* emerge, they are clothed in a dense, soft, white fur. The first buds open before the leaves have developed and the lush, purple flowers face the sky on stems up to 15 cm tall. Later blooms nod slightly and open above the newly expanding foliage, which, unlike that of *P. vulgaris*, remains sparsely hairy throughout the summer. *Pulsatilla halleri* has been divided into several subspecies that occur in isolated populations across Central and south-east Europe.

CUSHION PLANTS, THE ULTIMATE ADAPTATION

In extreme conditions, plants may only be able to survive if they huddle close to the ground and make a rounded, cushion shape. This shape exposes the minimum surface area to hostile weather conditions and presents little resistance to wind. The cushion is composed of a network of stems, each one ending in a cluster or rosette of leaves at the outer surface of the plant. These rosettes can sometimes be tiny, so the cushion is composed of hundreds of them densely packed together, giving the plant a virtually smooth surface. Inside the cushion, the stems often remain clothed with the dead leaves of previous seasons, so the whole plant is like a sponge, which gives it resistance to drought. Some specimens are surprisingly hard.

The characteristics that make cushion plants so good at surviving extremes also present serious problems when they are transferred to lowland gardens. A dense cushion may be remarkably resistant to ice, wind and falling rubble, but in a mild, wet winter it will soak up moisture like the spongy mass it is. The thin stems covered with dead leaves soon begin to rot and the plant's demise will usually follow. There are various ways to overcome this, including growing the plants in tufa to provide perfect drainage, planting them in vertical crevices in a rock garden or on a wall, and growing under glass so watering is controlled. One thing you soon learn if you grow a number of cushion plants is that regular propagation is essential to keep a collection going. The supply of young plants will replace the ones you kill, but the ultimate aim is to keep the older plants going and produce that perfect cushion.

FAR LEFT
An upturned cushion of *Draba rigida*, showing the internal structure and 'growth rings' corresponding to the three years of its life.

LEFT
Silene acaulis sheltering among rocks in Norway.

From high meadows in the mountains of central Europe comes one of the glories of the Alpine spring, *Pulsatilla alpina*, which was introduced to cultivation in 1652. This superb species has upward-facing flowers of pure white, on stems that can reach over 30 cm tall. These shallow bowl-shaped blooms are 4–6 cm wide and the rounded petals are sometimes backed with bluish-purple. Just as beautiful is *P. alpina* subsp. *apiifolia* (sometimes called *P. sulphurea*), which displays sulphur-yellow blooms, held above the long-stalked, ferny leaves.

One of the true alpines of the genus is *Pulsatilla vernalis*, which grows at altitudes of 1,300–3,600 m (4,265–11,811 feet) throughout much of Europe and is sometimes called the 'lady of the snows'. This is a fairly small plant with evergreen leaves forming low, compact mounds. The basal leaves are divided pinnately into broad segments. The stem leaves are hairy and held in a whorl behind the solitary flower. These goblet-shaped flowers are relatively large, up to 6 cm wide, and pearly white within, stained with violet or blue on the back and coated in soft, tawny hairs. Wild plants seldom produce more than five blooms. They are nodding when they first appear but become erect as they open. The whole plant is only 5–15 cm tall at flowering time but the stems can reach 35 cm tall when in fruit.

Pulsatilla vernalis requires better drainage than the other species of the genus, and care should be taken to prevent it becoming overcrowded by surrounding plants. It is ideal for a raised bed or rock garden scree but the soil should retain some moisture in the spring and summer. A position in full sun will encourage the production of flowers but this charming species can be shy to bloom in cultivation, although specimens with more than 50 flowers have been cultivated.

CLASSIC CUSHIONS

The low, compact shape of *Pulsatilla vernalis* is typical of many high-altitude alpine plants. More extreme is the formation of a tight cushion or bun shape, a characteristic found in several genera that have alpine representatives, such as *Dianthus*, *Silene* and *Primula*. This is an adaptation for surviving extreme conditions, whether on windswept plains, icy mountain slopes or vertical rock walls. These cushion plants are fascinating to grow. A perfectly formed cushion so smothered with flowers that the foliage is completely hidden is what serious growers strive for. A cushion plant can quite rightly be called a 'classic' alpine, regardless of the genus to which it belongs.

One of the best-loved cushion plants is a member of the genus *Primula*. This is an important genus of alpine, rock garden and woodland plants, but of the 430 or so species in the world, only around 34 are found in Europe. However, one of these is *P. allionii*, the only cushion-forming species.

In the wild, this plant is restricted to a few locations in the Maritime Alps in south-east France and north-west Italy, growing on shady limestone cliffs and in caves, sometimes on overhangs. It has been in cultivation for over a century. The reason this species is so popular, apart from its obvious beauty, is the variation it exhibits. The flowers are typically primrose-like but they sit directly on top of the mound of dark green, slightly sticky, rounded leaves and come in colours ranging from dark purple and deep pink to violet, mauve, pale pink and white. The white 'eye' at the centre of the flower varies in size and the petals may be notched at their tip or have wavy margins. The petals may also be either rounded, wide and overlapping or more rectangular and clearly separate from each other. The flowers range in size from under 1.5 cm to over 2.5 cm wide. Not surprisingly, hundreds of forms have been named.

Although this species can survive outside, it generally does better under glass where it is protected from rain. Careful watering to avoid the foliage and good ventilation are important. It does well in pots and can also be grown in vertical rock crevices or in tufa. Propagation from seed or cuttings in spring or early summer is simple.

Primula allionii is classified in section *Auricula*, which comprises 22 species, all native to Europe, including *P. marginata*, *P. auricula* and *P. hirsuta*. The latter two have been

BELOW
Primula allionii
'Claude Flight'.

Androsace pubescens
Family: Primulaceae

Androsace pubescens is one of the high-altitude, cushion-forming species in the genus *Androsace*. It belongs to *Androsace* section *Aretia*, which, apart from two Asian species (*A. delavayi* and *A. lehmannii*), are all European plants. The section is characterised by having flowers that arise from the leaf axils rather than from the centre of the leaf-rosette, and it contains some of the most desirable European cushion plants.

Section *Aretia* started out as a genus, described by Linnaeus in 1753 and containing only one species, *Aretia alpina* (now known as *Androsace alpina*). Linnaeus separated *Aretia* from *Androsace* on the basis of its solitary flowers. In 1805, in the third edition of *Flore Français*, Augustin de Candolle described the solitary-flowered *Androsace pubescens* and included *Aretia* within the genus *Androsace*. The German botanist Wilhelm Koch (1837) was the first to publish *Androsace* section *Aretia*, in his *Synopsis Florae Germanicae et Helveticae*.

Since Koch described section *Aretia*, this group has been enlarged and divided into two subsections (Smith & Lowe, 1997). *Androsace pubescens* is in subsection *Aretia*, which contains the species with solitary flowers. Species with flowers held on a peduncle, either singly or in an umbel, are in subsection *Dicranothrix*, which contains some easy and widely grown androsaces, such as *A. halleri* and *A. laggeri*.

The shallow cushions of *Androsace pubescens* are composed of open rosettes of leaves, each one up to 12 mm across. The withered basal leaves don't persist, so the cushions do not become as hard and dense as those in some other closely related species, such as *A. cylindrica* and *A. helvetica* (Ferguson, 1972). The individual leaves are elliptic and covered in simple or forked hairs. The solitary flowers are borne on short pedicels and each rosette can have up to five. The flowers are 4–6 mm wide and white with a yellow eye.

Androsace pubescens should be planted in a free-draining soil, with a mulch of grit or rock chippings at least 2.5 cm deep applied around and under the cushion. This will help to keep moisture away from the foliage and allow some air circulation under the cushion. In addition, a pane of glass over the plant in the winter will keep off rain. In spring and early summer, as the plant comes into growth, it needs a plentiful supply of water. As long as they receive enough moisture when in growth, most androsaces prefer a position in good light.

Cuttings of *Androsace pubescens* can be taken in early to mid summer. Remove individual rosettes with a short portion of stem and insert them in moist sand. Plants can easily be propagated from seed. The single capsules are held on their short stems just above the cushion. They split open when dry to reveal a few seeds, 1–2 mm in diameter. *Androsace* hybrids often occur in collections, and in the wild crosses between *A. pubescens* and *A. helvetica* have been recorded (*A.* × *hybrida*). The true species is presently very rare in cultivation.

Curtis's Botanical Magazine, plate 5808 (1869). Artist: Walter Hood Fitch.

crossed to produce the 'garden auriculas' (*P.* × *pubescens*) that were so popular in Britain from the seventeenth to the nineteenth century. Today, the National Auricula and Primula Society still holds several shows a year in England.

Also in the primrose family (Primulaceae) is *Androsace*, a genus of around 100 species that is best known for its cushion-forming plants. These plants occur naturally at high altitudes, often growing on screes or sheltering in cracks and crevices on sheer rock faces. In spring, when the snow and ice begins to melt, these high mountain species receive a steady supply of water and burst into life, often producing masses of small pink or white primrose-like flowers that can completely cover the plant.

Nearly all androsaces occur in the northern hemisphere, from sea level to over 5,000 m (16,404 feet). Habitats range from high mountains to pastures and woodlands. There are mat- and tuft-forming species, often with umbels of flowers held on long stems; annuals and biennials exist in addition to the perennial cushion-forming plants. Plants from higher altitudes tend to be tighter and more compact, with the flowers having no visible stem so that they are held close to the cushion. The genus has been divided into six sections, although one of these, the North American section *Douglasia*, is sometimes treated as a separate genus.

In 1869, *Androsace pubescens* was featured in *Curtis's Botanical Magazine* where it is described as a "lovely little alpine, belonging to a genus notoriously difficult to keep in cultivation" (Hooker, 1869). Since then, understanding of the needs of androsaces in cultivation has improved and many species are now well-established in alpine plant collections. In general, it is the high-altitude, dense cushion-forming species of section *Aretia*, which includes *A. pubescens*, *A. alpina*, *A. cylindrica*, *A. hirtella* and *A. pyrenaica*, that present problems in cultivation. Nevertheless, some are quite easy, so long as basic precautions are taken to keep them dry in mild, damp, lowland winters, and red spider mite attacks in late summer are dealt with.

Raised beds are useful for growing many of the cushion-forming androsaces because the soil mix can be specially prepared and water drains away easily. On a rock garden, the existing soil structure can be modified by the addition of extra grit and leaf mould (a very gritty mixture with low loam content should be the aim) or the plants can be planted in crevices, tufa or scree beds.

Growing androsaces in a cold frame allows greater control over their environment but they must be well-ventilated. In spring and summer, the frame lights are best be taken off to avoid overheating. Plants in pots should be grown in a loam-based soil mix with additional sharp grit. A deep grit mulch is important to keep the cushion away from wet soil. Clay pots can be plunged in moist sand,

which will provide a steady supply of water and prevent rapid drying of the soil in hot weather.

Similar treatment is required for other cushion plants, such as those in the genera *Draba* and *Dianthus*. The genus *Draba* contains well over 300 species and most are mountain plants, forming cushions or mats of foliage. They are distributed across the Northern Hemisphere and the mountains of South America. The flowers are white or yellow, with the four petals characteristic of the family Cruciferae (Brassicaceae). These flowers are often held on spindly stems

TOP
The Pyrenean *Androsace hirtella* growing on tufa.

ABOVE
Draba bryoides in a rock garden crevice.

above the cushion of green or grey leaves. Some of the more commonly grown species, such as *Draba bryoides*, *D. longisiliqua* and *D. mollissima*, come from the Caucasus and Turkey. The white-flowered *Draba dedeana* is a Spanish species described by Edmond Boissier and George Reuter in 1845 in the second volume of *Voyage Botanique dans le Midi de L'Espagne*. It grows in rocky places and crevices from the Cordillera Cantábrica and Picos de Europa, to the Pyrenees in Navarra and south to Teruel in Aragón.

The genus *Dianthus* is best known for pinks and carnations but there are a few good cushion-forming plants among the 300 or so species. Many species are from the Balkans and Mediterranean region but there are some from the Alps, including *D. pavonius* and *D. alpinus*. The former, from the French Alps, is arguably the pick of the bunch, with short, spiky, grass-like leaves forming a low, bright green cushion, and wide pink flowers held close to the foliage on short stems.

When discussing European alpine cushion plants, mention must be made of the 'king of the Alps', *Eritrichium nanum*. It has an almost legendary status, largely because of its striking blue flowers but also due to the high elevations which it inhabits in the wild, and its long-attested difficulty in cultivation. It usually occurs at altitudes of 2,500 m (8,202 feet) or more, growing in screes, cracks and crevices, and often flowering as the snow melts. It is the vivid flower colour of this species that sets the pulse racing, especially after a long hike to the cold, bleak, rocky peaks that are its home.

This species appeared in *Curtis's Botanical Magazine* in 1870, a year after *Androsace pubescens*. Joseph Hooker wrote the description and was obviously in awe of this plant: "In intensity of colour the blue of *Eritrichium nanum* is equalled only by that of the Alpine gentians, whilst it is of a much

more azure hue than any of these, approaching most nearly to the deepest blue of the sky, at a point of the heavens opposite the suns position, as seen on a cloudless day from the elevation the plant itself inhabits." (Hooker, 1870).

Eritrichium nanum was described by Heinrich Schrader in 1828, in the second volume of Gaudin's *Flora Helvetica*. It forms a low, compact mat, some 10 cm across (rarely more), made up of branched stems with a woody base. The leaves are up to 1 cm long and covered with white silky hairs. The inflorescence can carry up to ten flowers, held just above the leaves. These flowers are pinkish-purple at first but then become bright blue, with a yellow eye. White-flowered forms are also known.

Eritrichium nanum is a plant for a light, well-ventilated cold frame or alpine house, where the amount of water it receives can be strictly controlled. As with many cushion or mat-forming, high-altitude plants, this species resents a damp atmosphere in winter when, in its natural habitat, it may be under snow and all water is frozen, keeping the plant dry. It needs a good supply of moisture in the spring and summer, corresponding to the period when water is readily available from snow melt in the wild, but water should be withheld when it is dormant in winter and none should touch the leaves. Use an open, free-draining soil mix for potting and a thick grit mulch to keep water away from the foliage. *Eritrichium nanum* is a good plant for growing in tufa because the moisture held in the rock means that overhead watering can be avoided. Nevertheless, it is hard to please and never approaches the beauty it attains in the wild. As Reginald Farrer (1919) wrote in *The English Rock Garden*, it is impossible "to make anything but a homesick exile, impossible to inspire with the air of his lost hills … or fill his veins with the blood of blueness that he draws from the blasts of the wind-swept arêtes where he has his home."

Alpines of the Mediterranean

You may not think the words 'alpine' and 'Mediterranean' go together but there are two good reasons why they do. First, the Mediterranean region is surprisingly mountainous; for example, the peaks on the island of Crete exceed 2,400 m (7,874 feet) in altitude, with snow covering them until late spring, and in southern Spain, only a few miles from the coast, the Sierra Nevada rises to over 3,400 m (11,155 feet). The second reason is that the cultivation requirements of hardy Mediterranean plants are very similar to those of alpines. Smaller Mediterranean species do very well on a rock garden, where they enjoy the sunny position and free-draining soil.

The Mediterranean Basin has a climate characterised by mild, wet winters and hot, dry summers. This weather pattern is also found in other parts of the world. These regions are all between latitudes of 30 and 45 degrees, and they are on the western side of a continent. In North America, California has a mediterranean climate, as does central Chile in South America. In South Africa, Western Cape experiences winter rain and summer drought. Parts of the southern and south-west coasts of Australia also experience this climate.

As well as sharing the same climate, the plants from these regions also share adaptations to the long, hot, dry summer, surviving the drought in various ways. Annuals complete their life cycle during the winter, flowering and setting seed before the soil dries up. Evergreen trees and shrubs have leaves with thick, waxy cuticles to slow water loss, whereas other plants, like the wire netting bush *Euphorbia acanthothamnos*, are summer deciduous, losing their leaves when water is scarce. One of the most common adaptations is to retreat underground for the summer, either as bulbs, corms and tubers or as fleshy roots and rhizomes. Once the autumn rains begin, growth commences and these plants usually flower in autumn or spring. If you are used to visiting the parched coast of southern Europe in the summer holidays, you may be surprised by the green hills and wild flowers of a Mediterranean spring.

The flora of the Mediterranean is one of the most diverse in the temperate world and many of the plants have been a part of our everyday life for hundreds of years. Mediterranean species have been spread across Europe by man, sometimes making their home far away from the climate in which they first evolved. The arrival of these plants in European gardens has not been the result of

BELOW
The Lefka Ori or White Mountains of Crete rise to 2,453 m (8,048 feet).

Anemone blanda
Family: Ranunculaceae

Anemone blanda is a beautiful species, only reaching 5–25 cm tall and displaying wide blooms, predominantly in shades of blue. It is native to mountainous regions of the Balkan peninsula, Cyprus and across Turkey to the Caucasus and Georgia, growing in semi-shade on rocky slopes or in scrub, sometimes reaching the snow line at over 2,000 m (6,562 feet).

The genus *Anemone* contains around 120 species. Characteristics include the radially symmetrical flowers made up of brightly coloured perianth segments; a whorl of three or four, often partially united, stem leaves below the flower; and seed heads that consist of a group of achenes (dry, one-seeded, indehiscent fruits), which are sometimes embedded in a mass of woolly hairs.

Anemone blanda was described by two Austrian botanists, Heinrich Schott and Theodor Kotschy, in 1854, from plants collected by Kotschy in the Taurus Mountains of Turkey. This species grows from rounded, tuberous rhizomes. The leaves are divided into three and each division is deeply lobed. The upper surface of the leaves is hairy but the undersides are hairless (glabrous) and often stained with purple, especially when young. The flowers are produced at the same time as the leaves, usually early in the year but as late as June at high altitudes in the wild (Strid, 1986). They are 2–5 cm across and composed of up to 18, normally lavender-blue, perianth segments; flowers in other shades of blue can be found, as can pink and white forms. In this species, the achenes are not woolly and the stem leaves are held on short petioles.

Anemone blanda is very close to the European *Anemone apennina*, which was described by Linnaeus a hundred years earlier. The ranges of these species overlap in the Balkans. Schott and Kotschy recognised the similarities between these two but distinguished *A. blanda* mainly on account of its leaves being glabrous beneath and the exterior perianth segments also lacking hairs. *Anemone apennina* has leaves that are hairy on both surfaces, the flowers usually have fewer perianth segments than those of *A. blanda* and the head of achenes is erect instead of nodding at maturity (Tutin & Chater, 1993).

Many colour forms of *Anemone blanda* are available commercially. The plant illustrated here is usually called *A. blanda* 'Atrocaerulea' and is of Greek origin, collected by J. J. Paton (No. 4267) between Tripolis and Olympia. Other named forms include the brilliant blue 'Ingramii', and 'Radar', which has deep reddish-pink flowers with a white centre.

Anemone blanda is ideal for a deciduous woodland garden, where it will flower early in the year, from February to April. It can also be grown on a rock garden, in a partially shaded gully or against west- or east-facing rocks. In summer, it dies down to its tuberous rhizomes. Colonies can be left to spread by seeding around the parent plant, and the seedlings will often produce flowers in a range of colours, from white and pale blue to dark blue and bluish-purple, particularly if different forms are grown near to each other.

Curtis's Botanical Magazine, plate 598 (1977). Artist: Margaret Stones.

groundbreaking expeditions by adventurous explorers or intrepid botanists, instead they have come gradually, introduced by successive waves of conquering civilisations since the days of the Roman Empire. Early civilisations in the Mediterranean region grew plants mainly to eat or for their medicinal properties. As these people moved around Europe, they carried plants like thyme, lavender and peony. Many of these ancient introductions are now established as familiar garden plants throughout Europe.

The basic requirements of Mediterranean plants in cultivation are good drainage and plenty of sunshine. Given these conditions, a vast range of Mediterranean species can be grown outside in cooler, wetter climates. The main restriction will be the plant's hardiness, and some coastal Mediterranean species will not survive a frost. However, being a mountainous region, you don't have to go far from the coast to find plants at higher altitudes that are hardy enough to be grown outside in Northern Europe or elsewhere. They may not be true alpines but their size and habit is in keeping with those of other rock garden plants.

In the highest mountains around the Mediterranean, plants have to cope with both a freezing winter and a dry summer. Growth, especially of the roots, will begin in autumn but slows or stops once temperatures drop, recommencing as the snow melts in spring. The highest peaks of Spain's Sierra Nevada are snow covered until early summer but plants do appear in patches of melting snow. These plants include the pale lilac-flowered *Crocus nevadensis*, which takes its name from these mountains. This crocus is also found elsewhere in Spain, Morocco and northern Algeria. It dies down to a corm to survive the dry summer. The summers in these regions may be longer than those in the high peaks of the Alps but the lack of moisture is another hurdle for these plants to overcome.

The north-facing slopes of the Sierra Nevada are colder than the southern slopes and snow may persist all year round in sheltered places. On the southern side of the range, including the steep valleys of Las Alpujarras, the climate is much warmer and drier. Here, the lower slopes are terraced for the cultivation of citrus fruits, almonds, walnuts, olives and other crops. These crops are sustained by the intricate irrigation system devised by the Moors over 500 years ago that utilises the trickling water from the melting snows, diverting it along narrow channels and ducts to the narrow fields and groves.

With its wide range of climatic conditions and associated plant communities, from near sea level to the alpine zone, the Sierra Nevada is recognised as one of the most important biodiversity hotspots in Europe. There are more than 70 plant species that are endemic to this mountain range, most of them found above the wooded slopes, at higher elevations. The isolation from other

LEFT
The terraced lower slopes of Spain's Sierra Nevada are often heavily cultivated but these mountains are still home to more than 70 endemic species.

LEFT
The arid southern slopes of the Sierra Nevada face the Mediterranean Sea.

mountain floras since the last ice age has resulted in over 40 endemic plants being found in the alpine and subalpine zones, including the grey-leaved glacier toadflax, *Linaria glacialis*, the mossy *Saxifraga nevadensis* and the rare daffodil *Narcissus nevadensis*.

In the subalpine zone of the Sierra Nevada there are populations of tough, low-growing, domed and spiny plants, forming the so-called 'hedgehog' zone between 1,700 m (5,577 feet) and 2,000 m (6,562 feet) (Polunin & Smythies, 1973). These plants are adapted to more arid mountain slopes and they include *Erinacea anthyllis* and *Bupleurum spinosum*. This distinctive zone of vegetation is also seen on other mountains in central and southern Spain, on the drier southern slopes of the Pyrenees and across the Mediterranean Sea in the Atlas Mountains of Morocco.

At lower altitudes, all around the Mediterranean, are plants that live on cliffs or in gorges. Although far from being alpines, the harsh conditions these plants have to survive, growing on near-vertical rocky surfaces with little soil and long periods with no rainfall, force them into compact forms in the same way that cold winds and snow affect plants from high mountains. These cliff dwellers, or chasmophytes, cling to the walls or narrow shelves by their deeply penetrating root systems and are often tough and slow-growing, creeping along ledges or nestling in cracks in the rock. Crete in particular is noted for its numerous gorges, the most famous being the Samaria Gorge, which cuts into the White Mountains (or Lefka Ori) and leads down to the south-west coast of the island.

One of the best known Cretan chasmophytes is dittany, *Origanum dictamnus*, which is endemic to the island. The small, rounded, silver-grey hairy leaves of this plant grow on wiry stems that emerge from crevices in calcareous rock, at altitudes up to 1,900 m (6,234 feet). It is not a common plant in the wild, surviving high up on inaccessible cliffs, out of the reach of man and grazing goats. Dittany has

BELOW LEFT
The sides of the Imbros Gorge in Crete are covered with a range of chasmophytes clinging to the vertical rock face.

BELOW
Linum arboreum is a typical chasmophyte, native to the Aegean islands and south-west Turkey.

Crocus sieberi
Family: Iridaceae

The genus *Crocus* contains around 80 autumn- or early-spring-flowering species. They grow from a corm and produce long, narrow leaves, usually with a pale stripe down their centre. These leaves may develop at or after flowering and they surround the flowers, which are held above the ground by the perianth tube. The corm is surrounded by a tunic made up of the expanded bases of the true leaves and the papery sheathing leaves, called cataphylls, which surround the aerial shoot. The characteristics of the corm tunic are important for identifying species.

Crocus sieberi was described by the French botanist Jacques Gay in 1831, from plants growing on the island of Crete and is named after Franz Sieber, the Czech naturalist who collected it. Gay was unaware of the mainland form of this species but *C. sieberi* is now known to occur in various forms throughout Greece and into southern Albania, Macedonia, southern Bulgaria and possibly western Turkey.

The *Crocus sieberi* known to Gay is endemic to Crete, where it grows on rocky slopes and in grass at altitudes of 1,500–2,700 m (4,921–8,858 feet). It flowers as the snow melts and can completely cover areas of grazed turf in April. The flowers can reach up to 8 cm tall and are white with a yellow throat and purple staining on the exterior of the outer perianth segments. This purple staining can vary from a narrow stripe down the centre of the segment to an almost complete covering. The branched styles are deep orange or yellow.

Brian Mathew (1982) recognises four subspecies of *Crocus sieberi*. The Cretan plant is subsp. *sieberi*, and although introduced in the nineteenth century, it is still quite rare in cultivation. By the 1940s, *C. sieberi* was widely grown in England but the plants usually offered in the trade had light mauve flowers (Burtt, 1949). These would have been one of the other subspecies, all of which have flowers in various shades of lilac or violet.

From the Attica region of Greece comes *Crocus sieberi* subsp. *atticus*. It has a more coarsely netted corm tunic than the other subspecies and lilac-blue or violet flowers with a yellow throat. Subspecies *sublimis* is from the Peloponnese to southern Albania, Macedonia and southern Bulgaria. It has pale lilac flowers with a pale yellow throat. Some forms with a deeper flower colour and a zone of white between the two colours have been called forma *tricolor*. Last, subsp. *nivalis* has lilac-blue flowers with a yellow throat, and occurs in the southern Peloponnese.

In the early 1990s, Melvyn Jope found a population of *Crocus sieberi* in the eastern Peloponnese, some members of which were autumn-flowering. This is very unusual but nonetheless is in line with several other typically spring-flowering plants of the eastern Mediterranean that have localised, autumn-blooming colonies.

Crocus sieberi makes a fine plant for a sunny position on a rock garden, flowering in late winter or early spring. The exception is subsp. *sieberi*, which needs to be kept drier than the other subspecies in summer and is best grown in a cold frame.

Curtis's Botanical Magazine, plate 6036 (1873). Artist: Walter Hood Fitch.

several medicinal properties and is cultivated by the people of Crete, as well as being found in the island's gorges. The leaves are thought to help cure wounds and it is used as an infusion to aid digestion. Dittany has been cultivated outside Crete since the sixteenth century, if not before, and is listed in William Turner's *The Names of Herbes* of 1548. It is not especially hardy and the hairy leaves can rot in wetter climates, so this plant will usually do best under glass, especially in a cold, damp winter. The small pink flowers appear from between rounded, membranous, leaf-like bracts in a compact inflorescence. In an alpine house or cold frame, it will bloom all summer long, each stem producing several cone-like inflorescences.

Another chasmophyte that has been in cultivation for a long time is the shrubby *Linum arboreum*, which displays bright yellow, five-petalled flowers in spring. This plant is also found on Crete but its range extends to the Aegean islands of Rhodes, Halki, Simi and Karpathos, and to the Datça Peninsula of south-west Turkey (Strange & Rix, 2007). It was featured in *Curtis's Botanical Magazine* in 1794, having been introduced in 1788 by John Sibthorp, the Professor of Botany at Oxford University. At that time, it was treated as a glasshouse plant but it is a fairly hardy species in Britain, as long as it is planted in a sheltered, sunny position. This is a variable plant and different variants from Crete have been described as *L. caespitosum* and *L. doerfleri*. The former is a very dwarf, low-growing plant from high altitudes, the latter is more compact and more densely leafy than typical *L. arboreum*, with stiff, succulent, overlapping leaves on the non-flowering rosettes. The variation found in these plants may be due to differences in altitude and the effects of grazing but they often remain in cultivation. Grown side by side in the same frame at Kew, plants of *L. doerfleri* and *L. arboreum* are clearly distinguishable. *Linum doerfleri* is named after Ignaz Dörfler, who collected specimens from Crete in 1904.

Chasmophytes are fascinating plants to seek out in the wild. The rugged environment in which they grow may be harsh for them but is often stunningly beautiful. The gorges around the Mediterranean, with their spring torrents of icy water and vertical cliffs adorned with plants clinging on to life, are often magical places. However, some of the most beautiful displays in the Mediterranean flora are produced by geophytes, which are plants that grow from a bulb, corm, rhizome or tuber. The brilliant red goblets of the crown anemone dotted among olive trees, a high meadow bejewelled with delicate crocus or a field stained pink by the waving flower stems of gladiolus are among the sights to be seen in a Mediterranean spring. Other geophytes, such as certain species of *Sternbergia*, *Colchicum* and *Cyclamen*, flower in the autumn at the beginning of their growing season.

The term geophyte covers any plant that dies down to an underground storage organ for part of its life, including many terrestrial orchids. True alpine habitats, with their short summers, have few bulbous plants. Nevertheless, among the more popular genera that have representatives occurring at elevations approaching 2,000 m (6,562 feet) or more are *Crocus*, *Chionodoxa* and *Galanthus*. These high-altitude species are snow-melt plants, bursting into life once the frozen ground thaws. Their flowering time can vary from late winter to early summer, depending on altitude and when the snow melt occurs. At lower altitudes, where summers are longer, warmer and drier, geophytes are encountered more commonly. As an adaptation to a long summer drought, the geophyte lifestyle is hard to beat, and all areas with a Mediterranean-type climate are rich in geophytes.

Geophytes are commonly referred to as bulbs, although they also include corms, tubers and rhizomes. They are easily transported when dormant and so are widely cultivated around the world. A true bulb is made up of swollen leaf bases, creating layers that are easily seen if it is cut in half. Genera that have true bulbs include *Narcissus*, *Allium*, *Scilla* and *Muscari*. A corm, found in plants such as *Crocus* and *Gladiolus*, is a compact swollen stem and is solid rather than layered. Unlike most bulbs, a corm is formed every year, all the reserves being used up when the plant begins growth. A new corm must be grown before the dormant season comes round again. A tuber is a swollen part of a stem or root and a rhizome is a horizontal, branching underground stem. Cyclamen, and some irises and anemones, have a form of tuber or rhizome. Whatever structure a geophytes has, the result is the same: a very successful way of living in a mediterranean climate.

Mediterranean geophytes

FAR LEFT
Scilla peruviana growing in a damp spring meadow in southern Spain.

LEFT
Colourful *Anemone coronaria*, the crown anemone, is found throughout the Mediterranean.

BELOW LEFT
The delicate spring flowers of *Cyclamen creticum*.

BELOW
A carpet of *Crocus sieberi* subsp. *sieberi* in Crete's White Mountains.

Bibliography and references

Bland, B. (2000). *Silver Saxifrages*. AGS Publications Ltd., Pershore.

Burtt, B. L. (1949). *Crocus sieberi*. *J. Roy. Hort. Soc.* 74: 12.

Crook, H. C. (1951). *Campanulas, Their Cultivation and Classification*. Country Life Limited, London.

Doncaster, E. D. (1943). *Campanula zoysii* and some variants. *Quart. Bull. Alpine Gard. Soc. Gr. Brit.* 11: 129–132.

Farrer, R. (1919). *The English Rock Garden*, 2 vols. Thomas Nelson and Sons Ltd., London.

Ferguson, I. K. (1972). *Androsace* L. In: *Flora Europaea*, vol. 3, ed. T. G. Tutin *et al.*, pp. 20–23. Cambridge University Press, Cambridge.

Gornall, R. J. (1987). An outline of a revised classification of *Saxifraga* L. *Bot. J. Linn. Soc.* 95: 259–272.

Halda, J. J. (1996). *The Genus Gentiana*. Dobré, Czech Republic.

Harding, W. (1970). *Saxifrages*. Alpine Garden Society, Woking.

Holubec, V. & Křivka, P. (2006). *The Caucasus and its Flowers*. Loxia, Prague.

Hooker, J. D. H. (1869). *Androsace pubescens*. *Curtis's Bot. Mag.* 95: t. 5808.

Hooker, J. D. H. (1870). *Eritrichium nanum*. *Curtis's Bot. Mag.* 96: t. 5853.

Koch, W. D. J. (1837). *Synopsis Florae Germanicae et Helveticae*. Frankfurt.

Lowe, D. (1995). *Cushion Plants for the Rock Garden*. B. T. Batsford Ltd., London.

Mathew, B. (1982). *The Crocus: a Revision of the Genus Crocus*. B. T. Batsford Ltd., London.

McGregor, M. (2008). *Saxifrages*. Timber Press, Portland.

Mitchell, P. J. (1973). *The Sempervivum and Jovibarba Handbook*. The Sempervivum Society, England.

Nicholls, G. (2007). *Dwarf Campanulas and Associated Genera*. Timber Press, Portland.

Paton, A. (1994). Three membranous-bracted species of *Origanum*. *Curtis's Bot. Mag.* 11: t. 248.

Polunin, O. & Smythies, B. E. (1973). *Flowers of South-West Europe, a Field Guide*. Oxford University Press, Oxford.

Praeger, R. L. (1932). *An Account of the Sempervivum Group*. The Royal Horticultural Society, London.

Sims, J. (1814). *Saxifraga ceratophylla*. *Curtis's Bot. Mag.* 40: t. 1651.

Smith, G. & Lowe, D. (1997). *The Genus Androsace*. AGS Publications Ltd., Pershore.

Stearn, W. T. (1992). *Dictionary of Plant Names for Gardeners*. Cassell Publishers Ltd., London.

Strange, K. & Rix, M. (2007). *Linum doerfleri*. *Curtis's Bot. Mag.* 24: t. 574.

Strid, A. (1986). *Anemone* L. In: *Mountain Flora of Greece*, vol. 1, ed. A. Strid, p. 208. Cambridge University Press, Cambridge.

Tutin, T. G. (1964). *Pulsatilla* Miller. In: *Flora Europaea*, vol. 1, ed. T. G. Tutin *et al.*, pp. 219–221. Cambridge University Press, Cambridge.

Tutin, T. G. (1972). *Gentiana* L. In: *Flora Europaea*, vol. 3, ed. T. G. Tutin *et al.*, pp. 59–63. Cambridge University Press, Cambridge.

Tutin, T. G. & Chater, A. O. (1993). *Anemone* L. In: *Flora Europaea*, vol. 1 (2nd edition), ed. T. G. Tutin *et al.*, pp. 262–264. Cambridge University Press, Cambridge.

Webb, D. A. (1977). *Saxifraga burseriana*. *Curtis's Bot. Mag.* 181: t. 747.

Webb, D. A. & Gornall, R. J. (1989). *Saxifrages of Europe*. Christopher Helm Ltd., Bromley.

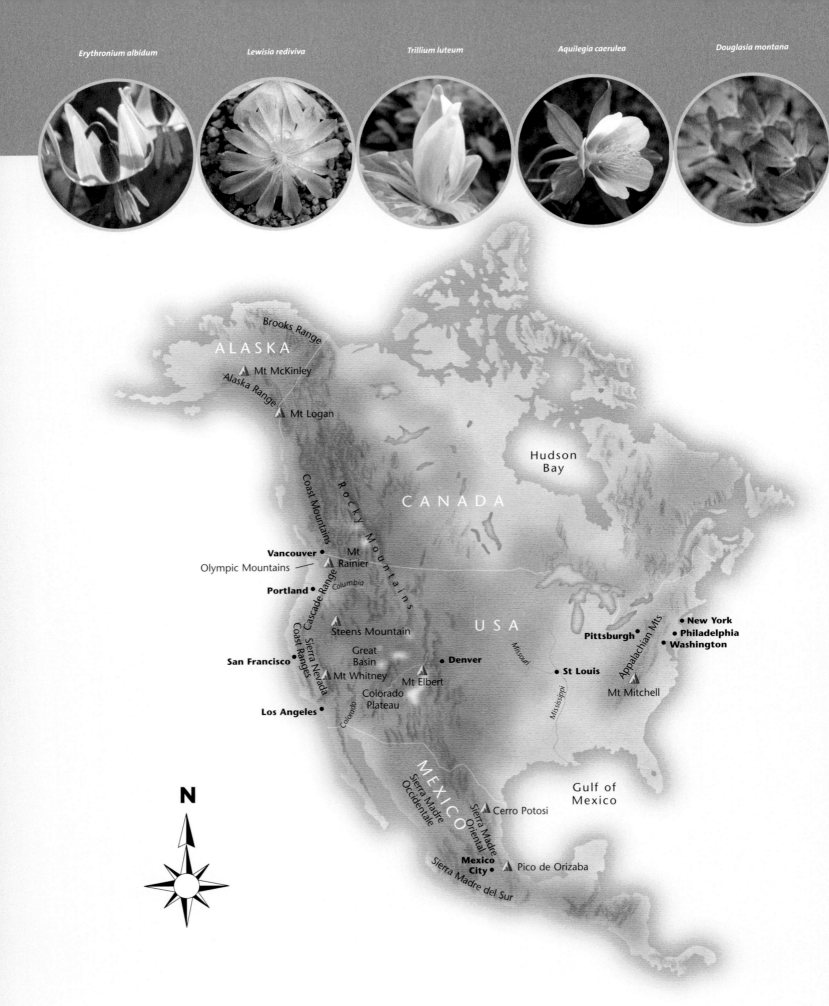

Erythronium albidum *Lewisia rediviva* *Trillium luteum* *Aquilegia caerulea* *Douglasia montana*

Brooks Range

ALASKA

▲ Mt McKinley

Alaska Range

▲ Mt Logan

Hudson
Bay

Coast Mountains

Rocky Mountains

CANADA

Vancouver ● ▲ Mt
Olympic Mountains — Rainier

Columbia

Portland ●

Cascade Range

Coast Ranges

▲ Steens Mountain

USA

Pittsburgh ●

Appalachian Mts

● New York
● Philadelphia
● Washington

San Francisco ●

Great
Basin

● Denver

Missouri

● St Louis

Sierra Nevada

▲ Mt Whitney

▲ Mt Elbert

Colorado
Plateau

Colorado

Mississippi

▲ Mt Mitchell

Los Angeles ●

MEXICO

Sierra Madre
Occidental

Sierra Madre
Oriental

▲ Cerro Potosi

Gulf of
Mexico

Mexico
City ●

▲ Pico de Orizaba

Sierra Madre del Sur

N

Chapter 4 **North America**

Slicing through Canada and the USA, the Rocky Mountains divide the continent of North America in two. From tundra and coniferous forests to canyonland and sagebrush country, this 3,200 km (2,000 miles) long mountain chain forms the continental divide and also marks a change in the landscape from east to west. The line of peaks looming on the horizon across the flat prairies and steppes of the Great Plains must have been a daunting sight to explorers venturing west in search of a route to the Pacific Ocean. What they found beyond this first line of mountains was a very different landscape, sometimes dramatic and beautiful, sometimes hostile and dangerous. The plants they found were as varied as the scenery, from cacti, colourful bulbs and high alpines, to the world's largest trees.

The Rocky Mountains (or Rockies) are made up of a complex series of ranges extending from the north of British Columbia in Canada to the Sierras of Mexico. They are at their furthest from the Pacific coast at a latitude of around 40° N in the USA, where the distance from the main peaks of the Colorado Rockies to the sea is over 1,600 km (994 miles). Nearer the coast is the Pacific Mountain System, which includes ranges such as the Cascade Range in Oregon and Washington and the Sierra Nevada of California. Between these and the Rockies is a vast region filled with high plains, dramatic canyons, deserts and volcanoes. Along the Pacific coast are the Coast Ranges and Olympic Mountains in the USA, and the Coast Mountains in Canada. These are the first peaks met by the moist air that blows inland from the Pacific Ocean and the highest precipitation levels in North America

occur in these mountains, in some locations exceeding 4,500 mm (177 inches) a year. Extensive conifer forests clothe the west-facing slopes of the Coast Ranges and include the tallest trees on the planet, the coast redwoods, *Sequoia sempervirens*.

The Canadian Rockies rise to 3,954 m (12,972 feet) at the summit of Mt Robson, but Canada's highest peaks are located in the Coast Mountains of British Columbia and the St Elias Mountains in the south-west corner of Yukon Territory. Canada's highest peak is Mt Logan at 5,959 m (19,551 feet) in the St Elias Mountains, a range that crosses over the border into Alaska.

BELOW
The Fortress (3,000 m; 9,843 feet) in the Kananaskis Range, part of the Canadian Rockies in Alberta. Photo: Kit Strange.

Alaska is a huge, sparsely populated state sitting mostly between the latitudes of 60° and 70° N, with roughly one-third of its mainland area sitting north of the Arctic Circle. The highest mountain in North America is Alaska's Mt McKinley, at 6,194 m (20,320 feet), one of the peaks in the Alaska Range. Between the Alaska Range in the south and the Brooks Range in the north is Alaska's interior, a vast, windy, cold plateau with mean annual temperatures ranging from -2°C to -6°C. The flora of the interior includes circumpolar species that are also found in the far north of Europe, with *Saxifraga oppositifolia*, *Silene acaulis* and *Cassiope tetragona* among the plants growing there.

From the Alaskan border, ranges such as the Mackenzie and Selwyn Mountains arch through Yukon Territory and the Northwest Territories towards British Columbia. Here is where the Rocky Mountains really begin, heading south through British Columbia and Alberta to the USA. The snowy peaks of the northern Rockies do not reach the altitudes found further south but they receive higher levels of precipitation.

The highest mountains in the Rockies are found in Colorado, USA, where there are more than 50 peaks above 4,300 m (14,108 feet) and the highest of all is Mt Elbert, at 4,399 m (14,432 feet). This region has a continental climate with fairly low precipitation, around 400 mm (15.7 inches) a year in Denver. Winters are generally bitterly cold but there are frequent mild spells followed rapidly by freezing conditions, with bright sunshine and strong, cutting winds.

From southern Utah and Colorado, the Rockies continue along the eastern edge of the Colorado Plateau, which takes its name from the Colorado River that has cut the Grand Canyon into these arid tablelands. Most precipitation here falls at higher altitudes, often as snow in the cold winters. To the west of this plateau are the Mojave and Sonoran Deserts and further south, the Mexican border.

Much of the region between the Rocky Mountains and the Sierra Nevada in the USA is taken up by the Great Basin, which covers an area of 520,000 km² (200,773 square miles) There is no outlet from this region to the sea, so precipitation ends up sinking into the ground or evaporating in marshes and salty lakes, such as the Great Salt Lake in Utah. Owing to the rain shadow effect of the Sierra Nevada and the southern Cascade Range, however, precipitation levels are low, from 150–300 mm (6–12 inches) a year over much of the area. The Sierra Nevada captures most of the moisture from the Pacific, and the southern Rockies are a barrier to moisture from the Gulf of Mexico. Plants that live in the Great Basin have to cope with both high levels of solar radiation, as a result of the high altitude, and the aridity. The mountains here, several of which reach over 3,500 m (11,483 feet), are like islands in a sea of dry scrubland and desert. Many of these isolated peaks are home to endemic plants, unable to spread due to the hostile conditions that surround the mountains on which they live. Examples include *Draba cusickii* var. *cusickii* and *Penstemon davidsonii* var. *praeteritus*, both of which are only found on Oregon's remote Steens Mountain (2,967 m; 9,734 feet).

The highest point in the contiguous USA is Mt Whitney, at 4,418 m (14,495 feet), in the Sierra Nevada, which extends along the eastern edge of California. This range is essentially a tilted block of granite, with steep slopes along the eastern flank and more shallow slopes facing west. These impressive mountains are home to the glaciated landscape of Yosemite National Park. Near the southern end of the range is Sequoia and Kings Canyon National Park, famous for its giant sequoias, *Sequoiadendron giganteum*, their impressive girth making them the largest (though not tallest) trees on Earth. The

ABOVE
Steens Mountain, south-east Oregon. Photo: Joanne Everson.

BELOW LEFT
Draba cusickii var. *cusickii*, endemic to Steens Mountain. Photo: Joanne Everson.

rest of California, below around 900 m (2,958 feet) altitude, has a mediterranean climate and the flora is rich in bulbous plants, such as *Erythronium*, *Fritillaria* and the wonderful mariposa lilies, *Calochortus*.

The Cascade Range is effectively a continuation of the Sierra Nevada northwards, stretching from northern California into Oregon, Washington and British Columbia, but these mountains differ geologically from the Sierra Nevada. The major peaks are volcanoes, including Mt Rainier (the highest) at 4,392 m (14,409, feet), Mt Shasta at 4,317 m (14,163 feet) and Mt Hood at 3,424 m (11,234 feet). Most famous of all is Mt St Helens, which erupted in May 1980 obliterating hundreds of square kilometres of forest and producing a massive cloud of ash that darkened the skies over eastern Washington State. This eruption destroyed the northern face of the mountain and reduced its height from 2,950 m (9,678 feet) to 2,550 m (8,366 feet).

Rainfall in the Cascades mostly occurs between October and May, and can be high, over 2,000 mm (78.7 inches) a year in some areas, but like the Sierra Nevada, these mountains cast a significant rain shadow. East of the Cascades on the Columbia Plateau, annual precipitation can be as low as 200 mm (7.87 inches).

Not all of North America's mountains are in the western half of the continent. Stretching over 2,000 km (1,243 miles) from south-east Canada to the north of Georgia, the Appalachian Mountains are the only significant topography in the eastern USA. This range includes the Great Smoky Mountains in Tennessee and North Carolina, the Allegheny Mountains in Pennsylvania, Virginia and West Virginia, the Adirondaks and Catskills in New York State, and the White Mountains in New Hampshire.

The Appalachians are very different from the Rockies and other ranges of western North America. These are ancient mountains, formed at the same time as the Scottish Highlands on the other side of the Atlantic, and millions of years of erosion have resulted in their more modest in altitudes. The highest point is Mt Mitchell at 2,037 m (6,683 feet) in the Blue Ridge Mountains of North Carolina. They are heavily wooded for most of their length. In the very north, the slopes are covered with dense coniferous forest but further south, broad leaf woodlands clothe the peaks and valleys.

Apart from on a few of the higher, more rugged peaks, the Appalachians are not home to true alpines but the region harbours a fascinating and beautiful woodland flora. *Trillium*, *Erythronium* and *Dodecatheon* are just some of the

Penstemon kunthii
Family: Plantaginaceae

The Mexican *Penstemon kunthii* was originally assigned to the genus *Chelone*, the turtleheads, and named *C. angustifolia* in 1818. It was collected by the German naturalist Alexander von Humboldt and his French companion Aimé Bonpland, near Real del Monte in the Mexican State of Hidalgo, in May 1803 (Humboldt, Bonpland & Kunth, 1818). These two explorers travelled extensively through South and Central America between 1799 and 1804, and the new plants they discovered, including *C. angustifolia*, were described by the German botanist Carl Kunth in seven volumes of *Nova Genera et Species Plantarum*. *Chelone angustifolia* was later transferred to the genus *Penstemon* by George Don, who named it *P. kunthii* in *A General History of the Dichlamydeous Plants* in 1838.

The genus *Penstemon* differs from *Chelone* in a number of respects. They both have more or less tubular flowers with four fertile stamens and one staminode (infertile stamen), but in *Chelone*, the flowers are held in a simple terminal spike and are virtually closed by the lower lip of the corolla. The upper lip is arched or hooded, resembling a turtle shell. These flowers have a staminode that is shorter than the four fertile stamens. Penstemons have flowers held in cymes, racemes or panicles, with the lower lip divided into three, normally spreading, lobes; the mouth of the flower is left open. The staminode is equal in length to the four fertile stamens and is often hairy at the tip. Other differences between these two genera include the shape of the seeds, which are flat and winged in *Chelone*, and wingless and rounded or angled in *Penstemon*.

The narrow tubular flowers of *Penstemon kunthii* come in shades of red or deep pink and are held in a panicle. Each flower is around 3 cm long, and the staminode usually has a beard of hairs at its tip. Branches from the main stem also produce an inflorescence, extending the flowering season. The narrow, sessile, bright green leaves are linear to lanceolate and have a serrated edge. The whole plant grows from a woody base and can reach over 80 cm tall.

This species has proved able to tolerate several degrees of frost and certainly survives the winter in southern England when grown in free-draining soil and full sun. Poor drainage is more likely to kill this species than cold. Also, it is better to cut back the old flower stems in early spring, just as new growth begins to sprout from the woody stems, rather than in autumn. The easiest method of propagation is from cuttings taken in summer or early autumn.

Penstemon kunthii is closely related to *P. campanulatus* (syn. *Chelone campanulata*) and the two have often been confused. *Penstemon campanulatus* has flowers in shades of purple and they are more widely dilated (bell-like) than those of *P. kunthii*. Confusion seems to have arisen because these two species hybridise so freely, resulting in many intermediate forms (Way & James, 1998). Hybrids occur in the wild, where their natural ranges meet in southern central Mexico. Named hybrids include the pale pink 'Evelyn' and the sugary pink 'Pink Endurance'.

Curtis's Botanical Magazine, plate 154 (1951). Artist: Lilian Snelling.

genera found there. Also, these mountains, and many of the plants that grow on them, were known to early settlers long before the western mountains were explored in the nineteenth century.

South of the USA, the mountains continue into Mexico as an extension of the Rockies. The two main Mexican ranges are the Sierra Madre Occidental in the west and the Sierra Madre Oriental in the east. Along the southern coast is the Sierra Madre del Sur and across the centre of the country, running from east to west just a few kilometres south of Mexico City, is the Trans-Mexican Volcanic Belt. This mountain belt joins the southern end of the Sierra Madre Occidental with the Sierra Madre Oriental and includes Mexico's loftiest peaks. The highest is Pico de Orizaba at 5,636 m (18,490 feet), the third highest mountain in North America after Mt McKinley and Mt Logan. The second highest mountain in Mexico is the active volcano Popocatépetl, at 5,426 m (17,802 feet), and third is Iztaccíhuatl at 5,230 m (17,159 feet).

The Sierras of Mexico are more modest in altitude than the volcanoes in the Trans-Mexican Volcanic Belt. Nevertheless, they reach 3,713 m (12,182 feet) on Cerro Potosi in the predominantly limestone mountains of the Sierra Madre Oriental, and around 3,300 m (10,827 feet) in the Sierra Madre Occidental, which has mostly volcanic-based rocks dissected by deep canyons. Between these two pine-clad ranges is the Mexican Altiplano, a high, arid plateau averaging between 1,000 m (3,281 feet) and 2,000 m (6,562 feet) above sea level.

Although half of Mexico is in the tropics, the high altitudes over much of the country mean that there are plants that are hardy enough to grow outside in more northerly climates, such as Britain's. One example is *Penstemon kunthii*, which may have been cultivated in England under the name *Chelone campanulata* as long ago as 1793 (Turrill, 1951). This species is distributed from western Chihuahua in north-west Mexico to Chiapas in the south. It is found in the Sierra Madre Occidental, the Sierra Madre del Sur and the southern end of the Sierra Madre Oriental (Straw, 1963) growing by roadsides, in fields and forests and on cliffs, to altitudes over 3,000 m (9,843 feet).

Penstemon kunthii is one of over 270 species of *Penstemon*, all found naturally in North America. They are best known in gardens, especially in Europe, as colourful, large-flowered hybrids, but the species come from a range of habitats, including prairies, screes, pine forests and high mountains. Many penstemons are adapted to arid conditions and poor soils. They are frequent along roadsides, and some of the more dwarf species are found growing on incredibly barren or rocky slopes, clinging to ledges or shifting screes. In cultivation, especially where water is more plentiful than in their natural habitat, a well-drained raised bed or rock garden is the ideal place to grow them.

South of Mexico, the high mountains of Guatemala still experience freezing conditions, so the plants found at these altitudes may also be frost hardy in cultivation. One such plant is the unusual, tuberous-rooted *Weldenia candida* in Commelinaceae (the *Tradescantia* family). It is native to the mountains of Mexico and Guatemala, growing on volcanic slopes and craters, in alpine meadows and in clearings in pine forests, at altitudes of 2,400–4,000 m (7,874–13,123 feet). This species, the only one in the genus, was first

ABOVE
Penstemon rupicola clinging to the side of Three Fingered Jack, Oregon, with the cone of Mt Jefferson (3199 m; 10,495 feet) in the background.
Photo: Joanne Everson.

LEFT
Penstemon procerus var. *tolmei*, native to Washington State and southern British Columbia, growing on the Rock Garden at Kew.

described in 1829, by the German botanist Julius Hermann Schultes. Another species, *W. schultesii*, described in 1841, appears to be synonymous with *W. candida* (Hunt, 1994). The first introduction into cultivation in Britain was in 1893. *Weldenia candida* came to the Royal Botanic Gardens, Kew from Guatemala, where it was collected in the crater of Volcan de Agua. With its peak at 3,760 m (12,336 feet), temperatures on this volcano can drop to -6°C.

Weldenia candida remained rare in cultivation until plants were reintroduced from Guatemala in 1934, by Dr P. L. Guiseppi (Bacon, 1981). One of these plants received an Award of Merit when exhibited by Guiseppi at the Alpine Garden Plant Conference in 1936. In May 2000, a large-flowered Mexican form, exhibited by Kew at the Chelsea Flower Show, gained a First Class Certificate.

North American plants have been introduced into cultivation in Europe since Europeans first discovered the New World at the end of the fifteenth century. Initially, there was just a trickle of new species, such as the northern white cedar, *Thuja occidentalis*, which was introduced by the French from Canada in 1536, and *Yucca gloriosa*, which came to Britain in the 1550s. Then, in the seventeenth and eighteenth centuries, more and more new plants from North America found their way to Europe. These early introductions were from the eastern side of the continent, and mostly trees and shrubs, but settlers began to venture further west as they extended their territory. It was when they met the Rocky Mountains, the mighty backbone of the North American continent, that many true alpines were found.

Weldenia candida
Family: Commelinaceae

Weldenia candida can be grown in the open garden in a raised bed or sunny border, but it is generally advisable to protect it from penetrating frosts and winter rainfall by keeping it in deep pots in a sunny, well-ventilated cold frame or cool glasshouse. This plant dies down for the winter and new growth will not appear until early spring.

The linear-lanceolate leaves are only a few centimetres long when the plant is flowering but can subsequently elongate to over 20 cm. They may be glabrous but are often hairy, particularly on their undersides. They can also have small tufts of whitish hairs on their upper surface, and this is particularly true of the Guatemalan forms. The inflorescence is a compacted cyme at the centre of the rosette of leaves. The three-petalled flowers have a distinctive, long corolla tube, 4–6.5 cm long. The petal lobes are 1–2 cm long, so each of the delicate white flowers can reach 4 cm wide. Individual flowers may only last a day but a succession is produced over several weeks in late spring.

Seed is hardly ever set in cultivation, as it seems that two clones are needed to allow for cross-pollination. Division in early spring is possible but the mass of tuberous roots can be difficult to part. The soil must be washed away from the roots and then individual growing points carefully teased apart but it is inevitable that some roots will be broken. Root cuttings can be taken in autumn and another method of propagation is to take side shoots as basal cuttings in summer.

The spring flowers of *Weldenia candida*.

So, the story of alpine plant introductions from North America mirrors the story of how this huge continent was explored. As expeditions headed west to find a route to the Pacific Ocean, more new plants were discovered. Of course, Native Americans had an extensive knowledge of their flora long before European settlers arrived. For example, the genus *Lewisia* is named in commemoration of one of the leaders of the Lewis and Clark expedition that crossed the Rocky Mountains to reach the west coast between 1804 and 1806, but these plants were already well-known to Native Americans. *Lewisia rediviva* is also known as bitterroot and was cooked and eaten by local people. Today, it is the state flower of Montana and here, in the north of the USA near the Canadian border, you will find the Lewis Range and, along the State border with Idaho, the Bitterroot Range.

The Lewis and Clark expedition is the most famous and celebrated of the early explorations of North America, and the plant specimens that were collected on that journey introduced many new and interesting species to the botanical world. Nevertheless, the story of plant introductions from North America begins in the east.

Alpines of eastern North America

By the late eighteenth century, the botanical exploration of North America had already resulted in the introduction of many species from the eastern half of the continent. In addition to the trees and shrubs, a few rock garden plants were brought across the Atlantic, including *Dodecatheon meadia*, cultivated in Britain since the late seventeenth century, *Sanguinaria canadensis*, grown in gardens as early as 1680, and the red- and yellow-flowered columbine *Aquilegia canadensis*, which was first introduced from Virginia by John Tradescant and was figured in Parkinson's *Theatrum Botanicum*, published in 1640.

Around 70 species of *Aquilegia* are found across the Northern Hemisphere and 21 of these occur in the USA and Canada. These perennial plants, commonly known as columbines or granny's bonnets, have divided, often ferny leaves and their flowers consist of five sepals and five petals. The petals have backward-pointing, hollow spurs with a nectary at their tip. The erect to nodding flowers come in a variety of colours, including reds, yellows, blues, purples and white and are often bicoloured. The greatest concentration of *Aquilegia* species in North America is in the south-west USA.

Aquilegia canadensis is the only columbine native to eastern North America (Nold, 2003). It was probably collected on John Tradescant the Younger's first expedition to Virginia in 1637. This species is a plant of open woods, rocky outcrops and forest margins, up to altitudes of 1,600 m (5,249 feet). The nodding flowers have

red sepals and the petals have a yellow blade, 6–8 mm long, and a straight red spur, 20–25 mm long. Growing to as much as 70 cm tall, this species is suitable for a large rock garden or partially shaded to sunny border but it does not like hot, dry conditions.

Dodecatheon is a genus that is almost entirely confined to North America, with just one species, *D. frigidum*, straying across the Bering Strait from Alaska into Siberia. With their swept-back petals and protruding cone of anthers, it is easy to see why these plants are commonly known as shooting stars. The reflexed petals are reminiscent of those in *Cyclamen*, but dodecatheons have dart-like flowers held in an umbel at the top the stem, above a basal rosette of leaves. After flowering in spring or early summer, the plants die down to fibrous-fleshy roots. A stylised *Dodecatheon* is the symbol of the North American Rock Garden Society, chosen because the genus has representatives in most states of the USA.

Dodecatheon meadia was described by Linnaeus in 1753, by which time this species was already becoming a well known plant in European gardens. Philip Miller refers to it in his *Gardeners' Dictionary* but uses the generic name *Meadia*, which commemorates the English

Shooting stars:
Dodecatheon or *Primula*?

The taxonomy of *Dodecatheon* has a long and complex history. Confusion over the naming of the various species, subspecies and varieties has often arisen through incomplete knowledge of these plants in the wild. Although local populations may be fairly uniform, they can show gradual variation over a wider area, which has led to the publication of a number of names for what is often best considered a single species. Reliable morphological characters are only found in the flowers and fruits, such as the size of the stigma, the texture of the anther connectives and the structure of the capsule teeth after dehiscence (Mitchem, 1991).

Today, the status of the whole genus is in doubt as a recent paper by Austin Mast and James Reveal (2007), which recognises 17 species of *Dodecatheon*, transfers all of the species of *Dodecatheon* into *Primula*. These authors state that molecular evidence from both chloroplast and nuclear DNA suggests that they are most closely related to *Primula* subgenus *Auriculastrum* and have descended from the most recent common ancestor of *Primula*. The 17 species are placed in section *Dodecatheon* of *Primula* subgenus *Auriculastrum*, and *Dodecatheon meadia* becomes *Primula meadia*, with no subspecies.

Although the flowers of *Dodecatheon* are distinctive, in all other respects, including the fruiting stages, these plants are remarkably similar to the primulas of subgenus *Auriculastrum*. Mast and Reveal state that both have chromosome numbers of 2n = 44, and that their valvate capsules are held on long scapes arising from a rosette of fleshy, lanceolate leaves with involute vernation (the young leaves are inrolled). However, at present, the names in the genus *Dodecatheon* are firmly entrenched in the rock gardener's vocabulary and it will probably be some time before any move to *Primula* is commonly accepted.

Dodecatheon pulchellum, from central and western North America, becomes *Primula pauciflora* in section *Dodecatheon* of subgenus *Auriculastrum*.

Primula rusbyi subsp. *ellisiae*, from New Mexico, is in section *Parryi* of subgenus *Auriculastrum*.

physician Dr Richard Mead. William Curtis included this species in the first volume of the *Botanical Magazine* in 1787, in which he states that according to Miller this plant was sent by "Mr Banister to Dr Compton, Lord Bishop of London, in whose curious garden he first saw it growing in the year 1709" (Curtis, 1787). Henry Compton imported many plants to his London garden at Fulham Palace and John Banister was one of the missionaries he sent to America. John Banister arrived in Virginia in 1678 and soon began studying the plants and animals of the region. He supplied many drawings, observations and plant specimens before his death in 1692. *Dodecatheon meadia* was also figured by Mark Catesby in his *Natural History of Carolina, Florida and the Bahama Islands* (2 volumes, 1730–1747).

Dodecatheon meadia is a widespread species in the eastern half of North America, ranging from Pennsylvania through Wisconsin and Georgia to Texas. It grows in a variety of habitats, including prairies, woods and moist cliffs, in sun or shade. The elliptic to oblanceolate, petiolate leaves can reach up to 30 cm in length, with the flower stem nearly twice that length. The numerous flowers are held on slender, arching pedicels and have five sharply reflexed petals, up to 2 cm long, in shades of magenta, lavender or white. The white-flowered forms are often listed as forma *album* or 'Album', whereas the form named 'Splendidum' has crimson flowers.

Dodecatheon meadia is one of the more easily grown species in the genus, requiring a humus-rich, moist but well-drained soil, in sun or part shade. Plenty of moisture should be available during the growing season, so a cool gully or alongside a rock garden pond or stream are ideal garden habitats. This is a hardy plant, surviving temperatures as low as -15 or -20°C. The leaves emerge in early spring and the umbels of flowers appear shortly after.

In 1878, the American botanist Asa Gray treated all the then known shooting stars as *Dodecatheon meadia*, which he divided into seven varieties (Gray, 1878). By contrast, Reinhard Knuth (1905) recognised 30 species in Engler's *Das Pflanzenreich*, dividing *D. meadia* into four subspecies. In a later study of the genus, Henry Thompson (1953) listed 14 species and recognised three subspecies of *D. meadia*: subsp. *meadia*, the smaller-flowered subsp. *brachycarpum* and subsp. *membranaceum*, which has more abruptly tapered leaves.

Trillium sessile has been grown in Britain for as long *Dodecatheon meadia*. This species featured in the second volume of the *Botanical Magazine*, where Curtis remarks that it was "as long standing in this country as the *Dodecatheon* but far less common" (Curtis, 1788). This species was also featured half a century earlier in Mark Catesby's *Natural History of Carolina*. Trilliums are now

LEFT
Aquilegia canadensis.

BELOW
The white form of
Dodecatheon meadia.

Trillium nivale

Family: Melanthiaceae

Trillium nivale, a species from the eastern USA, was first described by John Riddell of Cincinnati in *A Synopsis of the Flora of the Western States*, published in 1835. Early in the nineteenth century, the 'Western States' covered an area from West Virginia to Missouri, and Riddell found *T. nivale* 'on the east bank of the Scioto river' in Ohio. He noted that its white flowers, which open from late February, were among the earliest to appear in the flora of the area. The common name of this plant is snow trillium, referring to its habit of flowering as the snow melts around it.

This species is found in scattered localities, mainly in an area stretching from the Allegheny Mountains of West Virginia and Pennsylvania, through Ohio, Indiana, Illinois and Iowa, to southern Minnesota, with outlying populations in Maryland, Michigan, Wisconsin and Nebraska (Case & Case, 1997). It grows in damp woodland, on slopes and rocky ledges or near streams, often on limestone.

Trillium nivale belongs to subgenus *Trillium*, in which the flowers are held on a stalk (pedicel), the petals are spreading and the leaves are usually plain green. The species with sessile flowers, erect petals and often mottled leaves are in subgenus *Phyllantherum*. *Trillium nivale* is a small species, growing from 5–15 cm tall and usually displaying wide, showy flowers with white petals, which are sometimes faintly veined with pale pinkish-purple. The pedicel is 1–3 cm long. These flowers are held erect at first but become nodding with age and are large for the size of the plant, reaching over 4 cm wide. The elliptic to ovate, petiolate leaves continue to expand as the flower fades, eventually attaining a length of around 5 cm.

Trilliums are often grown in the dappled shade and moist soil of a woodland garden. Because of its small size, *Trillium nivale* is well-suited to cultivation in a rock garden if grown in partial shade and neutral to alkaline, gritty, humus-rich soil. It also makes a fine plant for pot cultivation, and housing it in a well-ventilated cold frame will protect its early blooms from wind and rain. Growth appears above ground early in the year and is susceptible to slug damage.

The best way to propagate *Trillium nivale* is from fresh seed. This normally needs two cold periods before germination, so seedlings may not appear for nearly two years. The seed may germinate straight away if sown just before it is ripe, but seed that has been stored may germinate erratically or not at all.

Seedlings can be left in their pot for a year or two before potting up in late summer. They will take three or four years to flower. This is a very long-lived species, available rarely but often seen in specialist collections, where plants over 20 years old are known.

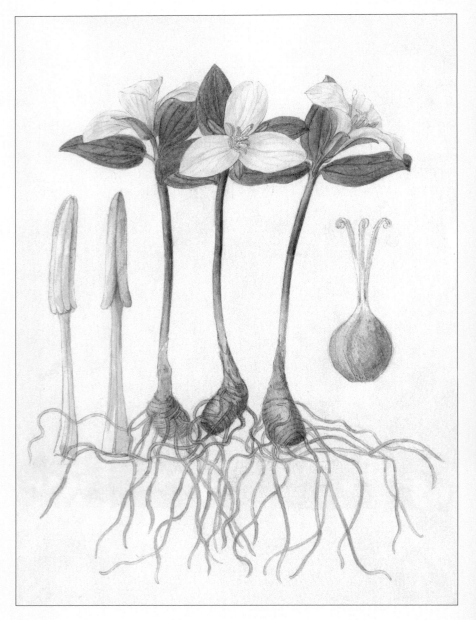

Curtis's Botanical Magazine, plate 6449 (1879).
Artist: Harriet Thiselton-Dyer.

amongst the most desirable of woodland plants, emerging in early spring to produce their broad, often attractively mottled leaves (technically leaf-like bracts) and solitary, three-petalled flowers in shades of pink, maroon, red, purple, white and yellow. They die down in summer to horizontal underground rhizomes. In the garden, in dappled shade and humus-rich soil, trilliums will gradually increase to form impressive clumps, but in the wild they can carpet a woodland floor.

As the generic name suggests, trilliums have parts arranged in threes. The herbaceous stem, which can reach 60 cm tall, grows from the horizontal rhizome and holds the three leaves, which may be sessile or petiolate. The single, terminal flower is composed of six perianth segments, divided into three mainly green sepals and three petals. These petals are erect or spreading and surround the six stamens and a superior ovary with three chambers. The fruit is a berry with several seeds. Trilliums are classified into two subgenera according to whether the flower is held on a stalk (pedicel) or is sessile. The pedicellate species are in subgenus *Trillium* and the sessile species in subgenus *Phyllantherum*.

Trillium sessile was described by Linnaeus in 1753. It is one of the sessile species and is found in the eastern states from Michigan and New York to Arkansas and northern Alabama, growing in deciduous woodland, often on calcareous soil. Linnaeus described three species of *Trillium*, the other two being pedicellate species, *T. cernuum*, from central and eastern Canada and the northern USA, and *T. erectum* from eastern Canada and eastern USA. The entry for *T. cernuum* gives the locality as Carolina and it seems that Linnaeus included features of two different plants in his description (Case & Case, 1997). The southern plant, which includes Carolina in its range, is now called *T. catesbaei*, honouring Mark Catesby.

There are now between 30 and 40 known species of *Trillium* distributed in three distinct geographical zones. Around five or six species grow in Asia, from the Himalaya to China and Taiwan and northwards to Japan, Kamchatka and Sakhalin. However, most are American: in the west there are about seven species, found in western USA and British Columbia, but the greatest concentration of species is in an area covering the eastern USA (particularly the Appalachian Mountains) and south-east Canada. All three zones have their own distinct species, with none occurring in more than one zone.

ABOVE RIGHT
Trillium erectum 'Kew Beauty' in Kew's woodland garden.

RIGHT
The pedicellate *Trillium catesbaei*, named after Mark Catesby in 1817.

Although many genera have species confined to either the east or west of North America, there are some plants that have more unusual distributions, such as the Dutchman's breeches, *Dicentra cucullaria*. This species is found in two distinct areas, one on each side of the continent. In the east, it is found from Nova Scotia and the Gaspé Peninsula south to northern Georgia and Alabama and west to North and South Dakota. In the west, it is found over a much smaller area in the Columbia River Basin of Washington and Oregon and in western Idaho (Stern, 1961). The western populations have been described as a separate species, *D. occidentalis*, or as a variety of *D. cucullaria*. These plants are, however, mostly indistinguishable from the eastern populations and are generally considered to be within the range of variation found in the species.

Dicentra cucullaria grows in deciduous woods and on gravelly stream banks, to altitudes of 1,500 m (4921 feet). It was introduced to Britain in the 1730s by Philip Miller, who probably received it from the Quaker botanist John Bartram of Philadelphia (Blunt, 1976). Bartram set up the first Botanic Garden in the USA, founded in 1731 in Philadelphia, a city that was to become the centre of North American botany by the end of the eighteenth century.

The delicate white flowers of *Dicentra cucullaria* resemble an upside-down pair of trousers (or breeches) but these flowers have also been likened to moths, butterflies and even a flight of birds. From 3–14 flowers are held in a raceme above finely dissected, ferny, glaucous foliage in early spring. Each flower consists of two deciduous sepals and four petals in two pairs. The outer pair of petals enclose the smaller inner petals except at their apex and they have diverging basal spurs, up to 13 mm long, giving

the flower its characteristic shape. The whole plant reaches 20–35 cm tall or more, before dying down in summer to a cluster of tiny bulbils.

Linnaeus described this plant as *Fumaria cucullaria* in 1753 but the genus *Dicentra* was proposed by Johann Bernhardi in 1833. It is clearly distinguished from *Fumaria* by its flowers possessing two spurs rather than one. There are now around 20 recognised species of these annuals, herbaceous perennials and climbers. They are distributed in temperate North America and eastern Asia, with nine species occurring in North America. *Dicentra cucullaria* is closest to *D. canadensis*, another species from eastern North America, which has rounded rather than pointed spurs and bulbils that are yellow and pea-shaped rather than white to pink and tear-shaped. It also has fragrant flowers that appear a week to ten days later than those of *D. cucullaria*.

Dicentra cucullaria was featured in *Curtis's Botanical Magazine* in 1808 and the specimen painted came from the Loddiges nursery in Hackney, London (Sims, 1808). This was one of the many new nurseries that sprung up in London in the second half of the eighteenth century selling exotic plants from around the world. Also among them was the American Nursery in Sloane Square, owned by John Fraser.

A Scotsman born near Inverness in 1750, Fraser made seven trips to North America between 1780 and 1810. After his first trip to Newfoundland, he made several expeditions to the southern and eastern States, the sixth and seventh trips with his son, also John. The American Nursery opened in the 1780s and here Fraser sold the plants he brought back from his expeditions. The catalogues produced for this nursery listed a range of species, many new to science and named for the first time.

The importance of the American Nursery catalogues in naming new species led to them being reprinted a century later. The catalogue produced after Fraser's fourth journey, around 1790, was reprinted in the *Journal of Botany* in 1899 (Britten, 1899). As you might expect, it included plenty of larger woody plants, such as *Cornus*, *Fraxinus*, *Ilex* and *Juglans* but also on offer were kalmias, *Lobelia cardinalis* and unspecified phloxes. A later catalogue, issued in 1813 by Fraser's son, stated that the "new and interesting plants" listed were collected "in Upper Louisiana, and principally on the River Missourie".

Alpines were not a prominent feature of these catalogues, but among those Fraser brought back were phloxes, including the moss phlox, *Phlox subulata*, from across eastern North America, which he brought to Britain in the 1790s. This species was already known to John Bartram, who may well have grown it in his botanic garden in Philadelphia. It is mentioned, as "fine creeping Lychnis" in a letter from Bartram to London businessman and plant enthusiast Peter Collinson, dated 1745 (Wherry, 1955). Fraser did introduce the creeping, mat-forming *P. stolonifera* to Britain. This species is found growing naturally in damp, open deciduous

BELOW
Phlox subulata 'Benita'.

Phlox stolonifera
Family: Polemoniaceae

This painting appeared in *Curtis's Botanical Magazine* in 1802, along with the original description of *Phlox stolonifera* by John Sims. The Scotsman John Fraser discovered and introduced this species. Sims writes: "We are informed by Mr John Fraser, of Sloane Square, Chelsea, that he first discovered this plant in Georgia, in the year 1786, together with *Phlox pilosa*, *setacea*, and *subulata*, but that living plants were not brought to Europe 'till 1801, his sixth voyage to North America, on botanical researches, in company with his son."

Sims gave his new species the common name of creeping phlox because this stoloniferous plant will form loose mats of evergreen foliage up to 60 cm across. The obovate to spathulate leaves are hairy, petiolate and up to 4.5 cm long; the leaves on the flower stems are shorter, sessile and more oblong. Each cymose inflorescence holds around six reddish-purple to lilac or violet, fragrant flowers that are 2.5–3 cm in diameter, with five spreading lobes and a narrow corolla tube, which is up to 2.5 cm long. The whole plant reaches around 25–30 cm tall.

In his monograph of *Phlox*, Edgar T. Wherry (1955) divides the genus into three sections, primarily on the basis of style characters and habit. Wherry places *P. stolonifera* in section *Phlox*, in which the styles are united for over half their length and often longer than the sepals, and the stamens equal the corolla tube in length. These are open, upright plants, rarely cushion or mat-forming. In this latter respect, they differ from the species in section *Microphlox*, such as *P. caespitosa*, which often form dense mats or cushions and have a few-flowered, sometimes single-flowered, inflorescence.

Within section *Phlox*, *P. stolonifera* is placed alongside *P. adsurgens* in subsection *Stoloniferae*. These two species come from opposite sides of the American continent (the latter is native to northern California and Oregon) but both have decumbent stems with elliptic to obovate, partly evergreen leaves. Their large flowers have a style that is as long as the pubescent corolla tube and stamens that are partly exserted. *Phlox adsurgens* has glabrous lower leaves, and flowers that have a pale eye and are slightly smaller than those of *P. stolonifera*.

Phlox stolonifera is a hardy plant but its flowers may be damaged by a late frost. It needs a humus-rich soil that is neutral to mildly acidic, and it should be planted in a cool situation, in partial shade, where it will gradually spread by rooting stolons. *Phlox stolonifera* can tolerate full sun if the soil remains moist but is more suited to a cool gully or to the dappled shade of a woodland garden. Propagation is by division after flowering. The variation in flower colour has led to the naming of several forms, including 'Ariane', which has pale green leaves and white flowers, 'Mary Belle Frey' with pink flowers and 'Blue Ridge' with deep violet-blue flowers.

Curtis's Botanical Magazine, plate 563 (1802). Artist: Sydenham Edwards.

woods in the eastern USA, particularly in the Appalachian Mountains and the Piedmont Plateau.

There are around 67 species of *Phlox* and, like the shooting stars, they are confined to North America with the exception of one species, in this case *Phlox sibirica*, which strays into Siberia. They range from stately herbaceous perennials such as *P. paniculata* to annuals and mat-forming subshrubs. Their flowers are held in cymes or panicles and have five spreading petals with a long, narrow corolla tube. The petals are often notched and come in shades of red, pink, blue, purple and white. Many of the ground-hugging species from western North America, such as *P. caespitosa* and *P. douglasii* make ideal rock garden plants that thrive in well-drained soil and a sunny position.

The 1813 American Nursery catalogue, reprinted in volume 2 of the journal *Pittonia* in 1890, was one of the first botanical publications of the botanist Thomas Nuttall, an Englishman born in Yorkshire in 1786. He emigrated to America in 1808, settling in Philadelphia. From there, he soon began botanising and collecting the American flora, mentored by the Professor of Botany and Natural History at the University of Pennsylvania, Benjamin Smith Barton. Unfortunately, most of the plants new to science that were listed in Fraser's 1813 catalogue were not described. Formal descriptions of

many of these new species were undertaken by the German botanist Frederick Pursh in *Flora Americae Septentrionalis*, published in 1814, but he sometimes used different names to those of Nuttall. One of the new species listed in this catalogue, and with a name credited to Nuttall, is *Eriogonum flavum*, the alpine golden buckwheat. *Eriogonum* is a large North American genus of approximately 250 species. The greatest diversity in this genus is found in the arid regions of western North America, and in Fraser's catalogue, Nuttall wrote that *E. flavum* was collected "in the vicinity of the Rocky Mountains". The botanical exploration of the west was already underway.

Heading west

Lewis and Clark lead the way

Scientific exploration of western North America really began with the Lewis and Clark expedition, from 1804 to 1806. Following the Louisiana Purchase in 1803, when America bought a massive area of land from France that vastly extended its territory westwards from the Mississippi to the Rocky Mountains and beyond, President Thomas Jefferson launched an expedition to find a route to the Pacific Ocean via the Missouri River. The aims of the expedition were to engage with the native people and study the plants, animals and landscape of the region. Jefferson

BELOW
The view from Iron Mountain in the Oregon Cascades.
Photo: Joanne Everson.

chose Captain Meriweather Lewis to lead this expedition, who then chose William Clark as his co-leader. Observing and recording the plants and animals of the region was an important objective, so Lewis was sent to Benjamin Barton at the University of Pennsylvania for a crash course in natural history.

The expedition set off from St Louis on 14 May 1804 and followed the Missouri River westwards. For six months, they followed the river upstream until winter set in and they established a camp at Fort Mandan, in present-day North Dakota. On 7 April 1805, a boat was sent down river with cargo for President Jefferson, including plant specimens. As yet no mountains, and hence no true alpines, had been encountered although the altitude increased as the expedition crossed the High Plains, now in parts of North Dakota and Montana. It was in July 1805 that the expedition met the Rocky Mountains, in present-day western Montana. In October 1805, they crossed the Columbia Plains, swept along by the Snake and Columbia Rivers. Passing through the Columbia River Gorge, the Cascade Range and the Coast Ranges, they reached the Pacific in November 1805. After spending the winter camped near the mouth of the Columbia River they set off for the homeward journey in late March 1806, arriving back in St Louis on 23 September 1806.

Although many collections were made during this journey, unfortunately they did not all survive. On more than one occasion, specimens were stored in bearskins for collection on the return journey only to be damaged or destroyed by water as the river rose unexpectedly high in the intervening period. As a result, hurried replacement collections were made on the return journey. The number of specimens that made it back to St Louis in 1806 may not be large but almost every plant they did bring back was new to science. In total, 239 specimens collected by Lewis and Clark exist today, representing 175 species of plant, and lost specimens account for a further 36 species (Phillips, 2003).

Thomas Jefferson passed the collections that had been sent downriver from Fort Mandan in 1805 on to Barton in Philadelphia. The collections made on the return leg of the journey were brought to Philadelphia by Lewis himself in April 1807. He passed them to Frederick Pursh, who had been working for Barton for a few years. Pursh was born in Germany in 1774. He worked in the Botanic Garden at Dresden before travelling to America in 1799. Barton had promised to help the explorers with their scientific discoveries but he appeared to be too busy, so Pursh was paid by Lewis to organise the plant collections, write descriptions and prepare drawings. The intention was to publish the new descriptions along with the journal of the expedition. Unfortunately, however, Lewis died in 1809 and Barton never did fulfil his promise. Meanwhile, Pursh took some of the collections to London, without Clark's knowledge, and eventually included them in his *Flora Americae Septentrionalis*, which was first presented to the Linnean Society in December 1813. The expedition journals were published in 1814 but without the scientific element.

LEFT
Erigeron compositus on Mt Eddy, Northern California.
Photo: Joanne Everson.

Pursh described 94 new species in his flora from collections made by Lewis and Clark, of which 40 are still accepted as he proposed them today (Reveal *et al.*, 1999). This flora was the first to cover the north-west region of the present-day USA, and among the new plants were several alpines and bulbs from the Rocky Mountains and Columbia Plains.

One of the many daisies growing in the western mountains of North America is the widespread *Erigeron compositus*, which was collected by Lewis on the "banks of the Kookoosky" now called the Clearwater River in Idaho, probably in the autumn of 1805 on the outward leg of the expedition. *Erigeron* is a huge genus with around 390 species worldwide and over 170 in North America. *Erigeron compositus*, known as the dwarf mountain fleabane, occurs from Greenland and Alaska, across Canada, south to California, Arizona and Colorado. It grows in various habitats from sagebrush to subalpine meadows, cliffs and screes, at altitudes of up to 4,300 m (14,108 feet), and flowers in summer. The solitary flower heads have white, bluish or pinkish ray florets around the yellow disc florets. A particular feature of this species is the finely cut foliage, with each leaf blade dissected into three narrow lobes. In its best forms, the leaves form a compact cushion topped by the flower heads on stems only 5 cm or so tall.

The area around the Clearwater River proved to be a rich hunting ground for new plants. On the return leg of the Lewis and Clark expedition, the team established Camp Chopunnish in this region, where they stayed from 13 May to 10 June 1806. The glacier lily, *Erythronium grandiflorum*, was one of the bulbous species collected here by Lewis and later described by Pursh. It has bright yellow flowers with reflexed tepals that are 25–30 mm long and held up to 30 cm above the plain green, lanceolate leaves.

Erythronium grandiflorum is found over a large area of western North America, from British Columbia south to Colorado, Utah and Oregon. It grows in open woods, forest margins and in short grass on subalpine slopes, often near melting snow, at altitudes up to 3,100 m (10,171 feet). In cultivation, it prefers a cool position, such as in the shade of a woodland garden.

Other bulb species found by the Lewis and Clark expedition include the diminutive *Fritillaria pudica*, described as *Lilium pudicum* by Pursh and later transferred to *Fritillaria* by Curt Sprengel in 1825. This short, delicate species has yellow, nodding flowers, with tepals around 1.5–2 cm long that become orange to reddish as they age. It is widespread in western North America, occurring from British Columbia to California, growing on grassy slopes or in woods, up to 2,100 m (6,890 feet) altitude. The expedition collected it on the Columbia Plains, near the Clearwater River in May 1806.

THE GENUS *Erythronium*

The genus *Erythronium* was described by Linnaeus in 1753 on the basis of the European *E. dens-canis*, the dog's tooth violet. The common name derives from the bulb, which is the shape of a canine tooth. There are now around 27 known species of *Erythronium*, 23 of which are found in North America. These American species are divided into two groups, the larger group in the west and a smaller group of six species in the east. Each group has its own characteristics and no species is found in both areas.

The *Erythronium* species in the eastern American group are more closely allied to the four Eurasian species than to the western group. They tend to have leaves that narrow at the base into a distinct, narrow petiole. The upper leaf surfaces display an irregular mottled pattern of purplish or brownish smudges, with the markings overlapping the leaf veins. The seeds have a fleshy appendage and the capsules are held on weak peduncles that bend down to the ground, allowing the dispersal of the seeds by ants.

The western species, from the Rocky Mountains westwards, have leaves that gradually taper to the base, are without a distinct petiole, and are either plain green or patterned with symmetrical markings that lie between the veins. The seed pods are held erect on stiff peduncles and the seeds have no enlarged appendage (Mathew, 2001).

Most species require a humus-rich, freely draining woodland soil, a sheltered position and partial shade. They are dormant for the summer but should not be too hot or dry at this time. All produce their charming flowers, with characteristically reflexed tepals and protruding anthers, in the spring.

FAR LEFT
Erythronium revolutum from the Pacific coast areas of British Columbia, Washington, Oregon and northern California.

LEFT
Erythronium americanum, from eastern USA and south-east Canada, was first described in 1808.

can reach 1.8–2 m tall. It grows on rocky slopes and in clearings in pine woods, where it can form spectacular populations that flower in early summer. The flowering of individual plants can be erratic and occurs only every 5–7 years, after which the flowering stem and leaves die. The range of this plant extends from southern British Columbia through Washington and Oregon to California, and it is also found in the mountains of northern Idaho and western Montana.

Among the Lewis and Clark collections described by Pursh were three new genera. A small bulb found by the expedition in May 1806 along the Clearwater River became the type for Pursh's new genus *Calochortus*. The name means 'beautiful grass', an apt description for this wonderful race of slender, bulbous perennials from western USA and British Columbia south to Guatemala. Another evocative name for these plants is mariposa lily, from the Spanish for butterfly. Pursh named this first species *C. elegans*. There are now 73 recognised species of *Calochortus*, with the highest concentration, over 40 species, found in California (Gerritsen & Parsons, 2007).

LEFT
Camassia quamash growing in a sunny border.

BELOW
Xerophyllum tenax.
Photo: Joanne Everson.

On the 'Quamash flats' at the foot of the Rockies, the expedition collected blue camas, *Camassia quamash*. The tall, blue-flowered racemes of this bulb were encountered on the outward journey and specimens were collected on the return, in June 1806. Occurring throughout much of the north-west USA and in south-west Canada, this was an important food crop for the Native Americans. A couple of weeks later, the creamy-white-flowered *Zigadenus elegans* was collected. This is known as the death camas because the bulbs, which are similar to those of *Camassia*, are poisonous. The two plants can grow together, so care had to be taken when harvesting the bulbs to eat. In the Pacific Northwest, *Zigadenus elegans* is a plant of subalpine meadows and moist screes, but it has a distribution ranging from Alaska to Texas and east to Quebec and Virginia. Specimens were collected in July 1806 on the west side of the pass now known as the Lewis and Clark Pass in Montana.

One of the most dramatic plants found by the expedition as they crossed the Rocky Mountains was beargrass or squaw grass, *Xerophyllum tenax*. Originally named *Helonias tenax* by Pursh, it was transferred to *Xerophyllum* by Thomas Nuttall in 1818 along with the only other species in the genus, *X. asphodeloides* from central eastern USA. The specimens used by Pursh to describe *Helonias tenax* were collected on 15 June 1806, along the Lolo Trail in Idaho.

Xerophyllum tenax produces tufts of long, linear, arching, evergreen leaves, each up to 1 m long. The inflorescence is a 50–70 cm long raceme of densely packed, creamy-white flowers held on a rigid stem that

Lewisia rediviva
Family: Portulacaceae

This wonderful painting by Walter Hood Fitch was the first colour illustration of a *Lewisia* to be published, in 1863 (Mathew, 1989a). There are now around 19 known species of *Lewisia*, occurring in western North America, from New Mexico to Alaska. These low-growing perennials have succulent leaves held in a rosette and may be evergreen or die down to thick fleshy roots. One species, *L. triphylla*, has a small, rounded tuber. Flowers vary in size from 1–7.5 cm across, have 5–20 petals and are held either singly or in a cyme, raceme or panicle.

The species name, *rediviva*, means 'brought back to life' and refers to this plant's ability to sprout new growth, even after long periods of desiccation. Pursh notes that a specimen taken from the Lewis herbarium was planted by the seed merchant Bernard McMahon of Philadelphia "and vegetated for more than one year". An even more remarkable story is told by William Hooker in *Curtis's Botanical Magazine*, concerning a specimen collected by David Lyall in British Columbia: "The specimen from which our figure was taken at Kew ... when gathered with a view of being preserved for the Herbarium...was immersed in boiling water on account of its well-known tenacity of life. More than a year and a half after, it notwithstanding showed symptoms of vitality, and produced its beautiful flowers in great perfection in May of the present year [1863], in the Royal Gardens of Kew."

Lewisia rediviva, the state flower of Montana, has one of the widest natural ranges in the genus, from southern California to British Columbia and east into Wyoming and Colorado. It grows in exposed sandy or rocky places and on screes, at altitudes of 1,300–3,000 m (4,265–9,843 feet). The habitats it favours have a dry climate, with a long cool growing season, and often with most of the annual precipitation falling as snow (Davidson, 2000). Growth commences in the cool of autumn, when the tuft of narrow, fleshy leaves emerges. The leaves reach up to 5 cm long but only 2–3 mm wide. The solitary, silky flowers, up to 7.5 cm wide, are held on short stems and are composed of 4–9 papery sepals and 12–20 petals surrounding a bunch of stamens. Pursh described the flower colour as white, but shades of rose or purplish pink are more commonly seen. The flowers open in late spring and after withering they become detached and blow along the ground, dispersing their seeds. The plant dies down for the dry summer.

Lewisia rediviva is a hardy species but it needs to be dry in summer so isn't suitable for growing outside unless summer rainfall is low. The main causes of death in cultivation are aphid infestation or too much moisture when the plant is dormant, leading to rotting of the rootstock. Plants are best repotted annually in late autumn in a lime-free, gritty, loam-based soil mix. As the tuft of leaves grows, the soil should be kept moist. The glorious, satin flowers will appear in late spring, and as they wither, so will the foliage. Watering must be reduced as the leaves die back and little or no water is needed throughout the summer.

Curtis's Botanical Magazine, plate 5395 (1863). Artist: Walter Hood Fitch.

LEFT
Xerophyllum tenax
growing among pines
on Mt Ashland, Oregon.
Photo: Joanne Everson.

BELOW
Calochortus elegans.
Photo: Joanne Everson.

The often deeply buried bulb of a *Calochortus* grows a single, sometimes branched stem and one linear basal leaf. The stem usually carries several smaller, alternate leaves and produces a cyme or loose umbel-like inflorescence of 1–7 flowers. The flowers may be almost flat, campanulate or globe-shaped and are held erect or nodding. The six perianth segments are held in two distinct whorls. The inner whorl is petal-like whereas the outer whorl is sepal-like, but both are often brightly coloured. At the base of the inner segments (petals) is a gland or nectary that is covered with hair-like structures (trichomes). In some species, these trichomes cover the whole of the segment, giving it a bristly or furry appearance. The flowers come in a variety of dazzling colours, from white and yellow to red, pink, purple and orange.

Calochortus elegans is called the cat's ear mariposa because the inside surface and margins of the white petals are covered in long, white and purple trichomes, resembling the hairs of a cat's ear. It belongs to a group of seven species, all with long-bearded petals, that are classified as subsection *Eleganti* of section *Calochortus*. This is one of three sections in the genus, which are distinguished in the classification of Marion Ownby (1940) by characters of the bulb tunic, seed and seed capsule. *Calochortus elegans* is found in Washington, Idaho and Montana, and south through Oregon to northern California, growing on grassy slopes and in open woods.

The other two new genera described by Pursh from the expedition were named after the two leaders. *Clarkia pulchella* is a pink-flowered annual that was collected near Camp Chopunnish in June 1806. Captain Meriweather Lewis is commemorated by the genus *Lewisia* and the remarkable *L. rediviva* or bitterroot. Pursh based his description of *L. rediviva* on a specimen collected by Lewis on 1 July 1806, on the return journey of the expedition. It was found near the junction of the Bitterroot River and Lolo Creek in Montana. Lewis had come across this plant on the outward journey as roots that were eaten by the local Native Americans. The common name of bitterroot refers to the taste of the roots, first sampled by Lewis in August 1805.

Discovering Rocky Mountain alpines

Further expeditions soon followed in the footsteps of Lewis and Clark. Thomas Nuttall left Philadelphia in 1810 and headed west. Later, he joined up with another Englishman, John Bradbury, on the Astorian Expedition, led by Wilson Price Hunt. This expedition aimed to follow the same route as Lewis and Clark, setting up trading posts along the way. Bradbury had been sent to America in 1809 by the Liverpool Philosophical Society and the Liverpool Botanic Garden to collect plants and to find new cotton-growing areas for the Lancashire cotton industry (Coats, 1969). Nuttall and Bradbury left St Louis in March 1811, but as they approached the Rockies, they decided not to cross them with the main expedition party. Bradbury accompanied the many plant specimens he had collected up to that point back downstream, and was later followed by Nuttall who had spent the summer of 1811 botanising around Fort Mandan.

Bradbury attempted to sail for England in 1812 but was prevented by the outbreak of the Anglo-American War. He eventually arrived home in 1817, but in the meantime, the specimens he had sent to William Roscoe at Liverpool Botanic Garden had been unwisely lent to Frederick Pursh. In Bradbury's absence, Pursh published the descriptions of the new plants in a supplement to his *Flora Americae Septentrionalis*. They included *Penstemon eriantherus*, the common wild buckwheat of the Great Plains: *Eriogonum pauciflorum*, and *Castilleja sessiliflora*, the semi-parasitic downy paintbrush.

Nuttall had been able to sail for England from New Orleans before the outbreak of war. As well as sending collections to Barton in Philadelphia, he brought back many specimens and seeds to Britain. Some of these plants went to Liverpool Botanic Garden, others were sold by the Frasers' American Nursery. Nuttall returned to America in 1815, and in 1818 published the two-volume *Genera of North American Plants*, an amazing achievement considering he had only arrived in America ten years before. However, it was 1834 before he made it to the Rocky Mountains, joining Nathaniel Wyeth's expedition to Fort Vancouver.

From 1819 to 1820, Major Stephen H. Long led an expedition from Pittsburgh to the Rocky Mountains, travelling along the Missouri and Platte Rivers to Colorado and then south to New Mexico. In terms of botanical collections, this venture was as successful as the Lewis and Clark expedition, resulting in the description of many new species, including the first true alpines recorded from the Rocky Mountains. The botanist, geologist and surgeon in the team was Edwin James from Vermont, who had studied under the botanist John Torrey at Middlebury College.

Among the new plants was *Aquilegia caerulea*, now the state flower of Colorado. It was found on 11 July 1820, in shady woods of pine and spruce on a divide between the Arkansas and Platte rivers in Colorado. The natural range of this species is now known to extend from south-west Montana to northern Arizona and New Mexico. It grows on rocky slopes and in light woodland, often near streams or in moist soil, at altitudes of 1,800–3,640 m (5,906–11,942 feet). In late spring or summer, the large, erect flowers are held on branched stems above the biternate, long-petioled leaves. Plants can reach over 80 cm tall. The flower is up to 8 cm wide, and the straight or slightly curved spurs usually reach around 5 cm long but can reach up to 7 cm. The spurs and sepals are normally deep to light blue and the petal limb is white or cream. In a revision of the North American species of *Aquilegia*, Edwin Payson (1918) describes a scene in Colorado: "...among the aspens, spruces, and firs, it is not uncommon to see a hillside meadow so completely covered with *A. caerulea* as to hide all other vegetation and to make it seem a fairyland of huge, dancing, blue and white stars".

On 13 July 1820, Edwin James, along with Joseph Verplank and Zachariah Wilson, began the ascent of Pikes Peak (4,302 m; 14,114 feet), now in El Paso County, Colorado. They reached the summit by the following afternoon. This was the first ascent of any of Colorado's 'fourteen-thousand footers' and James was able to make the first collections of true alpine plants above the treeline in the Rocky Mountains, a significant moment in American botanical history (Williams, 2003). Among these were *Primula angustifolia*, *Trifolium nanum*, *Telesonix jamesii* (first described as *Saxifraga jamesii* by Torrey) and, near the zone of perpetual snow, a cushion-forming *Androsace* first named *A. carinata* but now considered a form of the circumpolar *A. chamaejasme*.

Other new finds of the Long expedition were the buckwheats *Eriogonum umbellatum* and *E. jamesii*, both collected in present-day Jefferson County, Colorado. Among the penstemons were *Penstemon glaber* var. *alpina* found in Colorado, *P. jamesii* on the Don Carlos Hills, New Mexico and *P. ambiguus* in Harding County, New Mexico. Many of these new species were described by Torrey in *Annals of the Lyceum of Natural History of New York*, from 1824 to 1827.

The Scotsman Thomas Drummond was assistant to naturalist Dr John Richardson on John Franklin's second expedition across Arctic America from 1825. Drummond was recruited because of his botanical knowledge and was recommended by William Hooker, Professor of Botany at the University of Glasgow. In Saskatchewan in August 1825, the team including Drummond split with the main party, which was headed beyond the Arctic Circle. They travelled instead to the Rocky Mountains, where the prospects for studying the plant life were much greater. Drummond then left the expedition completely in October and spent the next eighteen months exploring and botanising in the Canadian Rockies. He returned to Britain in the autumn of 1827, and from 1828 to 1831 he was Curator of the Belfast Botanic Garden. He then set off for America again and this time slowly made his way to Texas, arriving in 1833. He died in Havana, Cuba in 1835.

Plants that honour Drummond include the annual *Phlox drummondii* from Texas and the alpine *Dryas drummondii*. The latter was found by Richardson in the Rocky Mountains and around Great Slave Lake in Canada's Northwest Territories. It grows across Canada and south to Oregon, on rocky ridges, cliffs, screes and along streams, often above the tree-line (Hitchcock & Cronquist, 1961).

Drummond's and Richardson's collections were used extensively by William Hooker for his *Flora Boreali Americana*, published between 1829 and 1840. In fact, on the title page, the flora is described as: "The botany of the northern parts of British America: compiled principally from the plants collected by Dr Richardson and Mr Drummond on the late northern expeditions, under command of Captain Sir John Franklin, R.N. To which are added (by permission of the Horticultural Society of London) those of Mr Douglas, from north-west America, and of other naturalists".

ABOVE LEFT
Eriogonum umbellatum.

BELOW
Dryas drummondii.

Silene hookeri
Family: Caryophyllaceae

In its best forms, this North American *Silene* is one of the most stunning species in the genus. It was originally described in 1838 by Thomas Nuttall, who named it after William Hooker. The description appeared in the first volume of *A Flora of North America* by John Torrey and Asa Gray and is based on a specimen collected by Dr Gardiner in the "woods of the Wahlamet, Oregon". This plant had three large white flowers, with each petal divided into four diverging lobes.

Thirty years later, Asa Gray (1868) described another species, *Silene bolanderi*, which was collected by Henry Bolander in Long Valley, Plumas County, California. This specimen had pale rose-pink flowers, with petals divided into 4–6 linear to lanceolate lobes. This plate, from *Curtis's Botanical Magazine* of 1873, clearly shows a plant matching the description of *S. bolanderi* but Joseph Hooker published it under the name *S. hookeri*. Hooker was aware of Gray's description of *S. bolanderi* but he treated it as a synonym.

Leroy Abrams (1944) reduced *Silene bolanderi* to a subspecies of *S. hookeri* in his *Illustrated Flora of the Pacific States*. He distinguished *S. hookeri* subsp. *bolanderi* from the typical form by its larger flowers, with petals that are 35–40 mm long and divided into 4–6 narrowly lanceolate lobes. Some modern authorities (e.g. Wilken, 1993) do not recognise *S. hookeri* subsp. *bolanderi* but the name is often encountered, usually in association with forms that have large, pure white, spidery flowers of 7 cm or more wide and deeply divided petals. A plant under this name received a First Class Certificate from the RHS in May 2003.

Silene hookeri is found in northern California and Oregon, growing in open oak woodland, in coniferous forest, on rocky slopes and in grassy areas, at altitudes up to 1,400 m (4,593 feet). It sends up tufts of soft grey-hairy leaves from a thick taproot and reaches 5–20 cm tall. The stems usually hold 3–7 flowers in a cyme, these varying in colour from deep pink to pure white. The petal limbs may be divided into four or six lobes. In some forms, the outer lobes are reduced to teeth on the side of the petal, whereas in others, the petal limbs are divided almost to the base and the lobes are very long and narrow. The white coronal scales at the base of each petal limb are divided into two teeth.

Hooker writes that this species was introduced into cultivation by Bolander. Plants first flowered at Kew in May 1873. This can be a demanding plant to keep alive as it does not like too much moisture in the winter. It can be grown outside in a sunny raised bed or rock garden scree, where the soil is very free-draining; but to protect it from too much moisture when it is dormant, it is safer to keep this species in a well-ventilated cold frame or alpine house. Plants are often short-lived, lasting only three or four years in the garden, so regular propagation is necessary. Cuttings of the young shoots can be taken in spring but plants are easily raised from seed.

Curtis's Botanical Magazine, plate 6051 (1873). Artist: Walter Hood Fitch.

Townsendia is one of the genera described by Hooker in this flora. There are 27 species of these annuals, biennials and perennials, and they are chiefly plants of the Rocky Mountains, from southern Canada, through the western USA to Mexico, with the highest concentration of species in Colorado and Wyoming. Their flower heads are composed of yellow disc florets and bluish, purple, pink or white (rarely yellow) ray florets. The flowerheads are often unusually large for the size of the plant. They may be sessile and surrounded by a rosette of spathulate to linear leaves or held on short, leafy stems. *Townsendia* species differ from those of *Aster* in having a pappus (the specialised calyx of hairs that aid seed dispersal) composed of scales rather than hairs, and in the presence of taproots rather than rhizomes, although one species, *T. formosa* from Arizona and New Mexico, has fibrous roots.

Hooker named the genus after David Townsend of Pennsylvania, who "studied and ably discriminated the numerous Pennsylvanian species of the allied genus *Aster*" (Hooker, 1834). Hooker's species, *Townsendia sericea*, is based on a specimen collected by Richardson during John Franklin's first expedition across Arctic America, from 1819 to 1822. It was collected at Carleton in Saskatchewan, Canada and Richardson originally named it *Aster exscapus*.

In his description of *Townsendia sericea*, Hooker also refers to a specimen collected by Drummond, but this collection and that of Richardson represent two distinct species. Drummond's specimen more closely resembles the description of *T. sericea* but Hooker designated Richardson's specimen as the type. In 1894, Thomas Porter renamed Richardson's plant *T. exscapa*, using Richardson's original specific epithet, with *T. sericea* as a synonym. It wasn't until John Beaman reviewed the genus in 1957 that the plant collected by Drummond was described. Beaman (1957) named this species *T. hookeri* in honour of the founder of the genus.

Hooker was extremely influential in the study of North American botany and was well acquainted with Asa Gray, who later published *A Flora of North America* with John Torrey (2 volumes published between 1838 and 1843). Once Hooker became Director of the Royal Botanic Gardens at Kew in 1841 his energies were diverted away from studying American plants, but his son Joseph became friends with Gray and the two met on several occasions. It is, however, the introduction of plants into cultivation that determines what we grow in our gardens, and only a small proportion of the important botanical collections made by the early expeditions across western North America resulted in the introduction of living alpine plants. It was the Horticultural Society of London, and their collector David Douglas (1799–1834), who introduced many living plants from America to the rest of the world and alpine plants were a significant part of that haul.

FAR LEFT
Townsendia exscapa.

LEFT
Townsendia parryi grows in meadows and screes from south-west Canada to Oregon, Nevada and Utah.

Lewisia rediviva, which survived despite becoming a herbarium specimen, was a rare exception of a living alpine plant introduction from the Lewis and Clark expedition. Nuttall brought back seeds from his travels but these were collected "in the vicinity" of the Rocky Mountains, not from the mountains themselves. It is the Scottish plant hunter David Douglas who is credited with introducing many western North American alpine plants and bulbs into cultivation. It was Douglas who introduced *Calochortus elegans*, collected by him in 1826, and *Erythronium grandiflorum*, gathered the same year. The seeds he collected of *Xerophyllum tenax* flowered in the Horticultural Society's garden in Chiswick, London in 1833. Although most famous for his tree discoveries, in particular the Douglas fir *Pseudotsuga menziesii*, Douglas is also commemorated in the names of several rock garden plants, including *Iris douglasiana*, *Phlox douglasii* and the genus *Douglasia*.

As a young gardener, Douglas came to the attention of William Hooker when he took up a post at the University of Glasgow Botanic Garden in 1820. Hooker recognised Douglas's interest in botany and invited him on treks to study plants in the Scottish Highlands. It was Hooker who recommended Douglas to the Horticultural Society of London when they were looking for a plant collector. As a result, Douglas set sail for New York in 1823. His task on this first trip was to investigate fruit growing and to collect samples of new trees to send back to the Horticultural Society (Mitchell & House, 1999). He was successful, and the Society was delighted with the plants he brought home at the beginning of 1824. By now, however, the western side of North America was generating more interest. Douglas's next expedition was to collect new plants from the far side of the continent.

In July 1824 Douglas set sail again, this time on a voyage to the Columbia Territories, via Brazil, Cape Horn and the Galapagos Islands. He arrived at the mouth of the Columbia River in April 1825 and began plant hunting. He did not return to London until October 1827.

Based at Fort Vancouver, near present-day Portland, Oregon, Douglas explored the Columbia River and its tributaries. He followed the route of Lewis and Clark towards the Rocky Mountains, trekked in the Blue Mountains in present-day north-east Oregon and south-east Washington, and also travelled south of Fort Vancouver, down the Willamette Valley to the Umpqua River. When he could, he sent seeds back to London. In March 1827, Douglas left Fort Vancouver and joined the 'Hudson Bay Express', a team of around 40 men with canoes who were the main communication link and supply chain for the Hudson Bay Company, travelling between the east and west of northern North America. With this band of hardy fur traders and hunters, Douglas crossed the Rocky Mountains in Canada and set off across the continent to Hudson Bay, from where he sailed back to England.

The Horticultural Society was overwhelmed by the quality and quantity of the seed collections sent back by Douglas and he was treated as a hero on his return. However, he soon became unsettled in London and wished to resume plant hunting. He sailed again for the Columbia Territories in October 1829, arriving in June 1830. On this third trip for the Horticultural Society, Douglas spent over a year in California, from the end of 1830 to August 1832. He explored the Canadian Rockies during a failed attempt to reach Alaska and Siberia in 1833 and he also sailed to Hawaii, where he climbed the volcanoes Mauna Kea, Kilauea and Mauna Loa. He was killed tragically early in life, in July 1834, when he fell into a wild bullock pit on the slopes of Mauna Kea.

BELOW
Phlox douglasii 'Rosea' in cultivation.

Both the Horticultural Society and William Hooker benefited from Douglas's collections. Hooker was able to study the specimens while preparing his *Flora Boreali Americana* and the Horticultural Society profited from the seeds he sent back. Seeds of larger trees were distributed to landowners with sizeable estates that could accommodate them, but many of the smaller shrubs, herbaceous plants, alpines and bulbs were tended in the Society's garden in Chiswick. In fact, between his second and third expeditions, Douglas sometimes looked after them himself.

Travelling thousands of miles by foot, horseback and canoe, Douglas often had to survive great hardship on his expeditions, including cold, near-starvation and almost drowning. When, on his third expedition in 1833, his canoe was wrecked on the Fraser River in Canada while attempting to reach Alaska, he lost around 400 plant collections and many personal possessions including his diary. Douglas was swept down the river and trapped in whirlpools for an hour and forty minutes. His determination and ability to survive harsh conditions is demonstrated by him being the first 'outsider' to complete the trans-continental trek with the Hudson Bay Express in 1827 on his second expedition. The results of his endeavours are the seeds of more than 880 species he sent to the Horticultural Society, of which more than 200 were new introductions (Mitchell & House, 1999).

The plant that was to be the first in a new genus named after Douglas was found in April 1827. While in the Rocky Mountains of British Columbia, Douglas noticed patches of brilliant purple flowers, peeping through melting snow. His first thought was that it could be a purple saxifrage, but on closer inspection he realised that it was apparently a new genus. On his return to England, Douglas submitted specimens to Lindley, who used them to describe the genus

THE PACIFIC COAST IRISES

The attractive group of North American irises known as the 'Pacific Coast Irises' are classified in series *Californicae* of the genus *Iris*. They occur throughout the Coast Ranges of Oregon, south to central California and north into Washington, west of an axis between the Cascade Mountains and the Sierra Nevada.

The first of the Pacific Coast Irises to be described was *Iris tenax*, discovered by David Douglas and described in 1829 by John Lindley in the *Botanical Register*. It flowered in the Horticultural Society's garden in 1828. Douglas found this species to be a common plant, growing in dry soils and open woods and flowering in April and May. It has a wide distribution, from south-west Washington southwards to south-west Oregon and northern California. It is common in unshaded or lightly shaded areas on the oak-covered hills of the Williamette and Umpqua Valleys (Lenz, 1958).

Douglas suggested the epithet *tenax* because the Native Americans used the fibres from the leaves to make snares, nets and other items requiring a tough fibre. Lindley (1829) even suggested that it could be grown as a substitute for New Zealand flax (*Phormium tenax*) as it is better suited to the British climate, but the idea never caught on and this species is not common in cultivation.

Lee W. Lenz of the Rancho Santa Ana Botanic Garden recognised 11 species in his revision of series *Californicae*. They grow from tough rhizomes with wiry roots, their leaves are generally slender and the stems are mostly unbranched. The beardless flowers have falls with blades that tend to spread out horizontally rather than turning down (Mathew, 1989b). The best-known species in this group are the low-growing, narrow-leaved *Iris innominata* and the tough, free-flowering *I. douglasiana*. Others include the creamy-yellow, Californian *I. purdyi*, and another pale yellow species, the slightly tender *I. chrysophylla*, from California and Oregon. Blue-purple *I. munzii* is the least hardy.

If planted in a well-drained, lime-free soil, in a sunny or lightly shaded position, the hardy species, especially the vigorous *Iris douglasiana*, will form strong clumps of tough, narrow leaves and will usually flower in late April or May. They can be grown on a rock garden or raised bed, as long as the soil doesn't dry out completely in the summer, although established plants can withstand some drought.

FAR LEFT
Iris purdyi.

LEFT
Iris tenax.

Douglasia. This first species was *D. nivalis*. It was raised from
seed collected by Douglas in California in a glasshouse in
the Horticultural Society's garden, where it flowered in July
1835 and again in April 1836 (Lindley, 1836).

Lindley noted that *Douglasia* was very close to *Androsace*
but differentiated it chiefly on the basis that the capsules
only contained 1–3 seeds, compared to several in *Androsace*.
Other distinguishing characteristics include the longer
corolla tube, extending to twice the length of the calyx, and a
style of variable length. *Douglasia* was described when few
androsaces were known outside Europe and America. In
their monograph of *Androsace*, George Smith and Duncan
Lowe (1997) follow the classification first proposed by Per
Wendelbo in 1961, in which the species of *Douglasia* are
placed in their own section within the genus *Androsace*.
Section *Douglasia* contains nine species, four of which are
found in north-west America; the other five occur in Alaska
and north-east Siberia.

John Lindley wrote up many of Douglas's new
introductions, including *Douglasia nivalis*, in the *Botanical*
Register in the late 1820s and 1830s. There,
you can see illustrations of the plants that flowered from
Douglas's seed in the Society's Chiswick garden and
cultivation details were sometimes provided.

As well as *Calochortus elegans*, Douglas collected several
other mariposa lilies, including *C. macrocarpus* and *C.*
nitidus from the Columbia region and *C. albus*, *C. luteus*,
C. pulchellus, *C. splendens* and *C. venustus* from California.
These bulbs are not usually thought of as garden plants,

needing a dry dormant season to survive, and are better suited to pot cultivation in a cold frame or alpine house. Nevertheless, the Horticultural Society of London seems to have had at least some temporary success in growing them outside. *Calochortus macrocarpus*, collected in dry barren ground near the Great Falls of the Columbia River, flowered in July 1827 in a "shady American border" (Lindley, 1828a). *Calochortus elegans* flowered in 1834 and *C. luteus*, received in 1831, is reported by Lindley (1833) to be hardy and to "succeed perfectly in a north border in sandy peat".

Douglas collected many penstemons on his expeditions, vastly increasing the number of species cultivated in Europe at the time. They included the reddish-purple *Penstemon richardsonii*, which is named after Dr John Richardson. This plant flowered in Chiswick in 1827, where it was "growing freely in peat among American plants" (Lindley, 1827). Other introductions from Washington and Oregon were the blue-flowered *P. ovatus*, the blue to violet *P. venustus* and the sprawling, lilac-purple *P. fruticosus* var. *scouleri*. The last was initially named *P. scouleri* by Douglas in 1829 in honour of Dr Scouler, a companion on his first voyage to the west coast of America. In California, Douglas found the tall, red-flowered *P. centranthifolius* and one of the easier and more long-lived species in cultivation, the blue-flowered *P. heterophyllus*.

Near the Great Falls of the Columbia River, in 1826, Douglas collected a dark purple-flowered plant with slender,

ABOVE LEFT
Olsynium douglasii.

LEFT
Eschscholzia californica
on the Rock Garden at
Kew.

unbranched stems to around 25–30 cm in length and narrow, rush-like leaves. This plant was initially named *Sisyrinchium grandiflorum* by Lindley in 1830. Of its cultivation, Lindley (1830) wrote that "it appears to love a peat border among bushes" and it does do well in moisture-retentive soil alongside a stream or rock garden pool. Lindley's name for this species had already been used for another plant, so in 1833, Albert Dietrich renamed it *S. douglasii* in honour of Douglas. It has since been transferred to *Olsynium* and *O. douglasii* is the only representative of the genus in North America; the other 18 or so species are South American.

Probably the best-known and most widely grown non-woody plant to be introduced into cultivation by Douglas is the Californian poppy, *Eschscholzia californica*. This bright orange- or yellow-flowered species was described in 1820 by Ludolf Karl Chamisso from specimens collected near San Francisco. It was Douglas, however, who in 1826 first sent seeds to Britain, having collected them in the Columbia region on open prairies along the banks of streams. This annual or short-lived perennial poppy occurs from south-west Washington, through western Oregon, California, Arizona and south-west New Mexico to Baja California and Sonora in Mexico. It is the state flower of California and is now seen in many gardens throughout the temperate world, enjoying any warm, sunny position.

Lindley (1828b), unaware of how willing this plant was to embrace cultivation, wrote in some detail about how to grow *Eschscholzia californica* from seed. His advice was to sow it in March, in small pots "placed in a frame, with a little heat. When the young plants have acquired ten or twelve leaves, and not before, they should be turned out of their pots in the open border". He was wise to warn against moving the plants once established as the roots are brittle and easily break but otherwise this species represents few problems in cultivation. Although not particularly invasive, it does spread by freely distributing its seed to create a glorious display in early summer.

Not all American plants are as easy to grow as *Eschscholzia californica*, some need special attention if they are to survive in cultivation. Nevertheless, our desire to grow North American alpines has not dimmed in the 180 years since Douglas began sending seeds to Britain. From the ephemeral woodlanders of the eastern states to the bulbs of California and the tight mats and cushions of the high Rockies, North American alpines can be found for most garden situations. Douglas was the first to collect their seeds in significant numbers but ever since, botanists and horticulturists have been scouring the continent, identifying, cataloguing and learning how to grow the glorious mountain plants of North America.

Bibliography and references

Abrams, L. (1944). *Illustrated Flora of the Pacific States*, 2: 162. Stanford University Press, California.

Bacon, L. J. (1981). Plant Portrait: *Weldenia candida*. *Quart. Bull. Alpine Gard. Soc. Gr. Brit.* 49: 70–73.

Beaman, J. H. (1957). The systematics and evolution of *Townsendia* (Compositae). *Contr. Gray Herb.* 183: 2–151.

Blunt, W. (1976). Poppycock: *Dicentras. The Garden* 101: 432.

Britten, J. (1899). Frasers' Catalogues. *J. Bot.* 37: 481–487.

Case, F. W. & Case, R. B. (1997). *Trilliums*. Timber Press, Portland.

Coats, A. M. (1969). *The Quest for Plants*. Studio Vista, London.

Curtis, W. (1787). *Dodecatheon meadia. Bot. Mag.* 1: t. 12.

Curtis, W. (1788). *Trillium sessile. Bot. Mag.* 2: t. 40.

Davidson, B. L. (2000). *Lewisias*. Timber Press, Portland.

Gerritson, M. E. & Parsons, R. (2007). *Calochortus: Mariposa Lilies and their Relatives*. Timber Press, Portland.

Gray, A. (1868). Characters of new plants of California and elsewhere, principally of those collected by H. N. Bolander in the State Geological Survey. *Proc. Amer. Acad. Arts* 7: 330.

Gray, A. (1878). *Synoptical Flora of North America*, 2(1). Ivison, Blakeman, Taylor & Co., New York.

Hitchcock, C. L. & Cronquist, A. (1961). *Vascular Plants of the Pacific Northwest*, 3: 103–104. University of Washington Press, Seattle.

Hooker, W. J. (1834). *Flora Boreali Americana*, 2: 16. Henry G. Bohn, London.

Humboldt, F. H. A., Bonpland, A. J. A. G. & Kunth, C. S. (1818). *Nov. Gen. Sp.*, 2: 365, t. 173. Paris.

Hunt, D. R. (1994). *Weldenia* Schultes f. In: *Flora Mesoamericana*, vol. 6, ed. G. Davidse *et al.*, p. 159. Universidad Nacional Autónoma de México, México, D. F.

Knuth, R. (1905). *Dodecatheon*. In: *Das Pflanzenreich IV*, part 237, ed. A. Engler, pp. 234–246. Leipzig.

LEFT
Phlox diffusa near Crater Lake in the Oregon Cascades.
Photo: Joanne Everson.

Lenz, L. W. (1958). A revision of the Pacific Coast Irises. *Aliso* 4: 1–72.

Lindley, J. (1827). *Penstemon richardsonii. Bot. Reg.* 13: t. 1121.

Lindley, J. (1828a). *Calochortus macrocarpus. Bot. Reg.* 14: t. 1152.

Lindley, J. (1828b). *Eschscholtzia californica. Bot. Reg.* 14: t. 1168.

Lindley, J. (1829). *Iris tenax. Bot. Reg.* 15: t. 1218.

Lindley, J. (1830). *Sisyrinchium grandiflorum. Bot. Reg.* 16: t. 1364.

Lindley, J. (1833). *Calochortus luteus. Bot. Reg.* 19: t. 1567.

Lindley, J. (1836). *Douglasia nivalis. Bot. Reg.* 22: t. 1886.

Mast, A. R. & Reveal, J. L. (2007). Transfer of *Dodecatheon* to *Primula* (Primulaceae). *Brittonia* 59: 79–82.

Mathew, B. (1989a). *The Genus Lewisia*. Christopher Helm, London.

Mathew, B. (1989b). *The Iris* (second edition). B. T. Batsford Ltd., London.

Mathew, B. (2001). *Erythronium japonicum. Curtis's Bot. Mag.* 18: t. 411.

Matuda, E. (1960). Algunas especies nuevas de la flora Mexicana. *Ann. Inst. Biol. Univ. Mex.* 30: 112.

McGary, J. (ed.) (2001). *Bulbs of North America*. Timber Press, Portland.

Mitchell, A. L. & House, S. (1999). *David Douglas, Explorer and Botanist*. Aurum Press, London.

Mitchem, C. M. (1991). A review of the genus *Dodecatheon. Plantsman* 13: 157–170.

Nicholls, G. (2002). *Alpine Plants of North America*. Timber Press, Portland.

Nold, R. (1999). *Penstemons*. Timber Press, Portland.

Nold, R. (2003). *Columbines: Aquilegia, Paraquilegia and Semiaquilegia*. Timber Press, Portland.

Ownby, M. (1940). A monograph of the genus *Calochortus. Ann. Missouri Bot. Gard.* 27: 499–502.

Payson, E. B. (1918). The North American species of *Aquilegia. Contr. U.S. Natl. Herb.* 20: 151–153.

Phillips, H. W. (2003). *Plants of the Lewis and Clark Expedition*. Mountain Press Publishing Company, Missoula.

Pursh, F. (1814). *Flora Americae Septentrionalis*. White, Cochrane & Co., London.

Reveal, J. L., Moulton, G. E. & Schuyler, A. E. (1999). The Lewis and Clark collections of vascular plants: names, types and comments. *Proc. Acad. Nat. Sci. Philadelphia* 149: 1–64.

Sims, J. (1808). *Fumaria cucullaria. Curtis's Bot. Mag.* 28: t. 1127.

Smith, G. & Lowe, D. (1997). *The Genus Androsace*. AGS Publications Ltd., Pershore.

Stern, K. R. (1961). Revision of *Dicentra. Brittonia* 13: 1–57.

Straw, R. M. (1963). The Penstemons of Mexico. III. Two subsections in the section *Fasciculus. Brittonia* 15: 53–56.

Thompson, H. J. (1953). The biosystematics of *Dodecatheon. Contr. Dudley Herb.* 4: 73–154.

Turrill, W. (1951). *Penstemon kunthii. Curtis's Bot. Mag.* 168: t. 154.

Way, D. & James, P. (1998). *The Gardener's Guide to Growing Penstemons*. David & Charles Publishers, Newton Abbot.

Wherry, E. T. (1955). *The Genus Phlox*. Morris Arboretum, Pennsylvania.

Wilken, D. H. (1993). *Silene*. In: *The Jepson Manual, Higher Plants of California*, ed. J. C. Hickman, p. 491. University of California Press, Berkeley.

Williams, R. L. (2003). *'A Region of Astonishing Beauty': The Botanical Exploration of the Rocky Mountains*. Roberts Rinehart Publishers, Lanham, Maryland.

Oxalis adenophylla

Tecophilaea cyanocrocus

Mutisia decurrens

Caiophora coronata

Calceolaria uniflora

Caribbean

COLOMBIA

Cordillera de Mérida

VENEZUELA

Cordillera Oriental

• Bogota

ECUADOR

Amazon

Lima •

PERU

BRAZIL

The Altiplano

BOLIVIA

Pacific Ocean

Antofagasta •

Atacama Desert

Paposo •

Andes

PARAGUAY

Rio de Janeiro •

La Serena •

Aconcagua

Valparaiso •

Mendoza •

C H I L E

Santiago •

ARGENTINA

Pampas

URUGUAY

• Montevideo

Buenos Aires

Atlantic Ocean

Concepción •

San Carlos deBariloche •

Patagonia

Falkland Islands

N

Tierra del Fuego

Cape Horn

Chapter 5 **South America**

Stretching from the tropical southern coast of the Caribbean at 12° north of the equator, to the icy peaks of Tierra del Fuego and Cape Horn, 55° south of the equator, the continent of South America contains almost every possible climate and habitat, from tropical Amazonian rainforest to frozen tundra. The topography is also extremely varied, with the high, snowy summits of the Andes contrasting with the flat grassland of the Argentinean Pampas. If you are looking for alpine plants in South America, the Andes will dominate your search. This extensive mountain chain stretches the whole length of the continent, from Venezuela in the north to the southern tip of Chile.

Rising to 6,960 m (22,834 ft), Aconcagua is South America's highest mountain. It is north-east of the Chilean capital, Santiago, but just over the border in Argentina. South of Aconcagua, the Andes gradually decrease in altitude towards the islands of Tierra del Fuego, although they still reach over 3,000 m (9,843 feet) in the famous Torres del Paine National Park. With many snow-covered volcanoes, forested slopes and hundreds, if not thousands, of lakes, the scenery of the southern Andes is stunningly beautiful. These slopes are home to the monkey puzzle tree (*Araucaria araucana*) and the southern beech (*Nothofagus*), as well as a range of wonderful alpine plants, many of them little known in cultivation.

To the north of Aconcagua, the Andes chain becomes broader until it splits in two, the western and eastern ranges enclosing the Altiplano, the bleak, desolate high plateau of northern Chile, southern Peru and western Bolivia. These ranges converge again in northern Peru and Ecuador before the Andes split into three main chains in Colombia. The eastern finger, the Cordillera Oriental, pushes into Venezuela, where it becomes the Cordillera de Merida, and still rises to over 5,000 m (16,404 feet) above sea level.

It can be hard to comprehend the extent of this huge mountain range. To help you gain some idea of its length, it may help to imagine it straddling the Northern Hemisphere. Place one end on Scotland and the Andes would stretch south across Europe, over the Mediterranean and into North Africa, across the vast

BELOW
The peaks of the Chilean Andes stretch endlessly into the distance.

Sahara Desert, through jungles of the Congo River and over the equator into Angola.

The western side of the temperate Andes receives plenty of rain, carried by the prevailing westerly winds. These slopes support southern Chile's humid temperate rainforest. In stark contrast, the eastern slopes are in the rain shadow and precipitation levels fall dramatically within a fairly short distance as the mountains give way to the cold, dry, windy steppes of Patagonia in southern Argentina. The Argentinian Lake District is spread along the border with Chile, around the town of San Carlos de Bariloche. Over the border is the corresponding Chilean Lake district, an area of blue waters, lush green fields and forests, and distant snowy volcanic peaks. In these mountains, rainfall is 600–1,000 mm (23.6–39.4 inches) a year but in central Patagonia it can be less than 200 mm (7.9 inches) (Erskine, 2001).

In central and northern Chile, the climate becomes mediterranean before giving way to semi desert and desert. Even here, the dry slopes of the Andes support a range of spring flowers, many of them bulbs, sprouting out of the ground among drought-tolerant cacti and the spiny leaf rosettes of puyas.

The Atacama Desert in northern Chile is a vast expanse of sand, rock and dry mountains, where in some places rain has never been recorded. Although incredibly dry, this desert is not especially hot because the sea along the coast of Chile and Peru is cooled by the Humboldt Current sweeping north from the Antarctic. This cooling of the water also reduces evaporation, so the air coming in off the sea does not hold a lot of moisture, hence the almost non-existent rainfall. When this air hits coastal mountains, however, it is forced up rapidly and any moisture it does hold condenses into low cloud or thick morning fogs, known as 'camanchacas'. The coastal mountains support an unusual flora that may have to survive long periods of drought and intense sunlight, obtaining moisture only from the morning fogs that swirl around the valleys. In Fray Jorge National Park in north-central Chile, almost permanent fogs shroud the coastal mountains and here a relict Valdivian forest survives. Valdivian forest mostly occurs along the coast of temperate central and southern Chile, where rainfall is higher and temperatures cooler. The coastal fogs of Fray Jorge National Park allow the last remaining stands of this vegetation to persist in the north of the country.

High in the Andes on the other side of the equator is another remarkable mountain flora. The alpine moors above the tree line in the high mountains of Venezuela, Colombia and Ecuador are known as the páramo zone of vegetation. Occurring above an altitude of around 3,500 m (11,483 feet) and extending up to the snow line, typically at

5,000 m (16,404 feet), the fragmented páramo ecosystem of the northern Andes is home to isolated plant communities, with high rates of endemism.

As you can imagine, the plants that grow along the Andes are as diverse as the climates, cultures and countries that the range passes through. Some are surprisingly familiar; for example, nasturtium (*Tropaeolum*), *Amaryllis* and many species of *Lobelia* are South American. There are, however, many lesser-known plants from the Andes and the horticultural potential of this flora has yet to be fully realised, especially when compared to the much more widely grown floras of the Alps and Himalaya.

TOP
The Andes near Vicuña, at the northern limit of Chile's Mediterranean zone.

ABOVE
The dry valleys of Fray Jorge National Park in north-central Chile are home to cacti as well as bulbous plants; clouds shroud the coastal hills.

Plant hunters in the Andes

Several famous naturalists explored the South American mainland in the eighteenth and nineteenth centuries, including Joseph Banks, Charles Darwin and Joseph Hooker, but their visits were brief stop-offs as they passed round Cape Horn on their way to the Pacific Ocean. It is the less celebrated naturalists, who spent many years travelling and studying the flora and fauna of this continent, who have made the greatest contribution to our knowledge and understanding of South America's natural history.

Among the earliest European explorers to study the plants of the Andes were the Spanish botanists Hipólito Ruiz and José Pavón, who travelled through Peru and Chile between 1777 and 1788. On their return to Europe, they embarked on a major project to publish a flora of these two countries. As an introduction to this project, they published *Florae Peruviana et Chilensis Prodromus* in 1794, in which they described many of the new genera found on their travels. In *Systema Vegetabilium Florae Peruvianae et Chilensis*, published in 1798, new species were described, and in the same year, the first volume of *Flora Peruvianae et Chilensis* appeared. The second volume was published in 1799 and the third in 1802. The project then ran into financial trouble. The plates for the fourth volume had been prepared and sets were distributed without the text, but it wasn't until 150 years later, in 1955, that the complete volume four was produced. A fifth volume was published in 1959.

Among the hundreds of plants Ruiz and Pavón described in these works were new genera, such as the daisy-like *Chaetanthera*, and *Eccremocarpus*, best known for the orange-flowered, half-hardy climber *E. scaber*, sometimes known as the Chilean glory flower. *Nierembergia* was first described in Ruiz and Pavón's *Prodromus*. This genus is closely related to *Petunia* and in the past has included the plant we now know as *Petunia patagonica*. *Conanthera*, a corm that is endemic to Chile, was also described by Ruiz and Pavón, as was *Fabiana*, which includes the compact, cushion-like *F. nana* from Patagonia and the wonderful Andean shrub *F. imbricata*, whose branches of tiny leaves are festooned with small tubular, pale pink to white flowers in late spring. Ruiz and Pavón described for the first time over 30 species of *Calceolaria*, including the diminutive *C. uniflora*, over 20 species of *Alstroemeria* and four new species of *Mutisia*, a captivating genus of South American, daisy-flowered climbers and scramblers.

Towards the end of the eighteenth century, the Bohemian naturalist Thaddaeus Haenke began his long exploration of the Americas. He eventually settled in Bolivia and never returned to Europe, but at one point it seemed he would never even begin his travels. Two ships, *Descubierta* and

ABOVE
The highest peaks in Fray Jorge National Park support a relict moist forest, living off the coastal fogs.

LEFT
Fabiana imbricata.

Mutisia subulata
Family: Compositae (Asteraceae)

Linnaeus the younger described the genus *Mutisia* in 1781, based on the Colombian *M. clematis*. It was named after the Spanish naturalist and physician, José Celestino Mutis, who studied the flora of Colombia in the late eighteenth and early nineteenth centuries. Around 62 species are now recognised, and most are found in Patagonia and along the length of the Andes, from Colombia to southern Argentina and Chile (Cabrera, 1965).

The flowers of mutisias come in shades of white, pink, violet, orange, yellow or red. They often have large ray florets that are evenly spaced around the outside of the flower head and they emerge from a thick, cylindrical or cone-like involucre. The alternate leaves are either simple or, less frequently, pinnately divided into several leaflets. Their margins are entire, toothed or deeply lobed; and in the climbing species, the leaf tips are elongated into curling tendrils that enable them to cling to other plants.

The glorious, crimson to vermilion, solitary flowers of *Mutisia subulata* are held at the ends of the branching, twining stems. In a revision of the genus, Ángel Cabrera divides *Mutisia* into six sections. *Mutisia subulata* is placed in section *Holophyllum*, along with six other species. These species have narrow, simple leaves with revolute margins and the ray florets are all female. The leaves of *M. subulata* are the narrowest in the genus, often less than 1 mm wide but up to 7 cm long. Their tips form thin, coiling tendrils and, if growing over other plants, this species can climb to 5 m or more. The flower heads have 7–10 ray florets with lanceolate petals that are around 3 cm long and slightly toothed at the tip. They surround the numerous yellow disc florets. The cylindrical involucre is 2.5–3 cm long.

In their description of *Mutisia subulata*, Ruiz and Pavón (1798) state that this species is common on dry, parched land between the coastal port of Talcahuano and the city of Concepción in Central Chile. A year later, the Spanish botanist Antonio José Cavanilles, apparently unaware of the description of *M. subulata*, also described this species and named it *M. inflexa*, using material collected near Valparaiso.

Mutisia subulata occurs in central Chile and the neighbouring Neuquén Province of Argentina. It grows in scrub, on dry, gravelly soils, slopes and screes, from near sea level to over 3,000 m (9,843 feet). At the higher end of the altitudinal range, *M. subulata* var. *rosmarinifolia* is more common. This form has shorter but broader leaves, up to 5 cm

long and 3 mm wide, with reduced or non-existent tendrils. It is found above 1,700 m (5,577 feet) and is a low, compact shrub with flowers the same size as those of var. *subulata*.

George Robinson introduced *Mutisia subulata* into Britain in 1928. As well as seed, Robinson brought back a potted specimen of *M. subulata* from Chile and this was the first plant to flower in this country, in 1929. A second introduction of this species was made in 1928 when seed was sent to William Balfour Gourlay after he had returned from an expedition to Chile with Clarence Elliott. This seed was germinated at the Royal Botanic Garden, Edinburgh (Elliott, 1930).

Curtis's Botanical Magazine, plate 9641 (1936). Artist: Lilian Snelling.

LEFT
Alstroemeria revoluta,
described by Ruiz and
Pavón in 1802.

Atrevida, set sail from Cádiz on 30 July 1789 on an expedition to visit and survey Spanish possessions in the Pacific. The expedition was commanded by the Italian Alessandro Malaspina, and Haenke was among the naturalists recruited for the voyage. Unfortunately, having travelled all the way from Vienna, Haenke arrived in Cádiz just hours after the expedition had left. Undeterred, he found another ship heading for Argentina and set sail on 19 August but his troubles were not over. After crossing the Atlantic, the ship capsized off the coast of present-day Uruguay, near Montevideo, and Haenke lost almost all his possessions, only managing to save a treasured copy of Linnaeus's *Genera Plantarum*. Furthermore, he had missed Malaspina's expedition, which had left Montevideo only a few days previously, on 15 November 1789.

Not surprisingly, these setbacks took their toll on Haenke and he spent a few weeks in Montevideo recovering from illness. He then moved to Buenos Aires and, at last, his luck began to change. In February 1790, Haenke set off over land to meet Malaspina on the west coast of South America. His journey through the Pampas and across the Andes resulted in more than 1,400 plant collections. At last, he met up with Malaspina in April 1790 in Valparaiso, and remained with the expedition for the next two years as it travelled up the coasts of South and North America, across the Pacific to the Philippines, Australia and New Zealand, and back to Chile. Haenke then left the expedition and remained in South America, travelling through Chile and Argentina to Bolivia, where he settled in 1796. He died in 1816.

Haenke described few species himself and much of his material from the Malaspina expedition was lost or damaged on its way to Europe. In 1821, however, seven neglected chests of specimens turned up, having been stored first in Cádiz and then in Hamburg. The National Museum in Prague acquired these chests and most of the plants were determined by the Prague-based botanist Carl Presl, who published over 900 plant names in two volumes of *Reliquiae Haenkeanae* that appeared in six parts between 1825 and 1835. Although 46 new genera were proposed in this work, only 18 are now accepted (Stearn, 1973). Among these is the South American genus *Caiophora* (Loasaceae), which now includes around 60 species. These have characteristically boat-shaped (cymbiform) petals and, like so many members of Loasaceae, a covering of irritating, stinging hairs, which makes them difficult plants to handle. On a more practical level, they are literally a pain to weed around.

One of the most famous early nineteenth century explorers is Alexander von Humboldt, not least because he has an ocean current named after him, as well as a river and a mountain range in Nevada, several plants and, of course, the Humboldt penguin. Humboldt was born in Berlin in 1769 and his expedition to South America with the French botanist Aimé Bonpland took place between 1799 and 1804. Humboldt was an all rounder, studying plants, animals, geography and meteorology. He is even credited with promoting the idea of using guano as a fertiliser. Between 1805 and 1817, Humboldt and Bonpland published two volumes of *Plantae Aequinoctiales*, which covered plants found in Mexico, Cuba, the northern Andes and the Amazon basin. From 1816 to 1825, seven volumes of *Nova Genera et Species Plantarum* were published by Bonpland, Humboldt and the German botanist Carl Sigismund Kunth. Kunth wrote most of the text, using material collected by Humboldt and Bonpland.

The cataloguing of South American plants continued throughout the nineteenth century as the number of European naturalists and plant hunters exploring the continent increased. Naturalists like Haenke and Humboldt studied a range of plants from diverse habitats, but in the mid nineteenth century, the British botanist Hugh Weddell looked specifically at the alpine plants of the Andes. Weddell was the botanist on the French scientific expedition led by Francis de Castelnau that travelled across South America from Peru to Brazil between 1843 and 1847. Weddell's plant descriptions were published between 1855 and 1862 in two volumes of *Chloris Andina*. The first volume was devoted entirely to Compositae (Asteraceae). Here you will find described, for example, 19 species of *Mutisia* and 11 species of the furry-leaved, rosette-forming *Espeletia*, from the high mountains of Venezuela, Colombia and Ecuador. The second volume describes an array of desirable alpines including 34 species of *Calceolaria* and 12 species of *Ourisia*. In both volumes, selected species were illustrated by beautiful and detailed line drawings, presumably created by Weddell himself.

As knowledge of South American plants increased and plants and specimens arrived in Europe, the more commercially minded collectors became interested. The famous Veitch nursery employed plant collectors to bring back new species to England, and their first collector, the Cornishman William Lobb, was sent to Chile in 1840. Lobb's best-known introduction was the monkey puzzle tree, but among the other plants he sent back were *Mutisia decurrens* and several species of *Tropaeolum*. These include the blue-flowered *T. azureum* and the summer-flowering *T. speciosum*, known as the Scottish flame flower because of its bright red flowers and because its preference for cool, moist conditions means it often does better in Scotland than further south in Britain.

Today, when talking about the introduction of alpine plants from the Andes, the name on most people's lips will be John Watson. From September 1971 to April 1972, Watson explored the Andes with Martyn Cheese and Ken Beckett. From this point onwards, he never looked back and began concentrating on plants from the Andes for his seed lists. He is now based in Chile, an hour from Santiago in the foothills of the Andes, where he and his wife Anita explore the mountains, study the plants and collect seed. Watson has done more than any other present-day enthusiast to raise the profile of South American alpines in the Northern Hemisphere. His extensive, detailed and often humorous accounts, particularly in the South American issue of the *AGS Bulletin* in September 1994 and in the *AGS Encyclopaedia of Alpines*, are fascinating to read. Nevertheless, there is still much to learn, especially when it comes to growing many of these plants successfully. Those that are established in cultivation tend to originate from the more southerly latitudes of South America, from the Andes of Chile and Argentina and from the dry steppes of Patagonia.

Plants of Patagonia and the Southern Andes

The Patagonian vegetation is a mixture of tussocks and ground-hugging mats and cushions, often with colourful flowers. These are plants adapted to high winds and often low levels of precipitation. Here, you can find myriad forms of *Nassauvia* (Asteraceae) and *Junellia* (Verbenaceae) or the intriguing *Petunia patagonica* huddling close to the ground. As a compact ground-hugger, *P. patagonica* looks nothing like the familiar, trailing, garish plants of hanging baskets and window boxes, but when it blooms you can immediately see its affinity. The flowers that sprout from this tiny-leaved cushion have a typical petunia shape but are smaller and cream-coloured, with speckles of brownish purple. The species was originally named *Nierembergia patagonica* by Carlo Luigi Spegazzini in 1897.

South America is one of the two main centres of diversity for the genus *Oxalis*, the other being South Africa. The greatest morphological variation and greatest number of taxa are found in South America, where there are around 250 species of *Oxalis* out of a worldwide total of around 500 (de Azkue, 2000).

LEFT
Mutisia decurrens, introduced by William Lobb.

One particular group of desirable Patagonian and Andean *Oxalis* species make fine rock garden or alpine house plants. They are *O. enneaphylla*, *O. adenophylla*, *O. squamoso-radicosa*, *O. laciniata* and *O. loricata*. All five species belong to *Oxalis* section *Palmatifoliae* and grow from scaly, rhizomatous or tuberous rootstocks. Their lobed, palmate leaves are topped by wide flowers in shades of pink, violet or white, often with darker veining.

Oxalis adenophylla differs from the others in having a bulbous, flask-shaped tuber. It occurs in the Andes of central and southern Chile, and from south of Mendoza Province to Santa Cruz in Argentina. It grows up to 2,600 m (8,530 feet) in altitude, sometimes above the tree-line but avoiding the hottest northern aspects, and it flowers on stony slopes as the snow melts (Erskine, 1998). The plant forms an attractive low mound of grey-green leaves, which arise directly from the tuber. The 9–22 heart-shaped leaflets have a prominent central vein, and as the leaves emerge in spring, the leaflets are folded in half along this vein, giving the leaf a pleated appearance. The flowers are usually deep violet-pink to pale rose-pink, with darker veining and a white base, but white-flowered forms also exist. This species was described by the Scotsman John Gillies in 1833, in an article by William Hooker and

George Arnott about the flora of South America and the islands of the Pacific, which appeared in *Hooker's Botanical Miscellany*. Hooker and Arnott (1833) were impressed by the work of Gillies, who lived for a time in Mendoza, Argentina and made several excursions across the Andes to the Pacific, and eastwards across the Pampas to the Atlantic.

Almost as popular in cultivation as *Oxalis adenophylla* is *O. enneaphylla*. In the wild, this species has a more southerly range than *O. adenophylla*. It grows on open heaths and windy steppe in the Falkland Islands, Tierra del Fuego, southern Patagonia and the Andes of southern Argentina. It is known as scurvy grass on the Falkland Islands because early sailors recognised its antiscorbutic properties. In cultivation, summer heat can be a problem so some shade may be needed. Flower colour varies from white to dark pink.

The other three species in the *Oxalis* section *Palmatifoliae* group are less commonly grown. The white- or pink-flowered *O. loricata* comes from the Andes, where it grows usually above the tree line in southern Patagonia and adjacent Chile. *Oxalis laciniata* and *O. squamoso-radicosa* are very similar and often combined under the first name. Growing from thin, pink, scaly rhizomes, they have flowers in white to pink or purple, with darker veining. The leaflets of *O. squamoso-radicosa* have attractively undulate margins. Both species occur in Patagonia, in the Argentinian Province of Santa Cruz, but *O. squamoso-radicosa* also occurs further north in Argentina and in southern Chile.

Hybrids between these species of *Oxalis* are known to occur in cultivation. One of the best known is *Oxalis* 'Ione

ABOVE
Petunia patagonica in cultivation at Kew.

LEFT
Oxalis adenophylla.

Hecker', raised in the mid 1960s by the plantsman E. B. Anderson, one of the founding members of the AGS. It is a cross between *O. laciniata* and *O. enneaphylla* and is easily grown, displaying its wide, blue-violet veined flowers in late spring.

The exposed, windswept, grassy steppes of Patagonia are home to the wonderful *Calceolaria uniflora*. There are around 270 species of *Calceolaria* in South America, and *C. uniflora* is among the most southerly, occurring in the subantarctic regions of southern Patagonia and Tierra del Fuego. The yellow flowers are deep, sagging pouches, mottled with red and held only a few centimetres above a neat mat of rounded green leaves. *Calceolaria fothergillii* is similar but has smaller flowers and a much hairier calyx. There have been reports of *C. fothergillii* occurring in Tierra del Fuego but it is only reliably documented from the Falkland Islands, where it is now considered endemic (Masco *et al.*, 2004). Both species have a characteristic white, fleshy appendage prominently displayed at the mouth of the lower lip of the flower. This appendage is sweet and eaten by birds, which pollinate the flower at the same time by brushing the top of their heads against the anthers located at the tip of the flower.

Calceolaria fothergillii, the lady's slipper, was named after Dr John Fothergill, who introduced it into Britain in 1777, along with several other Falkland Island plants (Curtis, 1796). The Falkland Islands are about 480 km north-east of Tierra del Fuego in the south-west Atlantic. They have a cool temperate climate, dominated by westerly winds and with a mean annual temperature of 5.6 °C. When Joseph Hooker visited the islands in 1842, during the Antarctic Voyage of

HMS *Erebus* and HMS *Terror* (see chapter on 'Australia and New Zealand'), he disparagingly described them as "amongst the bleakest spots on the globe" (Hooker, J. D., 1885). He found only three plants he considered of horticultural merit: *Calceolaria fothergillii*, *Oxalis enneaphylla* and *Olsynium filifolium*.

Olsynium filifolium was originally named *Sisyrinchium filifolium* by French botanist Charles Gaudichaud-Beaupré, who visited the Falkland Islands in 1820. Gaudichaud nearly lost his herbarium specimens when the ship he was on, the *Uranie*, was wrecked off the coast

Unique plant communities

Species from the temperate Andes of southern Chile and Argentina provide most of the South American alpines that are grown in gardens and alpine houses. However, some extraordinary and fascinating plant communities have evolved in the mountains of South America, and they include some species that have become established in cultivation despite being adapted to survive unusual and extreme conditions. These plants live in fog-zones along the coast or in high equatorial mountains.

The high alpine moors of Venezuela, Colombia and Ecuador, known as the páramo, are home to plants, such as the furry-leaved espeletias, that have to cope with low, sometimes sub-zero temperatures at night and intense sunlight, drying winds and soaring temperatures during the day. They obtain much of their moisture from dense fogs, caused by the dramatic temperature changes that occur at such high altitudes near the equator.

LEFT
A white form of *Olsynium junceum* on the Rock Garden at Kew.

BELOW
The slopes of the coastal mountains near Paposo, Chile, are home to the unique fog-zone vegetation.

of the Falkland Islands on 14 February 1820. He managed to salvage part of his collection and produced the first flora of the islands on his return to France. He described *S. filifolium* in 1825.

Olsynium (Iridaceae) is a genus of around 18 species from South America and one from North America. It was established in 1836 by Constantine Rafinesque of Philadelphia, based on *O. grandiflorum*, which is now treated as a synonym of the North American *O. douglasii*. This genus was not universally accepted, but in a recent study (Goldblatt *et al.*, 1990), *Olsynium* was revived and now includes plants previously classified in the genera *Phaiophleps*, *Chamelum* and *Ona*, as well as some of the species formerly in *Sisyrinchium*.

General characteristics used to separate *Olsynium* from *Sisyrinchium* include the thickened roots and rush-like leaves that are circular (terete) or elliptic in cross-section. They also differ in their leafless, unbranched flower stems and in having brownish, angular seeds as opposed to blackish, globose seeds.

Olsynium filifolium has 2–8 creamy-white flowers with purplish veins and a greenish or yellowish base. The flowers are around 2.5 cm across and held in a cluster at the end of the terete stem. The thin leaves are elliptic in section and up to 32 cm long. This species is found in Tierra del Fuego as well as the Falkland Islands. *Olsynium junceum*, from mainland temperate South America is very similar but with terete leaves and slightly smaller flowers that are pink to white, with a yellow throat.

Espeletia schultzii
Family: Compositae (Asteraceae)

The genus *Espeletia* is found in the mountains of Venezuela, Colombia and northern Ecuador. These plants generally occur at altitudes above 2,800 m (9,186 feet), and can be the dominant form of vegetation in the alpine moors above the tree-line, known as the páramo zone of vegetation. In these habitats, temperatures can fall to near or below freezing at night and fog or dense mist is not uncommon. Also, they are growing just north of the equator, exposed to intense sunlight and high temperatures during the day. None of the species is widespread, but each area of páramo is home to one or more endemics, each isolated by the surrounding lower mountains (Smith & Koch, 1935).

The genus *Espeletia* is in need of revision, but in the *Botanical Magazine*, Kew botanist Dr Nicholas Hind states that in its broadest sense *Espeletia* contains over 100 species, which are normally divided into two groups. The first group contains shrubby or tree-like plants whereas the second contains the rosulate species. *Espeletia schultzii* is in the latter group. *Espeletia* are fascinating plants, forming wide rosettes of long, furry leaves, often at the top of a stout trunk. The pappus that many plants in the Compositae have to aid seed dispersal is absent. This limits their ability to migrate, so individual populations spread slowly.

The genus *Espeletia* was named by José Celestino Mutis and described in 1809 by Alexander von Humboldt and Aimé Bonpland in *Plantae Aequinoctiales*. Mutis found the type species, *E. grandiflora*, near Bogota, in present-day Colombia (Humboldt & Bonpland, 1809). He named the genus after Don José de Espeleta, who was viceroy of New Granada, an area now covered by Colombia, Venezuela, Ecuador, and Panama. Humboldt and Bonpland added a further two species that they had discovered on their travels: *E. argentea* and *E. corymbosa*.

Espeletia schulztii was described in 1856 by the British botanist Hugh Weddell in *Chloris Andina*, an account of South American mountain plants. Weddell states that this species is common in the high-altitude páramo vegetation of the Cordillera of Mérida, in present-day Venezuela. It also occurs in the Venezuelan state of Trujillo and grows at altitudes of 3,000–4,700 m (9,843–15,420 feet). This species forms wide rosettes of many leaves, on a short or subterranean trunk that is clothed with old leaf bases. The narrow, silvery leaves reach 45 cm long and are covered in a dense layer of grey-white, woolly hairs. These hairs reflect some of the intense sunlight that the plants are exposed to high up in the equatorial mountains and

may also trap a warm layer of air to help them survive freezing night-time temperatures. The densely hairy, axillary flower stems can reach more than 50 cm in height, and each branch holds a few erect to nodding flower heads. The flower head is around 3.5 cm wide or more, with numerous yellow ray florets surrounding the disc florets.

Curtis's Botanical Magazine, plate 158 (1990). Artist: Ann Farrer.

A unique range of plants is also found in isolated communities on the flanks of the otherwise dry coastal mountains of northern Chile and southern Peru. Driving along the Pan-American Highway through the Atacama desert, you can travel for hundreds of miles seeing hardly a single plant, not even a scrubby bush by the roadside. But head for the hills along the coast and the situation changes. Cacti begin to appear, and in spring you may even detect a slight green tinge on the hillsides. This is the fog-zone vegetation, which survives almost solely on moisture from the fogs that envelop the lower slopes. These hills, called Lomas formations, host species that have to survive long periods with little or no water, often as underground bulbs or tubers. When moisture is available, usually in spring, they grow and flower, bringing the dry slopes alive with their greenery. Delicate climbers and soft-leaved herbaceous perennials grow alongside tough, spiny cacti.

The small village of Paposo lies on the coast of Chile, 50 km (31 miles) north of Taltal and 150 km (93 miles) south of Antofagasta. Behind this humble collection of small dwellings and government offices, the mountains rise dramatically, cut by steep-sided valleys that catch the morning fog. The richest fog-zone flora in northern Chile has developed here, starting at around 300 m (980 feet) above sea level and continuing up to around 900 m (2,950 feet). Above and below this, cacti are dominant, particularly the round barrels of *Copiapoa cinerea*, *C.*

eremophila and the upright columns of *Eulychnia iquiquensis*. Within the fog zone, the flora is much more diverse. Plants obtain water from the fogs, known as camanchacas, but in winter, meltwater coming down from the high mountains, sometimes as a short-lived but raging torrent, provides a boost, resulting in a rich display of spring flowers and surprisingly lush growth in the gorges and narrow valleys.

A spring hike in these remote valleys gives you an idea of the conditions these plants have to deal with. The silence is only punctuated by sporadic bird song and the sound of your feet on the rocks and gravel. The morning mist hangs around for a while, the tiny droplets drifting in the still air and leaving a film of life-giving moisture on everything they touch. The mist soon lifts, and as the clouds part, the intense sun beats down from a clear blue sky. The narrow, twisting valleys, with their steep, rocky sides continually reveal new plants as you climb.

The remarkable flora of these isolated hills has caught the attention of keen naturalists and scientists. Occasional groups are taken through the valleys behind Paposo in spring. Checklists of the plants growing here have been compiled, but there are so many of these valleys along the coast between Taltal and Antofagasta that you can't help thinking that some of them may never be properly explored, and these Lomas formations extend even further north into Peru.

THE LION'S PAW:
Leontochir ovallei

In the same family as *Alstroemeria* is a remarkable plant that is only known from the coastal mountains of Chile, particularly those in the Parque Nacional Lanos de Challe, northwest of Vallenar at the southern end of the Atacama. Known as 'mano de leon' or lion's paw, *Leontochir ovallei* is a scrambling perennial. It grows from a thin, delicate rhizome that links together rounded swollen roots. The long stems, of up to 1 m in length, are densely clothed with elliptic to lanceolate, slightly twisted, sessile leaves. The end portion of the stem is leafless and thickened, supporting an umbel-like cyme of bright red flowers. Each flower is composed of six free, clawed, leathery tepals.

The common name seems to come from the shape of the inflorescence, with the flowers representing the pads of a lions foot (Wilkin, 1997). This plant was described by Rudolph Amando Philippi in 1873. It is the only species in the genus, although yellow forms have recently been found in the wild and named var. *luteus* (Muñoz Schick, 2000). The specific name commemorates Javier Ovalle, who collected the type specimen in December 1866. It is rare in cultivation and requires a light, airy, frost-free situation. Growth begins in autumn and flowering is in late spring, after which the plant dies down. When repotting in late summer, it is essential to keep the delicate rhizomes that link the heavy swollen roots intact, otherwise new shoots will not form.

Leontochir ovallei
flowering in the Davies
Alpine House at Kew.

Some of the species that are known from the valleys behind Paposo are endemic to the region, such as the rare *Dalea azurea*, a small, blue-flowered, brittle shrubby legume with less than 200 known individuals in the wild. Shrubs, such as *Balbisia peduncularis*, *Oxalis gigantea* and *Euphorbia lactiflua* join the cacti on the slopes. Large, floppy rosettes of blue-grey leaves give rise to the magenta flowers of *Calandrinia cachinalensis*, and the yellow, orange or occasionally reddish trumpets of *Argylia radiata* are held above loose mounds of divided foliage.

On a more 'alpine' scale are the mats of *Cruckshanksia pumila*. The *Cruckshanksia* genus (Rubiaceae) is named after Alexander Cruckshanks, an English naturalist who lived in Chile in the first half of the nineteenth century and sent collections to William Hooker. Looking like a flattened euphorbia, this fascinating species spreads out over the gravel of the valley floor. It is an annual, and has acid yellow or sometimes creamy-white bracts that surround the insignificant flowers. Another annual, *Chaetanthera glabrata*, produces yellow, daisy-like flowers, only a couple of centimetres across, close to the ground, their outer petals backed with coppery-red. The neatly arranged, small rounded leaves are blue-green with faint purple margins.

Violas also grow here, but not the kind you normally see. These form compact, flattened rosettes of tightly packed leaves and are known as rosulate violas. They belong to *Viola* section *Andinium*, and many species are distributed along the Andes of Chile and Argentina, in Patagonia, and further north in Peru and Bolivia and even Ecuador. Their form may not be anything like the violets you are used to, looking more like sempervivums, but when they flower, their affinity is immediately obvious. From between the tiny leaves, the typical *Viola* blooms emerge, often in a ring around the plant like a jewelled necklace.

Not surprisingly, these violas have become extremely desirable plants to grow but they represent a challenge to cultivation, being used to poor, stony soil on dry, windswept ridges and slopes, and resenting any root disturbance. Some success has been achieved by sowing seed sparingly in long pots and not pricking out the seedlings. Left alone to send down their long roots and watered carefully to avoid waterlogging the soil in the oversized pots, they can be coaxed into flower.

With a long, dry summer to survive, it is not surprising that many of the plants found in these Lomas formations are geophytes, growing from bulbs, corms or tubers. The magenta-pink *Rhodophiala laeta* can be found near Paposo, growing from bulbs buried deep in the pure sand on the low slopes not far from the coast. Higher up the valleys, it occupies ledges and rocky hillsides. Up to six glorious trumpet blooms are held on a stem that ranges from 10–30 cm tall.

ABOVE
The rare *Dalea azurea*.

LEFT
The orange flowers of *Argylia radiata* among the barrel-shaped cactus *Copiapoa eremophila*.

The fog zone vegetation of northern Chile

ABOVE LEFT
The flora near Paposo is an unusual mixture of plants, including cacti, drought-tolerant shrubs and bulbs.

ABOVE RIGHT
Chaetanthera glabrata.

FAR LEFT
The annual *Viola litoralis* is only 3–4 cm across and its minute cream flowers peer from between the dark grey-green leaves.

LEFT
Cruckshanksia pumila.

Rhodophiala is a genus of bulbous perennials that, although not confined to Chile, is characteristic of the flora of this country. There are around 35 species, possibly more (Watson, 1994), from Chile, Argentina, Paraguay, Uruguay and Brazil. Around 18 species are found in Chile. *Rhodophiala* is in Amaryllidaceae and closely related to, and sometimes included within, the genus *Hippeastrum*. Two or more trumpet-shaped flowers, comprising six flaring, slightly reflexed tepals surrounding the same number of elegantly curving stamens, are held at the top of a sturdy, leafless stem. The narrow, strap-like leaves usually appear as the flowers fade.

Although not commonly grown, a few species have a tentative hold in cultivation. The winter-growing *Rhodophiala bifida* (syn. *Hippeastrum bifidum*), from northern Argentina and Uruguay, is a reasonably easy plant to try, flowering in late summer with scarlet to deep red blooms. Introduced around 1825, it was originally called *Habranthus bifidus*, the specific epithet referring to the two-cleft spathe (Herbert, 1825). In fact, this splitting of the spathe is now used to separate *Rhodophiala* from *Habranthus*. In the latter, the spathe forms a tube at the base of the pedicel of the solitary flower. Hardy enough to be grown outside in Britain, *R. bifida* just needs a sunny position and fairly free-draining soil but not one that is baked dry in summer. The leaves appear after flowering and remain until late spring.

Other species in cultivation include the bright pinkish red *Rhodophiala advena*, also a winter grower, which occurs in central and southern Chile, from Valparaiso and Santiago to the Araucanía region. This species was first introduced into Britain in 1808, as *Amaryllis advena*, and flowered in the Vineyard Nursery of James Lee and Lewis Kennedy in Hammersmith, London (Ker Gawler, 1808). The pale yellow-flowered *R. elwesii* is a winter grower from the Andes of southern Argentina and Chile. It was discovered by Henry Elwes in 1902, near Lake Nahuel Huapi in the Argentinian Lake District, and flowered in his garden at Colesborne the following year (Prain, 1915).

Species from high altitudes, such as the beautiful white- or pink-flowered *Rhodophiala rhodolirion*, which grows at elevations of up to 3,500 m (11,483 feet), may spend the winter under snow. This species comes from the mountains above Santiago, south to Araucanía, and over the border into Argentina. In cultivation, it should be kept on the dry side in winter and have a wet spring to simulate its more alpine habitat.

From the north of Chile come some desert species, such as *Rhodophiala laeta* and the golden-yellow *R. bagnoldii*, which grows in the sands of the southern Atacama desert. In cultivation, these species will probably need some protection from frost, in a cold frame or alpine house. Many South American amaryllids have a tendency to flower erratically or not at all in

FAR LEFT
Rhodophiala bifida in cultivation.

LEFT
Rhodophiala laeta growing amongst cacti near Paposo.

The genus *Tropaeolum*

Tropaeolum is mostly a genus of climbing annuals and tuberous perennials. Linnaeus described three species in 1753, all of them annuals. Of these, *T. majus* (the common nasturtium or Indian cress) and *T. minus* were already well-established in cultivation, the latter since the sixteenth century. The third species, *T. peregrinum*, the canary creeper, was introduced in the late eighteenth century. In a recent revision of the genus, the Swedish botanists Benkt Sparre and Lennart Andersson recognised 86 species, all from Central and South America (Sparre & Andersson, 1991).

Characteristics of the genus include alternate leaves that generally have long, twining petioles, with which they attach themselves to other plants as they climb, although a few species, such as *Tropaeolum polyphyllum*, are prostrate, scrambling herbs. The leaf blades are rounded, angled or lobed and often deeply dissected. Most species have solitary flowers that arise from the leaf axils and are held on pendant stalks. The calyx forms a spur of variable length behind the flower and there are normally five petals. The upper two petals differ in shape from the lower three, although in some species they are almost equal. The fruit is divided into three, one-seeded carpels.

Sparre and Andersson divided *Tropaeolum* into ten sections. Most of the cultivated species are in section *Chilensia*, which contains 18 tuberous perennials, including *T. polyphyllum*, *T. speciosum*, *T. brachyceras*, *T. ciliatum*, *T. tricolor* and *T. azureum*.

Tropaeolum speciosum, known as the Scottish flame flower, is the most widely cultivated of the tuberous species. If this Chilean climber is given the cool, moist conditions it prefers, a profusion of scarlet flowers will be draped over shrubs and small trees in summer. It can be hard to establish, but once settled in it will become quite vigorous and can even become a nuisance.

Another hardy species is *Tropaeolum polyphyllum*. The blue-grey stem and leaves of this species trail over the ground and it is best grown on a rock garden or raised bed, in free-draining soil. In late spring, it produces large, yellow flowers towards the stem tip. The tubers can delve down a long way into the soil as this species becomes established, and it is not unusual to find them buried more than a metre deep.

Several species, including *Tropaeolum speciosum* and *T. polyphyllum*, were collected by William Lobb in the 1840s. Lobb was the first plant collector employed by the Veitch Nursery and one of his most striking collections was *T. azureum*. This species is easily distinguished from the others by the colour of

its flowers, which are violet-blue. It gained Veitch a silver medal at a meeting of the London Horticultural Society held on 4 October 1842, only two months after the tubers arrived in this country. The autumn flowering of this normally spring-flowering species was a result of the tubers arriving from Chile just after the southern hemisphere winter.

ABOVE
Tropaeolum speciosum, the Scottish flame flower, growing in a woodland garden.

ABOVE
Tropaeolum azureum.

TOP LEFT
Tropaeolum tricolor
growing through cacti
near Paposo, Chile.

LEFT
Tropaeolum polyphyllum.

In the wild, *Tropaeolum azureum* grows on dry hillsides and in scrub, up to 1,600 m (5,249 feet), in central Chile. It was named by the Italian botanist Carlo Guiseppi Bertero, who collected it near Valparaiso, and was formally described in 1832 by another Italian, Luigi Colla. In May 1995, this species received an Award of Merit from the RHS and in April 2000 it gained a First Class Certificate. Both award plants were grown by Ian and Margaret Young of Aberdeen.

cultivation. Finding the correct watering regime is important, but the plants do not always behave how you want them to and you may have to force them into dormancy. In the case of these desert species, a sandy, free-draining soil and a good summer baking might make them feel more at home, followed by a good dose of water in winter to get them started into growth.

The genus *Tropaeolum* includes several tuberous species. For example, the climbing *T. tricolor* grows from a pinkish-red, rounded tuber. Its slender, leafy stems scramble through shrubs and cacti in the fog zone of the coastal mountains of Chile. The small, tubular, daintily spurred flowers are orange-red and held on thin pedicels along the stem. They are pollinated by humming birds. After flowering and setting seed, the stems die back and the plant retreats underground for the dry summer. The genus *Tropaeolum* contains many of these exquisite perennial species, apart from the annual nasturtium, that deserve to be grown on a rock garden, climbing through shrubs or in pots in an alpine house.

The endemic bulbs of Chile

As in other regions with mild, wet winters and long, dry summers, such as California and the Mediterranean Basin, the central zone of Chile has a flora rich in bulbous plants. This mediterranean climate zone is found between the latitudes of 27°S and 42°S and covers roughly one-third of the length of Chile. In the northern part of this region, around the coastal resort of La Serena, the mediterranean climate begins to give way to semi-desert conditions that, nevertheless, still support many bulbs and corms. It is remarkable how little water some of these plants appear to need to grow and flower, and you can still find bulbs poking out of the sand right into the Atacama Desert.

Chile's bulb flora is very rich, and many of the species are endemic to this region. The Andes to the east and the Atacama Desert to the north have combined to ensure that many Chilean bulbous plants have evolved separately from their close relatives and are prevented from spreading further by these formidable geographical barriers. Of these endemic bulbs, the most colourful and showy are found in the genus *Leucocoryne*. They, and *L. ixioides* in particular, were christened 'Glory of the Sun' by the nurseryman Clarence Elliot in the late 1920s. In Chile, they are known as 'Huilli'.

Leucocoryne (Alliaceae) contains around a dozen or more species, although their taxonomy is far from settled. In a series of papers published in his own leaflet periodical, *Onira*, between 2000 and 2005, the South American botanist Pierfelice Ravenna described nearly 30 new species. It seems unlikely that most of these names will be accepted by the botanical or horticultural community, but Ravenna's work does demonstrate the variability that is found in the genus.

The genus *Leucocoryne* dates from 1830, when it was established by John Lindley in the *Botanical Register* (t. 1293). Lindley described three species, *L. odorata*, *L. alliacea* and *L. ixioides*. The first was found in November 1825 on a mountainside near Valparaiso by James McRay, who was working for the Horticultural Society of London. This collection was sent to England, where it flowered in the summer of 1826. The latter two species were based on plants previously classified as species of *Brodiaea*, which is now treated solely as a western North American genus (and has been placed in a different family, Themidaceae). *Brodiaea ixioides* was described by John Sims in *Curtis's Botanical Magazine* (t. 2382) in 1823 from a plant grown by John Walker of Southgate, in north London; unfortunately the origin of this plant is not stated. *Brodiaea alliacea* was found by the British botanist John Miers, who travelled in South America in the early nineteenth century. He mentions it in his *Travels in Chili and La Plata* (Miers, 1826).

LEFT
Leucocoryne narcissoides, growing near Paposo, northern Chile.

LEFT
Leucocoryne purpurea for sale in a native plant nursery near Santiago. The price is in Chilean Pesos, not dollars!

Leucocoryne plants produce a few long, narrow, linear leaves in late autumn and the flowers open in late spring, usually in late April and May, just before the plants die down for the summer. These flowers are held in an umbel of up to 12 blooms, 20–60 cm above ground on a thin, leafless stem. The umbel is subtended by two long papery bracts. The six tepals of the flower are fused to form a tube that opens out at the end to form a star-like bloom that can reach 4–5 cm across. There are three fertile stamens and three sterile staminodes, which can be quite swollen and club-like. For example, in *L. coquimbensis*, the staminodes are bright yellow and protrude from the white throat of the otherwise purplish-blue flower. Some species have appendages on the tepals, as in *L. narcissoides*, which has white tepals that have prominent, fleshy, orange-yellow appendages around the mouth of the flower that resemble the corona of a *Narcissus*. Flower colour in the genus ranges from white to purple and blue. One of the most distinctive species is *L. purpurea*, which has violet-purple flowers that have a deep maroon-purple centre.

A few species of *Leucocoryne* are in general cultivation; *L. purpurea* has received the RHS Award of Garden Merit. They are usually grown under glass to protect them from freezing in winter and excess rainfall in summer. Some appear to be fairly resilient to frost and are worth trying in the open in a sheltered, sunny position. These include *L. ixioides* and *L.*

coquimbensis, which both originate from the middle and southern parts of the range of the genus. Species from the north of the range, such as *L. macropetala* and *L. narcissoides*, will be less easy to please in the open because they are used to minimal rainfall and are often found growing directly out of the sand of the desert.

The family Alliaceae is divided into three subfamilies (Fay & Chase, 1996) and subfamily Gilliesioideae contains all eleven of the South American genera in the family. *Leucocoryne* belongs in tribe Ipheieae, along with *Ipheion*, *Tristagma* and *Nothoscordum*; all these have more or less radially symmetrical (actinomorphic) flowers. The species in tribe Gilliesieae have flowers that exhibit bilateral symmetry (zygomorphism). These are placed in four genera, all of which are endemic to Chile: *Gethyum*, *Gilliesia*, *Miersia* and *Solaria*. Of the plants in this tribe, the most unusual flowers belong to *Gilliesia* as each one bears a remarkable resemblance to an insect. If these flowers have evolved to mimic an insect in order to attract other insects to carry out pollination, they are the only non-orchid monocots to demonstrate sexual deceit as part of the pollination mechanism (Rudall *et al.*, 2002).

ABOVE
Leucocoryne coquimbensis in cultivation.

LEFT
Leucocoryne macropetala growing in sand near the town of Vallenar.

FAR LEFT
*Gethyum
atropurpureum.*

LEFT
The flower of *Gilliesia
graminea.*

BELOW
Miersia chilensis.

The genus *Gilliesia* was named by John Lindley in the *Botanical Register* (t. 992) in 1826 in honour of John Gillies. Lindley described *G. graminea*, probably the only species in cultivation. Like *Leucocoryne odorata*, this species was discovered near Valparaiso by James McRay. It first flowered in England in September 1825, a few weeks after its arrival. It is not an especially attractive plant, with long, narrow, untidy leaves that hang down from the pot, and small, insignificant flowers. It can, however, be extremely floriferous and the intriguing, fly-like blooms are certainly interesting to look at. Grown under frost-free glass, it will flower in late winter. The genus *Miersia*, with two species, *M. chilensis* and *M. cornuta*, was also named by Lindley, at the same time and in the same publication (sub t. 992) as *Gilliesia*. This genus honours John Miers. *Miersia chilensis* grows well under frost-free glass and flowers in January in Britain. It is similar to *G. graminea* in general appearance but is much smaller, shorter and less ungainly, reaching only 10–15 cm tall. The tiny flowers are zygomorphic but do not have the same striking resemblance to an insect seen in *Gilliesia*. Recently, a new colour form has been described, *M. chilensis* var. *bicolor*. Instead of having the typically green

Tecophilaea cyanocrocus
Family: Tecophilaeaceae

Every once in a while, a species is introduced into cultivation that captures the public's imagination and subsequently spreads rapidly throughout the horticultural world. For species with a limited natural range, this new-found attention can become a hazard, especially when combined with other threats, such as grazing pressure. Plants are removed from their natural habitat at such a rate that wild populations cannot recover. Just such a fate was alleged to have befallen the beautiful Chilean blue crocus, *Tecophilaea cyanocrocus*.

The stunning, deep blue flowers of this species ensured that it became highly sought after when it was first introduced in the second half of the nineteenth century. The subsequent decline of this bulb in the wild may be due to a number of factors apart from over-collection. The fact that the corms are edible has been cited as one reason for its apparent disappearance. It is only in the past few years that this rare species has been rediscovered in the wild, in the mountains just south of Santiago. Here, at just over 2,000 m (6,562 feet) altitude, a small population was found in the southern hemisphere spring of 2001 (Eyzaguirre & Garcia de la Huerta, 2002).

The German nurserymen Haage and Schmidt were the first to flower this species in cultivation in 1872. Further plants were introduced in the 1880s and 1890s, notably by Max Leichtlin of Baden-Baden in Germany, and it received a First Class Certificate from the RHS in 1882. By the 1930s, however, *Tecophilaea cyanocrocus* was becoming hard to find in the wild. In *Hardy Bulbs*, Charles Grey (1938) wrote: "A nurseryman in Valparaiso who knew its habitat well wrote to me three or four years ago that cattle were on the uplands just before the flowers appeared and that there was not a trace of it to be found."

In cultivation, this plant is surviving well and corms can be purchased, at a price, from specialist bulb nurseries. It can be grown in the open garden in mild or sheltered areas, in a sunny position and in rich, well-drained soil, but this is generally a bulb for a sunny, well-ventilated cold frame or alpine house. Plenty of moisture should be available in the late winter and spring, but as the leaves die down, watering should be reduced and the soil kept barely moist in summer.

The common name comes from the solitary crocus-like flowers, which can reach 4–5 cm across and are held on 7–10 cm long stems in early spring. The form named 'Violacea' has flowers of a dull violet-purple. In the flowers of *Tecophilaea cyanocrocus* 'Leichtlinii', named after Max Leichtlin (who introduced it), the white of the throat spreads along the tepals.

The first species of *Tecophilaea* to be described, in 1836, was *T. violiflora* from Chile and Peru. The Italian Carlo Guiseppi Bertero named the genus after Tecophila Billotti, the daughter of fellow botanist Luigi Colla (Grey, 1938). *Tecophilaea cyanocrocus*, the only other species in the genus, was collected and described by the German botanist Friedrich Leybold in 1862; he found it at around 3,000 m (9,843 m) in the Andes, at Paso de la Dehesa, north of Santiago.

Curtis's Botanical Magazine, plate 8987 (1923). Artist: Lilian Snelling.

tepals, the tepals are dark purple with pale, whitish, hyaline margins. This form was found at an altitude of 400 m (1,312 feet) in the Metropolitan region of central Chile, at Laguna de Aculeo.

One of the most stunning Chilean endemic geophytes is a corm, *Tecophilaea cyanocrocus*, in the family Tecophilaeaceae. This very rare species is well-known in cultivation but another Chilean endemic genus in this family, *Conanthera*, is less familiar. Hipólito Ruiz and José Pavón first described this genus and the species *C. bifolia* in the third volume of *Flora Peruvianae et Chilensis*, published in 1802. There are perhaps a dozen species but, like *Leucocoryne*, a lot more fieldwork needs to be done before the genus is fully understood.

No species of *Conanthera* is commonly grown, but the one you are most likely to come across is *C. campanulata*. This species has an extensive range in the wild, stretching from the coast of the Atacama Desert to south of Santiago, and has been the one most frequently collected. This corm is not difficult to grow in a cold frame or alpine house. As with many of these Chilean bulbs and corms, the leaves are long and narrow, and grow throughout the winter. These leaves can become untidy, but *C. campanulata* flowers at the end of its growing season, in early summer, as the leaves are dying back. The inflorescence has thin wiry stems and can reach 60 cm tall, holding over 90 pendant flowers that vary from 1–3 cm across and are bell-shaped with flared perianth lobes. They are violet-purple but with a few white hairs along the margin of the lobes near the mouth of the flower.

Conanthera trimaculata and C. bifolia are also tall species, reaching 30 cm or more. The former has flowers up to 4.5 cm across and with more flared and elongated lobes than C. campanulata. These lobes are violet purple, darker on the outside, and the inner lobes have a dark purple blotch near their base. Conanthera bifolia has distinctive reflexed tepals with dark spots near the base of each strap-like lobe and a long pointed cone of yellow anthers pointing downwards from the centre of the flower. Conanthera sabulosa is another taller species and has pale bluish-white, bell-shaped flowers with rounded lobes. The shorter species, such as C. minima, C. urceolata and C. johowii, will be more appealing to alpine plant enthusiasts but they have a limited range in the wild and do not appear to be in cultivation at present.

Finally among the Tecophilaeaceae endemic to Chile is the genus Zephyra, with one or two species. Zephyra elegans was described by David Don in 1832. It inhabits mainly coastal areas in the northern third of Chile, growing in sand and scrub and flowering in spring. Plants reach anything from 10 to 60 cm tall, with the narrow leaves up to 38 cm long. The starry flowers, up to 2.5 cm across, are white with a hint of blue towards the tips and on the backs of the tepals. There are four fertile and two infertile stamens. In 2001, a second species, Z. compacta, was described with shorter, wider leaves and smaller flowers. These plants may well turn out to fall within the range of variation found in Z. elegans. As for all of the Chilean geophytes, the taxonomy of the genus is likely to change as more is discovered about the different species and forms that occur along the length of this beautiful and diverse country.

Bibliography and references

Cabrera, A. L. (1965). Revisión del género *Mutisia* (Compositae). *Opera Lilloana* 13: 5–227.

Curtis, W. (1796). *Calceolaria fothergillii. Bot. Mag.* 10: t. 348.

de Azkue, D. (2000). Chromosome diversity of South American *Oxalis. Bot. J. Linn. Soc.* 132: 144.

Elliott, C. (1930). Some Mutisias. *Gard. Chron.* ser. 3, 88: 274.

Erskine, P. (1994). With the AGS in the Andes. *Quart. Bull. Alpine Gard. Soc. Gr. Brit.* 62(3): 255–292.

Erskine, P. (1998). *Oxalis enneaphylla* and its cousins. *Quart. Bull. Alpine Gard. Soc. Gr. Brit.* 66: 348.

Erskine, P. (2001). Alpines in the Southern Andes. In *Alpines 2001, Proceedings of the Seventh International Rock Garden Plant Conference*, eds. C. Brickell *et al*. pp. 24–28. SRGC & AGS.

Eyzaguirre, M. T. & Garcia de la Huerta, R. (2002). *Tecophilaea cyanocrocus* Leyb. (Tecophilaceae) rediscovered in its natural habitat. *Gayana, Bot.* 59 (2): 73–77.

Fay, M. F. & Chase, M. W. (1996). Resurrection of Themidaceae for the *Brodiaea* alliance, and recircumscription of Alliaceae, Amaryllidaceae and Agapanthoideae. *Taxon* 45: 441–451.

Goldblatt, P., Rudall, P. & Henrich, J. E. (1990). The genera of the *Sisyrinchium* alliance (Iridaceae: Iridoideae): phylogeny and relationships. *Syst. Bot.* 15: 497–510.

Grey, C. H. (1938). *Hardy Bulbs* 2: 162–3. Williams & Norgate Ltd., London.

Herbert, W. (1825). *Habranthus bifidus. Curtis's Bot. Mag.* 52: t. 2597.

Hooker, J. D. (1885). *Sisyrinchium filifolium. Curtis's Bot. Mag.* 111: t.6829.

Hooker, W. J. & Arnott, G. A. W. (1833). Contributions towards a flora of South America and the islands of the Pacific. *Bot. Misc.* 3: 129–30.

Humboldt, F. H. A. & Bonpland, A. J. A. G. (1809). *Plantae Aequinoctiales* 2: 10, t. 70–72. Paris.

Ker Gawler, J. B. (1808). *Amaryllis advena. Curtis's Bot. Mag.* 28: t. 1125.

Lindley, J. (1826). *Gilliesia graminea. Bot. Reg.* t. 992.

Lindley, J. (1830). *Leucocoryne odorata. Bot. Reg.* t. 1293.

Mascó, M., Noy-Meir, I. & Sérsic, A. N. (2004). Geographic variation in flower color patterns within *Calceolaria uniflora* Lam. in Southern Patagonia. *Pl. Syst. Evol.* 244: 77–91.

Miers, J. (1826). *Travels in Chili and La Plata*, 2 volumes. London.

Muñoz-Schick, M. (1985). *Flores del Norte Chico*. Direccion de Bibliotecas Archivos y Museos, Chile.

Muñoz-Schick, M. (2000). Novedades en la Familia Alstroemeriaceae. *Gayana, Bot.* 57 (1): 55–59.

Muñoz-Schick, M. (2003). Three new monocots discovered in Chile: *Alstroemeria mollensis* M. Muñoz & A. Brinck (Alstroemeriaceae), *Miersia chilensis* var. *bicolor* M. Muñoz (Gilliesiaceae) and *Calydorea chilensis* M. Muñoz (Iridaceae). *Gayana, Bot.* 60 (2): 101–106.

Prain, D. (1915). *Hippeastrum elwesii. Curtis's Bot. Mag.* 141: t. 8614.

Rudall, P. J., Bateman, R. M., Fay, M. F. & Eastman, A. (2002). Floral anatomy and systematics of Alliaceae with particular reference to *Gilliesia*, a presumed insect mimic with strongly zygomorphic flowers. *Amer. J. Bot.* 89 (12): 1867–1883.

Ruiz, H. & Pavón, J. (1798). *Systema Vegetabilium Florae Peruvianae et Chilensis*. Madrid.

Ruiz, H. & Pavón, J. (1798–1802). *Flora Peruviana et Chilensis*, 3 volumes. Madrid.

Smith, A. C. & Koch, M. F. (1935). The genus *Espeletia*: a study in phylogenetic taxonomy. *Brittonia* 1: 498.

Sparre, B. & Andersson, I. (1991). A taxonomic revision of the Tropaeolaceae. *Opera Bot.* 108: 18–125.

Stearn, W. (1973). *An Introduction to K. B. Presl's Reliquiae Haenkeanae (1825–1835)*. A. Asher, Amsterdam.

Ward, B. (2004). *The Plant Hunter's Garden*. Timber Press, Portland.

Watson, J. (1994). South American alpines. *Quart. Bull. Alpine Gard. Soc. Gr. Brit.* 62 (3): 293–352.

Weddell, H. A. (1855–1861). *Chloris Andina*, 2 volumes. Paris.

Wilkin, P. (1997). *Leontochir ovallei. Curtis's Bot. Mag.* 14 (1): t. 308.

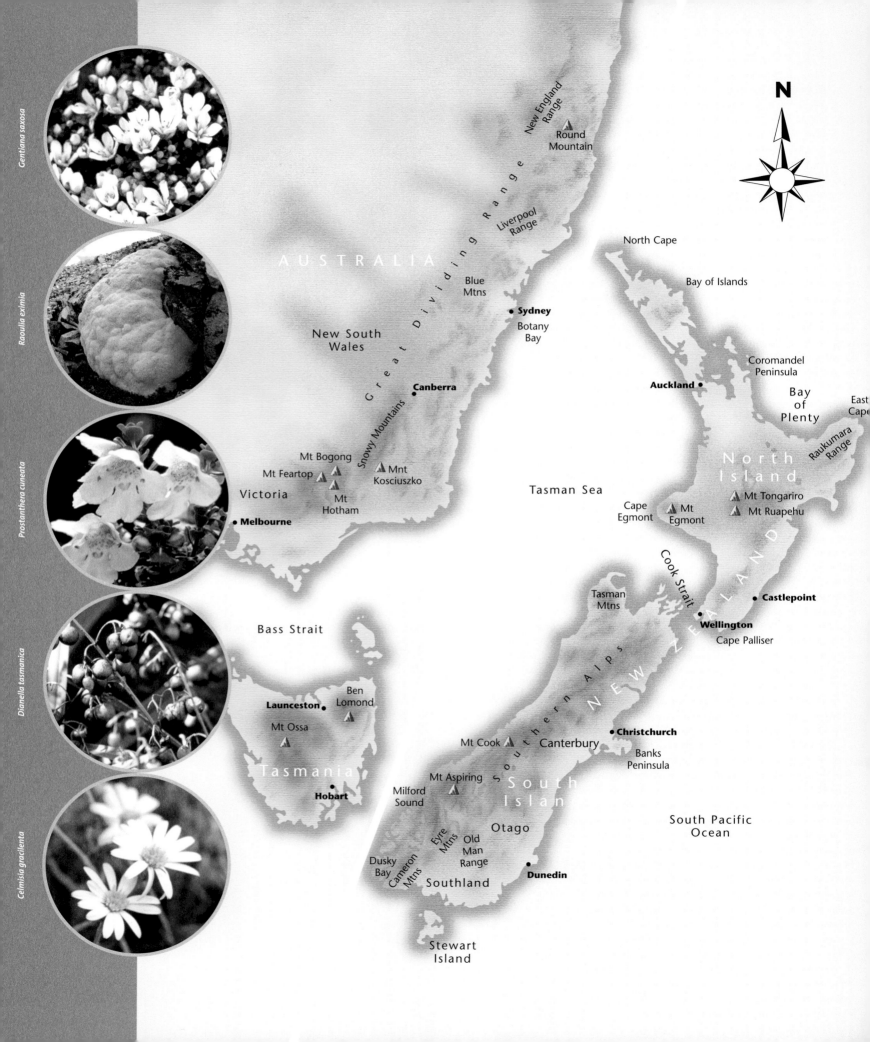

Gentiana saxosa

Raoulia eximia

Prostanthera cuneata

Dianella tasmanica

Celmisia gracilenta

N

AUSTRALIA

New England
Range

Round
Mountain

Liverpool
Range

Great Dividing Range

Blue
Mtns

Sydney

New South
Wales

Botany
Bay

Canberra

Mt Bogong

Mt Feartop

Snowy Mountains

Mnt
Kosciuszko

Victoria

Mt
Hotham

Melbourne

Tasman Sea

North Cape

Bay of Islands

Coromandel
Peninsula

Auckland

Bay
of
Plenty

East
Cape

North
Island

Raukumara
Range

Cape
Egmont

Mt
Egmont

Mt Tongariro

Mt Ruapehu

Cook Strait

NEW ZEALAND

Tasman
Mtns

Castlepoint

Wellington

Cape Palliser

Bass Strait

Ben
Lomond

Launceston

Mt Ossa

Tasmania

Hobart

Southern Alps

Mt Cook

Canterbury

Christchurch

Banks
Peninsula

Mt Aspiring

South
Island

Milford
Sound

Eyre
Mtns

Old
Man
Range

Otago

South Pacific
Ocean

Dusky
Bay

Cameron
Mtns

Southland

Dunedin

Stewart
Island

Chapter 6 Australia and New Zealand

The history of botanical exploration in Australia and New Zealand is a relatively short one. It was in April 1770 that Captain James Cook made his famous landing at Botany Bay in south-east Australia, during the three year voyage of the *Endeavour* (1768–1771). On this voyage, Joseph Banks was Cook's Scientific Officer and he and his assistant, the Swedish naturalist Daniel Solander, were the first European botanists to collect specimens of Australian plants. The genus *Banksia*, in Proteaceae, is named after Banks but like many Australian plants they are not reliably hardy in Britain.

There are few high mountains in Australia. The highest is Mt Kosciuszko at 2,230 m (7,316 feet), in the Snowy Mountains region of the Australian Alps in southern New South Wales. The Australian Alps are part of the Great Dividing Range, which stretches from Melbourne to Brisbane and then curves inland before continuing north through Queensland, mostly at altitudes of less than 1,000 m (3,281 feet). Other high points in this chain are the Blue Mountains, inland from Sydney, and the New England Range in north-east New South Wales, which reaches 1,615 m (5,299 feet) on Round Mountain. There are numerous other ranges in Australia but they are mostly in the continent's interior, the vast region of desert and semi-desert that covers most of the country. Australia's flora is remarkable and unique but alpines do not form a significant part.

The alpine and subalpine environments of mainland Australia, also known as snow country because they regularly experience persistent snow, cover around 5,200 km² (2,008 square miles), with 2,500 km² (965 square miles) in the

Snowy Mountains, although only 250 km² (96.5 square miles) are truly alpine (Costin *et al.*, 2000). The tree line occurs at 1,830 m (6,004 feet) on Mt Kosciuszko. Alpine zones also occur in the Alps of Victoria, particularly around the peaks of Mt Bogong (1,986 m; 6,516 feet), Mt Feartop (1,922 m; 6,306 feet) and Mt Hotham (1,860 m; 6,102 feet).

The island of Tasmania, to the south of Australia, has a total area of 64,000 km² (24,711 square miles) but being further south it has a more temperate climate. An area of 6,500 km² (2510 square miles) in Tasmania is snow country and there are more than 60 peaks above 900 m (2,953 feet) in altitude, with the highest point on Mt Ossa at 1,617 m (5,305 feet). The tree line in south-west Tasmania occurs at roughly 800 m (2,625 feet), but in the north-east it is at 1,400 m (4,593 feet). This tree line is not always clear and the subalpine or eucalypt forest gradually changes to alpine heath. Much of the central plateau of Tasmania is at altitudes of 1,000–1,200 m (3,281–3,937 feet) and has a treeless subalpine flora. The largest contiguous area of true alpine flora in Tasmania is around Ben Lomond in the north-east (Kirkpatrick, 1997).

The flora of Tasmania includes many hardy species and has much more potential than that of Australia for the alpine gardener. The western side of the island has a wetter climate than the east, with annual precipitation levels ranging from 760 mm (29.9 inches) in the north-west to 1,750 mm (68.9 inches) in the south west. In the east, the precipitation ranges from 500 to 800 mm (19.7–31.5 inches), apart from in the north-east highlands, which receive 1,200 mm (47.2 inches) of rain a year (Simmons,

Wapstra & Wapstra, 2008). Rainfall occurs all year round but with a winter peak, and most Tasmanian mountains receive over 1,200 mm (47.2 inches) of rain a year.

The eastern side of Tasmania has a higher average summer temperature than the west. There are no areas of permanent snow cover but the high peaks, mountain slopes and plateaus have seasonal snow cover and the montane vegetation experiences severe frosts. Of 2,500 species of flowering plants growing on Tasmania, 500 are endemic. Endemic montane plants include small shrubs such as the creeping pine, *Microcachrys tetragona* and the mountain riceflower, *Pimelea sericea*. Low-growing and creeping herbs include the Ben Lomond cushion plant *Chionohebe ciliolata*, which also occurs in New Zealand, and snow everlasting, *Helichrysum milliganii.*

The level of endemism in the Tasmanian flora is high, but nowhere near the level found in New Zealand where endemism is somewhere between 80 and 90 percent of the flora. These islands are 1,610 km (1,000 miles) from Australia, the nearest mainland. The mountains are higher than in Australia and are mostly at a more southerly latitude. The highest point on New Zealand's North Island is Mt Ruapehu at 2,797 m (9,177 feet) but most of the high mountains, and therefore most of the alpine plants, are on New Zealand's South Island. Mountain ranges extend the whole length of South Island, from the Tasman Mountains in the north, through the main ranges of the Southern Alps, to the Eyre Mountains, Kaherekoau Mountains and Cameron Mountains in the south. The highest point is Mt Cook in the Southern Alps, which reaches 3,754 m (12,316 feet). The western coast, especially towards the south, is indented with flooded valleys and includes the Fjordland National Park. The alpine zone is extensive, making up around 15% of the total land area (Mark, 1995).

Running down the centre of South Island, the Southern Alps have a huge influence on the climate of the island. The prevailing north-west winds cause high levels of precipitation on the western side of the range, where the slopes are heavily forested, mainly with southern beech, *Nothofagus*. The average precipitation over the whole country ranges between 750 mm and 1,500 mm (29.5–59 inches), but on the mountains it rises to around 5,000 mm (197 inches) and large areas of the Southern Alps average

FAR LEFT
Microcachrys tetragona, endemic to Tasmania.

LEFT
Mt Cook, at 3,754 m (12,316 feet), is New Zealand's highest mountain.
Photo: Joanne Everson.

7,000 mm (276 inches) (Allan, 1961). East of this main divide, precipitation is around 750 mm to 1,000 mm (29.5–39.4 inches). The driest region of South Island is in the basin of central Otago, in the south, where only 330–500 mm (13–19.7 inches) of rain fall per year.

The tree line on North Island is at around 1,500 m (4,921 feet) but on Stewart Island, which is off the southern end of South Island, it occurs at 900 m (2,953 feet). The relatively low altitude at which the tree line occurs on mountains in both Australia and New Zealand is due to the effect of the sea. The South Pacific Ocean, off the east coast of New Zealand, and the Tasman Sea, between New Zealand and south-east Australia, have a moderating effect on temperatures. The average temperature of the warmest month is lowered and so the tree line is found at lower altitudes. On the heavily forested slopes, the tree line is abrupt and conspicuous, but in other areas, particularly the drier rain shadow regions of South Island, the forest is replaced by subalpine shrubs that gradually give way to alpine vegetation. Above the climatic tree line are shrubs and tussock grassland.

The alpine zone in New Zealand, which spans an altitudinal range of around 1,000 m (3,281 feet) from the tree line to the permanent snow, can be divided into the low alpine zone and the high alpine zone. The low alpine zone is characterised by tall snowtussocks (*Chionochloa* species) growing with shrubs such as *Podocarpus*, *Hebe*, *Dracophyllum* and *Coprosma*. Dominant herbs in this zone include species of *Celmisia*, *Phormium*, *Aciphylla* and *Astelia*. As altitude increases, the shrubs become shorter, giving way to a vegetation cover of snowtussock and herbs, known as herbfield. Permanently wet areas are common in the low alpine zone, with bogs supporting various species of mosses, sedges, rushes and cushion plants.

TOP
Rob Roy glacier, below Mt Aspiring (3,030 m; 9,941 feet), north-west Otago.
Photo: Joanne Everson.

MIDDLE
Tussock grassland in Old Man Range, Otago.
Photo: Joanne Everson.

LEFT
Herbfield dominated by spiny *Aciphylla aurea*.
Photo: Joanne Everson.

The vegetation of the high alpine zone varies according to habitat. Fellfield has sparse, low-growing plants among stable rocks. Scree slopes are another habitat type, comprising loose rocks and stones and supporting a different flora of specialised plants that are adapted to the shifting substrate. Cushionfield is found on the windy plateau summits of Central Otago and is largely made up of dwarf, mat or cushion-forming species. Snowbanks, where snow accumulates and persists well into the normal growing season, is a fourth alpine habitat type (Mark, 1995).

The plants of the fellfields vary according to the underlying rock type and the amount of rainfall, but cushion plants are a feature in most areas. On the drier, eastern slopes of the Southern Alps, the fellfields are home to species that become so large that they are often referred to as vegetable sheep. These plants are mostly from the genera *Raoulia* and *Haastia*. They have pale-coloured, grey or silvery foliage, and when they form large, rounded cushions, it is quite understandable that they could be mistaken for sheep at a distance.

Another characteristic of the New Zealand flora is the high proportion of white-flowered species, and this is especially true of the alpine flora. In the New Zealand flora as a whole, 61% of species have white flowers, and this rises to 78% in the mountains (Richards, 1995). Many of the white-flowered species in New Zealand belong to genera that have different coloured flowers in other parts of the world. This suggests that these white-flowered plants evolved after New Zealand became isolated from the continental landmass over 60 million years ago. The most likely reason for this unusually high proportion of white flowers is that New Zealand has few specialist pollinators. For example, there are no social bees in New Zealand and few butterflies. The advantage of attracting specialist pollinators is that the flower needs to

produce less pollen as there is a much greater chance of that pollen being carried to a flower of the same species. However, if there are few or no specialist pollinators around, it makes more sense to attract generalist pollinators, produce more pollen and hope for the best. White flowers attract generalist pollinators, including flies and beetles. They also tend to be bowl-shaped and trap the heat of the

ABOVE LEFT
A mosaic of mat-forming plants, Old Man Range.
Photo: Joanne Everson.

ABOVE RIGHT
Raoulia eximia, a species of vegetable sheep, in dry fellfield, central south Island.
Photo: Joanne Everson.

LEFT
A white New Zealand 'gentian', *Gentianella corymbifera*.
Photo: Joanne Everson.

sun, a distinct advantage when encouraging insects to visit on a high, windswept mountain. Although New Zealand alpine plants often have white flowers, this doesn't make them any less beautiful. Soon after these islands were first explored by European expeditions, their plants were being sent back to be grown and enjoyed in gardens and glasshouses on the other side of the world.

The first Europeans arrive

The first voyage of Captain James Cook set off from Plymouth, England in 1768 to observe the transit of Venus across the sun's disc from the South Pacific Ocean, which would take place in June 1769. The measurements taken were intended to help scientists calculate the distance of Venus from the sun and to improve navigational techniques at sea. As well as astronomy, the scientists on board the *Endeavour* would study the botany and zoology of the places they visited. Joseph Banks was the Scientific Officer and provided, at his own expense, all the equipment and stores needed to make collections during the voyage. He also recruited the Swede Dr Daniel Carl Solander, a student of Linnaeus, to accompany him, as well as eight other staff.

The *Endeavour* sailed around Cape Horn early in 1769. By April that year, the expedition reached Tahiti, where they stayed for three months and carried out the necessary astronomical observations. Before leaving England, Cook

had been given secret orders by the King, George III, to search for a southern continent, so on leaving Tahiti in July 1769, the *Endeavour* set sail to look for this *Terra Australis*. In October they found land, not a continent but the North Island of New Zealand. For the following six months, Cook navigated round both main islands, a total of 3,860 km (2,398 miles) of coastline, and Banks and his team made hundreds of botanical collections.

Stylidium graminifolium
Family: Stylidiaceae

Stylidium is an almost entirely Australian genus of over 140 species of annuals, perennials, subshrubs and climbers. The genus was established by the Swedish botanist Olof Swartz and was first described in 1805 in the fourth edition of *Species Plantarum*, which was edited by Carl Willdenow. Plants of this genus are commonly known as trigger plants because of their remarkable pollination mechanism. This mechanism was first studied on *Stylidium graminifolium* and is described in detail by John Sims (1817) in *Curtis's Botanical Magazine*, where he refers to it as the "singular irritability of the column".

The flowers of trigger plants have two stamens and a style, which are joined together to form a mobile column. This column is initially bent back, but when touched near the base by a visiting insect, it suddenly springs up. This action showers the insect with pollen, which is then transferred to the stigma of another flower when the insect moves on in search of more nectar. After a short time, the column gradually resumes its former position. Once the pollen of a flower has been dispersed, the stigma becomes ripe and sticky. The trigger mechanism continues to operate so that the now-receptive stigma can pick up pollen from insects that have just visited other, younger flowers.

Stylidium graminifolium grows naturally in south-east Australia, in Queensland, New South Wales, Victoria, South Australia and Tasmania, where it occupies heathland, grassland, bogs, woodland and open forests, from near sea level to over 1000 m (3,281 feet). It is a summer-flowering, tuft-forming perennial with stiff, grass-like leaves and numerous flowers held in a simple raceme. The erect stems can reach 75 cm tall but are often only half this height. The pale pink to deep lilac flowers are around 1 cm across and have five petals, but one of these, the labellum, is smaller and reflexed. This is a variable plant in the wild and several forms have been described, including var. *album* (with white flowers) and var. *angustifolium* (with narrower leaves).

John Ker (1816) writes that *Stylidium graminifolium* was found by Joseph Banks in New South Wales and later by Robert Brown in Tasmania. Seed was collected by Peter Good, Brown's assistant on the voyage of the *Investigator*, and sent to England in 1803. It was grown in the Vineyard Nursery of James Lee and John Kennedy in Hammersmith, London.

The hardiness of *Stylidium graminifolium* depends upon its provenance; it is best grown in a well-ventilated, cool glasshouse or cold frame. The plants should have plenty of light and can be grown in full sun, although some light shading may be necessary on hot, sunny days. The flower spikes first appear in late spring but the fascinating flowers can still be opening in early autumn. The narrow leaves are evergreen.

This species can be grown in the open, in a sunny position on a rock garden, where it will require frequent watering. Forms originating from high altitudes are most likely to survive freezing temperatures but they will not normally survive a severe winter.

Curtis's Botanical Magazine, plate 1918 (1817). Artist: unknown.

On 1 April 1770, Captain Cook turned the *Endeavour* west and continued his search for the southern continent. Only seventeen days later, the coast of Australia was spotted and on 29 April 1770, the ship anchored in the inlet that would be named Botany Bay.

Cook's famous first voyage marked the beginning of the botanical exploration of Australia and New Zealand. Plant collections were mainly made near the coast so alpines were not part of the first haul of specimens. There were a few exceptions however, as plants like *Leptospermum scoparium* grow both on the coast, where specimens were collected by Banks, and in the mountains, where they have a more prostrate habit. This shrub grows in Australia, Tasmania and New Zealand. Banks also collected specimens of the grass trigger plant, *Stylidium graminifolium*, a locally abundant plant that is found from near sea level to alpine moorland, growing in a variety of habitats, from bogs, heathland and grassland, to woodland and open forests.

Banks and Solander concentrated on recording what they saw and taking specimens of the plants they found. They did not introduce many species to cultivation, although by the end of the eighteenth century plants from Australia, then known as New Holland, were becoming popular and *Banksia serrata* was claimed to be the first plant raised in Britain from Botany Bay seed (Coats, 1969). Gradually, as more naturalists explored these newly discovered lands, more plants were introduced, including some alpines. Not long after returning to England in 1771, Cook was off on a second voyage, this time to find the Antarctic continent. Two ships, the *Resolution* and the *Adventure*, set sail from Plymouth in 1772, and the naturalist on board was Johann Reinhold Forster. His son, Georg Forster, came with him as his artist. On a stopover at the Cape of Good Hope, the botanist Dr A. Sparrman, another student of Linnaeus, joined the crew. Having unsuccessfully searched for the Antarctic continent, the ships sailed into Dusky Bay at the southern end of New Zealand's South Island in March 1773, later moving on to Queen Charlotte Sound at the north end of the South Island. The Forsters and Sparrman made many collections of New Zealand plants during the voyage, including species of the daisy-flowered genus *Celmisia*, gentians, hebes and spiny *Aciphylla*.

At the end of the voyage, the Forsters moved back to their native Germany and published several books, including *Characteres Generum Plantarum* in 1776. This publication is an account of the new genera discovered on the voyage. Among the new genera established in this work are *Aciphylla*, *Phormium*, *Leptospermum* and *Coprosma*. In 1786, Georg Forster published *Florulae Insularum Australium Prodromus*, in which many new species found on the voyage were described for the first time.

The first New Zealand gentians observed by Europeans were named *Gentiana montana* and *G. saxosa*; both were discovered on Cook's second voyage and described by Georg Forster in 1777. The taxonomic position of these species has long been unclear and they have sometimes been classified as belonging to the genus *Gentianella*, primarily because their flowers lack the pleats or lobes of tissue (plicae) between the petal lobes that are found on true gentians. Many botanists have regarded the New Zealand species as being sufficiently different from *Gentianella* not to be classified as such. The *Flora of New Zealand* (Allan, 1961) states that further study is required before they are definitely assigned to *Gentianella*. However, more recent studies (e.g. Von Hagen & Kadereit, 2001) have concluded that they should indeed be classified as species of *Gentianella*, a genus of around 244 species distributed across Asia, North and South America, Australia and New Zealand.

The flowers of New Zealand 'gentians', including those of *Gentianella saxosa*, are mostly white with purplish veins, although they may rarely be shades of red, purple or violet and some species have flowers with a pale lemon-yellow or sulphur tinge. The first major revision of New Zealand gentians was by Thomas Kirk (1895). Placing them in the genus *Gentiana*, he grouped *G. saxosa* with *G. cerina*, *G. antarctica* and *G. antipoda*, all of which share the characteristic of having petiolate rather than sessile stem leaves.

BELOW
Gentianella saxosa in cultivation.

In the second edition of his *Manual of the New Zealand Flora*, Thomas Cheeseman (1925) recognised 24 annual and perennial species of gentian from New Zealand, and this number is maintained in the *Flora of New Zealand*. *Gentianella saxosa* is the most commonly cultivated New Zealand species, and it flowers in July and August in the northern hemisphere. *Gentianella cerina* is the closest species to *G. saxosa* but has longer, more leafy stems and flowers with prominent crimson veins. *Gentianella bellidifolia* is also very similar but the stems are generally a little more erect and its habitat is damp, subalpine herbfields and grasslands, whereas *G. saxosa* grows on rocky shores and sandhills, at or near sea level. *Gentianella montana* is primarily a mountain plant, although it can also be found near sea level. It has long, ascending stems that can reach 60 cm.

The genus *Aciphylla* was described by Forster in 1776 and the first species was *A. squarrosa*. Also known as Spaniards or speargrass, there are now around 40 recognised species of *Aciphylla* and all but two are endemic to New Zealand. The plants form rosettes or tufts of incredibly vicious, stiff, spine-tipped leaves that can make moving or working around them a very painful experience. The small flowers are produced in umbels that sprout from the axils of the leaf-like bracts on the tall spike-like inflorescences. Individual plants have either male or female flowers. A sunny position and a well-

ABOVE LEFT
The inflorescence of *Aciphylla squarrosa*. Photo: Joanne Everson.

LEFT
The spiny leaf rosette of *Aciphylla scott-thomsonii*. Photo: Joanne Everson.

drained, deep soil to accommodate their long taproots are needed to grow these plants successfully. Some species, such as *A. horrida* and *A. aurea*, both from South Island, can grow quite large with leaves 70 cm long or more; others are much smaller and species such as *A. monroi* are less than 30 cm tall. The foliage of aciphyllas is usually yellow or gold tinged and the rosettes can make a dramatic feature in a rock garden.

Many of the early botanical explorers who visited Australia and New Zealand were members of sea-based voyages. Captain Mathew Flinders led a voyage to Australia from 1801 to 1805 on the *Investigator*, and was accompanied by the Scottish botanist Robert Brown, the botanical artist Ferdinand Bauer and the Kew gardener Peter Good. Following this voyage, Brown published *Prodromus Florae Novae Hollandiae* in 1810. The Frenchman Jules Sebastien Cesar Dumont d'Urville sailed on the *Coquille*, later named the *Astrolabe*, on three voyages to Australia and New Zealand. The second of these, which set sail from France under d'Urville's command in April 1826, was the most significant and resulted in the publication in 1832 of *Voyage de Decouvertes de l'Astrolabe Botanique*. The plants collected on these ocean-bound expeditions were mostly coastal species and the mountains were little explored. It was mainly land-based explorers who ventured further inland, and one of the most notable was Allan Cunningham.

Cunningham was from a Scottish family but was born in Wimbledon, south London, in 1791. He worked for William Aiton, Curator at Kew, and in 1814 was sent to Rio de Janeiro to collect plants. After nearly two years there, he was instructed to move on to Australia, arriving in Sydney in December 1816. He spent fifteen years in Australia, and his numerous expeditions included crossing the Blue Mountains several times, tracing the course of the Lachlan and Macquarie Rivers, crossing the Liverpool Range and reaching as far north as the Darling Downs in southern Queensland and Moreton Bay, where the port of Brisbane was established. He even spent five months on New Zealand's North Island, from August 1826 to January 1827. In 1831, Cunningham returned to England, settling near Kew. He was soon offered the post of Colonial Botanist in Sydney but turned it down in favour of his younger brother Richard, who arrived in Australia in January 1833. At the end of that year, Richard too visited New Zealand but covered little new ground before returning to Sydney in May 1834. He did, however, find the unusual *Fuchsia procumbens*, a creeping, lowland species described by his brother Allan in 1839. In April 1835, Richard was part of an expedition to explore the Darling River but he became lost and was killed by aborigines. Allan Cunningham later returned to Australia in 1837, taking over from his brother as Colonial Botanist, and this

second period also included a second trip to New Zealand in 1838. By this time though, he was very ill and after returning to Sydney, he died in 1839.

On both of Allan Cunningham's visits to New Zealand, he met the Cornish missionary William Colenso, who had been sent to the Bay of Islands (at the tip of North Island) in 1834 by the British and Foreign Bible Society. While carrying out his mission work, Colenso also observed the flora of the country and this pursuit was encouraged by Cunningham. Colenso must have built up a good reputation because when the young naturalist Joseph Hooker arrived in New Zealand in August 1841, on the British Antarctic Voyage of Captain James Clark Ross, his father William Hooker had recommended he use Colenso

ABOVE
Prostanthera cuneata, the alpine mint bush, collected by Ronald Gunn in Tasmania in 1842 and described by Bentham in 1848.

NEW ZEALAND FUCHSIAS

Most of the 100 or so species of *Fuchsia* are to be found in Central and South America, but New Zealand is home to four species (Allan, 1961). All the New Zealand species belong to section *Skinnera*. They have alternate leaves, funnel-shaped flowers with reflexed sepals, small or non-existent petals, often well-exserted filaments and blue pollen. They include the tree fuchsia *F. excortica*, which can reach 12 m tall, and at the other extreme, the creeping *F. procumbens*.

Fuchsia procumbens occurs in the northern part of New Zealand's North Island, from North Cape to the Coromandel Peninsula, where it grows in sandy or gravelly places and among rocks or grass near the coast. It was found in March 1834 on a sandy beach near the village of Matauri on the east coast, by the British botanist Richard Cunningham. It is a trailing or scrambling plant with slender stems and more or less circular leaves around 1 cm across. The small flowers appear in summer and have no petals, but the pale orange or greenish-yellow calyx splits into four reflexed lobes that are tipped with purple. Pinkish-red berries develop in late summer.

Fuchsia procumbens is an endangered species in the wild (Given, 1981). Threats include trampling and grazing by goats and other animals, erosion and an increase in tourist developments. It was introduced into cultivation in the first half of the nineteenth century, and William Hooker featured it in *Icones Plantarum* in 1842. It wasn't until 1980 that *F. procumbens* received an Award of Merit from the RHS, as a flowering plant on 5 August and for its fruits on 18 November. It is not reliably hardy and is generally grown as an alpine house plant, but it can be grown outside in milder areas of Britain.

Fuchsia procumbens
with flowers and fruit.

as a guide to the local flora. The two men made several excursions to study plants during Hooker's three-month stay. The British Antarctic Voyage, from 1839 to 1843 was the first major expedition undertaken by Joseph Hooker and the discoveries he made were published in six impressive, illustrated volumes under the overall title of *The Botany of the Antarctic Voyage*. These publications were a significant milestone in the study of the flora of Australia and New Zealand, and Hooker's role in advancing the knowledge of this region's flora cannot be underestimated.

Joseph Hooker and the British Antarctic Voyage

Two ships, HMS *Erebus* and HMS *Terror*, left England on 30 September 1839 on a voyage that was to last four years. Captain James Clark Ross was in command, and Joseph Hooker was his assistant surgeon and naturalist. Hooker sailed on the *Erebus* and another naturalist, David Lyall, sailed on the *Terror*. The aim of the voyage was to explore the southern oceans and to search for the continent of Antarctica, and Hooker was to make collections at every stop on the way.

In August 1840, the two ships arrived in Hobart, Tasmania, then still known as Van Dieman's Land. There they stayed for three months during which Hooker was able to botanise extensively, guided by Ronald Campbell Gunn, a correspondent of William Hooker. Gunn had a keen interest in natural history. He was born in South Africa and emigrated to Tasmania as an assistant superintendent of convicts in 1829. He remained in Tasmania working as a public servant and politician until he died in 1881.

In November, the ships of the Antarctic Voyage departed for the Lord Auckland Islands, Campbell Island and then the continent of Antarctica, which was first sighted on 11 January 1841. Five months after leaving Hobart, the ships returned and stayed for a further three months, during which they were repaired and refitted. They then set off for a short stay in Sydney before heading for New Zealand, arriving in The Bay of Islands in August 1841. After another three-month stay, a second tour of Antarctica was undertaken, and from there the ships sailed to the Falkland Islands and Tierra del Fuego. The third and last exploration of the Antarctic began in December 1842, and the *Erebus* and *Terror* eventually arrived back in England in September 1843. The Antarctic Voyage was a great success in many ways, and thanks to Joseph Hooker, the botany of the expedition was very well documented.

After returning home, Joseph Hooker wrote *The Botany of the Antarctic Voyage*, in three parts of two volumes each, beautifully illustrated by Walter Hood Fitch. The first,

ABOVE
Raoulia australis, the first species in the genus described by Joseph Hooker in 1846.

LEFT
Raoulia hookeri, named after Joseph Hooker by Harry Allan, author of *Flora of New Zealand*.

Flora Antarctica, was completed in 1847 and covered the flora of the islands of the southern oceans, such as the Falkland Islands, Kerguelen Islands and the Auckland and Campbell Islands. In the first volume, were plants described by Hooker whereas the second volume included plants already described by other botanists. In 1848, Hooker departed England for India and the Himalaya (see chapter on 'China and the Himalaya'), but on his return he worked on *Flora Novae Zelandiae*, which appeared in installments between 1852 and 1855. With 1,767 species described in this work, Hooker relied upon the specimens collected by more than 30 botanists, including David Lyall and William Colenso. In the autumn of 1855, the first installment of *Flora Tasmaniae* came out. This was eventually completed in 1859.

The Botany of the Antarctic Voyage includes descriptions of 5,340 species of flowering plants, fungi, algae, lichens and mosses, with 528 plates by Fitch (Desmond, 1999). Among them were rock garden plants such as *Dianella tasmanica*, celmisias and several veronicas that were later transferred to other genera, particularly *Hebe* and *Parahebe*.

Hooker also described one of the genera of vegetable sheep, *Raoulia*. He named this genus after the French botanist Etienne Raoul, who visited New Zealand in the 1830s and was one of the first to study the flora of the east side of South Island. Not all species of *Raoulia* form large 'sheep-like' mounds. Hooker's first species was *R. australis*, a low-growing, mat-forming species from lowland to mountain habitats, on bare ground and river banks, on North and South Island. It was collected by Raoul and described by Hooker in Raoul's *Choix des Plantes de la Nouvelle-Zélande*, published in 1846. In *Flora Novae Zelandiae*, Hooker added four more species: *R. subsericea*, *R. glabra*, *R. tenuicaulis* and *R. grandiflora*. Raoulias can be grown in the open garden but need very good drainage to survive damp winters. They will do best in crevices between rocks. *Raoulia australis* is one of the more reliable species and has tiny leaves not more than 2 mm long that form a hard, dense mat that seems resistant to winter rain. Twenty species of *Raoulia* are included in *Flora of New Zealand* (Allan, 1961) and one of these, *R. hookeri*, was named after Hooker by Harry Allan.

BELOW LEFT
The berries of *Dianella tasmanica*.

BELOW RIGHT
Parahebe lyallii, named *Veronica lyallii* by Joseph Hooker in 1853.

Dianella tasmanica was described in 1858 by Hooker in *Flora Tasmaniae*. This species is found in New South Wales, Victoria and Tasmania, growing in a variety of locations, from coastal dunes to the alpine zone, often in shallow, sandy soils, sheltered among rocks and shrubs or in damp, shady forests. The specimens Hooker studied were sent to him by Ronald Gunn, who collected them in north-west Tasmania. The genus *Dianella* was first proposed by the French botanist and zoologist Jean-Baptiste Lamarck in 1786. There are now 25–30 known species distributed from south-east Africa and south-east Asia to Australia, New Zealand and the Pacific Islands. They are rhizomatous perennials with strap-like leaves and compound inflorescences of blue, purple or white flowers. Australia is home to 15 species and 11 of these are endemic, including *D. tasmanica* (Henderson, 1987). This species flowers in early summer but its most striking feature is the large, purple-blue berries that develop in late summer and autumn. Although a large and potentially invasive plant, its fruits make a dramatic display towards the end of the year in a woodland or rock garden. It is not a reliably hardy species and Hooker referred to it as a greenhouse plant. It will, however, withstand several degrees of frost for short periods and can be successfully grown outside in milder parts of Britain if the soil remains moist in summer.

Hooker (1853) included 24 species of *Veronica* in *Flora Novae-Zelandiae*. Although initially classified in *Veronica*, the southern hemisphere species have long been placed in separate genera, separated by morphological characters such as the way the seed capsule opens (dehisces) and their woody or semi-woody stems. They range from large evergreen shrubs or small trees in the genus *Hebe*, with racemes or panicles of flowers, to cushion-forming plants in the genus *Chionohebe*, which have tiny overlapping leaves and solitary, terminal flowers.

One of Hooker's species is *Veronica lyallii*, named after his companion on the Antarctic Voyage, David Lyall. Lyall found this plant while surgeon on the voyage of HMS *Acheron*, which surveyed the coast of New Zealand from 1847 to 1849. *Hebe* was the first of the southern hemisphere 'veronica' genera to be accepted and, for a short time, *Veronica lyallii* was known as *Hebe lyallii*.

The genus *Parahebe* was proposed in 1944 by Walter Oliver, Director of the Dominion Museum, Wellington, and he formally transferred *Hebe lyallii* to his new genus. Oliver used several characters to separate *Parahebe* from *Hebe*. In *Parahebe*, the capsules are laterally compressed, with the dividing septum across the narrowest diameter and, in most species, the leaves have a toothed or serrate margin. In *Hebe*, the capsules are usually dorsally compressed, with the dividing septum across the broadest diameter, and the leaves are generally entire. Hebes are woody subshrubs or rarely trees with usually erect stems, whereas parahebes are subshrubs, with woody or semi-woody stems that are often prostrate or decumbent.

Parahebe lyallii is common on New Zealand's South Island, growing in subalpine or lowland rocky places and beside streams at altitudes up to 1,400 m (4,593 feet). In summer, the flowers are produced in axillary racemes up to 8 cm long. Each flower is around 1 cm across and the four

ABOVE
Hebe macrantha, from the Southern Alps of New Zealand.

Celmisia spectabilis
Family: Compositae (Asteraceae)

Celmisia spectabilis is one of the more widespread species in the mountainous areas of New Zealand, where it is commonly known as the cotton daisy. Joseph Hooker described it in 1844, in the first volume of his *Flora Antarctica*. The specimens he studied were collected by John Bidwill in 1839 on Mt Tongariro, on New Zealand's North Island. Its range is now known to extend from the Raukumara Range on North Island to South Canterbury on South Island, generally east of the main divide. It grows in alpine and subalpine tussock grassland, herbfields and fellfields, up to 1800 m (5,906 feet) altitude. It can occupy vast areas of hill country and is an early coloniser of disturbed sites (Evans, 1987).

The leathery leaves of this species are ovate to lanceolate or narrowly oblong and can reach 30 cm long. They have a shiny green upper surface, with prominent parallel grooves, but their undersides are densely covered in soft, whitish or buff-coloured hairs. The leaf bases are overlapping and compacted to form a stout pseudostem. The flower stems reach 30 cm tall and are densely covered with white hairs. At the end of each stem is a beautiful solitary flower head, 3–5 cm across, with numerous white ray florets and yellow disc florets. Plants can form mats of up to 2 m across.

Celmisia spectabilis is a variable species; in *Curtis's Botanical Magazine* Hooker writes: "The specimen of *C. spectabilis* here figured gives no idea of the stature which the species attains, or of the curious dwarf forms it sometimes assumes. In its largest state, the base of the stem, clothed with silky leaf-sheaths, is as thick as a child's wrist, and the leaves a foot long and 20–30 in number; whilst the smallest forms have only a few leaves, and these little more than one inch long."

In *Flora Novae-Zelandiae*, Hooker described *Celmisia spectabilis* var. *lanceolata*, which has narrowly lanceolate leaves. It is found in the south-east corner of North Island, from Cape Palliser to Castlepoint. The larger forms of the species are found on South Island and were described as var. *magnifica* by Harry Allan in 1947. The leaves of the typical variety are generally around 9 or 10 cm long and 1.5 cm wide, but in var. *magnifica*, the leaves can reach 30 cm long and 4.5 cm wide. These varieties were raised to subspecies of *C. spectabilis* by the New Zealand botanist David Given (1984).

Hooker writes that *Celmisia spectabilis* was the only species of *Celmisia* that was introduced into cultivation in Britain at the time it was featured in the magazine. The painted plant came from the Veitch Nursery, where it flowered in May 1882. It is a hardy species but it needs to be grown in a cool position in the open garden. Two different clones are generally required to produce fertile seed. Large clumps of this plant will benefit from dividing as they can begin to degenerate in the centre, especially if conditions are damp and there is little air movement.

Curtis's Botanical Magazine, plate 6653 (1882). Artist: Matilda Smith.

unequal corolla lobes are white to pink, with fine lilac veining and often a pinkish-red eye. The whole plant grows 10–20 cm tall and is one of the best rock garden plants in the genus. It does best in free-draining soil that retains some moisture or where the roots can grow under large rocks that keep the soil cool and prevent it from drying out completely. However, this plant will be lost in winter if the soil is too wet. It does well planted between vertical or sloping rocks so that the roots are protected from the heat in summer but the stems can trail down in full sun.

Parahebe ×*bidwillii* is a natural hybrid between *P. lyallii* and *P. decora*. It was first described as *Veronica bidwillii* by William Hooker in 1852 and is named after the Englishman John Bidwill, who became the first Director of the Royal Botanic Garden, Sydney in 1847. *Parahebe decora* is a prostrate plant with small, entire or once-lobed leaves less than 0.5 cm in length. *Parahebe* ×*bidwillii* is intermediate between the two parent species, having smaller leaves and a more prostrate habit than *P. lyallii*.

The name *Hebe* was first suggested in 1789, by Philibert Commerson in Antoine Jussieu's *Genera Plantarum*, but it was not until 1921 that the American plant taxonomist Francis Pennell revived the genus. General acceptance of *Hebe* was confirmed when Leonard Cockayne and Harry Allan transferred many of the New Zealand species of *Veronica* to *Hebe* in 1927. Pennell (1921) used several characteristics to separate *Hebe* from *Veronica*, such as their shrubby habit, their southern hemisphere distribution and the dehiscence of the seed capsules. In *Hebe*, the capsules initially dehisce septicidally, that is to say they split open along the line of the septum that separates the two carpels. Pennell states that in *Veronica* this form of dehiscence has been virtually lost and the capsules open by first splitting along the middle of the carpel wall (loculicidal dehiscence).

There are now more than 100 known species of *Hebe*. They are found in South America, south-east Australia and New Guinea but by far the greatest number are native to New Zealand, where they form an important part of the flora. The separation of genera such as *Hebe*, *Chionohebe* and *Parahebe* from *Veronica* has, however, recently been challenged and there are strong arguments to return them to *Veronica* (e.g. Garnock-Jones *et al.*, 2007; Albach, 2008). Apart from DNA evidence that suggests they are part of the genus *Veronica*, the arguments also state that the morphological characters used to define the separate

TOP RIGHT
Hebe raoulii, from the hills and mountains of Canterbury, South Island.

RIGHT
Celmisia gracilenta, described by Joseph Hooker in *Flora Antarctica*.

genera cannot always be used reliably. For example, a species like the large-flowered *Hebe macrantha* has the general appearance of a *Hebe* but the capsules are more like those of *Parahebe* in that they are laterally compressed and the septum is across the narrowest diameter (Allan, 1961). *Hebe macrantha* also has toothed leaves, as do other *Hebe* species, such as *H. hulkeana* and *H. raoulii*, a characteristic used to define *Parahebe*. Although it seems that the southern hemisphere species will once again belong to *Veronica*, it will be a long time before the name *Hebe* disappears from nurseries and garden centres.

One of the most characteristic plants of the New Zealand mountains is *Celmisia*, and Hooker described 13 species of this genus in *The Botany of the Antarctic Voyage*. The genus *Celmisia* was established by the French botanist Henri Cassini in 1825, based on the Australian *C. longifolia* (Cassini, 1825). There are now 65–70 known species, with around 60 occurring in New Zealand and the remainder in south-east Australia. They are perennial, evergreen herbs or subshrubs, with leaves forming dense tufts or overlapping along the branches. The daisy-like flowers are white with a yellow or rarely purple centre. In *Curtis's Botanical Magazine*, when writing about *C. spectabilis*, Joseph Hooker described the genus as "one of the most beautiful of the New Zealand flora", with many "extremely handsome" species.

The publication of *Flora Novae Zelandiae* marked a new era in the history of the botany of New Zealand. The range of plants included and the accuracy of the descriptions laid the foundation for further study of these islands' flora and there was much activity in botanical research in the years following its publication. The rapid colonisation of South Island resulted in the exploration of the mountains and the discovery of the rich alpine flora. Botanists like Claude Monro, William Travers, Julias Haast, Lauder Lindsay and John Buchanan all studied the flora of South Island in the second half of the nineteenth century, and they are frequently remembered in the names of the plants. These new discoveries led the New Zealand Government to arrange for Joseph Hooker to write a new, concise flora of the country. Hooker's *Handbook of the New Zealand Flora* appeared between 1864 and 1867. Thomas Cheeseman, author of *Manual of the New Zealand Flora*, first published

in 1906, states that "the clearness and excellence of the descriptions and their general accuracy are most noteworthy especially when it is considered that a large proportion of the species have been examined and described by the author alone."

ABOVE
Celmisia traversii, named after the Irish naturalist William Travers by Joseph Hooker in his *Handbook of the New Zealand Flora*.

Bibliography and references

Albach, D. C. (2008). Further arguments for the rejection of paraphyletic taxa: *Veronica* subgen. *Pseudolysimachium* (Plantaginaceae). *Taxon* 57: 1–6.

Allan, H. H. (1961). *Flora of New Zealand*, 1. R. E. Owen, Wellington.

Cassini, A. H. G. (1825). *Celmisia*. In: *Dictionnaire des Sciences Naturelles*, 37, ed. F. G. Levrault, p. 259. Paris.

Cheeseman, T. F. (1906). *Manual of the New Zealand Flora*. John Mackay, Government Printer, Wellington.

Cheeseman, T. F. (1925). *Manual of the New Zealand Flora* (2nd ed.). New Zealand Board of Science and Art, Wellington.

Coats, A. M. (1969). *The Quest for Plants*. Studio Vista, London.

Costin, A., Gray, M., Totterdell, C. & Wimbush, D. (2000). *Kosciuzko Alpine Flora* (2nd ed.). CSIRO Publishing, Collingwood.

Desmond, R. (1999). *Sir Joseph Dalton Hooker, Traveller and Plant Collector*. Antique Collectors' Club, Woodbridge.

Evans, A. (1987). *New Zealand in Flower*. Reed Methuen Publishers Ltd., Auckland.

Garnock-Jones, P., Albach, D. & Griggs, B. G. (2007). Botanical names in Southern Hemisphere *Veronica* (Plantaginaceae): sect. *Detzneria*, sect. *Hebe*, and sect. *Labiatoides*. *Taxon* 56: 571–582.

Given, D. R. (1981). *Rare and Endangered Plants of New Zealand*. A. H. & A. W. Reed Ltd., Wellington.

Given, D. R. (1984). A taxonomic revision of *Celmisia* subgenus *Pelliculatae* section *Petiolatae*. *New Zealand J. Bot.* 22: 144–147.

Hooker, W. J. (1842). *Fuchsia procumbens*. *Icon. Pl.* 5: t. 421.

Hooker, J. D. (1853). *Flora Novae-Zelandiae*, 1: 196. Lovell Reeve & Co. Ltd., London.

Hooker, J. D. (1864). *Handbook of the New Zealand Flora*. Reeve & Co., London.

Ker, J. B. (1816). *Stylidium graminifolium*. *Bot. Reg.* 1: t. 90.

Kirk, T. (1895). A Revision of the New Zealand Gentians. *Trans. & Proc. New Zealand Inst.* 27: 330–341.

Kirkpatrick, J. (1997). *Alpine Tasmania*. Oxford University Press, Australia.

Mark, A. F. (1995). The New Zealand alpine flora and vegetation. *Quart. Bull. Alpine Gard. Soc. Gr. Brit.* 63: 245–259.

Musgrave, T., Gardner, C. & Musgrave, W. (1998). *The Plant Hunters*. Ward Lock, London.

Pennell, F. W. (1921). 'Veronica' in North and South America. *Rhodora* 23: 2–5.

Richards, J. (1995). White flowers and the flora of New Zealand. *Quart. Bull. Alpine Gard. Soc. Gr. Brit.* 63: 275–278.

Simmons, M., Wapstra, H. & Wapstra, A. (eds.). (2008). *A Guide to Flowers and Plants of Tasmania* (4th ed.). Reed New Holland, Sydney.

Sims, J. (1817). *Stylidium graminifolium*. *Curtis's Bot. Mag.* 44: t. 1918.

Von Hagen, K. B., & Kaderiet, J. W. (2001). The phylogeny of *Gentianella* (Gentianaceae) and its colonization of the southern hemisphere as revealed by nuclear and chloroplast sequence variation. *Org., Divers. & Evol.* 1: 61–79

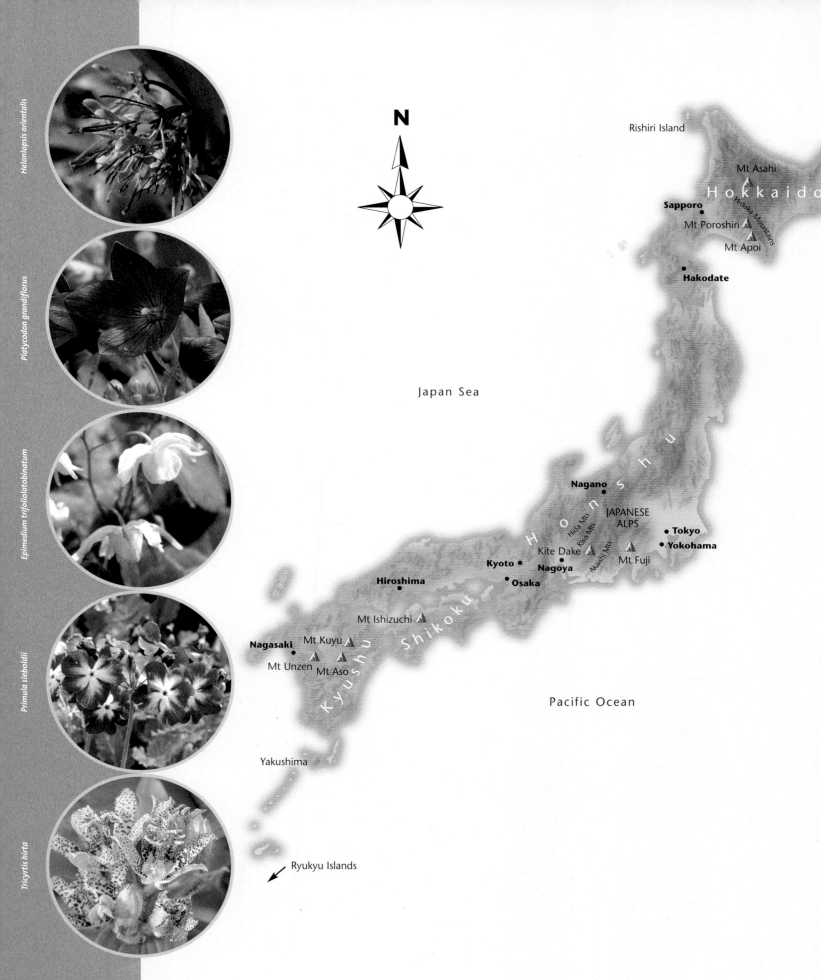

Heloniopsis orientalis

Platycodon grandiflorus

Epimedium trifoliolatobinatum

Primula sieboldii

Tricyrtis hirta

N

Rishiri Island

Mt Asahi

H o k k a i d o

Kurile Islands

Sapporo

Hidaka Mountains

Mt Poroshiri

Mt Apoi

Hakodate

Japan Sea

Nagano

H o n s h u

JAPANESE ALPS

Hida Mts

Kiso Mts

Tokyo

Yokohama

Kite Dake

Akaishi Mts

Mt Fuji

Kyoto

Nagoya

Hiroshima

Osaka

Mt Ishizuchi

S h i k o k u

Nagasaki

Mt Kuyu

K y u s h u

Mt Unzen

Mt Aso

Pacific Ocean

Yakushima

Ryukyu Islands

Chapter 7 Japan

Lying off the east coast of Asia, between the latitudes of 25° and 45° N, are more than 3,000 islands that make up the country of Japan. The total area of Japan is over 377,000 km² (145,560 square miles). Although a relatively small area compared to the other regions covered by chapters in this book, the wide latitudinal range and varied topography of these islands, as well as the influence of the North American and Asian floras, ensures that the plants of Japan are interesting, diverse and sometimes unique.

The four main islands of Japan are, from north to south, Hokkaido, Honshu, Shikoku and Kyushu, with Honshu being the largest. Extending south from Kyushu towards Taiwan on the Tropic of Cancer are the subtropical Ryukyu Islands, also known as Nansei-shoto. Japan's densely populated cities are mostly located on coastal plains and much of the rest of the country (over 70%) is mountainous, much of it forested. Several of these mountains reach over 3,000 m (9.843 feet) in altitude, with the highest being the volcano Mt Fuji at 3,776 m (12,389 feet), situated near the capitol, Tokyo. The rest of Japan's highest peaks are found in the granite mountains of the Japanese Alps, which stretch 225 km (140 miles) across central Honshu. They comprise three main ranges: the Northern Alps, also known as the Hida Mountains, the Central Alps or Kiso Mountains, and the Southern Alps or Akaishi Mountains. Kite Dake, in the Akaishi Mountains, is the highest peak in all the Japanese Alps and the second highest in Japan, reaching 3,192 m (10,472 feet).

The highest mountain on the northern-most of the main islands, Hokkaido, is the volcano Mt Asahi in the Daisetsuzan National Park at 2,290 m (7,513 feet). In south-east Hokkaido are the Hidaka mountains, with the highest point at the summit of Mt Poroshiri at 2,052 m (6,732 feet). This range also includes Mt Apoi (810 m; 2,657 feet), which is known for a number of endemic plants that grow on its slopes. Despite its relatively low altitude, Mt Apoi has a well-developed alpine flora along its ridge due to the summer fogs that come off the sea, cutting out solar radiation and keeping temperatures down.

The highest point on the island of Shikoku is Mt Ishizuchi (1,982 m; 6,503 feet) and on Kyushu it is Mt Kuyu (1,788 m; 5,866 feet). On Kyushu is also Japan's most active volcano, Mt Aso (1,592 m; 5,223 feet). South of Kyushu is the small island of Yakushima, which is only 500 km² (193 square miles) in area but reaches an elevation of 1,935 m (6,348 feet). At sea level, Yakushima has a subtropical climate but the mountains of this island are often snow-capped in winter.

The climate of Japan varies with latitude, and the Ryukyu Islands in the south have a subtropical climate with high precipitation, particularly during the rainy season. The rainy season in Japan begins in May in the south, working its way northwards until reaching Hokkaido in late July. In addition, typhoons develop in late summer, moving from the south-west to the north-east and bringing heavy rain. Prevailing winds and sea currents also affect the climate of Japan. The Kuroshio Current, also known as the Japan Current, brings warm waters from the tropics to the eastern, Pacific coast of Japan. The Pacific coast also experiences warm south-easterly winds in summer and so the summer months are hot and humid. Winters are cold but with little snow. On the Japan Sea side of the country, the north-westerly winter winds bring very heavy snowfall. Summers are cooler than on the Pacific side. Further north in Hokkaido, winters are longer and summers cooler.

The alpine zone in the Japanese mountains is found above roughly 2,500 m (8,202 feet) in central Honshu but further north, in Hokkaido, it occurs lower down the slopes, beginning at about 1,500 m (4921 feet) (Ohwi, 1984). This alpine zone is characteristically populated by the shrubby pine, *Pinus pumila*. Several rhododendrons are also found in the alpine scrub, including the brick-red-flowered, evergreen *Rhododendron kaempferi*, which is found on all the main islands, and the yellow-flowered, prostrate evergreen shrub *R. aureum*, which also occurs in Korea, Sakhalin, Kamchatka and eastern Siberia. Alder and birch extend into the alpine zone as stunted shrubs, and the foliage of the endemic rowan, *Sorbus matsumurana*, provides splashes of bright-orange autumn colour. The Japanese alpine flora has a strong link to that of eastern Siberia, Alaska, the Aleutian Islands and Kamchatka. Circumpolar species, such as *Loiseleuria procumbens* and *Cassiope lycopodioides*, are also found here. Between 440 and 580 Japanese species have been described as alpine plants, and this alpine flora has a high endemism rate of 51.3% (Fuji & Senni, 2006).

With their extensive wooded slopes, it is no surprise that the Japanese mountains have contributed many beautiful plants to woodland gardens around the world. The deciduous woodland floor is home to bulbous and rhizomatous species that bloom as the snow melts, usually in March and April in northern Japan. They include plants like the purple-rose-flowered *Erythronium japonicum*, also found in Korea, Sakhalin, the Kurile Islands and China, *Adonis amurensis* with its finely dissected leaves and golden-yellow flowers, and hepaticas, long grown as pot plants in Japan and with over 500 cultivars now recognised.

Flora Japonica

The earliest Japanese plants grown in Western gardens were those that are also found outside Japan, such as *Camellia japonica*, which also grows in China. Exploration of Japan was largely forbidden to outsiders until the nineteenth century, but among the Japanese rock garden plants that found their way into cultivation before then is *Platycodon grandiflorus* of the Campanulaceae. Sometimes known as the balloon flower because the buds expand like a balloon before opening, it was introduced into cultivation in Britain in 1782 by John Bell, a land steward to the Duke of Northumberland at Syon House in Middlesex (Desmond,

FAR LEFT
Loiseleuria procumbens, a circumpolar species found in Japan.

LEFT
Erythronium japonicum.

1994). It is possible, however, that Bell only reintroduced this species. It could have been known in Europe long before the eighteenth century if the "Blew Bell-flower of China", mentioned in Gerard's garden list of 1599, is the same plant (Coats, 1968). A dwarf form has been collected from Mt Apoi on Hokkaido and named *P. grandiflorus* 'Apoyama'. It received an Award of Merit from the RHS in 1961. The original plants have long died out but seed-raised dwarf forms are now classified in the Apoyama Group.

Platycodon grandiflorus is a striking, summer-flowering perennial from north-east China, eastern Siberia, Korea and Japan, where it grows on grassy and rocky slopes and among shrubs at up to 2,000 m (6,562 feet). Japanese plants of this species were first described as *Campanula glauca* in 1784 by Carl Thunberg in his *Flora Japonica*. Thunberg was a Swedish physician and naturalist who studied under Linnaeus at Uppsala. He arrived in Japan in 1775 to work as physician for The Dutch East India Company, which had a base on an artificial island called Deshima in the bay of Nagasaki, southern Japan.

This Dutch trading post was established in 1641 and, at this time, only the Dutch and the Chinese were allowed to trade with Japan. Early in the seventeenth century, missionaries from other European countries had been accused of being intolerant and cruel, even supporting local revolutionary movements. This led to their expulsion and to the closure of the ports to all foreigners; the Japanese were also forbidden to leave their country. Only the Chinese and Dutch, who had not sent missionaries, were allowed some trading concessions. The products the Dutch exported from Japan included silver, gold, copper and pottery. Imports were mainly medications. Foreigners were closely watched and access to the mainland over the bridge linking Deshima to Nagasaki was mostly forbidden. However, the Japanese were keen to learn about western medical practices and the physicians who stayed on Deshima were occasionally permitted into Japan, where some were able to collect plant specimens.

Long before Thunberg arrived in Deshima, another physician with an interest in the plants of Japan had stayed on the artificial island while working for The Dutch East India Company. Engelbert Kaempfer arrived to take up his post in 1690 and stayed until November 1692. Knowing of his interest in botany, the Japanese brought him specimens of plants growing around the bay of Nagasaki, both wild and cultivated. Kaempfer illustrated and described them meticulously. In addition, he was required to travel with the Dutch governor to Yedo (Tokyo) once a year in spring to appear at the Imperial Court. This long journey by land and sea lasted around 12 weeks in total, including the 30 or so days spent in Yedo, and was a welcome change to the monotony of everyday life on the small island of Deshima. Kaempfer travelled to Yedo twice and took these opportunities to collect plant specimens along the way. He was also allowed to leave Deshima once or twice a year, under supervision, to explore the Bay of Nagasaki.

LEFT
Adonis amurensis, grows in deciduous woodlands on Hokkaido, Honshu and Kyushu, as well as Continental Asia.

BELOW
The plant now known as *Hosta sieboldiana* is included in Kaempfer's *Amoenitates Exoticae* of 1712.

Naming the balloon flower

Platycodon grandiflorus displays wonderful, broadly bell-shaped flowers that can be up to 7 or 8 cm across and are purplish-blue with darker veining. They open wide from balloon-like buds that are produced at the end of the herbaceous stems.

Johann Georg Gmelin, of the University of St Petersburg, found this plant in Siberia in 1754. However, it was 1776 before it was formally given a name, *Campanula grandiflora*, by Nicolaus Jacquin (1776). Jacquin included it in his *Hortus Botanicus Vindobonensis*, in which plants from the Botanic Garden at Vienna are described and illustrated. Alphonse de Candolle created the genus *Platycodon* in 1830 and described two species, *P. grandiflorus* and *P. homallanthinum*. The first is Jacquin's *Campanula grandiflora*, but the second was removed from the genus in 1839 and initially placed in *Wahlenbergia* in de Candolle's *Prodromus*. More recently, this species was listed as a synonym of *Astrocodon expansa* in the *Flora of the USSR* (Fedorov, 1972). *Platycodon* differs from the closely related *Campanula* in having seed capsules that open by five apical valves opposite the calyx lobes, rather than from basal or median pores.

In 1851, John Lindley and Joseph Paxton described plants collected in China by Robert Fortune as *Platycodon chinense* (Lindley & Paxton, 1851). These, along with other species, such as *P. glaucus* and *P. autumnale*, are now regarded as synonymous with *P. grandiflorus* and the genus is widely considered to be monotypic. More compact forms have been found in Japan and have been given cultivar names, such as 'Apoyama'.

The seeds are dispersed from apical valves.

Platycodon grandiflorus.

In 1712, back in Germany, Kaempfer published an illustrated account of his travels, *Amoenitates Exoticae*. The botanical content of this work is found in the fifth section, where 232 plant species are described, both native and introduced, but all observed by Kaempfer in Japan. Among them are plants now known as *Camellia japonica*, *Ophiopogon japonicus* and *Hosta sieboldiana*, and introductions from China, such as *Paeonia suffruticosa* and *Chimonanthes praecox* (Stearn, 1999). This important work can be regarded as a preliminary flora of Japan and was used by Linnaeus as the only source of information about Japanese plants until Thunberg returned to Sweden from Japan in 1778.

Thunberg also had the pleasure of accompanying the annual embassy to Yedo and he too collected plants along the way. Restrictions on his movements appeared to be more relaxed than those during Kaempfer's time 80 years earlier. As well as travelling to Yedo and visiting a plant nursery on the return leg, he was able to explore the area around Nagasaki many times, even twice a week in the spring (Coats, 1969). He cared for his plants in a small garden on Deshima and managed to send some back to Holland. Once back in Europe, Thunberg published his descriptions in *Flora Japonica* in 1784. Like Kaempfer's work, Thunberg's *Flora Japonica* included a great number of newly described species.

Many of the plants that appeared in *Flora Japonica* have now had changes of name. Among them is *Convallaria japonica*, named "Mondo & Biaks Mondo" by Kaempfer and now known as *Ophiopogon japonicus*. He lists *Asarum virginicum* , first described by Linnaeus in 1753, but the plants known to Thunberg in Japan were a different species, later named *Heterotropa asaroides* by the Belgian botanists Charles Morren and Joseph Decaisne in 1834 and now known as *Asarum asaroides*.

Thunberg lists only two species of *Scilla* in *Flora Japonica*: *S. japonica* and *S. bifolia*. The latter plant he subsequently renamed *Scilla orientalis* in 1794 (Thunberg, 1794), but this and *S. japonica* were later transferred to *Heloniopsis*, a genus established by the American botanist Asa Gray in 1859. Thunberg's scillas are now both treated as synonyms of *H. orientalis*, a clump-forming perennial found in Japan, Korea and Sakhalin.

The plant now known as *Heloniopsis orientalis* was eventually introduced into cultivation after being collected by Charles Maries in the mountains of Japan and brought to the Veitch Nursery in England, where it first flowered in the spring of 1881. Maries spent three years collecting for Messrs. Veitch in China and Japan, from 1877 to 1880.

When describing the genus *Heloniopsis*, Asa Gray named only one species, *H. pauciflora*, from a dried specimen collected in north-west Hokkaido. Gray (1859) compares

this species to the American genus *Helonias* but states that it has fewer flowers and a single, slender style, rather than three separate styles. Further species were soon described, including *H. japonica* and *H. breviscapa*, both named by the Russian Carl Johann Maximowicz in 1867. These are now considered synonyms of *H. orientalis*, which was described by Tyôzaburô Tanaka in 1925.

Heloniopsis breviscapa, from the mountains of Kyushu, is treated as a variety of *H. orientalis* in Ohwi's *Flora of Japan* (Ohwi, 1984). It differs from the typical form in its white to pale rose-pink flowers that have shorter perianth segments. Ohwi also recognises another variety, the slightly taller, white-flowered var. *flavida* from Honshu.

Heloniopsis leucantha and the late summer- to autumn-flowering *H. kawanoi* are found in the Ryukyu Islands, whereas *H. umbellata* is native to Taiwan. *Heloniopsis* is now thought to contain four or five species; a full list of synonyms for this genus is given in a revision by Noriyuki Tanaka (1998). However, Tanaka transfers all the species of *Heloniopsis*, and the closely related *Ypsilandra*, to the previously monotypic genus *Helonias*. It remains to be seen whether this revised classification will be generally accepted by taxonomists.

Asarum asaroides
Family: Aristolochiaceae

Asarum is a genus of rhizomatous perennials distributed across the temperate regions of the northern hemisphere, with the highest concentration of species in China and Japan. They are woodland plants, often growing in deep shade, in valleys or ravines and on north-facing hillsides. Their usually evergreen, long-stemmed leaves can be attractively patterned, and from beneath them, on short stalks, peer the curious, sometimes sinister-looking flowers. These are commonly in shades of dull purple, brown or green and consist of three perianth lobes that are united at least at the base, sometimes forming a distinct tube.

Taken in its broadest sense, the genus *Asarum* contains around 100 species. In the past, however, it has been split into several smaller genera separated by minor differences in floral morphology. The genus *Heterotropa* was established by the Belgian botanists Charles Morren and Joseph Decaisne in 1834. They described one species, *H. asaroides*, on the basis of the plant incorrectly named *Asarum virginicum* in Thunberg's *Flora Japonica*. It was given the name *Asarum asaroides* by Tomitaro Makino in 1910.

Around 50 species of *Asarum* are found in Japan and the Ryukyu Islands. Many of them are endemic to Japan, including *A. asaroides* which occurs in south-west Honshu and Kyushu. Asarums have been cultivated in Japan for hundreds of years. They are believed to offer protection from earthquakes and storms if planted at the front of houses or hung from the eaves (Boyce, 1994).

Asarum asaroides was introduced to Europe by Philipp von Siebold on his return from Japan in 1830. The spotted and mottled leaves are broadly ovate to roughly triangular in outline and up to 12 cm long. They persist throughout much of the year, but the main growing period is spring and summer. The dark, dull purplish-green flowers appear in early spring. They have a pear-shaped tube of 2–2.5 cm in length and three spreading, rounded to triangular lobes. Around the mouth of the tube, the perianth lobes are wrinkled; the ridges are lighter purple or crested with white. The flowers have also been described as "perfumed somewhat like a ripe apple" and "large as a walnut" (Graham, 1840).

Although *Asarum asaroides* can tolerate a few degrees of frost, it is best grown in a cold frame to keep off rain in the winter and to provide some protection during particularly cold spells. Use an acidic, humus-rich, free-draining soil mix and place the rhizomes just below soil level. During the winter, keep the soil just moist; but once growth begins in spring, increase watering and never let the soil dry out throughout the spring and summer. If this species is tried in the open garden, plant it in a cool, shady, sheltered spot.

This is a slow-growing plant, but older clumps can be carefully divided in spring by cutting off portions of the rhizome with roots and a growing point. If seed is produced, it should be collected and sown immediately, before it dries out. Germination will usually occur in early spring but may take more than a year.

Curtis's Botanical Magazine, plate 4933 (1856). Artist: Walter Hood Fitch.

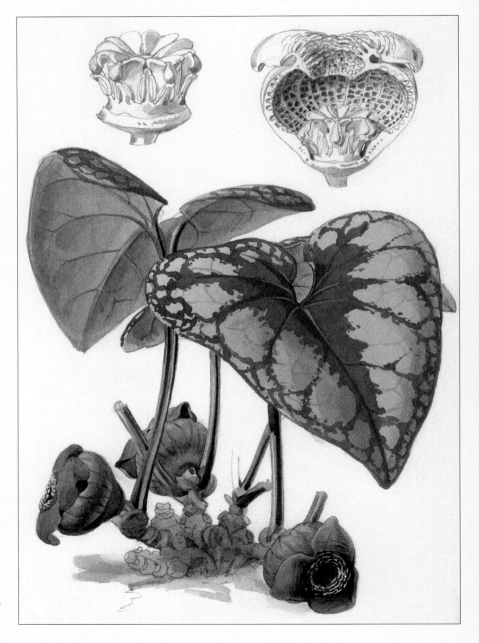

Heloniopsis orientalis
Family: Melanthiaceae

Heloniopsis orientalis grows at altitudes of 50 m (164 feet) to over 2,000 m (6,562 feet). At lower altitudes, it is often found in deep shade in forests, amongst leaf litter, besides streams or on peaty banks. In the mountains, it tends to inhabit more open positions, in moist meadows, in scrub and on stony slopes.

This is a hardy species that can be grown outside in peaty, moist but never waterlogged soil, in a cool, shady position. It can withstand temperatures as low as −10 °C to −15 °C. It is an evergreen, but in spring new leaves emerge along with the flower stems from fat buds at the centre of the clump.

The flower stems grow 10–20 cm tall but can elongate to around 60 cm after flowering. The racemes hold 2–10 nodding flowers in shades of pink to rose-purple or red. The narrow perianth segments are free to the base, around 1–1.5 cm long and spreading in the upper half when fully expanded. These flowers are held above often untidy rosettes of evergreen, oblanceolate leaves that are green, tinged with brownish-purple and up to 15 cm long. Propagation is best by division in autumn or late winter.

Heloniopsis orentalis.

In August 1826, 50 years after Thunberg left Japan, the German doctor Philipp Franz von Siebold arrived on Deshima. As well as being a well qualified and skilled physician, he had a keen interest in natural history and plant collecting. He also went on to publish a *Flora Japonica*, in collaboration with Joseph Zuccarini. This work was published in two illustrated volumes between 1835 and 1842.

Siebold was eventually expelled from Japan for attempting to export prohibited maps, but only after spending a year in prison from December 1828 to December 1829. Nevertheless, he still managed to arrange for a consignment of plants to be sent to Holland in January 1829; and when he left Japan in January 1830, he took with him a further 485 plants, among them hostas, epimediums, hydrangeas, lilies, bamboos and camellias. With these, he established a nursery in Leiden and so made a major contribution to the introduction of Japanese plants to nineteenth century horticulture in Europe.

Primula sieboldii was introduced by Siebold and grown in his Leiden nursery. It was named after him by Charles Jacques Édouard Morren in 1873. This is one of the most colourful and variable species in cultivation. In the wild, its range extends from eastern Siberia through Manchuria and

LEFT
Primula sieboldii in cultivation.

Korea to Japan, where it is found in wet grassy places on Hokkaido, Honshu and Kyushu. The flower colour is rose, white or rose purple often with a large white central eye.

Primula sieboldii was grown in Japanese gardens long before it was introduced into Europe. Many cultivars have been produced and some have made their way into cultivation outside Japan. It is a creeping, deciduous species that spreads to form large clumps of oblong to oval leaves with flower stems up to 30 cm tall holding one or occasionally two whorls of flowers in spring. It is easily propagated by division in early spring before flowering.

Among the plants described by Siebold and Zuccarini in their *Flora Japonica* are a few that wouldn't look out of place on a large rock garden. These include *Daphne genkwa* of the Thymelaeaceae. Although native to China and Korea, this shrub has long been grown in Japanese gardens. Prostrate forms in particular can make good specimens for a rock garden.

The genus *Deutzia*, of the Hydrangeaceae, was described by Thunberg in 1781 using *Deutzia scabra* as the type species. The genus comprises deciduous or semi-evergreen shrubs from Asia and Mexico that have attractive flowers. Siebold and Zuccarini described two endemic Japanese species, *D. crenata* and *D. gracilis*. Both display racemes of five-petalled, white flowers in May and June. Siebold and

Zuccarini also described a lily, *Lilium callosum*, which has yellow to orange-red nodding flowers on stems anything from 30 to 100 cm tall. This species is native to Japan but also occurs in China, Korea, Taiwan and Manchuria.

It was Siebold and Zuccarini who named the plant that has come to be known as the Japanese anemone. Thunberg described this autumn-flowering herbaceous perennial using the name *Atragene japonica*, but it was Siebold and Zuccarini who gave it the name *Anemone japonica*. This plant was later reduced to a variety of *Anemone hupehensis*, but the name 'Japanese anemone' is now widely used for a popular group of hybrids that come in a range of colours, from white to deep pink and maroon. These hybrids are based on crosses between *A. hupehensis* and *Anemone vitifolia*, neither of which are native to Japan but come from China. *Anemone hupehensis* is naturalised in Japan, hence Thunberg's description. In fact, it is clear that many of the plants described by the foreign physicians based on Deshima were found growing in Japanese gardens. The tight restrictions imposed on the movements of these physicians, from the mid seventeenth century to the early nineteenth century, meant that botanical exploration was often limited to gardens and nurseries. The long history of Japanese horticulture meant that a wide range of plants were being cultivated, both from Japan and other countries in eastern Asia.

FAR LEFT
Deutzia gracilis, endemic to Japan and described by Siebold and Zuccarini in 1835.

LEFT
Anemone hupehensis, naturalised in Japan and one of the parents of the 'Japanese anemones' of gardens.

It was only when Japan opened her ports to European and American trade, and allowed more freedom of movement for foreigners, that large numbers of Japanese plants were introduced to Europe. Once the restrictions were lifted, it did not take long for the richness of Japan's flora to be fully appreciated outside the country.

Arrival of the plant hunters

From 1853, Japan began to open her ports to foreign trade. The American Perry Expedition of 1852–1854 led to the change in international relations and resulted in the signing of the Treaty of Kanagawa in 1854, allowing the USA to trade with Japan. In 1858 Russia, France, Holland and Britain signed similar treaties.

Restrictions were still imposed on travel inland but botanists soon arrived and began collecting the flora of the country. The Royal Botanic Gardens, Kew sent a collector, Charles Wilford, to the Far East and he arrived in Japan, having travelled via Hong Kong and Taiwan, in 1859. No plant introductions appear to have resulted from this trip, but he did collect herbarium specimens and is remembered in the names of several plants, including the low-growing *Geranium wilfordii*. This species is certainly a suitable size for a rock garden if a little invasive when allowed to romp around unchecked. It spreads by its small rounded tubers to form a mat of leaves topped by purplish-pink flowers.

Carl Johann Maximowicz arrived in Japan in September 1860 to study the flora and stayed for over three years. He sent 72 chests of herbarium specimens home to St Petersburg (Barnes, 2001), as well as bulbs and seeds that resulted in the introduction into cultivation of many new plants, such as *Berberis thunbergii*. Plants that are named after him include the tuberous aroid *Arisaema maximowiczii* from the woods of the Unzen Peninsula on Kyushu, described in 1924. This is one of several arisaemas from Japan. They include one of the most widely cultivated arisaema species, *A. sikokianum*, which has a white, swollen spadix surrounded by a dark purple spathe.

The name of Veitch consistently turns up when discussing nineteenth century plant introductions into Europe and the arrival of Japanese plants is no exception. Through their two nurseries in Exeter and Chelsea, this famous family had a huge influence on British and European horticulture for over a century. It was the 21-year-old John Gould Veitch, based in Chelsea, who set sail for Japan, arriving in Nagasaki on 20 July 1860. So soon after Japan had relaxed her restrictions on foreign visitors, it must have been a sign of the times that when he found a place to stay in a Buddhist temple he was lodging with three other Englishmen.

Veitch was permitted to travel only ten miles from his base in Nagasaki, but in this area he was able to find plenty of plants to interest him, growing wild and in gardens. He was even allowed to grow his living collections in part of the temple garden, and when he was away he asked his compatriots to look after them. However, he really wanted to visit the area around Tokyo so at the end of August he set sail for Yokohama. There, he met with the British Consul, Sir Rutherford Alcock, who invited him to join an excursion to Mt Fuji as 'Botanist to Her Britannic Majesty's Legation at Yedo' (Coates, 1969). This was the first time Europeans had been allowed to climb this sacred mountain. Veitch took the opportunity to collect seed and specimens of many species, including several conifers.

After this excursion to Mt Fuji, Veitch re-visited Yokohama and also visited Hakodate, at the southern tip of Hokkaido. He then stayed with Alcock in Tokyo, but his movements there were very restricted and he had to use local collectors to find plants for him in the surrounding area. He left Japan at the end of November 1860, but his stay in Tokyo overlapped with the visit of Robert Fortune, already a veteran of four successful plant-hunting expeditions to China.

Although successful in many other ways, Veitch's trip to Japan did not result in many alpines being sent back to Britain. Among the few plants that could be grown on a rock garden, however, was one of the most dramatic introductions of the second half of the nineteenth century. If you didn't know any better, upon seeing *Lilium auratum* growing in a garden, you would assume it was a flamboyant hybrid bred in cultivation, but this wonderfully extravagant plant is a true wild species from the hills and mountains of Honshu. It caused a sensation when shown by the Veitch's Chelsea Nursery at the show of the Horticultural Society of

The oriental lilies

The genus *Lilium* contains around 100 species that are distributed across the northern hemisphere, mostly in the temperate regions. There are 13 species listed in *Flora of Japan* (Ohwi, 1984). Until Harold Comber (1949) published his new classification of the genus in 1949, lilies were grouped according to their flower shape. Comber, the son of James Comber (the first head gardener at Nymans in Sussex), used a number of characters to divide up the genus. The oriental lilies were placed in section *Archelirion*, which has the wonderful Japanese *Lilium auratum* as its type species. Characteristics of the lilies in this section include the rooting stems, the entire bulb scales, the distinctly petiolate, alternate leaves and hypogeal germination, which is usually delayed so the first leaf to appear is a true leaf. This may be 18 months after sowing because growth is initially below ground, where a small bulb forms; growth above ground is delayed until after a cold period. Other oriental lilies include the well-known *L. speciosum* from Shikoku and Kyushu, *L. rubellum* (the maiden lily), which is endemic to northern Honshu, *L. japonicum* from Honshu, Shikoku and Kyushu and the Chinese *L. brownii*. *Lilium japonicum* and *L. speciosum* were both described by Thunberg; the former in his *Flora Japonica* in 1784 and the latter in 1794.

   Lilium rubellum and *L. japonicum* have soft rose-pink, funnel-shaped flowers; but in *L. japonicum*, they are longer, to 15 cm, with dark brown rather than yellow anthers. *Lilium japonicum* also has longer leaves and grows up to 1 m tall. *Lilium rubellum* grows 30–80 cm tall, with scattered, lanceolate to oblong-elliptic leaves. It was imported from Japan by Messrs Bunting of Chelmsford in February 1898. Stock was purchased by the nurseryman and lily specialist Robert Wallace of Colchester and exhibited at the RHS Temple Show on the 25–27 May 1898, where it received a First Class Certificate. It was described by John Baker in the *Gardeners' Chronicle* of 28 May 1898 but this plant was already well-known in its native country. It was figured by the Japanese artist Iwasaki Tsunemasa in the *Honzo Zufu*, an illustrated flora of Japan in 96 volumes that includes 2000 coloured drawings, which was published in 1828.

Lilium speciosum.

London (soon to become the Royal Horticultural Society) on 2 July 1862. The huge, saucer-shaped, strongly fragrant, ivory-white flowers are dotted with purple-red spots, and broad yellow bands extend from the tips of the perianth segments towards the centre of the flower, giving this plant the names 'gold-banded lily' and 'golden-rayed lily'.

Although needing plenty of moisture during its summer growing period, *Lilium auratum* is better suited to the well-drained and relatively poor soil of a rock garden than the moist humus-rich soil of a woodland garden where lilies are often grown. A healthy, well-grown specimen of this lily can display more than 20 blooms at the end of a leafy stem that reaches 1.5 m tall. The scent is intoxicating. John Lindley described this "glorious" lily in the *Gardeners' Chronicle* on 12 July 1862, the same day it was exhibited at the show of the Massachusetts Horticultural Society (Nelson, 1999). It is the type species of section *Archelirion*, the 'oriental lilies'.

When Robert Fortune met the young John Veitch in Tokyo in 1860, he was already one of the more influential plant collectors of the time, having made many plant introductions from China. Unlike his previous expeditions, however, Fortune's trip to Japan, from 1860 to 1861, was undertaken on behalf of neither the Horticultural Society of London nor the East India Company. Fortune probably financed it himself as one of the purposes of this trip was to collect works of art. He also collected plants but this pursuit was almost entirely limited to what was growing in Japanese gardens and nurseries. It seems likely that he had an arrangement with Mr Standish's nursery at Bagshot, Surrey, to distribute the plants on his return (Cox, 1943). In the 15 March 1862 edition of the *Gardeners' Chronicle*, it is stated that Mr Standish was "engaged in rearing the very interesting series of plants recently introduced by Mr Fortune from Japan".

Among the plants growing in Standish's Bagshot nursery was an autumn-flowering *Saxifraga* that Joseph Hooker named after Fortune in 1863. *Saxifraga fortunei* is a leafy, perennial species usually found growing along streams and among wet rocks in shaded areas at altitudes of 2,000–3,000 m (6,562–9,843 feet), and producing sprays of white, spidery flowers. It also occurs in Korea and the Chinese provinces of Sichuan, Hubei, Jilin and Liaoning.

Saxifraga fortunei makes a fine plant for a woodland garden, a shady gully on a rock garden or pots in a shaded frame, where it will flower from late summer. The round leathery leaves have lobed margins and are bright green early in the season, with red undersides that gradually become bronze-red. The sprays of white, spidery flowers are produced on branched stems up to 50 cm tall. Several cultivars of *S. fortunei* are available and some, such as 'Wada' and 'Rubrifolia', have their foliage suffused with red throughout the season.

LEFT
Saxifraga stolonifera.

BELOW
Saxifraga fortunei.

Saxifraga fortunei belongs to section *Irregulares*, which contains around 15 species. All of the plants in this section have asymmetrical flowers, a unique feature in the genus. One or two of the lower petals are much longer than the others, up to three or four times longer. The flowers are held in elegant panicles well above the kidney-shaped to rounded leaves. *Saxifraga fortunei* is not stoloniferous but some species in this section are, such as the widely grown *S. stolonifera*, commonly known as 'mother of thousands', which forms new leaf rosettes at the end of long stolons. *Saxifraga stolonifera* occurs on Honshu, Shikoku and Kyushu, as well as in China, Korea and Taiwan and is also suited to woodland conditions.

Fortune is also credited with the introduction of the magenta-flowered 'candelabra' *Primula japonica*, which he first saw growing in gardens in Tokyo. He was so enamoured with this plant that he called it the 'queen of the primroses'. Fortune collected seeds and sent them to England but they failed to germinate. He also sent plants but these were lost on the voyage. It was 1870 before seeds did germinate in England, and according to Joseph Hooker (1871), they came from W. Keswick Esq. of Hong Kong and Messrs. Walsh Hall & Co. of Yokohama, "which gentlemen have the honour of introducing a very lovely plant into English gardens". This species was named in 1859 by Asa Gray from specimens collected in 1855 by Charles Wright, one of two botanists on the Ringgold and Rodgers US North Pacific Exploring Expedition, 1853–1856. The other botanist was J. Small, commemorated in the Japanese *Trillium smallii*.

Trillium smallii is just one of the many woodland plants that have made their way from Japan to the gardens of Europe and North America. The early collector's mentioned here and those that followed, sent back plants from the wooded hills and mountains of Japan but the true alpine flora has been relatively neglected. One reason for this is

that extensive arctic-alpine areas are not represented in Japan. There are, however, plenty of woodlands, giving way to pine, alder and birch scrub, and ground cover of *Sasa*, a dwarf bamboo, at higher altitudes. It is notable that when Veitch had the honour of climbing Japan's highest mountain, Mt Fuji, in 1860, it was seed of conifers that he brought back, not alpines. Also, the links the Japanese flora has with those of Asia and North America mean that most genera of Japanese mountain plants are also found elsewhere in the Northern Hemisphere. One exception is the very rarely cultivated, monotypic genus *Japonolirion*, which is usually placed in the same family as *Heloniopsis* (Melanthiaceae) but more recently has been moved to Petrosaviaceae, an eastern Asian family of only two genera, the other being *Petrosavia*. *Japonolirion* is the only endemic genus of the Japanese alpine zone (Ohwi, 1984). Nevertheless, there are around 1,950 endemic plants in Japan, some of them belonging to genera that are much more diverse in other parts of the world. Many of these endemics come from the alpine meadows and wooded slopes of Japan's mountains.

Japanese endemic mountain plants

The alpine zones of Japan are distributed across the country, especially in central Honshu and Hokkaido, like islands in a 'sea' of temperate vegetation. During interglacial periods, the plants in these distinct alpine zones have diversified in isolation, resulting in a high proportion of endemic species. In glacial periods, these alpine zones joined together, particularly in the northern half of Japan, and lower sea levels led to the formation of land bridges allowing plants to migrate to Japan from the rest of Asia and North America. Then, as the climate warmed again, sea levels rose, the land bridges linking the Japanese islands to the mainland disappeared and the alpine zones shrunk, becoming isolated from one another once again. As a result, the Japanese alpine flora includes many relicts from the Asian and North American floras and has strong links with them.

Japanese endemic mountain plants include both true alpines and woodland plants. Those from the alpine zone include the rare, greenish-yellow *Papaver fauriei*, from the gravelly slopes of the dormant volcano Mt Rishiri (1,721 m; 5,646 feet) on Rishiri Island, north-west of Hokkaido. This small, hairy, perennial species is related to *P. nudicaule* (often called the 'Iceland poppy' although it comes from the mountains of central and northern Asia). *Papaver fauriei* grows 10–20 cm tall with a solitary flower around 2.5–4 cm across. Very similar and often confused with *P. fauriei* is *P. miyabeanum*, which is also yellow-flowered and comes from the Kurile Islands, a volcanic archipelago that extends from

north-east Hokkaido towards Kamchatka. *Papaver miyabeanum* has larger flowers and a slightly larger seed capsule than *P. fauriei*, and its leaves are mostly pinnately divided instead of bipinnate and have more rounded lobes (Gardner, 1999). Both species are attractive, dainty alpine poppies, short-lived but easily increased by seed.

The columbine *Aquilegia buergeriana* grows in mountain meadows and forest edges in Honshu, Shikoku and Kyushu. The genus *Aquilegia* contains around 70 species distributed throughout the temperate regions of the Northern Hemisphere. In *Flora of Japan*, Ohwi lists just three Japanese species and *A. buergeriana* is the only one that is endemic. It was described by Siebold and Zuccarini in 1846 and has brownish purple sepals and yellowish petals. One of the finest aquilegias is the Japanese *A. flabellata*, also described by Siebold and Zuccarini in 1846. It occurs in Korea, in Sakhalin and in the alpine regions of Hokkaido, Honshu and the Kurile Islands. The dwarf form from northern Hokkaido, named *A. flabellata* var. *pumila*, may reach only 15 cm tall and has purple-blue petals often tipped with white. Plants sold under the name *A. flabellata* 'Nana' are really the same as var. *pumila*. Those named 'Nana Alba' are white-flowered.

BELOW
The dwarf *Aquilegia flabellata* var. *pumila*.

Glaucidium palmatum
Family: Ranunculaceae

This distinguished herbaceous perennial, from wooded slopes in the mountains of Japan, can easily be mistaken by the casual observer for some strange *Anemone* or poppy. When Philipp von Siebold and Joseph Zuccarini described *Glaucidium palmatum* in 1845, they placed it in Ranunculaceae, but it has since been placed in Paeoniaceae, Podophyllaceae and even in its own family, Glaucidiaceae (e.g. Tamura, 1972). More recently, the classification of the Angiosperm Phylogeny Group, based on DNA studies, has returned it to Ranunculaceae but in its own order, Glaucidioideae.

Glaucidium palmatum is the only species in this genus. It occurs sporadically in Hokkaido, northern Honshu and the Japan Sea side of central Honshu, growing in deciduous forests high in the mountains, sometimes in deep shade but often in glades or areas of re-growth following tree felling (Halliwell, 1987). It is dormant for the winter months but in spring the new shoots push through the ground, with the tightly folded leaves surrounding the flower buds.

The flowers open when the stems are around 15–20 cm tall and often before the leaves are fully developed. The unbranched stems can eventually reach 60 cm tall and hold two or occasionally three pale green leaves. These are broadly palmate, 8–20 cm across and with 5–11 lobes. The leaf margins are coarsely toothed and the central lobes are split again into two or three shallow divisions. At the end of the stem is the solitary flower, subtended by a leafy bract. These beautiful, wide bowl-shaped flowers are made up of four thin, petal-like sepals in shades of mauve, violet, lavender blue or rarely white. They are up to 8 cm wide and, usually, at their centre are two carpels surrounded by a boss of bright yellow anthers.

Glaucidium palmatum was introduced to cultivation in Britain early in the twentieth century and received an Award of Merit in April 1954 and a First Class Certificate in April 1963. A white-flowered form of this species was described as *G. palmatum* var. *leucanthum* by Tomitaro Makino in 1910. This is often listed invalidly as *G. palmatum* 'Album'. Only a proportion of seed from these plants will produce offspring with white flowers.

Glaucidium palmatum needs an open, moist, humus-rich, lime-free soil and a cool, partially shaded position in which it is sheltered from the wind. It will suffer in high summer temperatures and strong sunlight. This is a hardy species that dies down by late autumn and overwinters as an underground rhizome. It generally does better in the open ground, in a woodland garden or a cool, shady gully on a rock garden.

Once established, *Glaucidium palmatum* is best left undisturbed, but it is possible to propagate this species by carefully dividing the rhizome in early spring. The best way to raise new plants is to sow the seed when fresh, but it may take two years or more to germinate. However, *G. palmatum* is very long-lived and plants of at least 60 cm in diameter and with 50 or more flowers have been recorded.

Curtis's Botanical Magazine, plate 159 (1936).
Artist: Lilian Snelling.

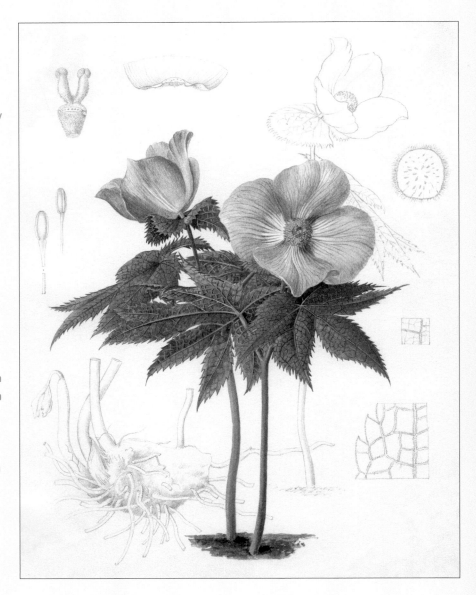

The European winter aconite, *Eranthis hyemalis*, is well known to gardeners and brightens up the winter months with its golden yellow blooms. Japan is home to a beautiful white-flowered species of *Eranthis*, the endemic *E. pinnatifida* from mountain woods in northern central Honshu. This species was described by Maximowicz in 1877. It has long petioled, grey-green leaves that are deeply divided into pinnatifid lobes, hence the name. The involucral leaves directly behind the flower are sessile but similarly divided. The flowers are around 2 cm across but the white sepals are the showy part and the tiny, yellow-tipped, lobed petals are shorter than the blue-tipped stamens. This delicate looking plant, growing only a few centimeters tall, is tougher than it first appears but its small size means that it can be lost in the garden and is better appreciated in a pot in a cold frame or alpine house.

The dappled shade and moist, humus-rich soil of a woodland garden are ideal for growing a range of Japanese herbaceous and bulbous plants. These are plants of the wooded hills and mountains, where rain falls in the summer months and the winters are cold enough to make these species hardy in many parts of Northern Europe and North America. *Japonolirion* may be the only endemic genus in the Japanese alpine zone but there are several endemic genera in the woodland zone. They include some that have only one species (monotypic genera), such as *Ranzania*, *Glaucidium* and *Pteridophyllum*.

The unusual fern-like poppy relative, *Pteridophyllum racemosum*, collected by Siebold in central Honshu and described in 1843, grows at altitudes of 1,000–2,000 m (3,281–6,562 feet) in shade, sometimes among moss, in alpine coniferous forests. The foliage of this plant looks remarkably like the fronds of a fern, hence the name *Pteridophyllum*, which means 'fern-leaved'. Only when the small, white, poppy-like flowers appear in mid- to late spring does its true identity become clear. Kew purchased this plant from the Yokohama Nursery Company in 1914, and this may well have been the first introduction of this species to cultivation in Britain.

Another fine garden plant from the woodlands of Japan is the aforementioned *Saxifraga fortunei*. It is not endemic but in Ohwi's *Flora of Japan*, three varieties of this species are recognised, chiefly on the basis of variations in leaf form. *Saxifraga fortunei* var. *incisolobata* has large, deeply lobed leaves, var. *obtusocuneata* has unlobed leaves with a broadly cuneate (wedge-shaped) base and var. *crassifolia* has shallowly lobed, fleshier leaves with longer hairs on the leaves and stems. The latter two varieties are endemic to Japan. In his book on saxifrages, Malcolm McGregor (2008) lists a further three varieties from Japan: var. *minima* with very small leaves 0.5–1.6 cm wide, var. *partita* with deeply divided leaves and particularly elongated petals, and var. *alpina*.

Tricyrtis flava and *T. latifolia*, both with yellow flowers spotted brownish purple inside, were described by Carl Maximowicz in 1867. The latter is also found in China. In 1888, Maximowicz added *T. macrantha*, which has arching stems and nodding yellow flowers. *Tricyrtis hirta* was originally described by Thunberg in 1784 as *Uvularia hirta* in his *Flora Japonica*. The genus *Tricyrtis* was established in 1826 by Nathaniel Wallich, based on a Nepalese plant (*T. pilosa*). In 1863, William Hooker transferred Thunberg's *Uvularia hirta* to the genus *Tricyrtis*, after seeing plants sent by Fortune from Japan to Standish's nursery in Bagshot, where they flowered in November 1862 (Hooker, 1863). *Tricyrtis hirta* produces pearly white flowers dotted with purple in late summer, in the axils of the upper leaves.

One of the largest bulbous genera in Liliaceae is *Fritillaria*, comprising around 120 species distributed across Asia, Europe and North America. Only a few species are found in Japan and one of these was described by Thunberg in 1784 as *Uvularia cirrhosa*. This plant was

LEFT
Saxifraga 'Cheap confections'.

BELOW
Tricyrtis hirta.

Several cultivars of *Saxifraga fortunei* have been introduced from Japan in recent years. Some of these have pink or purple flowers, such as 'Cherry Pie' with purple-red flowers and 'Black beauty' with deep pink flowers that are held above very dark red to almost black leaves. Other cultivars, such as 'Cheap confections', have wide, expanded petals with deep notches; double forms, cream-coloured and even variegated-leaved selections are also available. Admittedly, these cultivars have a novelty value but it is hard to beat the pure elegance of the unadorned species.

Saxifraga fortunei is closely related to another endemic Japanese species, *S. cortusifolia*, which was described by Siebold and Zuccarini in 1843. It has smaller flowers than *S. fortunei* and the upper petals are broadly ovate, rather than linear or lanceolate, narrowing to a distinct claw and with a yellow spot at the base. It also flowers a few weeks earlier than *S. fortunei* in cultivation.

It is hard to imagine a woodland garden without hostas, now classified in Agavaceae. These magnificent and popular perennials are at their most diverse in Japan, where most of the 40 or so species in the genus are found. They range from the magnificent blue-grey-leaved *Hosta sieboldiana*, from Honshu, to the tiny *H. venusta* from Japan and Korea, with leaves only 2–4 cm long.

A woodland genus in the lily family that is particularly diverse in Japan is *Tricyrtis*, the toad lilies. Over half of the 18 or so species are Japanese, most of them endemic, and they include some now quite commonly grown woodland plants. Although their popularity will never reach the levels enjoyed by hostas, there are some attractive species, such as *T. perfoliata* and *T. affinis*, and these offer the added bonus of producing their often spotted and usually upward-facing flowers in late summer and autumn.

transferred to *Fritillaria* in 1867 and renamed *F. thunbergii*. It is cultivated in Japan and not native, probably coming from Central Asia and naturalised in China (Rix, 2005a), from where it was imported to Japan as a medicinal plant.

Also in Japan is *Fritillaria camschatcensis*, with dark brown-purple, nodding flowers and a distribution that ranges from Honshu and Hokkaido, through the Kurile Islands, Kamchatka and the Aleutian Islands to Alaska, British Columbia and Washington (Rix, 2005b). What better plant to illustrate the link between the floras of North America and Japan?

A further eight fritillaries are found in Japan and these are all endemic. They form a distinctive group and all have similar bulbs, stems and leaves. They differ mainly in floral characteristics. These are woodland species that require different growing conditions to most other fritillaries. They flower in spring but require some moisture all year round, even when dormant, and are best kept in a cool shady frame. The best known of this relatively little-grown group is *Fritillaria koidzumiana*, sometimes classified as *F. japonica* var. *koidzumiana*. *Fritillaria japonica* and *F. koidzumiana* both come from Honshu and both have broadly campanulate flowers, the latter with fimbriate margins to the tepals. The other endemic species are

F. amabilis, which has more tubular flowers; the similar *F. shikokiana*, with tessellated tepals; the recently described *F. tokushimensis*, with more pointed 'shoulders' to the flowers; *F. ayakoana*, which has more conical, umbrella-like flowers; *F. kaiensis*, distinguished by its faintly chequered flowers and yellow-green nectar; and *F. muraiana*, which is similar to *F. japonica* but has more rounded shoulders and vividly chequered and shorter tepals (Naito, 2005). The flowers of all these endemic species vary from creamy white to yellowish and rusty peach, marked to a greater or lesser extent with tessellations outside and purple spots inside. Provided with moisture, a leafy soil and a cool situation, these species should do well in cultivation, but at present most are little-known outside Japan.

Some genera of Japanese mountain plants have their centres of diversity on the adjacent mainland of continental Asia, particularly in the eastern Himalaya and China, and are represented by only a few species in Japan. Among these few Japanese species, however, the proportion of endemics can be fairly high. This supports the theory that these plants migrated to Japan from continental 'hotspots' when the land bridges allowed and have since diversified once separated from the mainland. This is particularly evident in genera such as *Primula* and *Epimedium*.

Around 78% of all *Primula* species occur in the Sino-Himalayan and adjacent ranges in Central Asia (Richards, 2002) where well over 300 species are found, but move away from China and the number of species drops dramatically. Ohwi lists only 13 species in the *Flora of Japan* but, of these, nine are probably endemic.

One endemic that is now doing well in cultivation is *Primula kisoana*, which is found in southern Japan, in Honshu and on the island of Shikoku, growing in woods and damp, shaded places in the subalpine and alpine zones. It is rare in the wild, only occurring in small numbers in a few scattered sites. Like the more widespread *P. sieboldii*, this species belongs to *Primula* section *Cortusoides*, a large group sometimes referred to as the 'woodland primulas'. These plants have soft, petiolate, usually hairy leaves that are oblong to ovate or circular in outline but with toothed or lobed margins. They are usually deciduous perennials. The whorl of purple, pink, white or rarely yellow flowers is held on a long stem above the leaves.

Primula kisoana was found by the Japanese botanist Ito Keiske in the mountains of the upper Kiso gava (now in Nagano Prefecture) in the early nineteenth century. It is known to have been cultivated in Japan since the early eighteenth century but wasn't formally described until 1867, by the Dutch botanist Friedrich Miquel, from material sent to him by Keiske in 1865 (Halda, 1992). It was grown at the Royal Botanic Garden, Edinburgh in 1918, when it was

painted for *Curtis's Botanical Magazine* (Stapf, 1938) but was then lost. Today, *P. kisoana* is well-established in cultivation and is an attractive species for a cool, shady site.

Primula kisoana has round to kidney-shaped leaves that are up to 7 cm across and covered in soft, long, white hairs. The petioles, stem and sepals are also hairy. The sturdy stem can reach 20 cm tall and holds a 2–8-flowered umbel. Some plants may have up to four superimposed umbels. The rose-purple flowers are 2–3 cm across and have petals that are deeply divided into two lobes. There is also a lovely pure white form in cultivation. Like *P. sieboldii*, this species can be divided in late winter or early spring.

The closest species to *Primula kisoana* is *P. jesoana*, another Japanese endemic, which differs in having more slender stems, smaller flowers and more markedly lobed leaves and in being less hairy. It also doesn't creep like *P. kisoana*. This species is found in the mountains of western Hokkaido and northern Honshu, and was introduced into Europe in 1932, when it was grown at the Royal Botanic Garden Edinburgh. *Primula kisoana* and *P. jesoana* are both in subsection *Geranioides* of section *Cortusoides*, in which the species have leaf veins that radiate from the base (the leaves are palmate). *Primula sieboldii* belongs to subsection *Cortusoides*, in which the leaves have veins branching from the mid-rib.

The *Berberis* family, Berberidaceae, is represented in Japan by both woody and herbaceous plants. Among the herbaceous species are several epimediums, otherwise known as barren worts, a group of ground-cover perennials with attractive foliage and delicate racemes of flowers. The range of the genus *Epimedium* extends from southern Europe, through North Africa and Asia to Korea and Japan. As for *Primula*, the centre of diversity is in China. In his revision of *Epimedium*, the late Professor William Stearn (2002) divides 54 species into two subgenera: subgenus *Epimedium*, with cauline leaves, and subgenus *Rhizophyllum*, containing two species (*E. pinnatum* and *E. perralderianum*) with leafless flower stems and all basal leaves. Subgenus *Epimedium* is divided into four sections. Section *Diphyllon* contains all the Chinese species, section *Polyphyllon* contains one Himalayan species (*E. elatum*), and section *Epimedium* contains the European *E. alpinum* and the Eurasian *E. pubigerum*. All of the Japanese species are in the fourth section, *Macroceras*.

Of the six species in section *Macroceras*, four are found in Japan, the exceptions being *Epimedium koreanum* from Korea and *E. macrosepalum* from far-eastern Russia. *Epimedium grandiflorum* occurs in China and Korea as well as in Japan and the other three species are Japanese endemics: *E. sempervirens*, *E. trifoliolatobinatum* and *E. diphyllum*.

Epimediums are perennial woodland herbs that can form a dense ground cover and spread by branching rhizomes just under the soil surface. The leaves may persist all year round, sometimes becoming attractively coloured in autumn, but in spring new growth produces a fresh flush of foliage and flowers. The leaves are compound, comprising from two to over 40 rounded to ovate or lanceolate leaflets, depending on the species. They are held on wiry stems and petioles. The racemes of numerous delicate flowers are held above the leaves. The two outer sepals of each flower usually fall as the flower opens. The four inner sepals and four petals form the showy part of the flower. The petals are spurred in several species and these spurs can be long, over 2 cm in some cases.

Epimedium diphyllum was introduced into cultivation in Europe in 1829, being part of Siebold's first consignment of plants to Leiden. It differs from the other Japanese species in having white, spurless flowers, and the leaves have just two leaflets. The Royal Botanic Garden, Edinburgh acquired a plant that was used by Robert Graham to describe this species in *Curtis's Botanical Magazine* in 1835. In Japan it grows on Kyushu, Shikoku and SE Honshu.

The flowers of *Epimedium trifoliolatobinatum* are also white but they have slender spurs of 10–15 mm in length. The leaves have four or six leaflets, arranged either as two pairs of leaflets or two sets of three leaflets. Stearn states that this species is undoubtedly the result of hybridisation

LEFT
Epimedium trifoliolatobinatum.

BELOW
Epimedium sempervirens var. *rugosum.*

species, *R. japonica*, is a rhizomatous, herbaceous plant that comes from the woodlands of Japan. It grows to 50 cm tall and has two opposite leaves on the stem. These leaves are divided into three palmately lobed leaflets and the 1–6 pale purple, drooping flowers are held between them on long pedicels.

Other genera of Berberidaceae in Japan include *Achlys*, *Caulophyllum* and *Diphylleia*. All three are rhizomatous, herbaceous, woodland perennials and have ranges that encompass both North America and eastern Asia. *Achlys* is treated by Stearn (2002) as comprising one species with three subspecies. *Achlys triphylla* subsp. *japonica* from Japan and Korea, and subsp. *triphylla* and subsp. *californica* from western North America. *Caulophyllum* has three species, two from eastern North America and one, *C. robustum*, from mixed woodland in eastern Asia, including Japan, Sakhalin and Korea. *Diphylleia* also comprises three species, one from the eastern USA, one from China and the third, *D. grayei*, endemic to Japan. This last species is named after Asa Gray, who in 1859 drew attention to the relationship of the Japanese flora to that of eastern North America.

The plants mentioned here are just a few of the endemic plants of Japan. Japanese alpines are generally not as widely grown as those from other regions but they form a distinctive and select group that enrich alpine plant collections, whether on a rock garden, in an alpine house or in a woodland garden. Japan has a temperate flora that is adapted to a climate not too dissimilar to that of western Europe, where many of the first plant introductions from Japan were made, so cultivation does not normally present many problems. It was the physicians working for the Dutch East India Company and the commercial plant collectors who followed them in the nineteenth century, who first alerted gardeners and botanists in the rest the world to the variety and beauty of Japan's flora. By the mid nineteenth century, however, another country with an extensive and diverse temperate flora had also just opened her borders to the world. China soon became a rich hunting ground for new introductions. For lovers of alpine plants, south-west China, together with the Himalayan Mountains, was now attracting great attention.

between *E. diphyllum* and *E. grandiflorum*. Stable populations of this intermediate plant have become established and can be found on the west side of Shikoku.

The third endemic Japanese species is *Epimedium sempervirens*, which is found on the western side of southern Honshu. It has large, long-spurred flowers held on flower stems of up to 60 cm tall. The flowers can reach 4 cm across and are white in var. *sempervirens* or reddish-purple in var. *rugosum*. This species differs from the other long-spurred Japanese species, *E. grandiflorum*, in its more elongated rhizome and evergreen leaves.

Epimedium grandiflorum is not endemic to Japan but two forms, one white-flowered and one violet, were the first long-spurred epimediums to be cultivated in Europe when introduced by Siebold, who brought them back on his return from Japan in 1830. They were grown in Ghent where they were propagated and then distributed to other European gardens. Since then *E. grandiflorum* has been hybridised with other cultivated species and is the parent of several popular hybrids, including *E.* × *rubrum* (with *E. alpinum*), *E.* × *versicolor* (with *E. pinnatum* subsp. *colchicum*) and *E.* × *youngianum* (with *E. diphyllum*).

In the same family as *Epimedium* is the monotypic genus *Ranzania*, which is endemic to Honshu and named after the Japanese naturalist Ono Ranzan (1729–1810). The only

Bibliography and references

Barnes, P. (2001). Japan's Botanical Sunrise. *Curtis's Bot. Mag.* 18: 117–131.

Boyce, P. (1994). Two Asian *Asarum* species. *Curtis's Bot. Mag.* 11: 59–65.

Coats, A. M. (1968). *Flowers and their histories* (2nd edn.). pp. 206–7. Adam & Charles Black, London.

Coats, A. M. (1969). *The Quest for Plants*: 63–85. Studio Vista, London.

Comber, H. F. (1949). A new classification of the genus *Lilium*. *The Lily Year Book* 13: 86–105.

Cox, E. H. M. (1943). Robert Fortune. *J. Roy. Hort. Soc.* 68: 161–171.

Desmond, R. (1994). *Dictionary of British and Irish botanists and horticulturists*. Taylor & Francis, London.

Fedorov, A. A. (1972). *Astrocodon* Fed., gen. nov. In: *Flora of the USSR*, 24, ed. B. K. Shishkin, pp. 269–272. Israel Program for Scientific Translations, Jerusalem.

Fujii, N. & Senni, K. (2006). Phylogeography of Japanese alpine plants: biogeographic importance of alpine region of Central Honshu in Japan. *Taxon* 55: 43–52.

Gardner, D. (1999). *Papaver fauriei. Curtis's Bot. Mag.* 16: t. 362.

Graham, R. (1840). *Heterotropa asaroides. Curtis's Bot. Mag.* 66: t. 3746.

Gray, A. (1859). Diagnostic characters of new species of phaenogamous plants, collected in Japan by Charles Wright, botanist of the U.S. North Pacific exploring expedition. *Mem. Amer. Acad. Art.* ser. 2, 6: 377–453.

Halda, J. J. (1992). *The Genus Primula, In Cultivation and the Wild*. Tethys Books, Denver.

Halliwell, B. (1987). Some Japanese plants for the rock garden. *Quart. Bull. Alpine Gard. Soc. Gr. Brit.* 55: 314.

Hooker, J. D. (1871). *Primula japonica. Curtis's Bot. Mag.* 97: t. 5916.

Hooker, W. J. (1863). *Tricyrtis hirta. Curtis's Bot. Mag.* 89: t.5355.

Jacquin, N. J. (1776). *Hortus Botanicus Vindobonensis*, 3: 4. t. 2. Vienna.

Lindley, J. & Paxton, J. (1851). The Chinese Platycode (*Platycodon chinense*). *Paxton's Fl. Gard.* 2: 121, t. 61.

McGregor, M. (2008). *Saxifrages*. Timber Press, Portland.

Naito, T. (2005). The endemic *Fritillaria* species of Japan. *Curtis's Bot. Mag.* 22: 189–196.

Nelson, E. C. (1999). So many really fine plants, an epitome of Japanese plants in Western European gardens. *Curtis's Bot. Mag.* 16: 52–68.

Ohwi, J. (1984). *Flora of Japan (in English)*. Smithsonian Institution, Washington, D.C.

Richards, J. (2002). *Primula* (second edition): 298–301. B. T. Batsford Ltd., London.

Rix, M. (2005a). North-western Chinese Fritillaries. *Alpine Gardener* 73:187.

Rix, M. (2005b). *Fritillaria koidzumiana. Curtis's Bot. Mag.* 22: t. 535.

Stapf, O. (1938). *Primula kisoana. Curtis's Bot. Mag.* 147: t. 8884.

Stearn, W. T. (1999). Engelbert Kaempfer (1651–1716), pioneer investigator of Japanese plants. *Curtis's Bot. Mag.* 16: 103–115.

Stearn, W. T. (2002). *The Genus Epimedium and other herbaceous Berberidaceae*. Royal Botanic Gardens, Kew.

Tamura, M. (1972). Morphology and phyletic relationship of the Glaucidiaceae. *Bot. Mag. Tokyo* 85: 29–41.

Tanaka, N. (1998). Phylogenetic and Taxonomic studies on *Helonias*, *Ypsilandra* and *Heloniopsis* III. Taxonomic revision. *J. Japan. Bot.* 73: 102–115.

Thunberg, C. P. (1784). *Flora Japonica*. Leipzig.

Thunberg, C. P. (1794). Botanical observations on the *Flora Japonica*. *Trans. Linn. Soc.* 2: 334.

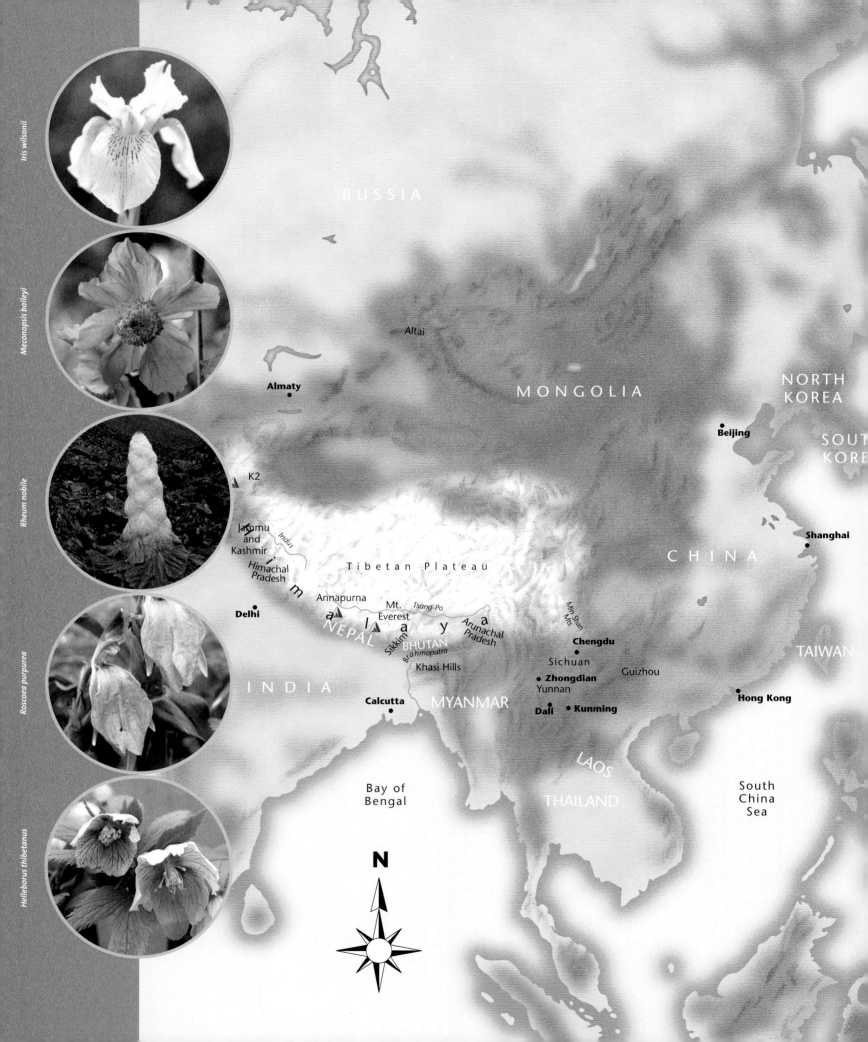

Iris wilsonii

Meconopsis baileyi

Rheum nobile

Roscoea purpurea

Helleborus thibetanus

RUSSIA

Altai

MONGOLIA

NORTH
KOREA

SOUT
KORE

Almaty

Beijing

K2

Shanghai

Jammu
and
Kashmir

Indus

CHINA

Himachal
Pradesh

Tibetan Plateau

H
i
m

Annapurna

Mt.
Everest

Tsang-Po

Mn Shan
Mts

Delhi

a

l

a

y

a

Chengdu

TAIWAN

NEPAL

Arunachal
Pradesh

Sikkim

BHUTAN

Sichuan

Guizhou

Brahmaputra

Khasi Hills

Zhongdian
Yunnan

INDIA

Hong Kong

Calcutta

MYANMAR

Dali

Kunming

Bay of
Bengal

LAOS

THAILAND

South
China
Sea

N

Chapter 8 China and the Himalaya

The Indus and Tsang-Po rivers both arise in the south-west corner of the Tibetan Plateau. Although their sources are relatively close, near Lake Manasarovar, they take very different courses to reach the sea. The Indus flows north-west before turning south through Pakistan and discharging into the Arabian Sea. The Tsang-Po flows east and then, doubling back on itself, it passes through remote winding gorges and a series of rapids and cascades. It drops over 3,000 m (9,843 feet) on its way to the Assam Valley where, as the Brahmaputra, it makes its way to the Ganges Delta in Bangladesh, on the Bay of Bengal. Between these two rivers is the mightiest mountain range on Earth. Extending over 2,400 km (1,500 miles) from the Northern Areas of Pakistan to Arunachal Pradesh in north-east India, the Himalayan Mountains take in Jammu and Kashmir, Himachal Pradesh, northern Uttar Pradesh, Nepal, Sikkim and Bhutan. The Himalaya may not be the longest range in the world, but includes many of the highest peaks on earth, receives the heaviest monsoon rainfall on the planet and is home to a huge variety of plant life, with influences from the Chinese flora in the east and the flora of Central Asia in the west.

The world's highest mountain, Mt Everest, reaches 8,848 m (29,035 feet) and is located on the border of north-east Nepal and Tibet (or the Tibet Autonomous region of China, also known as Xizang). It is worth noting that the highest mountain in the Alps, Mont Blanc, is 4,808 m (15,774 feet) high, North America's highest mountain, Mt McKinley, reaches 6,194 m (20,322 feet) and South America's Aconcagua reaches 6,960 m (22,835 feet); yet there are more than 100 mountains in the Himalaya that exceed 7,200 m

(23,622 feet) in altitude. These peaks form the southern rim of the Tibetan Plateau, a vast region of 2.3 million km² (888,035 square miles) known as 'the roof of the world', with an average elevation of over 4,500 m (14,764 feet).

The richness of the Himalayan flora is a result of the huge range in altitude and the varied topographies, climates and habitats found there. In the lower foothills and deep valleys of northern India and Nepal, the climate is subtropical. At higher altitudes, the climate is temperate with broadleaf woodlands, evergreen oaks, conifers and rhododendrons.

BELOW
The snowy peak of
Mt Jhomolhari
(7,313 m; 23,993 feet)
in NW Bhutan near the
Tibetan border.
Photo: Joanne Everson.

This temperate zone begins at around 1,800 m (5,906 feet) in Nepal but in the Western Himalaya, which is at a more northerly latitude, it begins lower down the slopes, at around 1,400 m (4,593 feet). The temperate zone extends to the treeline, which is at an altitude of 3,700–4,000 m (12,139–13,123 feet), and from here on up to the permanent snow is the alpine zone. The permanent snow may not occur until 6,000 m (19,685 feet) above sea level.

The pattern and amount of precipitation have a massive influence on how plants grow in the Himalaya and on how gardeners should treat these plants in their gardens. These mountains are subjected to a summer monsoon along their south-facing slopes. Warm, moisture-laden air flows north from the Bay of Bengal and the Arabian Sea and is forced upwards when it meets the first mountains of the Himalaya. The highest rainfall figures occur in the eastern Himalaya and the Khasi Hills of Meghalaya in north-east India where the amount of rain that falls is scarcely believable. The Khasi Hills run 241 km (150 miles) west to east and with nothing but low-lying land between them and the sea, they bear the full brunt of the monsoon winds blowing inland from the Bay of Bengal. The wettest place on Earth is said to be Mawsynram in these hills, which has an average annual rainfall of an astonishing 11,872 mm (39 feet). Nearby Cherrapunji holds the record for the highest rainfall in a single year, 26,461 mm (86 feet 9 inches) between August 1860 and July 1861. The most rain in a 24-hour period, 1,563 mm (61.5 inches) on 16 June 1995, was also recorded at Cherrapunji (Middleton, 2001); this rainfall in a single day is well over twice the amount of precipitation that falls on the south of England in a whole year.

These record-breaking levels of rainfall only occur in a narrow band on the windward side of the mountains; at Mawsynram, this is at around 1,400 m (4,593 feet) altitude. Such high levels of precipitation do not fall on the alpine zone, but there too, rainfall is greatest in the summer, with low cloud and damp conditions persisting four months or more in some areas. The monsoon begins in early June in the eastern Himalaya and spreads westwards, so that by early July it has affected all the Himalayan mountains.

The rain shadow cast by the high peaks of the Himalaya also has a significant effect: mountains like Annapurna (8,091 m; 26,545 feet) form a massive barrier that prevents the monsoon reaching the higher, inner valleys. The rainfall in some parts of the Himalaya may be less than 100 mm (3.9 inches) a year, yet only a relatively short distance away are locations that are swamped by 2–3 m (78–118 inches) of rain in a year. The plants that grow in these dry hills and inner valleys experience conditions very different to those in the monsoon zone, and elements of the flora of

the dry Tibetan Plateau extend into these dryer parts of Nepal and the Western Himalaya. The Tibetan Plateau generally has an arid climate, with annual precipitation of between 200–500 mm (7.9–19.7 inches). The landscape is mainly high-altitude steppe, semi-desert or desert, although some southern areas have a higher rainfall because low valleys in the Himalaya allow some of the monsoon rains through.

The Western Himalaya have a shorter monsoon period than the mountains further south and east, from early July to early September. There is also significant winter precipitation. In areas sheltered from the monsoon in the west, such as the Kashmir Valley, the summer can be fairly dry and winter is the wettest time of year. This rainfall pattern combined with the more northerly latitude means that elements of the Central Asian flora are found in the Western Himalaya. Bulbous or tuberous species, adapted to survive the dry summer, such as *Eremurus himalaicus* and *Tulipa clusiana*, are not uncommon here (Polunin & Stainton, 1984). Snow can last until April or May on the mountains and spring flowers appear as the snow melts, but the alpine flora is best during the monsoon season in July and early August.

The flora of the Western Himalaya is distinct from that found in central and eastern Nepal and the mountains further east, regions that are nearer the tropics and experience a true monsoon climate. The monsoon months in Nepal are June to September, when most of the annual precipitation falls. The rainy season is followed by the cold season from October to December and the hot season from January to May. Spring flowers bloom from April to June in the temperate zone, with rhododendrons taking centre stage. The peak flowering season is from June onwards but the alpines in the high meadows and screes are at their best in July and August. This means that plant hunters have to endure being soaked through by the monsoon rains, day after day, if they want to see a good range of Himalayan alpines in flower. It also means that any seed collections are extremely difficult to dry out, and many have undoubtedly been lost over the years even before being transported down the mountain.

Looking further east, the mountains continue into south-west China as a series of limestone ranges arching south through Sichuan and Yunnan, and these also experience the summer monsoon, with over half the annual precipitation falling in the months of June to August. This part of China has an incredibly rich flora that wasn't fully appreciated in the west until explorers like Ernest Wilson and George Forrest collected in this area in the late nineteenth and early twentieth centuries. Between 1843 and 1950, these and other collectors sent back plants from the hills and mountains of south-west China that were to have a profound impact on the garden flora in Europe and America. Hardy trees, shrubs and herbaceous perennials, including magnolias, rhododendrons, primulas and lilies, caused great excitement when introduced to cultivation, and it is hard to find a garden today in which plants from China have no influence on the planting scheme. The same is true of rock gardens, with androsaces, meconopsis and gentians all coveted by alpine growers. The rage for rock gardening in the first half of the twentieth century, can largely be attributed to this influx of new and exciting Sino-Himalayan species during 'the golden age of plant hunting'.

The British influence

Many of the early explorers in the Himalaya were British, a direct result of Britain's colonial status on the Indian subcontinent in the nineteenth century and the role of the British East India Company. However, although Britain ruled much of India, her influence only extended to the foothills of the Himalaya. Foreigners were generally not welcome in the principalities of Nepal, Sikkim and Bhutan, and permits to travel in these regions were difficult to obtain. Assam came under British control only in 1826, and Kashmir and the Punjab in the 1840s. Nevertheless, the East India Company ran the botanic garden at Calcutta in Bengal and this became the base for the botanical exploration of the Indian Himalaya (Coats, 1969).

Calcutta was the seat of the Government of British India. In 1786, Colonel Robert Kyd, Military Secretary to the Government, proposed the formation of a nursery to grow useful plants, which would then be distributed throughout British India. The site was chosen near Calcutta on the Hooghly River, and plants from around the world, including sago, date palm, sandalwood, teak and coffee, were requested so that they could be grown there. Under the management of Kyd and his successors, this nursery became a true botanic garden and pleasure park. After Kyd's death in 1793, Dr William Roxburgh, an Assistant Surgeon to the East India Company, was invited to become superintendent of the garden, a position he held until 1813, although he was plagued by ill health and often had to take sick leave. In 1809, the Danish surgeon Dr Nathaniel Wallich was appointed as his assistant.

BELOW
The Himalaya at Rangalti, Himachal Pradesh.
Photo: Joanne Everson.

Nathaniel Wallich, 1786–1854

Nathaniel Wallich was born in Copenhagen in 1786. He qualified as a surgeon in 1806 and a year later took a position in the Danish settlement of Serampore on the Hooghly River, Bengal. In addition to his duties as a surgeon, he was also commissioned to collect plants and seeds for Copenhagen Botanic Garden. When the British annexed Serampore in 1808, Wallich became a prisoner of war, but the following year he was released to work with William Roxburgh at Calcutta Botanic Garden where he became acting Superintendent in 1814. In 1817, with support from Joseph Banks at Kew, his appointment became official. In return for this support, Wallich sent many seeds and plants to Banks, as well as to other notable gardens in Britain and Europe.

During his time in charge at Calcutta, Wallich travelled to collect and study plants, visiting several countries including China, Singapore, Nepal and Burma. During a period of leave in 1828, he brought his entire herbarium of over 8,000 specimens to London, where they were housed in the East India Company's museum. There, they were sorted, labelled and made available for study by botanists in Britain and Europe.

As well as providing new plant descriptions for Carey's printing of Roxburgh's *Flora Indica*, Wallich produced an illustrated account of the flora of Nepal, *Tentamen Florae Napalensis Illustratae*. It was published in parts between 1824 and 1826. Then, from 1829 to 1832, he published his account of the Indian flora, *Plantae Asiaticae Rariores*, subtitled 'descriptions and figures of a select number of unpublished Indian plants'. Desmond (1992) described this as the "last of the ambitiously conceived, extravagantly produced Indian floras". Wallich returned to Calcutta in 1833, eventually resigning his post as superintendent in 1846.

As well as all the plants Wallich described himself, a huge number of the plants in his herbarium were described by other botanists and many were named after him. Among the alpine and rock garden plants are *Allium wallichii*, *Geranium wallichianum*, *Meconopsis wallichii* and *Euphorbia wallichii*.

BELOW LEFT
Allium wallichii.

BELOW RIGHT
Geranium wallichianum.
Photo: Joanne Everson.

Roxburgh studied Indian plants in preparation for a flora and he also sent material to the Royal Botanic Gardens, Kew, including herbarium specimens, drawings, seeds and plants. When he left India, he left the unpublished manuscript of his *Flora Indica* with his close friend, the missionary William Carey. After Roxburgh's death in 1815, Carey resolved to publish the flora (De Candolle & Radcliffe-Smith, 1981). Wallich, who by then had become Superintendent of Calcutta Botanic Garden, volunteered to bring the manuscript of *Flora Indica* up to date with additional material of his own.

The East India Company also maintained a botanic garden at Saharanpur in the Punjab, now in Uttar Pradesh. Established in a former pleasure ground, this botanic garden became the most important on the subcontinent after Calcutta. Saharanpur is located the foothills of the Himalaya, where the climate is suitable for growing a range of more temperate species and tea was successfully cultivated there. The garden's first superintendent was George Govan, a civil surgeon at Saharanpur who took up the post in this new botanic garden in 1817. He returned to Europe in 1821 on sick leave and was eventually succeeded by John Forbes Royle, who took over in 1823.

Royle was born in Cawnpore, now Kanpur in Uttar Pradesh, in 1799. He was educated in Edinburgh and became an assistant surgeon for the East India Company in India in 1820, before taking the post at Saharanpur from 1823 to 1831. One notable development at the garden during Royle's time was the establishment of a nursery higher up the mountains, in the hill station of Mussoorie at 2,000 m (6,562 feet) altitude. There, Forbes grew medicinal plants and also alpines, before moving them down to the botanic garden in Saharanpur. Royle rarely had time to visit the mountains himself but employed his gardeners to collect plants for him. When he left the Saharanpur garden in 1831 there were 30,000 plants growing there, representing around 4,000 species. The knowledge of the plants he grew and studied was put to good use when he wrote his pioneering mountain flora.

Royle's *Illustrations of the Botany and other Branches of the Natural History of the Himalayan Mountains: and of the Flora of Cashmere*, to give it its full title, was published between 1834 and 1839. The plants included were mainly from Kashmir and Kunawar on the Tibetan border, and he also consulted the collections of other botanists, including those of Wallich and Govan. His descriptions were accompanied by notes on the geographical distribution of the plants and their usefulness to man, as economic botany was his main interest. He noted the similarity of the European and Himalayan mountain floras, a themed to be picked up by Joseph Hooker during his time in Nepal and Sikkim several years later.

Royle's *Illustrations of the Botany...of the Himalayan Mountains* and Roxburgh's *Flora Indica*, as well as the works of Wallich, were among the first publications to document the plants of the Himalaya for European botanists. They were preceded, however, by James Edwards Smith's *Exotic Botany*, published in two volumes between 1804 and 1808. This publication displayed coloured illustrations by the botanical artist James Sowerby, alongside scientific descriptions of 'new, beautiful or rare plants as are worthy of cultivation in the gardens of Britain' (Smith, 1804).

Smith, the founder and first President of the Linnean Society, described plants from around the world in *Exotic Botany*; he included plants from South Africa, America, Europe and Australia, and also consulted the collections of Dr Francis Buchanan from Nepal. Buchanan was born in Scotland and became a ship's surgeon for the East India Company. In 1794, he became an assistant surgeon in

BELOW
Roscoea purpurea.

Primula denticulata
Family: Primulaceae

Most of the Sino-Himalayan primulas now in cultivation were introduced in the twentieth century; a few, particularly species from the western and central Himalaya, found their way into gardens in the nineteenth century. Early collectors in this area included Joseph Dalton Hooker, Nathaniel Wallich and John Forbes Royle, who introduced seed of the subject of this plate, *Primula denticulata*, the drumstick primula.

James Edward Smith described *Primula denticulata* in the second volume of *Exotic Botany* on the basis of a drawing made in India. Smith reports that this species was collected by Dr Francis Buchanan "in moist parts of the hills about Chitlong" in Nepal, where they flowered from February to April. It was some years later that seed of *P. denticulata* reached Britain. Professor Isaac Bayley Balfour (1913), Regius Keeper at the Royal Botanic Garden Edinburgh, states that this species was introduced into cultivation by Messrs Veitch in 1842.

Primula denticulata has a wide distribution in the wild, ranging from eastern Afghanistan and northern Pakistan, across the Himalaya to Yunnan, Sichuan and Guizhou in China, growing in open, wet places. It is the most common Himalayan *Primula* and by far the most widely cultivated species in section *Denticulata*. The species in this section are perennial, deciduous, clump-forming plants that bear compact heads of many flowers and that overwinter as large, above-ground buds with thick roots.

The winter buds of *Primula denticulata* are surrounded by large, leathery scales. In spring and summer, the oblong, wrinkly leaves can grow up to 30 cm long and have a toothed margin. The spherical flower head, held on a stem up to 30 cm tall, is up to 8 cm across and composed of usually stalkless flowers. Flower colour varies from deep purple or blue to pink or white, but the normal colour is pinkish-purple or lilac, with a yellowish eye. *Primula denticulata* subsp. *sinodenticulata*, from northern Burma and western China, is a robust plant with an elongated flower stem, up to six times the length of its leaves (Richards, 2002).

Of the other species in section *Denticulata*, *Primula cachemeriana* (syn. *P. denticulata* var. *cachemeriana*) from Kashmir is most often seen in cultivation, but it is not widely grown. This species differs from *P. denticulata* in its pointed, yellow-mealy resting bud and the narrow, very mealy leaves, which remain smooth until after the plant has flowered. Some authors classify this as a form of *P. denticulata*, but Richards (2002) maintains it as a separate species.

Primula denticulata is an easy, hardy garden plant that can be grown in a variety of soils but will not tolerate drying out in the summer months. It thrives in heavy garden soil in a border and is ideal for small gardens. It also does well in dappled shade. It is a clump-forming species that can be propagated by division in summer or autumn. Fresh seed can be sown from autumn to early spring. Root cuttings can also be taken when the plant is dormant.

Curtis's Botanical Magazine, plate 3959 (1842). Artist: Walter Hood Fitch.

Bengal, and from April 1802 to March 1803, he was stationed in Kathmandu, Nepal, as surgeon to Captain Knox. Knox became the first British Resident in Nepal after the signing of a treaty between the British and the Nepalese Gurkhas in 1801 but he was recalled in 1803 due to the increasing hostility of the Nepalese. As well as sending plants and seeds to Calcutta, Buchanan presented his specimens to Smith on his return to London in 1805, in the hope that Smith would use them in *Exotic Botany*. In the end, Smith only used twelve of Buchanan's plants but among them were *Primula denticulata*, now one of the more commonly grown primulas in gardens, *Androsace umbellata* (described as *A. rotundifolia* by Smith, but this was an invalid name because it had already been used in 1799 for another Himalayan plant) and *Roscoea purpurea*, the type species of this genus.

Twenty species of *Roscoea*, occurring along the Himalayan range and into south-west China, are now known. They belong to the ginger family (Zingiberaceae) and are typical of plants from a monsoon climate: they are summer growers, surviving the winter underground as small rhizomes with long, fleshy roots. In the wild, they flower in the monsoon season. In cultivation, different species can be in flower from late April to September or even October in suitable conditions. It is usually the more eastern Chinese species, such as *R. cautleyoides* and *R. humeana*, that flower first with the Himalayan species following in July and August. Indeed, *R. purpurea* may not emerge from the ground until June in cultivation in southern England. The unusual flowers of roscoeas emerge from the top of the stem, sometimes on a long peduncle, depending on the species. The 'stem' is technically a false stem, made up of the overlapping leaf sheaths, and the flowers are composed of two small, narrow lateral petals, an erect or hooded dorsal petal and a larger lower lip or labellum. Flower colour ranges from yellow to white, violet, dark purple and rarely red

Buchanan collected *Roscoea purpurea* in 1802 at Narainhetty, a Hindu Temple opposite the Palace in Kathmandu now called Narayan Hiti (Cowley, 2007). This plant was described and illustrated in the second volume of *Exotic Botany*. Smith named the genus after the Liverpool lawyer and banker William Roscoe (1753–1831), who founded the Liverpool Botanic Garden, which opened in 1803. This garden obtained seeds and plants from the many trade ships that docked in the growing port of Liverpool. Botanic gardens, nurseries and collectors including Carey, Roxburgh and Wallich also sent plants to this new garden.

It was Wallich who collected a second species of *Roscoea* during his time in Nepal, from 1819 to 1822. This was the Nepalese endemic *R. capitata* and it too was described by Smith, in 1822. In 1839, Royle described another

ABOVE
Roscoea capitata, originally collected by Wallich in Nepal.

LEFT
Roscoea bhutanica, on the road to Docu La, western Bhutan.
Photo: Joanne Everson.

Himalayan species, *R. alpina*, in his *Illustrations of the Botany...of the Himalayan Mountains*. New species of *Roscoea* are still being named. One of the most recent is *R. bhutanica*, described in 2000. *Roscoea ganeshensis* is a Nepalese species found by the Oxford University expedition to Nepal in 1992. It was described by Jill Cowley in *Curtis's Botanical Magazine* in 1996. This expedition also discovered a prized red-flowered form of *R. purpurea*, a colour not seen in the genus before, subsequently named *R. purpurea* forma *rubra* 'Red Gurkha'. All these Himalayan species are great for adding summer colour to the rock garden or alpine house.

In the second volume of *Exotic Botany*, Smith also described two species of *Epidendrum*. These orchids are now classified in the genus *Pleione*, popularly known as 'window-sill orchids'. Smith called his first species *Epidendrum praecox* or the 'purple-fringed epidendrum' and the second, *E. humile*, the 'dwarf hairy-lipped epidendrum'. Both of these epiphytic orchids were discovered growing on mossy tree trunks in Upper Nepal by Buchanan.

David Don later transferred these two species of *Epidendrum* to a new genus, *Pleione*, which he described in *Prodromus Florae Nepalensis*, published in 1825. However, John Lindley (1821) considered them to be species of his new genus *Coelogyne* and published the names *C. praecox* and *C. humilis*. It wasn't until the beginning of the twentieth century that Robert Allen Rolfe (1903) resurrected the genus *Pleione*. While acknowledging the similarities between *Coelogyne* and *Pleione*, Rolfe notes differences in the shape and details of the lip of the flower, the differently shaped, annual pseudobulb, and the thin, deciduous leaves and distinctive inflorescence of *Pleione*.

Pleiones produce one or occasionally two flowers, which consist of three petal-like sepals, two showy lateral petals and one modified petal that forms a lip. The lip is brightly coloured to attract pollinators and normally has a callus of hairs, ridges or papillae on its upper surface. The flowers are usually pink or purple, less commonly white and in *Pleione forrestii* they are yellow. The pseudobulb (a swollen stem internode) is replaced annually and the shoot emerges from its base.

The genus is divided into two sections. Section *Pleione* contains the autumn flowering species, including *Pleione praecox*. These flower once the leaves have died down, at the beginning of the winter dormant period. The spring-flowering species, such as *P. humilis*, are in section *Humiles*, and their flowers appear before their leaves (Zhu & Chen, 1998). The eighteen or so species of *Pleione* are distributed from Nepal, east to Taiwan and from central China south to Myanmar (Burma), northern Thailand and Laos. *Pleione humilis*, from Nepal, north-east India, Bhutan and Myanmar, at altitudes of 1,850–3,200 m (6,070–10,499 feet), was introduced in 1849 by Thomas Lobb, who sent it from the Khasi Hills to Messrs James Veitch and Sons in Exeter.

More alpine plants can be found in Roxburgh's *Flora Indica* including, for example, the summer-flowering

FAR LEFT
Pleione formosana, a Taiwanese species in this popular orchid genus.

LEFT
Androsace lanuginosa in cultivation.

Androsace lanuginosa. This species was one of Wallich's additions to Roxburgh's work and it appeared in the second volume of *Flora Indica* in 1824. It is a mat-forming species, covered in silky hairs. Wallich describes his specimen as "caulescent, somewhat branchy and adscending, every part of it covered with white, soft, long, shining wool". Rosettes of short, grey-green, lanceolate leaves, give rise to reddish stems. Each stem can be up to 30 cm long, with sessile leaves scattered along its length and a rosette of leaves at its tip. Further rosettes frequently appear in the leaf axils, which leads to branching of the stems. The inflorescence grows from the stem tip and comprises an umbel of 10–15 flowers, held at the end of a 4–10 cm long peduncle. The 10 mm wide flowers are usually pale pink with a greenish yellow eye but various shades, from deeper pink to almost white with a dark pink eye, can be seen within each umbel. This species is now known to occur from Kashmir to western Nepal, in the north-west Himalaya.

Seeds of *Androsace lanuginosa* were sent to Dublin Botanic Garden by Royle, where they first flowered in August 1842 (Hooker, 1843). In 1885, a form of this species received a First Class Certificate from the RHS, when shown by the German horticulturist and plantsman, Max Leichtlin. This plant, now known as 'Leichtlinii' or var. *leichtlinii*, had white flowers with a yellow or pink eye and the leaves were less woolly than those of the typical form (Harrow, 1890).

Androsace lanuginosa belongs in section *Chamaejasme*, a large, mainly Asian section, in which the leaves generally have entire margins and the inflorescence arises from the centre of each leaf rosette (Smith & Lowe, 1997). This section also includes the widely grown *A. sarmentosa*, which is closely related to *A. lanuginosa* and was also described by Wallich in *Flora Indica*. The stoloniferous *A. sarmentosa* has a range stretching from Kashmir eastwards to western Nepal. It has petiolate summer leaves that are larger (up to 7 cm long) than the sessile leaves of the overwintering rosette and it flowers a little earlier than *A. lanuginosa*.

Androsace sarmentosa requires similar conditions in the garden to *A. lanuginosa*. Both species are best planted in a crevice or a sunny, narrow planting pocket on a rock garden, with soil that is well-drained but doesn't dry out in summer. They are hardy and make a fine display on a rock garden, at a time of year when many alpines have finished flowering.

Wallich was responsible for the introduction of another popular summer-flowering rock garden plant, the herbaceous *Potentilla nepalensis*. The bright colour of the flowers, combined with their appearance late in the season, makes *P. nepalensis* a worthy addition to a rock garden, despite its long stems and often sprawling nature. It was introduced into cultivation in Britain in 1822 and flowered at the Royal Botanic Garden Edinburgh in July 1823 (Hooker, 1825). It was described by William Hooker in 1825, in the second volume of his *Exotic Flora*. Over 100 years later, in 1929, it was featured in *Curtis's Botanical Magazine* where Otto Stapf suggests that the specific epithet of *P. nepalensis* may be a misnomer as there is no specimen from Nepal in Wallich's collection and no mention of it in his Catalogue. However, there is a specimen from Kumaon (Uttar Pradesh) and Stapf (1929) goes on to say "The flora of Inner Nepal has, indeed, so much in common with that of Kumaon, that the

ABOVE LEFT
Androsace sarmentosa in Himachal Pradesh.
Photo: Joanne Everson.

BELOW
Potentilla nepalensis.

occurrence of *P. nepalensis* in Nepal might safely be anticipated." *Potentilla nepalensis* is now known to occur extensively in the western Himalaya, from northern Pakistan through Kashmir to central Nepal. It is found on sunny hillsides and in open woodland at altitudes of 2,000–2,700 m (6,562–8,858 feet).

Potentilla is a large and varied genus containing around 500 species of shrubs, perennials and annuals, but Hooker was not aware of any other *Potentilla* with which *P. nepalensis* could be confused. He considered the rose-red flowers to be of a colour unlike that of the flowers of any other species published at that time. The flowers are held in loose panicles at the end of purple-red, hairy stems that are usually 30–60 cm tall, but if growing among other plants these stems can reach 1 m long. Each flower is 1.5–3 cm across and usually deep crimson to rose-red but can also be cherry-pink, orange or occasionally white. A similar species to *P. nepalensis* is *P. atrosanguinea*, which is found from Afghanistan to Sikkim. This species has red or yellow flowers and all the leaves are divided into three rather than five leaflets, which are densely covered with white hairs on their undersides. It was the first species William Hooker wrote about in *Curtis's Botanical Magazine*, in 1826, and he also painted it. This species was described in 1823 by Conrad Loddiges, in his rival publication the *Botanical Cabinet*. The plant Hooker painted was collected in Nepal by Wallich.

A hybrid between *Potentilla nepalensis* and *P. atrosanguinea*, with deep purple-red flowers, was raised by W. Russell in his nursery at Battersea in 1827. It became known as *P. × russelliana*. Hooker (1836) describes it as "far exceeding in size and beauty of its blossoms either of its parents". Another plant often considered a clone of *P. nepalensis*, but arguably of hybrid origin, is the popular 'Miss Wilmott', which is a shorter plant, to 30 cm, with rose-crimson flowers.

Wallich's *Tentamen Florae Napalensis Illustratae* was published between 1824 and 1826. Among the species described in this work is the magnificent bulb now known as *Cardiocrinum giganteum*, which is found in forests at altitudes of 1,200–3,600 m (3,937–11,811 feet) in China, Bhutan, Myanmar, northern India, Nepal and Sikkim. Wallich found it in moist shady places and notes that it didn't survive one season in the heat of Calcutta. He named it *Lilium giganteum* and it was introduced to cultivation by Thomas Lobb, who was collecting in India for the Veitch nursery in 1850. This lily relative grows to 2 m tall or more, displaying glistening white trumpets in early summer. The first plant to flower in Europe was at the Comely Bank Nursery in Edinburgh, in 1852. In cultivation, this species prefers the cool shade and moist soil of a woodland garden. The huge, shiny bulbs that sit at or just below the surface can take seven years to reach flowering size from seed. Japanese botanist Tomitaro Makino transferred this species to *Cardiocrinum* in 1913.

FAR LEFT
Cardiocrinum giganteum, originally named *Lilium giganteum* by Wallich.

LEFT
Arisaema speciosum.

Wallich also described several Himalayan arums that were later transferred to the genus *Arisaema*. They include *Arisaema nepenthoides*, *A. costatum* and *A. speciosum*. The floriferous *Primula floribunda* is another of Wallich's new species. This has small golden yellow flowers held in whorls on a stem that reaches 10–15 cm tall. It occurs from the Khyber Pass between Afghanistan and Pakistan, to south-west Nepal, at 500–2,700 m (1,640–8,858 feet). This is an interesting species in that it may be a link between the mainly western Asian *Primula* section *Sphondylia*, to which it belongs along with species such as the Arabian *P. verticillata* and the Afghan *P. edelbergii*, and the Sino-Himalayan section *Prolifera*, the candelabra primulas, which include *P. bulleyana*, *P. japonica* and *P. cockburniana* amongst others (Richards, 2002). *Primula floribunda* has been in cultivation for over 100 years and does best under glass in the UK, protected from excessive damp and cold.

Royle's *Illustrations of the Botany and other Branches of the Natural History of the Himalayan Mountains: and of the Flora of Cashmere* is an impressive work, in eleven parts, with 100 plates. It contains descriptions and paintings of fossils, animals, insects and birds, as well as plants. Many species were described and illustrated for the first time in this work, among the Himalayan plants are *Roscoea alpina*, *Campanula cashmiriana*, the blue-flowered *Meconopsis aculeata*, which first bloomed at Kew in 1864, and *Corydalis cashmeriana*, also blue-flowered, which was not introduced for another hundred years but which caused a sensation when exhibited at the Alpine Garden Society Spring Show in 1934 (Sealy, 1968).

Royle also described two species of Himalayan delphiniums, *Delphinium cashmerianum* and *D. brunonianum*. There are around 250 annual, biennial and perennial species of *Delphinium*, or larkspurs, distributed across Europe, Asia and North America, with a few in Africa and South America. Several smaller species from the Himalaya are ideal for a rock garden, raised bed or alpine house.

The striking, large-flowered *Salvia hians* was also featured in Royle's *Illustrations*. This species is distributed along the western Himalaya, from Kashmir to Nepal, usually growing on open, rocky slopes and scrub, at altitudes of 2,400–4,000 m (7,874–13,123 feet). It was described in George Bentham's account of the Indian Labiatae in Royle's collection, published in William Hooker's *Botanical Miscellany* in 1833. Royle received specimens of this species from his plant collectors, who found it in Kashmir.

Salvia hians first flowered in England at the Horticultural Society of London's garden in 1840. It was featured in the *Botanical Register* in 1841, with an account by John Lindley (1841), who writes that it was introduced to cultivation by the Court of Directors of the East India Company. This

Delphinium cashmerianum
Family: Ranunculaceae

Delphinium cashmerianum comes from the western Himalaya, occurring in northern Pakistan, north-west India and Tibet (Xizang). It grows 10–60 cm tall and in the wild is found on grassy slopes and among rocks at altitudes of 2,700–5,000 m (8,858–16,404 feet). It was described by John Forbes Royle in 1834, and he stated that he received specimens from "the garden of Shalimar" in Kashmir. The plant painted for *Curtis's Botanical Magazine* in 1875 was probably the first introduction of this attractive species to cultivation.

Most species of *Delphinium* have flowers in shades of blue or purple, but there are also red-, yellow- and white-flowered species. Their palmate leaves are often toothed and may be divided into narrow lobes. The flowers consist of five petal-like sepals, with the upper sepal elongated into a spur behind the flower. At the centre of the flower are four petals, the upper two with nectar-secreting projections that extend into the spur.

Delphinium cashmerianum has large bluish-purple flowers, around 3.5 cm wide, with a mostly straight, 12–15 mm long spur. The petals can be light blue but are often darker than the sepals, forming a dark eye at the centre of the flower. The hairy leaves can reach 10 cm across and are palmately divided into 5–7 toothed lobes. This is a variable species, particularly in leaf-shape, petal-colour and pubescence. In general, these plants are glabrous in the lower part and pubescent in the region of the inflorescence but the amount of pubescence varies considerably (Qureshi & Chaudhri, 1988).

Delphinium brunonianum, also described by Royle, is similar but has more kidney-shaped leaves and can grow up to 1 m tall, though it is often shorter. The upper leaves are like leafy bracts and the upper portion of the plant is covered with glandular hairs. The petals are black and the inflorescence usually holds more flowers than *D. cashmerianum*. It also has a musky smell.

Delphinium cashmerianum is a perennial species but it is usually short-lived and often dies after flowering. It is hardy and can be grown in the open if planted in a free-draining but moisture-retentive soil. The soil should be moist in the summer when the plant is in growth; some shade, especially at the roots, will prevent it drying out too quickly, otherwise this species can be grown in full sun.

Collect seed and raise new plants every year. The seedlings can flower in their first year but they often die in the autumn. If the first season's flower buds are pinched out, the plant is more likely to behave as a perennial, but it will still be short-lived so regular propagation is necessary.

Curtis's Botanical Magazine, plate 6189 (1875). Artist: Walter Hood Fitch.

Incarvillea subgenus Amphicome contains only I. arguta and I. emodi. Both have woody-based stems and their flowers are smaller than those of the more widely grown, showy herbaceous species, such as I. delavayi and I. mairei, which are in subgenus Pteroscleris.

Incarvillea emodi is primarily a western Himalayan species. It is found from eastern Afghanistan, through north-west Pakistan and Kashmir, to northern India and western Nepal, growing in rocky places and crevices at altitudes of 600–2,500 m (1,969–8,202 feet). It can reach up to 50 cm tall when in flower and the short, unbranched stems have greyish, pinnate leaves that grow to 15–25 cm long. From 6 to 18 flowers are held in a one-sided raceme at the end of the each stem. These flowers are around 3.5 cm in diameter and rose pink to pinkish purple, with a yellow throat. The corolla tube can be more than 5 cm long. The more widespread Himalayan and Chinese I. arguta has smaller flowers than I. emodi but the branched stems can reach more than 1 m long.

Many of the plants featured in the publications of Smith, Roxburgh, Wallich and Royle made it into cultivation, either soon after they were described or when recollected by plant hunters several years later. However, the scale of Himalayan introductions stepped up a level when Joseph Hooker spent three years in these mountains from 1848 to 1851. Furthermore, with the help of his father William back home at Kew, Hooker's travels resulted in the publication of two illustrated accounts of the plants he found, plus his *Himalayan Journals*, one volume of *Flora Indica* co-authored by Thomas Thomson, and finally the *Flora of British India*, published in seven volumes between 1872 and 1897.

LEFT
Incarvillea emodi.

BELOW
Incarvillea arguta.

herbaceous perennial has thick, hairy quadrangular stems that can grow from 30 to 100 cm tall. Each whorl (verticillaster) has four to six flowers, each up to 5 cm long and 1.5 cm wide, with an inflated corolla tube and spreading lobes; *hians* means 'gaping'. The lower lip is often white, but in striking contrast, the rest of the corolla is a spectacular deep blue, violet or purple.

The genus *Amphicome* was proposed by Royle but, on the advice of the botanist Robert Brown at the British Museum, he reduced it to a subgenus of *Incarvillea*. Royle (1836) states: "The genus *Incarvillea*...found hitherto only in China and Japan, has also (at least the subgenus *Amphicome*) been discovered in the Himalayas, where Dr Wallich's *I. emodi* was found, near Srinuggur [Srinagar], and by myself on the Suen range...The Himalayan species are too closely allied to be separated into a genus distinct from the Chinese *Incarvillea*, but are yet sufficiently distinguished to constitute a subgenus." However, George Don (1837) revived the genus *Amphicome* and this treatment was followed by subsequent authors, including Hooker, Lindley and de Candolle. In 1948, Debabarta Chatterjee concluded that *Amphicome* should not be maintained as a genus distinct from *Incarvillea*, and formally published the combination *Incarvillea emodi*, with *Amphicome emodi* as a synonym.

Hooker left England in November 1847, arriving in Darjeeling via Calcutta in April 1848. While waiting for permission to enter Sikkim, he explored the hills around Darjeeling, finding the first of many rhododendrons and the beautiful *Magnolia campbellii*. Eventually, he set off in October 1848 with permission to enter eastern Nepal and return via Sikkim. He headed for the Wallanchoon and Yangma passes, to the west of the mighty Kanchenjunga (8,586 m; 28,169 feet), at the time thought to be the world's highest mountain. Hooker was the first European to see this part of Nepal and he also managed to find a way into Sikkim, over the western border, before returning to Darjeeling in January 1849. On this expedition, Hooker and his team climbed to over 4,600 m (15,092 feet) on the Tibetan border. Among the alpine plants he collected was the bizarre *Saussurea gossipiphora*, with its large, spherical, cotton wool-like inflorescences that cling to the stony slopes.

In May 1849, Hooker set off for a much longer exploration of Sikkim, only returning to Darjeeling the following December. He made scientific observations, took measurements and drew accurate maps of this remote and little-known region, as well as collecting plants and seeds. After a winter of writing up notes and sorting his collections, he set off again in May 1850 with his friend Thomas Thomson for a nine-month expedition to Assam and the Khasi Hills. This was not an unexplored region but the plant life is incredibly lush and diverse, no doubt due to the high rainfall in these hills.

Hooker departed India for England in January 1851. His three years in India had been hugely productive. He collected over 3,000 species in Sikkim and Bengal and many more in Assam, as well as completing over 700 drawings of plants in addition to sketches and maps (Desmond, 1999). From a horticultural point of view, Hooker's exploration of the Himalaya had a far greater impact than the Antarctic expedition. He sent back seeds of many new *Rhododendron* species, which caused a great deal of excitement in Britain and have had a significant impact on the garden landscape. This excitement was fuelled by the beautiful paintings in *Rhododendrons of Sikkim-Himalaya*, the first part of which was published in 1849, edited by William Hooker while Joseph was still in India. Two further parts were published in 1851. The plates were executed by Walter Hood Fitch and in all 31 species were portrayed.

Illustrations of Himalayan Plants was published in 1855 and portrays a mixture of plants from the alpine zone to the subtropics. One of the most spectacular is the giant alpine rhubarb, *Rheum nobile*, which was painted by Fitch from Hooker's sketches. Hooker found this remarkable plant at 4,260 m (14,000 feet) altitude in the Lachen Valley of Sikkim.

TOP
Saussurea gossipiphora, growing at 4,850 m (15,912 feet) altitude in Bhutan.
Photo: Joanne Everson.

LEFT
Potentilla cuneata, Himachal Pradesh.
Photo: Joanne Everson.

Rheum nobile

One of the wonders of the plant kingdom, this giant rhubarb grows to nearly 2 metres tall on screes and boulder fields at altitudes of 3,600–4,600 m (11,811–15,092 feet), where all other vegetation is merely centimetres tall. The inconspicuous white flower clusters are hidden behind the pale creamy-white, overlapping, drooping bracts that clothe the stout stem forming a "vegetable greenhouse" (Baker, Henderson & Birks, 2004). At the base of the plant is a skirt of large green leaves that clasp the ground.

Rheum nobile is found in the high mountains of eastern Nepal, Sikkim, Bhutan and south-east Tibet. It was first described by Joseph Hooker and Thomas Thomson in Hooker's *Illustrations of Himalayan Plants*, which was published in 1855.

Rheum nobile at 4,600 m (15,092 feet) altitude just below Yelia La, Bhutan. Photo: Joanne Everson.

Among Hooker's alpine plant introductions is the wonderful *Primula sikkimensis*, which he saw forming carpets of yellow in the high meadows of Sikkim. He sent seed of *Inula hookeri* from the valleys of Sikkim to Kew, where it flowered in 1851, although it wasn't named until 1876. *Primula capitata*, with its globular heads of lilac-purple flowers, was another of Hooker's introductions and he also sent the mat-forming, yellow-flowered *Potentilla cuneata* back to the UK. Hooker was responsible for introducing the first Himalayan blue poppy to flower in cultivation. It was named *Meconopsis wallichii* by William Hooker, after Nathaniel Wallich who discovered it in Nepal. The plants flowered at Kew in 1852 and were featured that year in *Curtis's Botanical Magazine* (Hooker, 1852).

It was some time before other Europeans followed in Hooker's footsteps, but when they did, they used his *Himalayan Journals* as a guide. For both political and geographical reasons, the eastern end of the Himalayan range, in Assam, Bhutan, Burma and south-east Tibet, was the last region of these mountains to be explored. Inaccessible valleys, treacherous rivers, imposing mountains and hostile tribes all conspired to make botanising and plant collecting very difficult. Hooker had made the first tentative steps into Sikkim, but it was not until the early twentieth century that any major plant collections were made further east. By then, the gardening public was being distracted by the new and exciting discoveries coming out of China and among them were many alpine and rock garden plants. The 'golden age of plant hunting' was well underway.

BELOW
Primula sikkimensis in southern Tibet. Photo: Joanne Everson.

China and the 'Golden age of plant hunting'

Although some plants from China arrived in Europe in the late eighteenth and early nineteenth centuries, it was really the signing of the Treaty of Nanking in 1842 that set the stage for the discovery and collection of China's botanical riches. This treaty marked the end of the First Opium War and resulted in the handing over of Hong Kong to Britain and the opening up for trade of four Chinese ports. It meant that travel in China for foreigners became easier.

The Horticultural Society of London was quick to take advantage of this new opportunity and employed Robert Fortune to travel to China and collect plants. Fortune arrived in China in 1843 and stayed for three years. He returned a further three times and as well as introducing new plants to horticulture in Europe, he was responsible for establishing the tea industry in Assam and Sikkim for the East India Company.

Many of the first western travellers in China in the late nineteenth century were French missionaries, such as Jean Pierre Armand David and Jean Marie Delavay. They were soon followed by collectors working for nurseries, who employed them to bring back new species that were then proudly exhibited and offered in their catalogues. This was the 'golden age' and our gardens have been all the richer ever since. Fortune was followed by a number of now famous plant hunters: Ernest Wilson, Reginald Farrer, Frank Kingdon-Ward and the team of Frank Ludlow and George Sherriff. As far as alpine plants are concerned, probably the greatest of all of these collectors was George Forrest.

The stories of plant hunters' travels and adventures in China have been extensively covered by books, journals and magazines, some of which are listed in the bibliography at the end of this chapter, but the following is a more detailed look at some of the plants these explorers introduced. Trees and shrubs often take top billing when the species introduced during this golden age are discussed, but the herbaceous and alpine flora of China, particularly in Yunnan and Sichuan is extraordinarily diverse. Below are examples of the rich pickings found by plant hunters in this fascinating period of garden history.

The names of plant collectors are remembered in the names given to the species they discovered. One example is *Aster delavayi*, described by French botanist Adrien Franchet in 1896 and named after the French missionary Jean Marie Delavay, who had collected it in Yunnan. Franchet (1896) describes this as a particularly desirable plant for the garden because of the intense colour of the flowers. This species is now treated as a synonym of *A. diplostephioides*, a species originally named *Heterochaeta diplostephioides* in 1836 by A. P. de Candolle. The genus *Heterochaeta* was created by de Candolle to contain species similar to asters but with single flower heads and double pappus (the specialised calyx of hairs that aid seed dispersal). In 1873, George Bentham reduced *Heterochaeta* to a synonym of *Aster*, in *Genera Plantarum* and Charles Baron Clarke published the combination *Aster diplostephioides* in 1876.

The appearance of *Aster diplostephioides* in *Curtis's Botanical Magazine* in 1883 probably marks the first recorded introduction of this species into cultivation.

LEFT
Aster diplostephioides,
Himachal Pradesh.
Photo: Joanne Everson.

Hooker (1883) writes, "The specimens here figured were raised from seed gathered in Sikkim by H. Elwes, Esq., and presented by him to the Royal Gardens. They flowered profusely in May and June, quite equalling the finest specimens from their native country."

This species grows in an area stretching from Kashmir, through northern India and Nepal, to Sikkim, Bhutan and China. It is found on grassy hills, screes, in scrub and forest clearings, at altitudes of 3,000–4,900 m (9,843–16,076 feet). This is a beautiful species, with flower heads up to 8 cm wide. The ray florets have mauve to blue-violet petals (ligules) and the disc florets are dark purple or blackish, turning bright orange-yellow as they open. It is easily grown in a sunny, rich scree if kept well-watered in the summer.

Ernest Henry Wilson is best known for his woody plant introductions, especially the handkerchief tree, *Davidia involucrata*, collected on his first expedition, but he also sent back several herbaceous plants from the hills of China. He worked for Messrs. Veitch and Sons and began his first expedition to China in 1899, at the age of 23, returning home in 1902. His second trip was undertaken from 1903 to 1905. He made a further two trips to China for the Arnold Arboretum, in Boston, USA and travelled twice to Japan in 1914–15 and 1917–19.

One of the main aims of his second journey to China for the Veitch Nursery in 1903 was to bring back to Europe the yellow-flowered *Meconopsis integrifolia*. This species had been introduced previously in 1895, thanks to the missionary Abbé Farges who sent seed to the French nurseryman M. Maurice L. de Vilmorin. It flowered in 1897 but no seed was produced and the species was lost to cultivation (Hemsley, 1905). Wilson found this plant in huge quantities at altitudes of 3,350–4,570 m (10,991–14,993 feet) in the alpine meadows of the mountains west of Tachienlu (now Kangding) on the Sichuan–Tibet border. Once the main object of the expedition had been found, Wilson could spend more time looking for other species, and he managed to find the extraordinary red-flowered *M. punicea*, the violet-blue *M. henrici* and the bristly *M. horridula*.

Among Wilson's other introductions was *Primula cockburniana*, one of the 'candelabra' species, which he found in alpine meadows west of Tachienlu at 2,740–3,350 m (8,990–10,991 feet). It first flowered at the Veitch's nursery in June 1905. Another species in this group, *P. pulverulenta*, was also collected by Wilson on his second expedition.

Lilium regale had already been found by Père Delavay in Yunnan in July 1888 but Wilson collected it in north-east Sichuan and it was named by him in 1913. This glorious species, with its long white trumpets, is strongly scented and makes a dramatic impact in the garden in early summer. Wilson found *Gentiana veitchiorum*, named after

**Plant introductions
of Ernest Wilson**

ABOVE LEFT
Meconopsis henrici.

ABOVE CENTRE
Primula cockburniana.

ABOVE RIGHT
Iris wilsonii.

LEFT
Lilium regale.

his employer by William Botting Hemsley, in 1909, and the yellow 'Siberian iris', *Iris wilsonii*, named after its discoverer by Charles Wright in 1907.

Around the same time that Wilson was in China, the Scotsman George Forrest was undertaking his first expedition. He travelled in China from 1904 to 1906 and explored the mountains of Yunnan and south-east Tibet (Xizang). He was employed by Arthur Kilpin Bulley, a Liverpool cotton broker who had a passion for plants and created Ness Gardens, now run by the University of Liverpool as Ness Botanic Gardens. Bulley also established a seed firm, Bees Ltd., in direct competition with the Veitch's, and Forrest was his first paid collector. Forrest began his second and last expedition for Bulley in 1910 but went on to make a further five trips to China before he died in 1932, at the age of 58.

Forrest was a remarkably successful plant hunter. Among his many new introductions were primulas, including *Primula forrestii*, *P. vialii* and the wonderful *P. bulleyana*. Forrest introduced *Androsace spinulifera*, *Roscoea humeana* and one of his greatest finds, the autumn flowering *Gentiana sino-ornata*, which flowered for the first time in cultivation, both at Ness and Edinburgh, in 1912. This gentian caused quite a stir in the horticultural world, its deep blue, funnel-shaped flowers, held on quickly spreading plants, being admired by many.

The fabulous, orange-yellow flowered *Primula bulleyana* was one of the many successful introductions by Arthur Kilpin Bulley's firm, Bees Ltd., from Forrest's collections in China. Forrest discovered this species in moist, open situations on mountain meadows on the eastern flank of the Lichiang (Lijiang) range, north-west Yunnan, in June 1906 (collection no. 2440), during his first plant hunting expedition for Bulley. He described it in 1908 and named it in honour of his sponsor. In his description he writes, "Like most of the alpine or subalpine primulas, this species grows in huge colonies, and to see several acres densely covered with such plants is a sight ever to be remembered."

Plants of *Primula bulleyana* first flowered in cultivation in 1909, and on 18 May of that year the species received a First Class Certificate from the RHS, when exhibited by Bulley. It caused great excitement at the time, and two photographs and a painting of this species were featured in the *Gardeners' Chronicle* of 10 July 1909. One photograph shows it flowering at the Royal Botanic Garden Edinburgh; the other was taken by Forrest in its natural habitat. In the wild, *P. bulleyana* grows in marshy meadows and beside streams and ditches, at altitudes of 2,500–3,300 m (8,202–10,827 feet), in north-west Yunnan and south-west Sichuan.

Primula bulleyana carries up to seven whorls of flowers that open over several weeks in late spring. The buds are brownish-crimson but open to form deep reddish-orange to orange-yellow flowers. Forrest also collected a form (no. 2449) with flowers of a 'crushed strawberry shade'. This species is one of the 'candelabra' primulas of section *Proliferae*, which also includes Ernest Wilson's *P. cockburniana*. Balfour (1913) was the first to coin the term 'candelabra', to encompass species that produce a cluster of primrose-like leaves and a tall scape, with whorls of stalked flowers at intervals, the number of these whorls varying from one to eight.

ABOVE
Roscoea humeana was introduced from Yunnan by George Forrest.

LEFT
Another popular Forrest introduction, *Primula vialii*.

Gentiana sino-ornata
Family: Gentianaceae

The autumn-flowering *Gentiana sino-ornata* was discovered by George Forrest during his first expedition for A. K. Bulley. He found it in 1904, growing in moist alpine meadows and at the borders of streams near the summit of the Michang Pass, between the Yangtse and the Zhongdian Plateau in north-west Yunnan. On his second expedition to Yunnan, Forrest collected seed of this species, sending it to Ness Gardens and to the Royal Botanic Garden, Edinburgh.

The plants introduced by Forrest were originally thought to be the Himalayan *Gentiana ornata*. The name *G. sino-ornata* was first used by Prof. Balfour when he described this species in 1918. Balfour recognised that the plants growing at Edinburgh were different from the true *G. ornata*. For several years, however, this species was grown under the name *G. ornata* and received an Award of Merit as such from the RHS in 1915.

Gentiana sino-ornata usually produces royal to sky blue flowers, with yellowish-white stripes leading from the calyx to the base of the corolla lobes; although in the wild, flower colour can vary from indigo blue to pale blue and white (sometimes flushed yellow or pink). From September to November, the flowers open at the end of long, leafy shoots that arise from a small overwintering rosette. These shoots or stolons can reach 18 cm in length and trail along the ground before turning up at the end. Secondary rosettes form from the rooting nodes and allow the plant to spread rapidly. The narrow, pointed leaves of *G. sino-ornata* are up to 3.5 cm long and 5 mm wide. The large, showy flowers are 5–6 cm long and have five corolla lobes and triangular, pointed plicae.

Gentiana ornata has short bell-shaped flowers that are a paler blue than those of *G. sino-ornata* and are produced from late August to September. They are held at the end of shoots that reach only around 10 cm in length, often less.

Grown in the right position, *Gentiana sino-ornata* is an easy, vigorous and free-flowering plant that has been described as one of the finest plant introductions of the twentieth century. It soon forms a carpet of foliage, and at its best will produce a mass of deep blue flowers from September until the first hard frost. Its main requirements are a cool, humid atmosphere and a moist, acidic soil, in sun or light shade. This species will not tolerate any lime in the soil, a characteristic shared by all its close relatives except *G. farreri*.

Gentiana sino-ornata is the parent of more hybrids than any other gentian. For example, *G. ×macaulayi*, the first hybrid to use this species, is a cross with *G. farreri*. It has pure deep blue flowers, borne in profusion, and like *G. farreri* will tolerate some lime in the soil. *Gentiana ×stevenagensis* is a cross between *G. sino-ornata* and the more compact *G. veitchiorum*, whose influence can be seen in the large, deep blue flowers.

Curtis's Botanical Magazine, plate 9241 (1931). Artist: Lilian Snelling.

tall, arising from the centre of a rosette of long, silky, pointed leaves. The flowers are held in a tight, almost globular umbel and vary in colour from magenta-red to rose-purple with a yellow eye that changes to red with age. This species overwinters as a compact, rounded rosette that looks like a small sempervivum. It is composed of short, sessile leaves only 5–20 mm long with a distinct spine-like tip. In spring, from the centre of the rosette, grow bristly, oblanceolate leaves that have a pointed tip and taper to a short petiole. These summer leaves can reach 18 cm long and 2 cm wide.

Androsace spinulifera is found in north-west Yunnan and western Sichuan, growing on stony slopes, dry grassland and in open woods, at altitudes of 2,400–4,500 m (7,874–14,764 feet). Forrest (1910) observed that plants from higher altitudes were more luxuriant, but the characteristic spine-like tips to the leaves were less prominent on these plants. He describes the most favourable situations as "...on the margins of pine forests, mostly with northern exposures; there in places, acres of ground were dominated by it to the exclusion of all other herbage, and in such places the plants attain their fullest beauty."

Androsace spinulifera is closely related to *A. strigillosa*, from the central Himalaya. Franchet described it as a variety of *A. strigillosa* in 1885, distinguishing it from the typical form of that species on the basis of its narrower leaves with rigid spines at their apex. The German botanist, Reinhard Knuth, raised Franchet's variety to species level, publishing the name in Engler's *Das Pflanzenreich* in 1905.

These two species can still be confused, with plants labelled as *Androsace spinulifera* often being the more widely grown *A. strigillosa*. The leaves of *A. strigillosa* lack a sharp tip, the flowers are usually white with a reddish

In May 1906, in the same area that he found *Primula bulleyana* but at a slightly lower altitude, Forrest collected a *Primula* with rose-carmine flowers and a yellow eye. He described it in 1911 as *P. beesiana*, naming it after Bulley's firm. He writes that it is almost identical to *P. bulleyana* but he never found the two growing together (Forrest, 1911). Recent fieldwork in the Yulong Shan (Yunnan) has modified this view; *P. bulleyana*, *P. beesiana* and *P. poissonii* sometimes occur together, forming vibrantly coloured hybrid swarms. In his monograph on *Primula*, John Richards (2002) reduces *P. beesiana* to a subspecies of *P. bulleyana*.

The Chinese *Androsace spinulifera* was introduced into cultivation by George Forrest in 1906. He collected it in May of that year from populations growing on very dry, barren, stony grassland at the north end of the Lijiang plain, under the collection number 2081 (Forrest, 1908). A later Forrest collection (no. 21242) was found in stony pastures in the mountains of south-west Sichuan.

This beautiful species is in section *Chamaejasme*. It produces one or more flower stems, generally up to 30 cm reverse and the umbel is more open with longer pedicels (up to 5 cm), the summer leaves have a longer petiole, equal in length to the blade, and they persist after withering, surrounding the winter rosette (Smith & Lowe, 1997).

Androsace spinulifera represents a challenge in cultivation, as it must be kept dry during the winter months but needs a plentiful supply of water when in growth. In the past, many growers thought it was monocarpic (dying after flowering) but this was more than likely due to the difficulty of keeping it alive during the winter. *Androsace strigillosa* is more tolerant of winter dampness and so is easier to grow, often producing many self-sown seedlings.

Bulley never employed Reginald Farrer as a collector but he did have dealings with him, purchasing shares in his seed collections. Farrer was a gardener and author, as well as a plant hunter. He travelled several times to the Alps, usually accompanied by gardening friends such as Edward Augustus Bowles and Clarence Elliott. He built a rock garden at Ingleborough in Yorkshire to grow the alpine plants he collected, and wrote nineteen books, including *My Rock Garden* in 1907, *Among the Hills* in 1911 and *The Rock Garden* in 1912, as well as contributing articles to the *Gardeners' Chronicle*. In 1913, he completed the frequently quoted *The English Rock Garden*, renowned for its 'flowery' prose and strong opinions. This encyclopaedia of alpine plants appeared in two volumes; its publication was delayed until 1919 by the First World War.

Farrer travelled in China from 1914 to 1915, accompanied by William Purdom. Purdom was a Kew-trained gardener and had previous experience of collecting in China, from 1909 to 1912, for the Veitch Nursery and the Arnold Arboretum. This expedition was supported not only by Bulley but also by the RHS and by keen gardeners, such as E. A. Bowles, an expert on bulbs who gardened at Myddelton House in Essex, and Frederick Stern, who created a famous garden on chalk at Highdown in Sussex. Introductions from this expedition include *Geranium farreri*, described by Otto Stapf in 1926, and *Gentiana farreri*. Farrer recounted his travels in *On the Eaves of the World*, published in 1917. In 1920, he died prematurely at the age of 40 while in Burma (Myanmar).

Geranium farreri was discovered by Farrer in August 1914 in the Min Shan Mountains of China, on the border of Gansu and Sichuan. The genus *Geranium*, with over 300 species, includes some of the most popular garden perennials. Many of the

Geranium farreri

Geranium farreri, named after Reginald Farrer, is a high alpine species from Gansu, where it grows on shale or limestone screes and rocky slopes at altitudes of around 3,900–4,500 m (12,795–14,764 feet). It dies down completely for the winter, but in early spring the new shoots emerge to form a low mound of foliage, which is topped by large, pale pink blooms, up to 3.5 cm across, with blue-black anthers. The whole plant reaches only 10–15 cm tall. The rounded petals are narrowed to a claw at their base, revealing the green sepals behind. The long-stalked leaves are 2–5 cm wide and deeply divided into seven segments, each subdivided into three broad lobes. *Geranium napuligerum*, which was discovered by Delavay in Yunnan in 1886, differs in having glandular rather than eglandular hairs, densely hairy sepals and filaments with long hairs.

This is a hardy species that grows well in a sunny position on a rock garden or in a raised bed if planted in free-draining soil. It resents too much moisture during its winter dormant phase, but from spring to autumn, the soil should never be allowed to dry out completely. The wide, pale pink flowers are held above the leaves in late spring or early summer. Plants often produce some late flowers and a new flush of leaves later in the year. The easiest way to propagate this species is in summer by

detaching a few shoots from the edge of the clump, just below ground level and inserting them into a pot of sandy soil. Some detached shoots may already have some roots and these can be pushed directly into the ground, where they will soon grow away if conditions are not too hot and dry.

Geranium farreri on the rock garden at Kew.

smaller species are suitable for a rock garden, raised bed or alpine house, but Farrer was particularly captivated by the plant he found. It is one of the most delicate and charming of all geraniums and was named after him by Otto Stapf in *Curtis's Botanical Magazine* 12 years later, in January 1926.

Farrer's original collection was made under number F. 201 but he only managed to obtain a couple of seeds. He tentatively named it *Geranium pylzowianum* var. *alpinum*. Seed of another collection, number F.170, was distributed freely and gave rise to two distinct plants at Kew. The first had slender rhizomes with tuber-like swellings at intervals along their length and narrowly dissected leaves. The second had a short, stout rhizome with thickened roots and leaves divided into short, broad lobes. It is the second plant that Stapf described as *G. farreri*.

In May 1921, this plant received an Award of Merit from the RHS as a pale-flowered form of *Geranium pylzowianum*, when shown by Clarence Elliott (Ingwersen, 1921). It received an Award of Merit again at the Chelsea Flower Show in May 1924, when it was called *Geranium* 'Farrer's Pink'. By this time, it was already known as *G. farreri* in the horticultural trade but the Floral Committee of the RHS considered it to be allied to and probably identical to *G. napuligerum*. Despite Stapf's subsequent formal description of *G. farreri*, the name *G. napuligerum* was incorrectly applied to this plant for many years. In his excellent book on hardy geraniums, Peter Yeo (1985) states that he can find no evidence that true *G. napuligerum* has ever been in cultivation.

Another of Farrer's collections from the Min Shan Mountains is *Stellera chamaejasme*. This species has a vast range in the wild, extending from the Altai Mountains, through Mongolia and northern China, south to the western Himalaya, the Tibetan Plateau and southwest China (Grey-Wilson, 1995). It is a beautiful, early-summer-flowering perennial that grows on stony mountain slopes, in scrub and open woodland, at altitudes of 1,800–4,300 m (5,906–14,108 feet), often forming extensive colonies.

The flowers of *Stellera chamaejasme* are held in a rounded, terminal head, at the end of the unbranched, herbaceous stems. These slender, leafy stems grow from a woody base and can reach over 40 cm tall. Throughout most of its range, this species has white flowers that are pinkish-red, lime green or pale yellow on the outside, but in the Chinese province of Yunnan especially, it often has yellow flowers. This yellow form was eventually described as forma *chrysantha* in 1985. As well as growing in Yunnan, its range extends into Xizang (Tibet) but Chris Grey-Wilson reports that it is never found growing with the white forma *chamaejasme* and appears to prefer areas with higher rainfall. Because of its geographical isolation, Grey-Wilson raised forma *chrysantha* to a variety, *S. chamaejasme* var. *chrysantha*, in 1995. However, there have recently been reports of the yellow form in Nepal's Marsyandi valley, atypically growing in mixed populations where the white form predominates.

Bulley launched the plant-hunting career of Frank Kingdon-Ward, who eventually made 22 journeys to hunt for plants between 1911 and 1957. His most famous collection must surely be *Meconopsis baileyi*, which he found on his expedition to explore the gorge of the Tsangpo-Dihang in Tibet and the Assam Himalaya, in 1924–5.

Kingdon-Ward wrote several books describing his travels, including *Land of the Blue Poppy* in 1913, *The Mystery Rivers of Tibet* in 1923 and *Riddle of the TsangPo Gorges* in 1926. Plants discovered by Kingdon-Ward include *Lilium mackliniae* and *Cassiope wardii*.

ABOVE LEFT
Stellera chamaejasme in Tibet.
Photo: Joanne Everson.

BELOW
The Himalayan blue poppy, *Meconopsis baileyi*.

The genus *Meconopsis*

The genus *Meconopsis* was established by L. G. Alexandre Viguier in 1814, for the yellow- or orange-flowered Welsh poppy, which had originally been described as *Papaver cambricum* by Linnaeus in 1753. Viguier distinguished *Meconopsis* from *Papaver* by the presence of a short style and the absence of a sessile stigmatic disc on the ovary. Today, *Meconopsis* contains around 50 species but *M. cambrica*, from western Europe, including Wales and south-west England, is the only one found outside the Himalaya and western China. This anomalous species is likely to be transferred to a separate genus, although this has yet to happen.

The genus is best known today for the beautiful blue-flowered species known as Himalayan blue poppies. *Meconopsis baileyi* (usually labelled *M. betonicifolia*) and *M. grandis* are among the most commonly grown. Both have wide, blue or purple flowers, but the latter can be distinguished by looking at the leaves. In *M. grandis*, the leaf bases are distinctly tapered, but in *M. baileyi* they are more truncated or heart-shaped. A hybrid between these two species arose in the garden of W. G. Sheldon in Oxted, Surrey, and this was named *M. ×sheldonii* by Taylor in 1936. Flower colour in the genus also includes white, yellow, orange and red forms. One of the most unusual species is the bright red-flowered *M. punicea*, which has flowers composed of crumpled paper-like petals that hang down like discarded tissues.

When grown in southern Britain, most species require woodland conditions, disliking summer heat, but further north they can be grown in more open positions. The main problems with cultivation result from pricking out the seedlings too late, letting them dry out (even for a short time) and planting in unsuitable locations, where it is too hot and dry in summer or too wet in winter.

TOP
Meconopsis cambrica.

ABOVE LEFT
Meconopsis grandis.

ABOVE RIGHT
Meconopsis punicea.

Of all the plant introductions from China and the Himalaya made in the early twentieth century, *Meconopsis baileyi* was arguably the most sensational. The glorious blue flowers, which are up to 10 cm across, captured the public's imagination. Today this plant is usually referred to as *M. betonicifolia* but Chris Grey-Wilson (2009) has recently revived the name *M. baileyi*, for the form of this blue poppy that grows in south-east Tibet and northern Myanmar; the form introduced by Kingdon-Ward. Within a few years of seed being sent back from Tibet by Kingdon-Ward, this poppy was well established in cultivation and reached a level of popularity that has been maintained to the present day. Each rose-lavender to sky-blue flower consists of four (sometimes five or six) petals that spread wide to expose the boss of yellow anthers at the centre. Plants can reach 1.5 m tall.

The true *Meconopsis betonicifolia* was discovered by Delavay in July 1886, growing in mountain woods at 3,200 m in north-west Yunnan and was described by Franchet in 1889. In July 1913, Captain Frederick Bailey, a Political Officer for the Indian Government, collected specimens of a blue-flowered poppy at Lunang, southeast Tibet, while exploring the Tsangpo River. This plant was described by David Prain in 1915 and named *M. baileyi* after its discoverer. It was very similar to *M. betonicifolia* but Prain (1915) separated *M. baileyi* on the basis that the ovaries were covered with bristly hairs and were not glabrous as in the Yunnan plants.

In March 1924, Kingdon-Ward left Darjeeling to explore the gorge of the Tsangpo-Dihang in Tibet and the Assam Himalaya. He found Bailey's blue poppy growing in woods on both sides of the valley of the Tsangpo River, flowering in May and June (Kingdon-Ward, 1926). It was from these plants that seed was introduced into cultivation, as *Meconopsis baileyi*. The plant that was featured in *Curtis's Botanical Magazine* in 1930 was grown from one of these collections (KW 5784) and flowered in a pot at Kew in 1926. This species received an Award of Merit from the RHS in April 1926 and a First Class Certificate in June 1927.

The hairiness of the ovary was found to be a variable characteristic, and in Taylor's monograph of *Meconopsis* published in 1934, *M. baileyi* is treated as a synonym of *M. betonicifolia* (Taylor, 1934). Virtually all the plants in general cultivation today have arisen from collections of the Tibetan form and, following Taylor's monograph, they are mostly given the name *M. betonicifolia*. However, having studied material from both Tibet and Yunnan, Grey-Wilson has noted several differences between the two forms, including the shape and size of the leaves (larger in *M. baileyi*), the size of the capsule (larger in *M. baileyi*) and the length of the style and stigma (both shorter in *M. baileyi*). Also, the plants from Yunnan are stoloniferous, while those from Tibet are not. The name *M. baileyi* has therefore been restored for the Tibetan plants, with *M. betonicifolia* occurring only in Yunnan.

Another of the discoveries made during Kingdon-Ward's exploration of the Tsangpo gorges in south-east Tibet in 1924 was *Cassiope wardii*. He found it growing on steep, grassy and rocky alpine slopes and ridges, at 4,200–4,500 m (13,780– 14,764 feet), fully exposed to the sun and wind. He collected specimens on two occasions in June 1924, both under number KW 5752. The first plants, on the Temo La, were not in flower, but a couple of weeks later, he found flowering plants on the Nyima La. For many years, travelling constraints have made follow-up fieldwork unfeasible, but recently *C. wardii* has been relocated by Peter Cox, although plants were not re-introduced.

The travels of Kingdon-Ward coincided with those of the partnership of Frank Ludlow and George Sherriff. These two met in Kashgar, India in 1929 and went on to travel extensively in the Himalaya and Tibet. The Second World War interrupted their explorations but they resumed in 1945 until Sherriff, the older of the two by fifteen years, retired to Scotland in 1950.

Ludlow and Sherriff reintroduced many plants that may have been lost to cultivation or had only a tentative hold. Among the new species they found were *Primula sherriffii* and *P. ludlowii*. They introduced *Euphorbia griffithii* and brought more stock of *Corydalis cashmeriana* into cultivation. Although described in 1866, the beautiful, white-flowered *Adonis brevistyla* was not introduced until 1936, when Ludlow and Sherriff introduced seed collected at Chösam, in the Tsari region of southern Tibet. In April 1940, a plant raised by T. Hay of New Lodge, Hyde Park, received an Award of Merit from the RHS, under the name *A. davidii*. Soon after, Frank Kingdon-Ward (1940) questioned the plant's identity, saying that it appeared to be *A. brevistyla*. He had seen this species in the Tsangpo Valley in 1924 and at Chösam in 1935. Adrien Franchet described *A. davidii* in 1885 and named it after its discoverer, the French missionary Armand David, who found it in Moupin (Baoxing), Sichuan, in 1869 (Franchet, 1885).

Study of the flora of the Himalaya and China continues up to the present day and this remarkable, botanically diverse

LEFT
Cassiope 'Muirhead', a hybrid between *C. wardii* and *C. lycopodioides*.

BELOW
Adonis brevistyla, introduced by Ludlow and Sherriff in 1936.

Cassiope wardii
Family: Ericaceae

In 1834, David Don removed five species from *Andromeda* to form a new genus, *Cassiope*. There are now 12 recognised species in this genus, distributed in arctic and subarctic Europe, Asia and North America. They are small, evergreen shrubs with wiry stems and bell- or goblet-shaped, pendent flowers. *Cassiope* is distinguished from *Andromeda* by solitary, lateral or terminal flowers and the sessile, usually overlapping (imbricate) leaves that clothe the stems. *Cassiope wardii* is often referred to as the finest species in the genus and is notable for the long silvery hairs on its leaf margins and tips. Cecil Marquand formally described *C. wardii* from Kingdon-Ward's specimens in 1929 and named it after its discoverer.

The sparsely branched stems of *Cassiope wardii* grow to 30 cm tall and are densely covered with four rows of overlapping, lanceolate leaves, with their characteristic hairs on the margins and tips. The white, pendulous flowers appear in spring and early summer. They are bell-shaped and up to 1 cm long, the corolla split into five short, triangular, recurved lobes. The sepals are tinged with red at their tips.

The closest relatives of *Cassiope wardii* are *C. pectinata*, from northern Myanmar (Burma) and western China, and the Himalayan *C. fastigiata*. The 1994 AGS China Expedition found *C. pectinata* to be common on exposed moorland throughout the Beima Shan and around Zhongdian, in north-west Yunnan. These plants generally had stems of up to just 10 cm tall (Grey-Wilson, 1996). *Cassiope pectinata* is similar to *C. wardii* but has deep green leaves with shorter, brown hairs on the margins and red pedicels. *Cassiope fastigiata* has comparatively slender shoots, clad with imbricate leaves whose finely ciliolate leaf margins are translucent (hyaline).

R. B. Cooke of Corbridge, Northumberland exhibited *Cassiope wardii* in May 1949 at the AGS Late Spring Show in London, where it received an Award of Merit, a Cultural Commendation and the Farrer Memorial Medal. Cooke obtained this plant in 1940 from J. Renton of Perth, Scotland, who raised it from seed collected by Dr (later Sir) George Taylor in Tibet (Xizang) in 1938. In 1982, *C. wardii* received a First Class Certificate when exhibited by H. Esslemont of Aberdeen. It is no coincidence that these award plants were grown in Scotland and the north of England, where the cooler, wetter conditions suit this species.

Cooke raised several *Cassiope* hybrids in his garden at Corbridge. They include *C.* 'Muirhead', which is a low-growing,

free-flowering plant that resulted from a cross between *C. wardii* and *C. lycopodioides*. From the 1980s onwards, Mike and Polly Stone in Askival, Scotland, have raised hybrids between *C. wardii* and three other species: *C. fastigiata*, *C. selaginoides* and *C. lycopodioides* (Stone, 1998).

Cassiope wardii is hardy but needs a cool, moist situation, with plenty of light and a humus-rich, acidic soil. On older plants, the leaves on the lower part of the stem will die and brown but an annual top-dressing of humus-rich soil with a little fertiliser, applied around the base of the plant, will encourage new shoots.

Curtis's Botanical Magazine, plate 168 (1951). Artist: Stella Ross-Craig.

Helleborus thibetanus
Family: Ranunculaceae

Helleborus thibetanus was known about long before its introduction into cultivation. It was described in 1885 by Adrien Franchet from specimens collected by Armand David, who found it in Moupin (Baoxing), Sichuan, growing on open, wet mountainsides at 2,400 m (7,874 feet) in March 1869. In 1885, the Russian naturalist Beresowski collected specimens in southeast Gansu. Beresowski's hellebore was described as *H. chinensis* by Carl Maximowicz in 1890 but is now considered to be synonymous with *H. thibetanus*.

Further specimens of *Helleborus thibetanus* were collected in the late nineteenth and early twentieth centuries but there are no records of seed ever being introduced. Then, in 1989, the Japanese botanist Mikinori Ogisu retraced David's steps and, with the help of local farmers, found a colony of *H. thibetanus* at Baoxing. Ogisu returned to the site in 1990 and 1991 and took the photographs that were shown at an RHS lecture by Roy Lancaster at Vincent Square, London (Lancaster, 1992). The plant painted for *Curtis's Botanical Magazine* in 1997 was raised from the first introduction of viable seed, which came from Prof. Kao Pao-chung of the Chengdu Institute of Botany in 1991.

The genus *Helleborus* contains around 20 species but *H. thibetanus* is separated geographically from all the others. The nearest species are *H. orientalis* and *H. vesicarius*, which are found in the Black Sea region and southern Turkey/northern Syria, respectively. *Helleborus thibetanus* occurs in the Chinese provinces of Sichuan, Gansu, Shaanxi and Hubei, growing among shrubs on damp hillsides and in shady forests at altitudes of 1,100–3,700 m (3,609–12,139 feet).

In overall appearance, *Helleborus thibetanus* is similar to the so-called 'stemless' species of section *Helleborastrum*, which include *H. orientalis*. However, it produces only two or sometimes three carpels on each flower, which is unusually few for the genus. Furthermore, pollen studies suggest a link to some of the 'stemmed' species, such as *H. foetidus*. Also, it is the only species to exhibit hypogeal germination. In all other hellebores, the cotyledons appear above ground after germination (epigeal germination), but in *H. thibetanus*, the cotyledons remain below ground and the first leaf to appear is toothed and consists of up to three leaflets (Mathew, 1992). For these reasons, *H. thibetanus* is placed in a section on its own: section *Dicarpon*.

As with all hellebores, it is the petal-like sepals that give the flowers their shape and colour and the petals are modified into nectaries. In this species, the flowers are 3–6.5 cm across and pale pink, fading to greenish-white, often with darker veins. Up to eight flowers per inflorescence have been recorded, appearing early in the year, sometimes even in December. The flowers are followed by one or two leaves, which are divided into 7–10 elliptic, toothed leaflets. In full leaf, the plant reaches 30–50 cm tall but it dies down by midsummer.

Helleborus thibetanus is not difficult to grow if provided with partial shade and plenty of moisture in its growing season. For pot-grown plants, use a leafy, loam-based soil that is never allowed to dry out completely, even when the plant is dormant.

Curtis's Botanical Magazine, plate 353 (1998). Artist: Joanna Langhorne.

region is still producing new plant species and introductions. Forms of the blue-flowered *Corydalis flexuosa* have become very popular garden plants, being easier to grow than *C. cashmeriana*. *Corydalis flexuosa* occurs in western Sichuan, at altitudes of 1,500–2,600 m (4,921–8,530 feet). It was originally collected by Armand David in 1869 but was only introduced into cultivation in the USA in 1986. This first introduction was named 'Blue Panda' and thousands of plants were produced by micropropagation to meet the demand for it in American gardens (Gardner, 1998). The craze soon spread across the Atlantic and several cultivars of the variable *C. flexuosa* are available in the UK as a result of new introductions from China. They include 'Purple Leaf', 'China Blue' and 'Père David'.

The end of the twentieth century also saw the first introduction of a Chinese species of one of the most-loved early-flowering perennials, the hellebore. *Helleborus thibetanus* is a distinctive and remote outlier in the genus, from the mountains of Sichuan, that was only introduced to cultivation in the early 1990s.

When *Helleborus thibetanus* first appeared in the UK, it caused a great deal of excitement in the horticultural world, in much the same way that plants such as *Gentiana sino-ornata* and *Meconopsis betonicifolia* did earlier in the century. In an article in *The Garden*, Roy Lancaster (1992) describes how there was an 'audible gasp' at an RHS lecture at Vincent Square, London, when he showed slides of it growing and flowering in the wild. Seeds were introduced from Sichuan in 1991 and since then many more collections have arrived. In a short period of time, this species has become well-established in cultivation. It received a Preliminary Commendation from the RHS on 21 January 1997 and an Award of Merit on 17 February 2001.

With continued exploration and improved access to the more remote regions of China and the countries along the Himalayan chain, there will inevitably be more new species discovered. Like Japan, the temperate climate and varied topography of this region ensures that many of the plants from these areas are likely to do well in cultivation in the gardens of Europe and North America.

ABOVE LEFT
Corydalis flexuosa 'China blue'.

ABOVE RIGHT
Helleborus thibetanus.

Bibliography and references

Baker, W. J., Henderson, S. & Birks, J. & H. (2004). On the Jhomolhari Trail. *Alpine Gardener* 72: 269–297.

Balfour, I. B. (1913). Chinese species of *Primula*. *J. Roy. Hort. Soc.* 39: 128–179.

Balfour, I. B. (1918). Some late flowering gentians. *Trans. & Proc. Bot. Soc. Edinb.* 27: 246–272.

Coats, A. M. (1969). *The Quest for Plants*: 63–85. Studio Vista, London.

Cowley, J. (2007). *The Genus Roscoea*. Royal Botanic Gardens, Kew.

De Candolle, R. & Radcliffe-Smith, A. (1981). Nathaniel Wallich, MD, PhD, FRS, FLS, FRGS, (1786–1854) and the Herbarium of the Honourable East India Company and their relation to the de Candolles of Geneva and the Great Prodromus. *Bot. J. Linn. Soc.* 83: 325–348.

Desmond, R. (1992). *The European Discovery of the Indian Flora*. Oxford University Press.

Desmond, R. (1999). *Sir Joseph Dalton Hooker, Traveller and Plant Collector*. Antique Collectors' Club, Woodbridge, Suffolk.

Don, G. (1837). *A General System of Gardening and Botany*, 4: 665. London.

Forrest, G. (1908). Primulaceae from western Yunnan and eastern Tibet. *Notes Roy. Bot. Gard. Edinb.* 4: 213–238.

Forrest, G. (1910). *Androsace spinulifera. Gard. Chron.* 47: 27.

Forrest, G. (1911). *Primula beesiana. Gard. Chron.* 50: 242–243.

Franchet, A. R. (1885). Plantae Davidianae ex Sinarum Imperio. *Nouv. Arch. Mus. Paris*, ser. 2, 8: 188.

Franchet, A. R. (1896). Compositae novae e flora Sinensi. *J. Bot. (Morot)* 10: 368–376.

Gardner, D. (1998). *Corydalis flexuosa. Curtis's Bot. Mag.* 15: t. 332.

Grey-Wilson, C. (1995). *Stellera chamaejasme*: an overview. *New Plantsman* 2: 43–49.

Grey-Wilson, C. (1996). *Cassiope. Quart. Bull. Alpine Gard. Soc. Gr. Brit.* 64: 189–190.

Grey-Wilson, C. (2009). Bailey's blue poppy restored. *The Alpine Gardener* 77: 217–225.

Harrow, W. (1890). *Androsace lanuginosa* and var. *leichtlinii. Gard. Chron.*, ser. 3, 8: 250.

Hemsley, W. B. (1905). *Meconopsis integrifolia. Curtis's Bot. Mag.* 131: t. 8027.

Hooker, J. D. (1883). *Aster diplostephioides. Curtis's Bot. Mag.* 109: t. 6718.

Hooker, W. J. (1825). *Exotic Flora*, 2: t. 88.

Hooker, W. J. (1836). *Potentilla atro-sanguinea*; hybrida, *Russelliana. Curtis's Bot. Mag.* 63: t. 3470.

Hooker, W. J. (1843). *Androsace lanuginosa. Curtis's Bot. Mag.* 69: t. 4005.

Hooker, W. J. (1852). *Meconopsis wallichii. Curtis's Bot. Mag.* 78: t. 4668.

Ingwersen, W. (1921). *Geranium pylzowianum. Gard. Chron.* 70: 275.

Jermyn, J. (2001). *The Himalayan Garden*. Timber Press, Portland.

Kingdon-Ward, F. (1926). Notes on the genus *Meconopsis* with some additional species from Tibet. *Ann. Bot.* 40: 540–541.

Kingdon-Ward, F. (1940). *Adonis davidii*: or *A. brevistyla? Gard. Chron.*, ser. 3, 107: 228–229.

Lancaster, R. (1992). *Helleborus thibetanus. The Garden* 117: 156–159.

Lindley, J. (1821). *Collectanea Botanica*: sub t. 37. London.

Lindley, J. (1841). *Salvia hians. Bot. Reg.* 27: t. 39.

Mathew, B. (1992). Germinating *Helleborus thibetanus. The Garden* 117: 518.

McLean, B. (1997). *A Pioneering Plantsman, A. K. Bulley and the Great Plant Hunters*. The Stationery Office, London.

Middleton, N. (2001). *Going to Extremes*. Channel 4 Books, London.

Musgrave, T., Gardner, C. & Musgrave, W. (1998). *The Plant Hunters*. Ward Lock, London.

Nicolls, G. (2006). *Dwarf Campanulas*. Timber Press, Portland, Oregon.

Polunin, O. & Stainton, A. (1984). *Flowers of the Himalaya*. Oxford University Press, Oxford.

Prain, D. (1915). Some additional species of *Meconopsis. Kew Bull.* (1915) 4: 161–162.

Qureshi, R. A. & Chaudhri, M. N. (1988). The Ranunculaceae of Pakistan. *Pakistan Syst.* 4: 76–77.

Richards, J. (2002). *Primula* (second edition). B. T. Batsford Ltd., London.

Rolfe, R. A. (1903). The genus *Pleione. Orchid Rev.* 11: 289–292.

Royle, J. F. (1836). *Illustrations of the Botany…of the Himalayan Mountains*. Wm. H. Allen & Co., London.

Sealy, J. R. (1968). *Corydalis cashmeriana. Curtis's Bot. Mag.* 176: t. 522.

Shephard, S. (2003). *Seeds of Fortune, a Gardening Dynasty*. Bloomsbury, London.

Smith, J. E. (1805–1808). *Exotic Botany*, 2 vols. R. Taylor & Co., London.

Smith, G. & Lowe, D. (1997). *The Genus Androsace*. AGS Publications Ltd., Pershore.

Stapf, O. (1929). *Potentilla nepalensis. Curtis's Bot. Mag.* 153: t. 9182.

Stone, M. (1998). The Askival hybrid Cassiopes. *Quart. Bull. Alpine Gard. Soc. Gr. Brit.* 66: 484–492.

Taylor, G. (1934). *An account of the genus Meconopsis*: 63–65. New Flora and Silva Ltd., London.

Yeo, P. F. (1985). *Hardy Geraniums*: 101–102. B. T. Batsford Ltd., London.

Zhu, G. & Chen S. C. (1998). *Humiles*, a new section of *Pleione* (Orchidaceae). *Novon* 8: 461–463.

Tulipa linifolia

Galanthus woronowii

Dionysia aretioides

Gentiana olivieri

Fritillaria chitralensis

St Petersburg

Moscow

RUSSIA

Siberia

Ural Mts

KAZAKHSTAN

Lake Balkhash

Aral
Sea

Dzung
Ala

Mt
Elbrus

Black Sea

Caspian Sea

Almat

Istanbul

Trabzon

Greater Caucasus

Karatau
Range

Tien Shan

Tbilisi

TURKEY

Pontic Mts

Lesser Caucasus

Baku

Kyzylkum
Desert

Tashkent

Anatolian
Plateau

Mt
Ararat

Karakum
Desert

Samarkand

Pamir
Alai

Kongkoe

Tibet
Plate

Taurus Mts

Talysh
Hills

SYRIA

Elburz Mts

Ashkhabad

Kopet Dag

Hindu Kush

Mediterranean
Sea

Tehran

IRAQ

IRAN

AFGHANISTAN

Kabul

Negev
Desert

Zagros Mts

PAKISTAN

Persian Gulf

Arabian
Peninsula

INDIA

Arabian Sea

N

Chapter 9 **Western and Central Asia**

This is a region defined, more than anything else, by its climate. By far the greatest proportion of Western and Central Asia experiences an arid to semi-arid, continental climate, characterised by very cold winters, hot, dry summers and often temperatures that fluctuate widely between night and day. To the north of the region, the extensive forests of Siberia take over, and to the south, are the deserts of southern Pakistan, Iran, Iraq, and the Arabian Peninsula. The few exceptions to this continental climate are found along the coastal areas of the Mediterranean Sea, Black Sea and Caspian Sea. The coasts of Turkey, Syria and Lebanon, at the eastern end of the Mediterranean, fall under the Mediterranean climate zone. They still experience hot, dry summers but the winters are generally mild, at least near sea level. Along the southern and eastern coasts of the Black Sea, the climate is much wetter, with rainfall possible all year round and precipitation levels approaching 4,500 mm (177 inches) a year in some locations. The southern coast of the Caspian Sea in northern Iran also has a climate that is wetter than that in much of the rest of this region.

With its long, dry summers, it is not surprising that a significant proportion of the plants introduced from Western and Central Asia are geophytes. These are plants that grow from a bulb, corm, tuber or rhizome, which allows them to become dormant during long periods of little or no rainfall. This dormant phase also makes them easy to transport so, not surprisingly, many of the most well-established introductions from this region have been bulbous plants, including species of *Tulipa*, *Iris*, *Fritillaria*,

Allium, *Crocus*, *Cyclamen* and *Corydalis*. They are found from the Mediterranean coast of Turkey to the deserts and mountains of Kazakhstan, Kyrgyzstan and Tajikistan in Central Asia. In fact, this part of Asia is often referred to as the 'bulb lands'.

This region encompasses many different and varied mountain ranges. In Turkey, the Taurus Mountains in the south and the Pontic Mountains in the north both have peaks of over 3,500 m (11,483 feet) altitude. Between these two ranges is the high Anatolian Plateau. The Pontic

Mountains run along the Black Sea coast of Turkey and extend into south-west Georgia, joining the Lesser Caucasus, which stretch through southern Georgia, Armenia and western Azerbaijan and reach 4,090 m (13,419 feet) on Mt Aragats in Armenia. Along the border of Georgia and Russia are the Greater Caucasus, which extend for around 1,500 km (932 miles) from the Black Sea in the west to the Caspian Sea in the east. The highest mountain is Mt Elbrus at 5,642 m (18,510 feet).

The Greater Caucasus are separated from the Lesser Caucasus by the river valleys of the Rioni in the west, which flows into the Black Sea, and the Kura in the east, which flows into the Caspian Sea. The Greater Caucasus are a watershed divide: the region to the north of the main ridge is known as Ciscaucasia and that south of the ridge is Transcaucasia. The climate in the Caucasus region is wetter in the west, near the Black Sea coast, where the lower slopes of the mountains are heavily forested and can receive 2,000 mm (78.7 inches) or more of precipitation a year. Further east, the climate is much drier, with annual precipitation as low as 206 mm (8.1 inches) at Baku on the Caspian Sea, and the flora has more in common with the treeless steppe of Central Asia.

The Great Steppe of Asia has a continental, semi-arid climate with temperatures ranging from 40 °C in summer to −40 °C in winter. South of the Aral Sea are the Karakum and Kyzylkum deserts in Turkmenistan and Uzbekistan, but it is the mountains that provide some relief from the heat and aridity of summer and are home to a diverse flora that is of interest to alpine gardeners.

In Iran, the Zagros Mountains dominate the western side of the country, from the border with Turkey south to the shores of The Persian Gulf. The northern third of the Zagros experiences heavier precipitation levels, around 900–1,000 mm (35.4–39.4 inches) a year, and includes volcanic peaks such as Sabalan, the highest at 4,811 m (15,784 feet). The southern two-thirds of the Zagros are drier and consist of fold mountains with several peaks over 4,000 m (13,123 feet).

Forming an arc around the southern end of the Caspian Sea are the Elburz (or Alborz) Mountains, which include Iran's highest mountain, the volcanic peak of Mt Damavand at 5,610 m (18,406 feet). West of the main Elburz range but still skirting the southern shores of the Caspian Sea are the Talysh Hills, which receive heavy rainfall that can, especially on the higher slopes, fall all year round, giving rise to thick vegetation. The highest precipitation in Iran is recorded along this south-west coast of the Caspian Sea, where nearly 2,000 mm (78.7 inches) a year can fall (Parsa, 1978). While the north-facing slopes receive high rainfall, on the southern slopes, facing away from the Caspian Sea, the rain shadow has a significant effect and precipitation levels are much lower.

North-east of Iran are the low deserts of Central Asia, but in eastern Uzbekistan and southern Kazakhstan, the land begins to rise again, leading to the complex of mountain ranges that make up the Pamir Alai and Tien Shan, mainly located in the countries of Tajikistan and Kyrgyzstan, respectively. These high mountains form the western rim of the Tibetan Plateau. The Pamir Alai in particular are a western extension of the Himalayan range, as are the mountains of the Hindu Kush in north-east Afghanistan. Several peaks in the Pamir Alai ranges reach over 6,000 m (19,685 feet) with Kongkoerh the highest at 7,649 m (25,095 feet).

ABOVE
The green northern slopes of the Elburz Mountains, northern Iran.
Photo: Christopher Ryan.

BELOW
The dry southern slopes of the Elburz Mountains.
Photo: Christopher Ryan.

There are mountain ranges all along the eastern border of Kazakhstan. In the far north-east, where the borders of Kazakhstan, Russia, Mongolia and China meet, are the Altai Mountains of southern Siberia. Mt Belukha at 4,506 m (14,783 feet) is the highest peak in this range. Many Central Asian ranges are little known outside the country in which they occur, but further exploration will undoubtedly reveal a host of plants from these mountains yet to be introduced to cultivation.

Botanical exploration of Western and Central Asia began in the sixteenth century when travellers interested in plants mentioned in the Greek and Latin classics were drawn to The Levant, the land of the sunrising, which at that time meant the Kingdom of Turkey (Coats, 1969). One of the first to collect botanical specimens was Leonhardt Rauwolf, a German physician who travelled through present-day Lebanon, Syria, Iraq and Israel between May 1573 and January 1575. He is remembered in the name of the small aroid *Eminium rauwolffii*.

The Frenchman Joseph Pitton de Tournefort travelled to the Greek islands, Constantinople (Istanbul) and on to eastern Turkey, Georgia and Armenia between 1700 and 1702. He was the first European to see and describe *Rhododendron ponticum* and *R. luteum*, and he is credited with introducing the oriental poppy, *Papaver orientale*, to cultivation. Another Frenchman, André Michaux visited Syria, Iraq and Iran from 1782 to 1785. He collected seeds and bulbs and is commemorated in the names of several plants, including the genus *Michauxia* and the cushion plant *Dionysia michauxii*, which was named after him by Edmond Boissier in 1846.

It was the publication of Edmond Boissier's *Diagnoses Plantarum Orientalium Novarum* between 1842 and 1859, followed by *Flora Orientalis*, between 1867 and 1884, that made the most significant contributions to the cataloguing of the varied flora in this region. Boissier travelled widely in Europe, the Mediterranean, Arabia, Syria and Turkey. In preparing *Flora Orientalis*, he used his own collections, both herbarium specimens and living plants growing in his private garden, as well as those of many other botanists who travelled in Western Asia in the early to mid nineteenth century. Among the botanists whose collections he studied are Theodoros Orphanides, Theodor von Heldreich, Theodor Kotschy, Alexander von Bunge and his close friend and frequent travelling companion, Georges-François Reuter. These botanists and travellers are often commemorated in the names of plants described by Boissier.

Boissier intended *Flora Orientalis* to be a practical guide for botanists and tourists travelling in the area who wanted to identify and classify the plants they found. The area covered stretches from the eastern Mediterranean, through Turkey, Transcaucasia, Armenia, Iran and into Afghanistan

and the borders of India. He was convinced that this area represented one floral region, a view supported at the time by William Hooker at Kew. Over the years, Boissier described 3,602 new species himself and a further 2,388 in collaboration with other botanists (Lièvre, 1994). The carefully catalogued specimens in his herbarium, L'Herbier Boissier, were available for subsequent botanists to study and so contributed to later floras of particular countries, such as *Flora USSR* in the 1930s, which includes significant parts of Western and Central Asia.

One of Boissier's collaborators, Alexander von Bunge, Professor at Dorpat, (now Tartu in Estonia), was entrusted

ABOVE
Mountains rising from the Central Asian steppe in Kyrgyzstan.
Photo: Kit Strange.

BELOW
Dionysia michauxii, found by André Michaux in the late eighteenth century.

by the German horticulturist and Director of the Imperial Botanic Garden in St Petersburg, Eduard von Regel, with sorting out the plants collected in Central Asia by his son, Albert von Regel. A physician based in Kuldja, Turkestan (now Yining in western China), Albert Regel sent his plant collections to his father in St Petersburg in the 1870s and 1880s. Among Regel's introductions were many bulbs including several tulips, such as *Tulipa kaufmanniana*, *T. linifolia* and *T. praestans*.

In the nineteenth century, Russian military expeditions explored the Caucasus and Central Asia and they also sent specimens and plants to St Petersburg where Eduard Regel, who was Director from 1855, was eagerly waiting for them. He described a huge range of species and distributed plants to botanic gardens in Europe. Many new plants, especially geophytes, from Central Asia were introduced into cultivation during the second half of the nineteenth century as a result of Regel's generosity. The flora of Western and Central Asia was very popular during this period with both amateur and professional botanists and many of the plants had become fashionable in gardens (Meikle, 1994). This interest continued to grow until the beginning of the twentieth century, when the new introductions from China diverted attention further east.

After the Second World War, there was a revival in the introduction of plants from the countries in Western and Central Asia. Collectors such as Paul and Polly Furse, Jim and Jenny Archibald, Per Wendelbo of Gothenburg Botanic Garden and Brian Mathew and Chris Grey-Wilson from Kew, explored this region, in particular Turkey, the Middle East, Iran and Afghanistan, and brought back many alpines and bulbs. This coincided with the preparation and publication of new floras such as the *Flora of Turkey and the East Aegean Islands*, *Flora Palestina* and *Flora Iranica*. Today, there is still a great deal of interest among alpine gardeners in the plants from this region. Holidays to study and enjoy the wild flowers of Western and Central Asia are as popular as ever. Two countries in particular have made significant contributions to the alpines and bulbs now established in cultivation: Turkey and Iran.

Turkey and the Caucasus

The flora of Turkey is so extensive that new species are still being discovered despite centuries of botanical exploration. This is a large, mountainous country, with the assorted habitats, varied topography and the effect of three major climate zones, all contributing to the diversity of plants that are found there. The estimated number of plant species in Turkey is over 8,600, with about one-third being endemic (Ekim & Güner, 2000).

ABOVE
Tulipa linifolia, introduced to cultivation by Albert Regel.

Turkey-in-Europe, or Thrace, covers only around 3% of the country's area. The rest of Turkey, Anatolia, is within Asia. Most of Anatolia is a plateau that rises towards the east and is bounded to the north and south by steep mountain ranges. Much of this plateau is at elevations of 800–1,000 m (2,625–3,281 feet), punctuated by higher peaks, but in the east, the level of the plateau reaches 1,700 m (5,577 feet). The highest point in Turkey is Mt Ararat at the far eastern end of the country, which reaches 5,137 m (16,854 feet). In the west, the plateau falls gradually to the Mediterranean coast. The northern Anatolian mountains fall steeply into the Black Sea and reach their highest in the Pontic Mountains south-east of Rize, with Kaçkar Dağ

BELOW
At its western end, the Anatolian Plateau falls gradually to the Mediterranean coast.

reaching 3,942 m (12,933 feet). The Taurus Mountains in the south of Anatolia, which reach 3,756 m (12,320 feet) on Mt Demirkazik, also fall steeply to the coast but experience a very different climate.

The flora of an area is closely linked to the climate it experiences and these characteristics are used to define phytogeographical regions. Three phytogeographical regions occur in Turkey: the Euro-Siberian, Mediterranean and Irano-Turanian. The first has the wettest climate and covers the northern coast of Turkey. Here, the average annual precipitation is over 1,000 mm (39.4 inches) and increases from west to east. The rainiest seasons are autumn and winter but rain can fall at any time of the year, although along the western part of the Black Sea coast there are enclaves of Mediterranean vegetation where summer drought does occur. The plants in Turkey's Euro-Siberian phytogeographical region are adapted to higher levels of precipitation that is more evenly spread throughout the year than in other parts of the country. The flora is therefore quite distinct from those of the other regions of Turkey.

The area of Anatolia covered by the Euro-Siberian zone is usually referred to as part of the Euxine province, which takes its name from Pontus Euxinus, the ancient name for the Black Sea. This region extends from southern Bulgaria and Thrace in the west, to western Georgia and Transcaucasia in the east. Humidity is high and the mountains are forested, with deciduous trees and evergreen shrubs on the lower slopes and conifers at higher altitudes. Above the treeline, the alpine flora of northern Turkey has close connections with that of the Caucasus.

The herbaceous and alpine flora of the Euxine province includes plants that are adapted to the damp, humid climate and often do well in cultivation in a woodland setting. In a humus-rich soil, under the shade of deciduous trees, plants like *Epimedium pubigerum* will thrive. This species was described in 1834 from material collected near Istanbul. It was introduced into cultivation in Britain in 1881 by Ellen Ann Willmott, who obtained a plant from Boissier's garden in Geneva (Stearn, 2002). It has tiny flowers with yellow petals and reddish to rose pink or whitish sepals, held on stems that can reach 75 cm tall. It occurs in wooded valleys from south-east Bulgaria, along the Black Sea coast of Turkey, into the Adjara region of western Georgia. The floriferous, yellow-flowered *E. pinnatum* is another Euxine species of which Stearn (2002) recognises three subspecies. All have leafless flower stems and flowers that are composed of four showy, yellow, rounded inner sepals and tiny brownish petals with short spurs. The form grown most commonly in gardens is subspecies *colchicum*, from western Transcaucasia near the Black Sea, in north-east Turkey and western Georgia. It was

ABOVE
The wooded hills and mountains of the Lesser Caucasus near the Black Sea port of Batumi.

LEFT
Epimedium pubigerum.

Campanula betulifolia
Family: Campanulaceae

Campanula betulifolia is a beautiful, large-flowered species from north-east Anatolia in the Euro-Siberian phytogeographical region of Turkey. It grows around 10–25 cm tall and carries pink buds that open to white or rarely pale pink flowers. These usually pendulous, campanulate flowers are held in clusters on spreading, branched stems in a corymb-like inflorescence beyond the tufts of leaves. The flowers are 3–4 cm long and have pointed corolla lobes that are around one fifth to one quarter of the length of the corolla. The specific epithet refers to the ovate to broadly ovate leaves, with sharply dentate margins, that are similar in appearance to those of *Betula* (the birches).

Karl Heinrich Emil Koch described *Campanula betulifolia* in 1850. Koch (1809–1879) was born near Weimar in Germany. He had a broad range of interests, including zoology, geography, anthropology, history and archaeology, but his main interest was botany. From an early age, he had a dream to see the Caucasus, and in 1836 he began the first of two expeditions to that region (Edmondson & Lack, 1977). It was possibly on his second expedition (1843–1844), which he began by travelling via Istanbul to Trabzon on the Black Sea coast of Turkey, that he collected *C. betulifolia*.

While preparing material for the account of Campanulaceae in the *Flora of Turkey*, Jürgen Damboldt revised the infrageneric classification of *Campanula* in Turkey. He recognised six subgenera in Turkey, of which subgenus *Campanula* and subgenus *Rapunculus* are the largest (Damboldt, 1976). *Campanula betulifolia* is placed in subgenus *Campanula*, section *Symphyandriformis*. In the younger flowers of plants in this section, the anthers are partly connate (fused) into a tube around the style. This characteristic makes the species in this section very close to the genus *Symphyandra*, in which the anthers are connate and form a tube, even in mature flowers. In fact, Damboldt (1978) states in the *Flora of Turkey* that *Symphyandra* should probably be considered a subgenus of *Campanula* but is retained "as a result of conservative tradition". There are three other Turkish species in section *Symphyandriformis*: *C. trogerae*, *C. choruhensis* and *C. seraglio*.

Campanula betulifolia was probably introduced into cultivation early in the twentieth century, and in 1937 a pink-flowered form received an Award of Merit at the Chelsea Flower Show. The white-flowered plant illustrated here was raised at Kew, from seed collected by Jim and Jenny Archibald in the province of Trabzon. *Campanula betulifolia* is a hardy species that can be grown in the open, if planted in a crevice or in very free-draining soil. However, the delicate nature of the flower stems means that this plant will look best if given the protection of an alpine house or cold frame. Although *C. betulifolia* can be kept for a number of years if fed regularly and given a large enough container, seed is best sown annually to provide a steady supply of young, vigorous plants. During the winter, most of the leaves die away and watering should then be reduced. New foliage appears the following spring and the plants will be in full flower by early summer.

Curtis's Botanical Magazine, plate 389 (2000). Artist: Joanna Langhorne.

FAR LEFT
Epimedium pinnatum
subsp. *colchicum*.

LEFT
A dark-purple-flowered
form of *Primula vulgaris*
subsp. *sibthorpii*.

BELOW
Helleborus orientalis in
south-west Georgia.

introduced to cultivation in Europe in 1842 as *E. colchicum* and is often used today as reliable, dense groundcover with the added bonus of racemes of bright, sunny flowers in March and April. *Epimedium pinnatum* subsp. *pinnatum* is geographically separated from subspecies *colchicum*, occurring at the southern end of the Caspian Sea, in northern Iran and in the Talysh region on the border with Azerbaijan. It was introduced from the Talysh region around 1830 but is much less well known in gardens than subspecies *colchicum*, from which it differs mainly in its shorter petal spurs, narrower, more obovate inner sepals and leaves with 5–11 rather than 3–5 leaflets. Subspecies *circinatum* is a little known form from the western end of the northern Caucasus.

Helleborus orientalis also forms colonies among the trees on the lower slopes of the mountains in the Euxine region. This species, with its wide flowers, has been used in the breeding of the various forms of garden hellebore that come under the name *Helleborus hydridus*. Wild forms mostly have flowers in shades of green, cream or occasionally pale pink to reddish purple with faint spots inside. In the western Caucasus, they grow and flower alongside *Galanthus woronowii*, *Cyclamen coum* and pink to purple flowered forms of *Primula vulgaris* subsp. *sibthorpii*. This subspecies of the common primrose is named after the English doctor John Sibthorp who travelled around the eastern Mediterranean collecting plant specimens and seeds between 1786 and 1795.

Galanthus woronowii is one of several snowdrops native to the Euxine province. It is widespread and often locally common in a variety of habitats, including deciduous and coniferous woodlands, on screes and cliff ledges, around the eastern end of the Black Sea. It was introduced in the 1880s under the name *G. latifolius* (Davis, 1999) and has shiny, bright green leaves that can carpet a woodland floor in late winter. *Galanthus rizehensis*, named after the

Turkish town of Rize on the Black Sea coast, has a narrower range than *G. woronowii* and is restricted to woodlands in high rainfall areas of north-east Turkey, western Georgia and southern Russia. It was described in 1956 by Sir Frederick Stern, who grew it in his garden at Highdown in Sussex. In the western and central regions of the Black Sea coast, *G. plicatus* can be found. This widely grown species has been in cultivation since the sixteenth century. It is easily identified by the rolled back leaf margins, a feature not found in any other species. At higher altitudes are *G. alpinus* and *G. krasnovii*. The former is a small species with glaucous foliage. It is a rare plant, typically found in small, isolated populations, although it has a wide range in the mountains of the Caucasus and northern Turkey, up to 2,200 m (7,218 feet) altitude. *Galanthus krasnovii* has an even more limited distribution, being restricted to a few localities in western Georgia. It is a distinctive species, with flared, pointed inner perianth segments and wide, shiny green leaves.

Cyclamen coum is a widespread species found from Bulgaria, across northern Turkey to the Caucasus and from south-east Turkey to northern Israel. Often growing in beech, oak or pine woods or on rocky ledges and in gullies, it is found from near sea level to altitudes of 2,150 m (7,054 feet). This is one of the most popular hardy cyclamen in cultivation, with only the autumn-flowering *C. hederifolium* being more widely grown in the open garden. It was described as long ago as 1768, by Philip Miller in the 8th edition of his *Gardeners Dictionary*. It is now classified in a series (series *Pubipedia*) with three other winter- and early-spring-flowering species: *C. parviflorum*, *C. elegans* and *C. alpinum* (sometimes called *C. trochopteranthum*). *Cyclamen coum* has a much wider distribution than the other three, with *C. parviflorum* being confined to the Pontic Mountains, *C. elegans* found only in northern Iran and *C. alpinum* limited to south-west Turkey. All four species are generally small, low-growing plants with rounded, rarely lobed leaves and velvety tubers that root from the middle of the base.

In contrast to *Cyclamen coum*, which has a broad natural range, the rarely cultivated, carmine-pink-flowered *C. colchicum* has a much more localised distribution, being endemic to a small area of western Transcaucasia in Georgia. This is a summer- to early-autumn-flowering species similar to the European *C. purpurascens* and has been treated as a subspecies of this plant, *C. purpurascens*

FAR LEFT
Galanthus krasnovii growing under deciduous trees in south-west Georgia.

LEFT
The flowers of *Galanthus woronowii*.

Variation in *Cyclamen coum*

Considering its wide distribution, it is not surprising that *Cyclamen coum* varies considerably across its natural range; and in his monograph of the genus, Grey-Wilson (2002) divides it into two subspecies. The characteristics of these subspecies represent extremes of form found across the species range, but there are many intermediate forms that blur the boundaries in the wild.

Cyclamen coum subsp. *coum* has kidney-shaped to rounded leaves and pink flowers with a dark basal blotch around a white 'eye'. The flowers are small, with petals only 8–14 mm long, and the leaves can be plain green, green with pale silvery patterning or completely silver. Flower colour varies from pure white, through various shades of pink to magenta. *Cyclamen coum* subsp. *caucasicum*, from north-east Turkey and the Caucasus, has heart-shaped leaves with a toothed margin. The petals are 12–20 mm long and the 'eyes' at their base are usually pink. Botanists have described many different species that cover the range of forms found in the Caucasus, but these are rarely upheld.

RIGHT
Cyclamen coum subsp. *coum* growing on a mossy cliff near Batumi, Georgia.

FAR RIGHT
Cyclamen coum subsp. *caucasicum* carpeting a woodland floor near Tbilisi, Georgia.

subsp. *ponticum*. However, its dark green, thick, leathery, more heart-shaped leaves, with fine but prominently toothed margins that give them a beaded feel, as well as the geographical separation, have contributed to its present recognition as a distinct species (Grey-Wilson & Wilford, 1998). In cultivation, this cyclamen is virtually evergreen when pot-grown in an alpine house and can produce the odd flower at any time, but the main flowering season is from late June to September. It requires some moisture all year round and the best time to re-pot is in spring, a couple of months before other species of *Cyclamen*, which are re-potted when dormant in early summer.

The Euxine province extends eastwards through the southern Caucasus, but gradually the levels of precipitation fall and much of south-east Georgia, Armenia and Azerbaijan has a dry, more continental climate. Rainfall increases again in the Talysh mountains of northern Iran, which have a damp and humid climate that extends round the southern end of the Caspian Sea. In fact, much of the Caucasus region has a dryer climate than the Euxine province, especially in

the east, although the southern slopes of the Greater Caucasus still receive around 1000–1500 mm (39.4–59.1 inches) of rainfall a year. It is the wide, flat valleys between the main ranges that experience hot, dry summers and are home to the Georgian wine-growing regions.

BELOW
Cyclamen colchicum in cultivation at Kew.

Above the treeline in the Caucasus Mountains, the alpine vegetation may not come into flower until late July or August and these plants have only a short growing season in which to produce seed before the snows return. The summer meadows are filled with sumptuous displays of flowering perennials, such as *Aquilegia olympica*, *Stachys macrantha*, *Scabiosa caucasica*, *Cephalaria gigantea* and *Geranium ibericum*. On more exposed rocky outcrops are low-growing alpines such as the silver saxifrage *Saxifraga paniculata* subsp. *cartiliginea* and cushions of *Minuartia caucasica*. The rarely grown, lemon-yellow-flowered *Gentiana verna* subsp. *oschtenica* is endemic to the western Caucasus, where it grows in rocky pockets, limestone screes and meadows of up to 2,800 m (9,186 feet) altitude. The most recent treatment of the flora of the Caucasus is the excellent *The Caucasus and its Flowers*, by Vojtûch Holubec and Pavel Kfiivka, published in 2006. Holubec has a passionate interest in the horticultural potential of the Caucasian flora and has introduced many species from this region.

Predating Holubec and Pavel's book by almost 200 years is *Flora Taurico-Caucasica* by Friedrich August Freiherr Marschall von Bieberstein, the first major flora of the

ABOVE RIGHT
The southern slopes of the Greater Caucasus from the Alizani valley in eastern Georgia.

RIGHT
Geranium ibericum in an alpine meadow in the Lesser Caucasus.

Caucasus. Volumes one and two appeared in 1808 and the third in 1819. This flora contains descriptions of over 2,300 plants, with 302 that were new to science at the time. *Anthemis marshalliana* and *Tulipa biebersteiniana* are named after Bieberstein, as is the genus *Biebersteiniana* in Geraniaceae.

According to Holubec and Kfiivka (2006), the flora of the Caucasus consists of 6,350 species of vascular plants of which 1,600 are endemic. Endemism is particularly high in the alpine flora and some genera in these mountains, including *Campanula*, *Saxifraga* and *Draba*, are very diverse.

TOP LEFT
Cephalaria gigantea.

BOTTOM LEFT
Minuartia caucasica.

BOTTOM MIDDLE
Stachys macrantha.

BOTTOM RIGHT
Gentiana verna subsp. *oschtenica*, endemic to the western Caucasus.

BELOW
Draba longisiliqua, endemic to the northern Caucasus.

The Mediterranean climate region of Turkey is very different to the Euxine province and extends along the western and southern coasts of Anatolia, continuing east into the coastal regions of Syria and Lebanon. The western Anatolian flora has strong links with that of the East Aegean islands. Plants would have migrated over land bridges between Turkey and these islands when the level of the Mediterranean Sea was lower. For example, several species once thought to be endemic to Crete have been found in south-west Turkey, including *Arum creticum* and *Tulipa saxatilis*. The southern part of Thrace is also in the Mediterranean region, as are the small enclaves along the western Black Sea coast. The Mediterranean climate is one of long, dry summers and mild, wet winters, and is markedly warmer than that of the Euxine province. The vegetation is characterised by tough, drought-tolerant, woody plants such as *Arbutus andrachne*, various *Cistus* species, spiny shrubs such as *Calycotome villosa*, junipers, pines and oaks. As in all countries bordering the Mediterranean, there are large numbers of geophytes in this region. Above the tree line, which is at around 1,700 m (5,577 feet) in the Taurus Mountains, are spiny shrubs and cushions, which are probably of Irano-Turanian origin (Ekim & Güner, 2000).

The spiny cushions found in the mountains of Turkey include several species of *Acantholimon*, a genus closely related to thrifts (*Armeria* spp.). They are found in the wild from south-east Europe, through Turkey, the Middle East and Central Asia, to the western Himalaya, with the main centres of distribution in Iran and Central Asia (Hedge & Wendelbo, 1970). The genus was described by Boissier in 1846, and at that time he recognised 22 species. When volume four of *Flora Orientalis* was published in 1879, the number had risen to 74. Today, there are thought to be around 130 species. Several have been introduced to cultivation, chiefly from Turkey, such as *A. hohenackeri* and *A. ulicinum*, but the two species that are most firmly established in cultivation are *A. venustum* and *A. glumaceum*. These four species were all described by Boissier.

The lax to dense cushions of *Acantholimon* are made up of narrow, usually spine-tipped leaves. In some species, the spring leaves are shorter, broader and flatter than the summer leaves. The inflorescence takes the form of a simple or branched spike and five-petalled flowers, which are surrounded by three or more bracts and are held in sessile spikelets. These spikelets can variously be spread evenly in two rows along the axis of the spike, concentrated towards the tip of the spike, held in a head (capitate) or rarely forming a panicle.

BELOW LEFT
Arum creticum is native to south-west Turkey as well as Crete.

BELOW
Acantholimon ulicinum in cultivation.

Acantholimon venustum was described from material collected by Theodor Kotschy in the Taurus Mountains. This species also occurs in northern Iraq, western Iran and western Syria. It holds its pink flowers on arching stems, above a mound of pointed, grey-green leaves. *Acantholimon glumaceum*, from Turkey and the Caucasus, has branched spikes with bright pink flowers clustered towards the apex.

The genus *Verbascum* is also well represented in Turkey. There are around 360 species of *Verbascum* distributed across Europe, North Africa and Asia, with at least 228 species occurring in Turkey alone. Of these, 176 are endemic to Turkey (Huber-Morath, 1978), including the popular garden biennials *V. olympicum* and *V. bombyciferum*, both described by Boissier, and the smaller, woody-based perennial *V. dumulosum*, a fascinating plant, described in 1952 by Arthur Huber-Morath and Peter Davis, editor of *Flora of Turkey and the East Aegean Islands*. A hybrid resulting from a cross between *V. dumulosum* and the Cretan endemic, *V. spinosum*, arose by chance at the RHS Garden, Wisley in 1960. It was named *Verbascum* 'Letitia' after the wife of

Ken Aslet, Foreman and later Superintendent of the Rock Garden Department. Its intricate, woody growth and lobed leaves resemble *V. spinosum* but it is more like *V. dumulosum* in its blue-grey, velvety foliage and racemes of flowers. This is a remarkably hardy and long-lived plant that has become more widely grown than either parent species.

The Mediterranean region of Turkey is home to a vast range of bulbous plants and attractive herbaceous perennials. Six species of *Paeonia* are native to the country, including the scarlet-flowered *P. peregrina*, found in the north-west and sold as a cut flower in the markets of Istanbul, and the widespread, pink-flowered *P. mascula*. In the south-west of turkey is the little-known *P. turcica*, described in 1965 from material collected by Peter Davis in 1941. This peony is endemic to the ancient regions of Caria and Lycia and grows in pine forest, on forest margins and in more open situations, at altitudes of around 1,500–1,800 m (4,921–5,906 feet) (Özhatay, Page & Sinnott, 2000). The flowers are magenta-rose, and in cultivation on the rock garden at Kew, it is always the first peony to flower, opening its blooms at the end of March above rapidly unfolding green leaves with a glaucous bloom.

Verbascum dumulosum
Family: Scrophulariaceae

When in full bloom in early summer, *Verbascum dumulosum* makes a beautiful, mound-forming subshrub that can reach 30 cm tall and over 60 cm across. The branched stems have a dense covering of soft, short, greyish-white or yellowish hairs, which are also present on both surfaces of the lanceolate to elliptic leaves. These leaves are arranged in lax rosettes at the ends of the short branches. The bright yellow, round flowers are 1–2 cm wide and up to 35 are held in each raceme. This species, one of around 176 species endemic to Turkey, is a component of the Mediterranean element of the flora but is only known from the original collection site. It grows naturally in the ruins of the ancient city of Termessus in Antalya, southern Turkey, at an altitude of around 950 m. In *Curtis's Botanical Magazine*, William Turrill writes: "Termessus was an ancient city that resisted and was by-passed by Alexander the Great...What may be the history of our plant, known only as growing on ancient ruins, an artificial habitat, is at present a matter for speculation."

Peter Davis collected specimens of this species in 1947 and 1949. Seed was introduced into cultivation from the second collection (*Davis* no. 15447), and this plant was widely grown by alpine gardeners in the 1950s and 1960s. In April of 1952, the same year this species was described by Davis, it was awarded a Preliminary Commendation by the RHS, and a year later, an Award of Merit. *Verbascum dumulosum* began to slip out of cultivation until Jim and Jenny Archibald collected and reintroduced seed in the 1980s, and in May 1999 it was awarded a First Class Certificate (Rolfe, 2000).

This is a hardy species, at least in British gardens, but it does resent dampness in winter. Cultivation is usually most successful under glass, and it is easily grown in a well-ventilated alpine house or a cold frame that is covered during wet weather to protect the downy leaves from the rain. On a rock garden, it will need to be planted in a sunny crevice to provide the best drainage, and the rosettes can be angled away from the horizontal to prevent rain water sitting on the leaves. New shoots will sprout from the woody stems, so any rotten rosettes can be cut away in late winter. Propagation can be by seed, although hybrids can occur easily if other *Verbascum* species are grown nearby. Alternatively, side shoots with a short portion of stem (i.e. taken with a 'heel') can be detached after flowering for use as cuttings. They often root in just a few weeks.

Verbascum dumulosum is closely related to another Turkish endemic, *V. pestalozzae*, which also comes from Antalya but which grows in limestone rocks at around 2,000 m (6,562 feet). This is a more dwarf species, with shorter, fewer-flowered racemes and slightly larger, yellow flowers.

Curtis's Botanical Magazine, plate 258 (1955). Artist: Ann Webster.

The greater part of Turkey is covered by the Irano-Turanian phytogeographical region. Inland from the Mediterranean and Black Sea coasts and shielded from moist maritime air by the high mountains around the rim of the Anatolian Plateau, the continental climate predominates. This region can be divided into two provinces, the Mesopotamian province in south-eastern Anatolia and the Syrian desert, and the Irano-Anatolian province that extends from central Turkey across Iran to Afghanistan. Much of central and eastern parts of Anatolia are treeless steppe, particularly in the areas centred on the salt lake Tuz Gölö and in the east around Erzurum and Lake Van. Other areas around the edge of the Anatolian Plateau support deciduous scrub and forest. As would be expected, geophytes are well represented, as are small tough herbs in genera such as *Teucrium*, *Salvia*, *Artemisia* and *Astragalus*. As seen in the Taurus Mountains, spiny cushion plants, including species of *Acantholimon*, are more widespread at higher elevations.

The Irano-Turanian flora is less well understood than those of the Mediterranean and Euxine regions. This may be due largely to difficulties in the identification of many of the genera found in the region, such as *Artemisia*, *Astragalus* and *Acantholimon* (Ekim & Güner, 2000). Another reason for the continued discovery of new species in Turkey is that a botanist has to travel on foot to really explore the different habitats in detail. The mountainous terrain is often hard to access and many of the plants flower early or late in the year, when the weather can cause problems for field work. Many of Turkey's endemic geophytes are only found in small, localised areas so it is not surprising that new species continue to be discovered as the various mountain ranges are explored.

A good example of a genus that has had several new Turkish species added to it in recent years is *Crocus*. These corms tend to flower very early or late in the year, and so the problems mentioned above are encountered when searching for them in the wild. New species of *Crocus* described in the last quarter of the twentieth century include *C. baytopiorum*, *C. asumaniae*, *C. abantensis*, *C. adanensis*, *C. antalyensis*, *C. paschei*, *C. mathewii* and *C. kerndorffiorum* (Mathew, 1998). There are bound to be more species found, in this and other genera, as the botanical exploration of this fascinating country continues.

Iran and the 'bulb lands'

The Irano-Turanian phytogeographical region extends east from Central Turkey, through parts of Iraq and Iran and into the Central Asian countries of Turkmenistan, Kazakhstan, Uzbekistan and Afghanistan. It is on the mountains that the diversity of plant life of this region is

BELOW
Fritillaria imperialis in the Chelgard Valley, Iran.
Photo: Christopher Ryan.

Crocus baytopiorum
Family: Iridaceae

The stunning pale blue flowers of the Turkish *Crocus baytopiorum* make it one of the most distinctive species of *Crocus*. It was discovered as recently as 1973 and described in 1974 by Brian Mathew, who named it in honour of Professors Turhan and Asuman Baytop of Istanbul University. Turkey is home to a remarkable number of *Crocus* species and new discoveries are still being made. Asuman Baytop first collected *C. baytopiorum* on Honaz Dağ, near Denizli in western Turkey. It was initially thought to be endemic to this mountain but other sites in south-west Turkey have since been found (Mathew, 1982). It grows on limestone screes and in rocky gullies in sparse *Pinus* and *Juniperus* woodland.

Crocus baytopiorum has a prophyll (a basal spathe around the scape), so in his 1982 classification of the genus, Mathew placed it in section *Crocus*. Although a distinctive species, *C. baytopiorum* appeared to be most closely related to four European spring-flowering species in series *Verni*, often called the 'vernus aggregate': *C. vernus*, *C. tommasinianus*, *C. etruscus* and *C. kosaninii*. These all have a single bract (floral spathe) at the base of the ovary and a corm tunic with reticulated fibres. The papery, white bract of *C. baytopiorum* is very conspicuous and often reaches the base of the perianth segments. Despite these morphological similarities, recent molecular analysis of the genus (Mathew, Petersen & Seberg, 2009) has concluded that *C. baytopiorum* is not part of this series and should be placed in a series of its own, series *Baytopi*.

The sky blue flowers, with delicate, slightly darker veining, together with the narrow leaves that only reach 1.5 mm wide, help to distinguish *Crocus baytopiorum* and make it easy to recognise. The flowers have a perianth tube that can reach 9 cm tall, with the perianth segments up to 3 cm long. The style is divided into three yellow or orange branches and the seeds are elongated and red.

The original collection by Baytop was made when the plants were flowering in February, but in cultivation, *C. baytopiorum* can flower in January or earlier. This painting was prepared from plants collected at the type locality, which flowered in cultivation on 23 January 1974.

Appearing so early in the year, the flowers can be damaged by wind and rain. Also the perianth tube can be fairly long and thin, and a shortage of sunny days can make it elongate further, causing the flower to fall over. A grower in Scotland (Bezzant, 1992) reports that some plants seem to want to flower very early, sometimes in December, and produce blooms that are very frail and short-lived, whereas plants that flower later produce much more flowers. To reduce the risk of the flowers collapsing, the corms can be given a free root run by planting them directly into open soil in a light, well-ventilated cold frame that is covered during adverse weather conditions. Pot-grown plants can also be housed in a cold frame or an alpine house.

Curtis's Botanical Magazine, plate 664 (1974). Artist: Mary Grierson.

at its greatest. At high altitudes, the summer temperatures are less intense and in spring there can be abundant moisture from melting snow. The cold winters and hot summers mean that there are effectively two seasons in which plant growth is inhibited, and most plants flower in either spring or autumn. Geophytes are well adapted to coping with this type of climate.

The bulbs of Central Asia have become such an integral part of our garden flora that it can be easy to forget where they come from. Bulbs such as irises, tulips and fritillaries are widely grown, but those that have become well established in cultivation represent a small proportion of the huge range of bulbous plants growing wild in the hills and mountains of this region. When looking at the conditions under which these plants grow in their native habitat, it is sometimes surprising that they do so well in a climate with heavier rainfall and much cooler, wetter summers.

One of the earliest plates in *Curtis's Botanical Magazine* shows the crown imperial, *Fritillaria imperialis*. According to Curtis, it was introduced in Vienna in 1576 and cultivated in Britain as early as 1596. This well-known bulb is native to south-east Turkey, Iran, Afghanistan, Pakistan and Kashmir, growing on rocky slopes and in scrub, up to 3,000 m (9,843 feet) altitude. It is frequently seen in gardens, having been imported into Europe via Constantinople in the sixteenth century. The large bulbs, which give off a strong 'foxy' smell, produce tall, leafy stems that can reach over a metre in height, topped by an umbel-like inflorescence of five to seven nodding, bell-shaped flowers in shades of orange or yellow, with perianth segments up to 5 cm long. Above the flowers is a distinctive top-knot of lanceolate, leaf-like floral bracts. The flowers, like many fritillaries, have prominent nectaries that can produce copious amounts of nectar to attract birds or insects.

Similar to *Fritillaria imperialis* and having the same umbel-like inflorescence of nodding flowers are three other species. Together these four species are classified in subgenus *Petilium*. *Fritillaria eduardii*, from Central Asia, has orange flowers that are more flared than those of *F. imperialis*. *Fritillaria chitralensis* occurs in eastern Afghanistan and the adjacent region of Chitral in Kashmir. For a long time, it was treated as a variety of *F. imperialis* and it has been grown on and off in Britain for a hundred years. Only in 1996 did Brian Mathew formally recognise it as a distinct species (Mathew, 1996). *Fritillaria chitralensis* is a shorter plant than *F. imperialis*, growing 20–45 cm tall and having fewer flowers that are a bright, rich yellow. The fourth species in the subgenus is the greenish-yellow-flowered *F. raddeana*, from north-east Iran and adjacent Turkmenistan, especially in the Kopet Dag, the range of mountains that runs along the border of the two countries. It has smaller and more numerous flowers than the other *Petilium* species and grows to a height

similar to that of *F. chitralensis*. *Fritillaria eduardii*, *F. chitralensis* and *F. raddeana* are not so accommodating as the crown imperial in cultivation, requiring a dry summer rest, which usually means growing them under glass, although *F. raddeana* can survive outside in a sunny, very well-drained border. They flower earlier then *F. imperialis*, usually in late winter, and make fine plants for the alpine house.

Fritillaria is a large genus with around 120 species, distributed across western North America, Europe, the Mediterranean basin and Asia. Their usually nodding, bell- to saucer-shaped flowers frequently come in shades of green, brown or purple, but they are often attractively marked with squares of dark and light colour (tessellated), as in the British native snake's head fritillary, *F. meleagris*. In addition, the inner surfaces of the six perianth segments can be delicately patterned, particularly around the nectaries, which are located near the base of each segment. The flowers are either solitary, held in a raceme or occasionally an umbel-like inflorescence, like those of the crown imperial. The subtle beauty of their flowers has ensured that fritillaries have become very popular with bulb growers.

BELOW
Fritillaria chitralensis in cultivation.

THE *Rhinopetalum* FRITILLARIES

Many Central Asian fritillaries really need protection from rain in the summer to do well. Among them are the five species once classified in a separate genus, *Rhinopetalum*. The main characteristic by which these species can be identified is the presence of deeply pitted nectaries that show as distinct bumps or 'noses' on the outer surface of the perianth segments. The five are *Fritillaria karelinii, F. gibbosa, F. stenanthera, F. bucharica* and *F. ariana*, all from Central Asia, Iran and Afghanistan. The genus *Rhinopetalum* was described by Lt. J. E. Alexander in 1830, but the name came from Dr Friedrich Ernst Ludwig von Fischer, Eduard Regel's predecessor as Director of the Imperial Botanic Garden, St Petersburg. Fischer sent bulbs of *R. karelinii* to the Chelsea Physic Garden in London, where they flowered in 1835. The species is named after the collector of these first bulbs, Grigory Karelin, who found them in the southern Urals, just north of the Caspian Sea. The species is distinctive in that only one of the six perianth segments in each flower has a large-horned nectary. Its range stretches from Iran to Xinjiang in western China.

The genus *Rhinopetalum* was not accepted by all authors. For example, Boissier and Kew botanist J. G. Baker both placed these species in subgenus *Rhinopetalum* of *Fritillaria*. It was Baker who published the name *Fritillaria karelinii* in 1874. Recent studies of their DNA have confirmed that these species are embedded within the genus *Fritillaria* (Rix, 2007a).

Probably the most attractive species in this group is *Fritillaria gibbosa*, which grows on steppes and rocky screes from Armenia and Iran to Afghanistan and Pakistan. The reddish to pink or apricot flowers are fairly flat for a fritillary, but their prominent nectaries on each perianth segment are clearly seen. It was described by Boissier in 1846, having been collected by Kotschy in 1842 near the ruins of Persepolis in south-west Iran (Rix, 2007b). Another distinctive member of the subgenus is *F. bucharica*, the only white-flowered species in the group.

BELOW LEFT
Fritillaria gibbosa.

BELOW MIDDLE
Fritillaria bucharica.

BELOW RIGHT
Fritillaria stenanthera.

Many fritillaries can be grown in the open garden, including a number from Central Europe and the Mediterranean. *Fritillaria imperialis* is one of a few Central Asian species in that can cope with the northern European climate. *Fritillaria pallidiflora* is another and is mainly found in the mountains along the border of Kazakhstan and China's Xinjiang Province, namely the Dzungarian Ala Tau and Tien Shan (Phillips & Rix, 1989). This species is cultivated on a large scale in China, where the bulbs are used medicinally. In the wild, it is found growing in meadows, on grassy slopes, in woodland clearings and among shrubs, at 1,000–3,000 m (3,281–9,843 feet) above sea level. At these altitudes, the winters are cold and the summers cool, which explains why *F. pallidiflora* does well outside in cultivation in northern Europe.

Fritillaria pallidiflora was described in 1841 by the Russian explorer Alexander Schrenk, from plants growing on the Dzungarian Ala Tau. It has broad, glaucous leaves and the large, pale greenish-yellow or creamy-white flowers have darker veins and a few reddish-brown spots. These broad, bell-shaped flowers are among the largest in the genus, reaching up to 5 cm long and 3 cm wide, and are held in a raceme of usually one to six flowers, with the pedicels arising from the axils of the upper leaves. The whole plant generally grows 30–45 cm tall but can reach up to 80 cm tall and hold up to 12 flowers (Rix, 1994).

One of the most successful *Fritillaria* species in cultivation is *F. uva-vulpis*, which is found mainly in meadows in northern Iraq but which also occurs in south-east Turkey and western Iran (Rix, 2000). This plant was introduced to cultivation by Rear Admiral Paul Furse and his wife Polly in 1962 but not named until 1975, when Martyn Rix described the species. The usually solitary flower is a distinctive colour, being a dusky glaucous, purplish-blue with yellow tips to the segments. The collection made by Paul and Polly Furse is still in general cultivation. It is a robust plant that produces many bulbils, making propagation simple.

The genus *Tulipa* also has many representatives in Central Asia. Tulips are one of the most popular garden bulbs but most of those in cultivation are hybrids that bear little resemblance to the wild plants. Wild tulips are incredibly diverse, with wide variations being found within single species, making their classification a nightmare for botanists. Across the hills and mountains of Central Asia, these resilient bulbs burst out of the ground in spring to decorate the meadows and rocky slopes with their colourful blooms in huge variety. It is hardly surprising that these plants have caught the imagination of gardeners and botanists. Coming from a region with hot dry summers, the species of *Tulipa* are not always easy to please in the garden. Given some protection from summer rain, however, most can be kept happy and many are well-established in cultivation. A few can be grown in a sunny spot in the open garden and among the most successful of these is *T. turkestanica*, a multi-flowered tulip from the mountains of the Pamir Alai and Tien Shan. It has small white flowers that have a yellow centre and are held on a stem that is 20–30 cm tall. Closely related is *T. tarda* from the Tien Shan, whose starry flowers are similar to those of *T. turkestanica* but on a much shorter plant that flowers later in the spring, usually in late March or April, when grown outside in southern Britain. *Tulipa praestans*, from the southern Pamir Alai, is one of the most widely grown tulip species. One bulb can produce several bright red flowers, and this species can live for many years undisturbed in the garden. *Tulipa linifolia* is also a good garden plant, and this is especially true of the named forms usually sold under the name *T. batalinii*, such as 'Bright Gem' and 'Bronze Charm'. Both *T. linifolia* and *T. batalinii* were described by Eduard Regel. The latter is yellow-flowered and is now considered a form of the red *T. linifolia*. This species has a wide natural range, being found from northern Iran to Afghanistan and the Pamir Alai.

The natural distribution of the genus *Tulipa* ranges from the Iberian Peninsula and North Africa to the mountains of the Tien Shan and Pamir Alai. There are around 70–100 species, and Central Asia is where they are most diverse.

The earliest tulip species to be introduced were from southern Europe and the Near East, but in the nineteenth century, many new introductions were made by Eduard and Albert Regel. In fact, Eduard Regel described more tulip species that any other botanist (Wilford, 2006). He also published a classification of the genus in 1873 and was the first to divide the genus according to the presence or absence of hairs on the filaments of the stamens, a characteristic still used today in the classification of *Tulipa* species.

The red-flowered *Tulipa albertii*, from the Tien Shan, was named by Eduard Regel in 1877 after his son, who discovered it in the mountains near Tashkent. Eduard Regel is commemorated by *Tulipa regelii*, a rare and unusual species from the Lake Balkhash region of south-east Kazakhstan. *Tulipa regelii* was first collected by Andrej Krasnow in 1886 and described by him in 1887. This is a very rarely grown and distinctive species. The usually single glaucous leaf lies close to the ground and has longitudinal, crest-like ridges on its upper surface, a character not seen in any other tulip (Mathew & Wilford, 2001). The small, solitary, funnel-shaped flowers are white with a yellow centre, indicating its close relationship with *T. turkestanica* and *T. tarda*. In the wild, *T. regelii* grows on stony limestone slopes in full sun. To succeed in cultivation, it is essential to protect it from summer moisture, so alpine-house or cold-frame conditions are needed.

FAR LEFT
Tulipa praestans is easily grown in the open garden.

LEFT
Tulipa regelii.

In the late nineteenth and early twentieth centuries, tulips became increasingly popular and Dutch bulb firms, such as C. G. van Tubergen, employed their own collectors to search out and send back tulips to Europe. The German plant collector Paul Sintenis was based in Ashkhabad and sent bulbs back to growers in Europe, including the wonderful scarlet *Tulipa montana*. Josef Haberhauer ran a hotel in the Central Asian city of Samarkand and was commissioned by C. G. van Tubergen to collect the impressive *T. fosteriana*, which grows in the hills surrounding the city. This wide-leaved tulip has huge, bright red flowers, reaching up to 12.5 cm from top to bottom and on stems 35–50 cm tall. It was described in 1906 and has been used in the breeding of many hybrid tulips in Holland. *Tulipa fosteriana* is one of the species that does well in the open garden, given a warm sunny position. Haberhauer also sent back different forms of *T. praestans*, including the popular 'Fusilier'.

Tulipa greigii is a widely grown species that comes in many differently named forms as a result of extensive hybridisation in cultivation. This species was described by Eduard Regel in 1873, from plants collected by Sewerzow and Fedschenko in the Karatau Mountains of southern Kazakhstan. He named it after General Greig, President of the Imperial Russian Horticultural Union. The wide, bowl-shaped flowers come in colours ranging from yellow to orange and red, and the leaves are characteristically marked with brownish or maroon streaks and spots. Paul Graeber, a collector based in Tashkent, sent bulbs of this

ABOVE
Habitat of *Tulipa montana* in Iran.
Photo: Christopher Ryan.

LEFT
Tulipa greigii.

tulip and of *T. kaufmanniana* to C. G. van Tubergen in the early twentieth century. From these collections, the breeding of the Greigii and Kaufmanniana hybrids began.

The genus *Iris* is larger than *Fritillaria* and *Tulipa* combined, with around 250 species. They are distributed across the Northern Hemisphere and grow from bulbs or rhizomes. Among the bulbous species are the 'reticulata' irises of subgenus *Hermodactyloides* and the 'juno' irises of subgenus *Scorpiris*.

The bulbous juno irises were previously classified in a separate genus, *Juno*, and they are distinguished quite easily from other irises. The bulbs have fleshy roots, a unique feature in *Iris*; the leaves are not arranged in the familiar fan shape that is usually found in garden irises, instead they are more like those of a leek, channelled and arranged in one plane; and the flowers also differ. All irises have six perianth segments making up the flower. Three arch downwards and are called falls, and three point upwards and are called standards. The standards are often large and showy but in the juno irises they are reduced in size, and held out horizontally or pointing downwards. Another general characteristic of the juno irises is that many are hard to grow. Most resent moisture in the summer and are prone to attack by fungal diseases in damp winters. A few of the more robust species can be grown in the open ground, including *Iris aucheri*, *I. bucharica* and *I. magnifica*.

Apart from *Iris planifolia*, the only European species, the juno irises are found from Central Turkey to Central Asia. They have been cultivated for many years and, in fact, the very first plate in *Curtis's Botanical Magazine*, in 1787, was

ABOVE
A dark purple form of *Iris aucheri*.

Iris persica, not from Iran as the name suggests but from southern and south-east Turkey, northern Syria and northern Iraq (Mathew, 1989). Curtis writes that it was grown in Holland. To survive its summer dormancy, this species (like most junos) has to be lifted and stored somewhere dry until late autumn, or alternatively grown in pots under glass to protect them from rain. Removing or damaging the fleshy roots when lifting will weaken the plant, so pot cultivation is preferable.

LEFT
Iris magnifica.

The reticulata irises are more amenable to cultivation than the juno irises, and several of the 12 or so species can be grown in the open garden. *Iris reticulata*, from northern and north-east Turkey, the Caucasus, northern Iraq and Iran, has variable flower colour and is an attractive, early-flowering garden bulb. The flowers come in shades of pale blue, violet and purple, sometimes with dark falls and pale standards. The bi-coloured variants are common in western Iran (Mathew, 1999). The name of this species, and the group, comes from the netted (reticulate) tunic that covers the bulb. *Iris reticulata* was described by Bieberstein in 1808, in the first volume of *Flora Taurico-Caucasica*. Most reticulata irises also have leaves with a square cross-section. The two exceptions are *I. bakeriana*, from southern Turkey, northern Iraq and western Iran, which has nearly cylindrical leaves, and *I. kolpakowskiana*, from the Tien Shan, which has narrow channelled leaves. *Iris histrioides*, from alpine slopes in northern Turkey, has the largest flowers in the group and they are blue-violet in colour. The hybrid *Iris* 'Katherine Hodgkin' is the result of a cross between *I. histrioides* and the yellow-flowered *I. winogradowii*. The latter is only known in the wild from a few sites in Georgia. It was discovered in 1923 growing in meadows on Mt Lomis Mta, near Borjomi, Georgia and it was distributed by Tbilisi Botanic Garden. It flowered at Glasnevin Botanic Garden, Dublin, in 1927.

The irises of section *Oncocyclus* grow from a rhizome and include some bizarre and flamboyant plants, such as *Iris iberica*, from the Caucasus and Turkey and the blackish purple *I. atropurpurea* from Gaza and Israel's Negev Desert. They are related to the bearded irises of section *Iris*. However, the onocyclus irises can be very difficult to maintain in cultivation, disliking damp winters and needing a dry summer rest. The group is distributed from Central Turkey and the Caucasus to the Kopet Dag mountains and south to the Sinai.

Where the range of the oncocyclus irises stops, the species of section *Regelia* take over. This is a group of around eight species distributed across Afghanistan and adjacent Central Asia. They are similar to the species in section *Oncocyclus* in that they grow from stout rhizomes, the seeds have a fleshy appendage (aril) and the flowers have a beard on the falls. The regelia irises differ in usually having two flowers per stem and they also have a beard on the standards. There are some regelia irises that can be grown in the open in well-drained soil and full sun, such as *Iris hoogiana* and *I. korolkowii*.

ABOVE LEFT
Iris persica.

ABOVE RIGHT
Iris reticulata in Iran.
Photo: Christopher Ryan.

RIGHT
Iris kolpakowskiana
in Kyrgyzstan.
Photo: Kit Strange.

Iris afghanica
Family: Iridaceae

Rear Admiral Paul Furse and his wife Polly made several expeditions to Western and Central Asia in search of plants in the 1960s. When in Afghanistan, in 1964, they came across this beautiful iris, growing on the northern side of the Salang Pass in the Hindu Kush, north of Kabul. They initially thought it was a form of *Iris darwasica*, but after finding it again on their second expedition to the region in 1966, they came to the conclusion that it must be a new species. Per Wendelbo, of Gothenburg Botanic Garden, eventually described it in 1972 and gave it the name *Iris afghanica*.

Paul and Polly Furse collected material of *Iris afghanica* and introduced it into cultivation. Wendelbo, Ian Hedge and Lars Ekberg also made collections during an expedition to Afghanistan in 1969 and it is from this material that Wendelbo described the species. Further collections were made by Chris Grey-Wilson and Tom Hewer in 1971, and although far from common, this species is now established in cultivation. The plant shown here was a Grey-Wilson and Hewer collection (*Grey-Wilson & Hewer* no. 698) that flowered at Kew in 1972.

Iris afghanica is a striking species. The bluish-green, slender leaves can be up to 30 cm long, though often shorter, and the outer ones are sickle-shaped. The flowers are around 8–9 cm across and have pointed falls that are creamy-white, heavily veined with purple-brown and with a solid purple patch in the centre. At the centre of the falls is a beard of yellowish or purple hairs. The pointed standards are pale yellow and they have a beard of greenish hairs on the lower part. Grey-Wilson (1974) has described this iris as "perhaps the finest introduction from Afghanistan, and the most superb of the regelia irises".

In the wild, *Iris afghanica* forms scattered colonies, with up to ten flowers per clump, growing among boulders and on steep rocky slopes at altitudes of 1,500–3,300 m (4,921–10,827 feet). At higher altitudes, the plants are more strongly coloured and around 10 cm tall, but at lower altitudes, the flowers are larger and softer coloured and the plants can reach 25–30 cm tall (Furse, 1968). It is endemic to north-east Afghanistan.

In its natural habitat, *Iris afghanica* experiences hot, dry summers and freezing winters, so it is perfectly hardy but must be kept dry when dormant. For this reason, it is best grown in a well-ventilated cold frame or alpine house that protects the rhizomes from rain in the summer. Regelia irises often do better if given a free root-run by planting directly into a frame bed. Some species, such as *I. hoogiana* and *I. korolkowii*, can be grown outside in a well-drained, sunny border. Plants can be increased by dividing the rhizomes in late summer when the plants are repotted. *Iris afghanica* is rare in cultivation and it is even rarer to find two clones growing together, so seed is very seldom available.

Curtis's Botanical Magazine, plate 668 (1974). Artist: Mary Grierson.

Apart from these more familiar genera, there are many other plants that have adapted to the Central Asian climate by evolving some sort of underground storage organ. The genus *Corydalis* contains more than 400 annual and perennial species distributed throughout the temperate regions of the northern hemisphere and as far south as Thailand and the mountains of East Africa. The perennial, tuberous corydalis represent less than a quarter of the total number of species but they are the most commonly grown. The largest group, with over 50 species, is section *Corydalis*, which contains the widely grown *C. solida*. In this section, the leaves are alternate and petiolate and the tubers are regenerated annually. In section *Leonticoides*, which contains around 21 species, the plants form an irregularly shaped, corky-coated, perennial tuber. The stem leaves are opposite, glaucous and generally sessile.

Members of section *Leonticoides* occur in Turkey and Central Asia, with outliers in Crete, Cyprus and the western Himalaya (Lidén & Zetterlund, 1997). They include *Corydalis popovii*, named after the Russian botanist and explorer Mikhail Popov, and *C. ledebouriana*, which was introduced into cultivation by Albert Regel and named after Carl von Ledebour in 1841 by Grigory Karelin and Ivan Kirilov. Ledebour was Director of the Botanic Garden at Dorpat and

author of *Flora Rossica*, which was published between 1841 and 1853. He discovered *C. ledebouriana* in the mountains of Tarbagatai in Kazakhstan.

The irregularly shaped tubers of the species in *Corydalis* section *Leonticoides* resemble those found in the genus *Leontice*, hence the name of the section. *Leontice* is a small genus of tuberous, yellow-flowered plants in the *Berberis* family (Berberidaceae) containing three species from southern Europe, North Africa and Western and Central Asia. They are closely allied to the species in two other tuberous genera, *Gymnospermium* and *Bongardia*. There are ten species in *Gymnospermium*, and they differ from those in *Leontice* in that the seeds have a membranous aril and emerge from the capsule long before they are ripe. Also, the racemes of flowers are terminal, whereas in *Leontice* they are both terminal and axillary. The similar genus *Bongardia*, with just two species, differs from these two in having only basal leaves.

The genus *Gymnospermium* was described in 1839 by the French botanist Édouard Spach, who transferred *Leontice altaica* to it. The genus was not widely accepted until William Stearn and David Webb (1964) maintained *Gymnospermium altaicum* in *Flora Europaea*. Then in 1970, Armen Tahktajan transferred five other species of *Leontice*

ABOVE LEFT
Iris iberica, in section *Oncocyclus*.

ABOVE RIGHT
Corydalis popovii.

Silene schafta
Family: Caryophyllaceae

Silene schafta is a loose mat-forming species, with slender stems that will tumble over rocks, providing some welcome colour in late summer. Its deep pink to reddish-purple flowers are produced from July to October. It is a commonly grown and quite vigorous rock garden plant that has long been in cultivation. In *Curtis's Botanical Magazine* in 1959, William Turrill writes that *S. schafta* was grown in Britain "at least as early as 1844". In 1846, a painting of this species appeared in the *Botanical Register*, where John Lindley (1846) writes: "It is seldom that so charming a recruit as this can be added to our hardy herbaceous species, for without any exception it is one of the prettiest of all border and rock plants…The Society received it from Dr Fischer, who obtained it from the Botanic Garden at Dorpat, and it has also found its way hither through France."

This is an easily grown, hardy species for the rock garden that is a native of the south-east Caucasus and northern Iran. It was described in 1838 from material collected on Mt Keridach (or Keridakhi) in the Russian Province of Talysh, now in southern Azerbaijan. From there, its range extends eastwards into the Iranian Provinces of Gilan and Mazanderan at the southern end of the Caspian Sea. It grows in rocky places at altitudes of 900–2,700 m (2,953–8,858 feet).

The prostrate to ascending stems of this species can reach 25–30 cm long, and they end in a loose dichasium (a cyme of three flowers with pedicels that are more or less equal in length); there may also be some solitary flowers. The narrow, pubescent, pale purple (rarely pale pink) calyx is up to 2.8 cm long. The spreading petal-limbs are around 1 cm long and shallowly divided into two lobes. At the base of each petal-limb is a coronal scale, and these form a raised ring at the centre of the flower.

This species needs to be placed carefully in the garden because it can spread quite rapidly and smother smaller plants. It should be planted in a sunny position, in a free-draining but moisture-retentive soil. It is best sited on a ledge so that the roots are shaded by the surrounding rocks and the stems can trail downwards, displaying their bright flowers from July until autumn. Growth continues throughout the summer and although this plant can tolerate some drought, it is better if the soil isn't allowed to dry out completely. A thick mulch of grit will keep moisture away from the foliage in winter. Cuttings of non-flowering shoots can be taken in summer and autumn, and this species can also be increased from seed sown in autumn or winter.

Curtis's Botanical Magazine, plate 336 (1959). Artist: Margaret Stones.

to *Gymnospermium*, including *L. albertii*, which was described by Eduard von Regel in 1881 (Regel, 1881). Regel named this plant after his son Albert, who discovered it in what is now Uzbekistan (then a part of W Turkestan).

Gymnospermium albertii is an unusual-looking plant from Central Asia, particularly the Tien Shan and Pamir Alai, where it grows on rocky hills and in scrub at around 2,000 m (6,562 feet). It flowers in April or May, as the snow melts. The yellow flowers are held in a dense raceme at the end of reddish stems. Initially, the stems are bent over as the flowers open, but as they elongate, they become erect and can reach 30 cm tall. As the flowers open, the one to three petiolate stem leaves gradually unfurl. They are pale green and palmately divided into five or more broadly elliptic segments. This species was introduced to cultivation in Britain when Eduard von Regel sent tubers to Henry Elwes.

It is not just geophytes that have attracted the interest of gardeners looking at the flora of Central Asia. The genus *Silene* for example, includes several attractive rock garden plants, including cushion- and mat-forming species. This huge genus comprises an estimated 500–700 annual, biennial and perennial species, distributed across Europe, Asia, Africa and the Americas, with the main centres of distribution in the Pamir Alai and Hindu Kush of Central Asia, and in an area covering Transcaucasia, eastern Turkey and northern Iran (Bittrich, 1993). From this latter region comes the bright-pink-flowered *Silene schafta*, an easy and floriferous species for the rock garden.

TOP
Gymnospermium albertii sprouting from ground in Kyrgyzstan.
Photo: Kit Strange.

ABOVE
Gymnospermium albertii in cultivation.

Gentiana is also a widespread genus with its centre of diversity in Asia. Of the Central Asian species in cultivation, *G. olivieri* must be one of the most attractive. It is often a common plant in the wild, where it can form drifts of blue in early summer and is found at altitudes of 200–2,800 m (656–9,186 feet), from eastern Turkey and Syria, through Iraq and Iran, to Afghanistan and the Pamir Alai. *Gentiana olivieri* is not so common in cultivation, a situation more than likely due to its need for a long, dry rest in summer, which makes its outdoor cultivation unreliable. It is most likely to survive outside if planted in a well-drained, sunny raised bed or scree. To withstand the long spells of intense heat and drought in its native habitat, this gentian has developed fleshy roots and a protective collar of fibres. It remains dormant during dry periods and starts to grow when there is an abundant supply of moisture, characteristics shared by many plants from this region.

Gentiana olivieri was first described by August Grisebach in 1838, from material collected in Iran. It was named in honour of its finder, Guillaume Antoine Olivier (1756–1814), a traveller and author. This species forms a rosette of leaves that reach 15 cm long but only around 1.5 cm wide. It has few cauline (stem) leaves, and these are relatively small and arranged in pairs. The uppermost pair clasp the cluster of three to ten, bell-shaped flowers, which open in late spring or early summer. The flowers are held in a cyme at the end of the stem and each one is up to 3.5 cm long, deep blue with a white to pale blue throat. The terminal flowers in the cyme are stalkless (sessile) but the side flowers are stalked (pedicellate). The stems are spreading at first but then turn upwards and can reach more than 20 cm in length. Paul and Polly Furse also report finding white and pale-blue-flowered specimens in the foothills of the Hindu Kush (Furse & Furse, 1969).

Gentiana olivieri is most closely related to two other Central Asian species, *G. kaufmanniana* and *G. dahurica*. In *Flora Iranica* (Schiman-Czeika, 1967), *G. olivieri* is placed in Section *Aptera*, along with four other species, including *G. kaufmanniana* and *G. cruciata*. The general characteristics of these species include a fibrous root-collar, lateral flowering stems and a basal rosette of large leaves. *Gentiana cruciata*, which is found throughout much of Europe and western Asia, differs from *G. olivieri* in having basal and stem leaves that are similar to each other and flowers with only four corolla lobes instead of five. *Gentiana kaufmanniana* and *G. dahurica* differ in having only sessile flowers.

BELOW LEFT
Gentiana olivieri.

BELOW RIGHT
Dionysia aretioides growing on a cliff in northern Iran.
Photo: Christopher Ryan.

No account of the plants of Central Asia should neglect to mention one of the most desirable, fascinating and exasperating genera in the region, *Dionysia*. These plants are desirable because, when in full bloom, the primula-like flowers in colours ranging from yellow to pink and violet, will cover the plant, completely hiding any foliage; fascinating because the majority form compact and sometimes very hard cushions, made up of hundreds of tiny leaf rosettes, held at the end of branching, woody stems; and exasperating because they do not cope with cultivation very well, often dying without any apparent reason. These are the cushion plants that alpine gardeners wish to grow successfully more than any other. Many species were introduced in the late 1960s and early 1970s but most were considered virtually impossible to grow and propagate. Since then, their cultivation has been largely mastered by those growers who can afford the time and effort to keep them alive, and their requirements are much better understood.

The genus *Dionysia* is closely related to *Primula*, exhibiting, in most cases, a relatively reduced height and leaf size. The 49 currently recognised species are mostly restricted to dry mountains in the Irano-Turanian region, particularly in Iran and Afghanistan but also in south-east Turkey, northern Iraq, northern Oman, the Pamir Alai and Pakistan. Most grow on shaded or semi-shaded limestone cliffs and slopes, often in gorges and chasms and sometimes in the crevices of overhanging rocks and caves, where they are sheltered from the intense summer heat. Water can percolate through the rock, providing the roots with moisture, especially as the snow melts in spring.

Some species of *Dionysia*, such as *D. mira* from Oman, with its long scapes bearing whorls of yellow flowers, resemble the primulas of section *Sphondylia*. In his monograph of *Dionysia*, Per Wendelbo (1961) states that there is no single characteristic to distinguish the two genera, but *Dionysia* can be separated from *Primula* by a combination of certain characters. These include the woody stems, the chromosome number, the characteristics of the pollen, the long, narrow corolla tube and the small subglobose, five-valved capsule. Wendelbo also observes that woolly farina (rather than powdery farina) and few-seeded capsules rarely occur in *Primula*. The species of

FAR LEFT
Dionysia aretioides in cultivation.

BELOW
Dionysia mozzaffarianii, a recently described species from Iran.

GROWING *Dionysia*

The three main problems associated with the cultivation of dionysias are *Botrytis* mould, aphid infestation and scorching of the foliage. A very free-draining soil mix should be used, and a mulch of grit or stone chippings at least 2 cm thick must be applied around and under the cushion. For most species, wetting the leaves is best avoided. Some shading will be needed on sunny days, particularly in spring and early summer, to prevent leaf-scorch. Any dying leaf rosettes and fading flowers should be removed to prevent rot spreading. Aphid attacks must be treated early with an insecticide. Nearly all the species need to be grown in a well-ventilated alpine house, where watering can be controlled and shading provided when necessary. Planting in vertical crevices or into tufa will provide perfect drainage.

A typical soil mix for dionysias in pots is (by volume) 1 part loam-based soil mix, 1 part grit and 1 part coarse sand, but different growers use a variety of mixes; perlite and fine-grade vermiculite are often incorporated. Overwatering must be avoided, but it is also important not to let the soil dry out when the plants are in growth. Clay pots are best plunged in moist sand so that water can be provided through the sides of the pot rather than by direct watering. The soil should be moist in spring and summer, and careful watering directly into the pots is needed in warm weather. For the rest of the year, when plants partially 'shut down' and will quickly rot if overwatered, it is usually only the plunge sand that needs to be kept moist. The cool, damp days of autumn and winter are when *Botrytis* is most likely to appear. Hardiness is not a problem, so the glasshouse can be well ventilated at all times and fans can be installed to boost air circulation.

Propagation is the key to successful cultivation of dionysias as it provides a constant supply of healthy young plants. Seed of most species is rarely produced in cultivation and germination is often poor, but propagation is relatively easy from cuttings of individual leaf-rosettes with a portion of stem taken after flowering (May to June).

Dionysia sarvestanica.

Young plants of *Dionysia*.

ABOVE
Dionysia involucrata
in Kew's Davies Alpine
House.

Dionysia form part of the broad concept of *Primula* (*Primula senso lato*) but they are a distinct group and the name of the genus is still maintained as separate from *Primula* (e.g. Lidén, 2007), a view welcomed by growers of these plants.

One of the easiest and most floriferous species of *Dionysia* in cultivation is *D. aretioides*. This species can form fairly large, soft cushions of greyish-green leaves, up to 40 cm in diameter. The yellow flowers, with notched petals, are generally solitary and held on short peduncles. In the wild, both farinose and non-farinose forms occur. This species was only introduced to cultivation in 1959, from seed collected by Wendelbo. Various forms have since been introduced and given cultivar names, such as 'Paul Furse', 'Gravetye' and 'Phyllis Carter'. They vary in the size and colour of the flowers and the tightness of the cushion.

Dionysia aretioides comes from the Elburz Mountains of northern Iran, growing on north-, west- or east-facing, shaded limestone cliffs, at altitudes of 300–3,200 m (984–10,499 feet). It was the first *Dionysia* to be discovered, by the German botanical explorer Carl Ludwig von Hablitzl in 1770, and was initially described as *Primula aretioides* by Johann Lehmann in 1817. The genus *Dionysia* was described by Eduard Fenzl in 1843, on the basis of material of *D. odora* collected by Kotschy in Kurdistan. Edmond Boissier transferred *Primula aretioides* to *Dionysia* in 1846, in *Diagnoses Plantarum Orientalium Novarum*.

Other *Dionysia* species that are well-established in cultivation include *D. tapetodes*, one of the most widespread species, which comes from the mountains of north-east Iran, the Kopet Dag and Afghanistan, growing on limestone cliffs, ledges and rocky slopes. The dense, domed cushions are covered with small, solitary yellow flowers in late winter. This species has been in cultivation since 1958 (Grey-Wilson, 1989). The pinkish-purple to violet-flowered *D. curviflora*, from volcanic or basalt cliffs in Central Iran, has the longest history of continuous cultivation, having been grown since 1932. One of the more distinctive cultivated species is *D. involucrata*, which grows wild in the Pamir Alai ranges in Tajikistan. It has wider leaves than many dionysias, reaching 12 mm long and 6 mm wide and having prominent raised veins so the individual leaf rosettes look like miniature cabbages. The loose cushions reach around 20 cm wide, and the bright pink flowers with a white eye are held in a short-stalked, three- to five-flowered umbel. This species produces plenty of seed, providing the easiest method of propagation for this plant.

New introductions of *Dionysia* are still being made and hybridisers have been working on the genus, creating a number of brightly coloured forms that are often more vigorous and easier to cultivate than the species. Recent introductions include the bright yellow-flowered *D.*

sarvestanica, which was described in 1989, having been found by the Iranian botanist Mozaffarian in the southern Zagros mountains in 1983. Another new Iranian species, *D. mozaffarianii*, was named after Mozaffarian by Magnus Lidén in 2000 and has also been introduced into cultivation. In a recent synopsis of the genus, Lidén (2007) described five new species following field work in Iran. They are *D. viva*, *D. zschummelii*, *D. cristagalli*, *D. zetterlundii* and *D. tacamahaca*.

The fascination with dionysias is an example of the continuing interest in the plants of Central Asia seen the second half of the twentieth century and beginning of the twenty-first. New introductions and reintroductions, as well as improved access to some countries, particularly those of the former Soviet Union, have ensured that the flora of the region is constantly springing new surprises on the gardeners of Europe and America. The botanists and collectors of the nineteenth century laid the foundations of our knowledge of this region's flora. Only when it was easier and more profitable for collectors to travel to the Himalaya and China, in the early twentieth century, was Western and Central Asia left largely unexplored. Luckily for us, a new band of plant collectors appeared after the Second World War and headed east to continue the traditions of those earlier explorers. Today, some countries, such as Iraq and Afghanistan, are obviously off limits for plant collectors but this extensive and varied region has more than enough to offer the modern plant hunter.

ABOVE
A hybrid between *Dionysia curviflora* and *D. tapetodes*, nestling between sandstone rocks at Kew

Bibliography and references

Bezzant, L. (1992). *Crocus baytopiorum. J. Scott. Rock Gard. Club* 22: 422.

Bittrich, V. (1993). *Silene* L. In: *The Families and Genera of Vascular Plants*, vol. 2, ed. K. Kubitzki *et al.*, p. 233. Springer-Verlag, Berlin, Heidelberg.

Coats, A. M. (1969). *The Quest for Plants*. Studio Vista, London.

Damboldt, J. (1976). Materials for a Flora of Turkey XXXII: Campanulaceae. *Notes Roy. Bot. Gard. Edinburgh* 35: 39–52.

Damboldt, J. (1978). *Campanula* L. In: *Flora of Turkey and the East Aegean Islands*, vol. 6, ed. P. H. Davis, pp. 2–64. Edinburgh University Press, Edinburgh.

Davis, A. P. (1999). *The Genus Galanthus*. Timber Press, Portland.

Edmondson, J. R. & Lack, H. W. (1977). The Turkish and Caucasian Collections of C. Koch 1: Turkey. *Notes Roy. Bot. Gard. Edinburgh* 35: 321–344.

Ekim, T. & Güner, A. (2000). The floristic richness of Turkey. *Curtis's Bot. Mag.* 17: 48–59.

Furse, P. (1968). *Iris* in Turkey, Iran and Afghanistan. In: *The Iris Year Book 1968*, pp. 61–73. British Iris Society.

Furse, P. & Furse, P. (1969). Flora of the Hindu Kush. *Quart. Bull. Alpine Gard. Soc. Gr. Brit.* 37: 283–298.

Grey-Wilson, C. (1974). Some alpines of the Central Hindu Kush. *Quart. Bull. Alpine Gard. Soc. Gr. Brit.* 42: 61–67.

Grey-Wilson, C. (1989). *The Genus Dionysia*. Alpine Garden Society, Woking, Surrey.

Grey-Wilson, C. (2002). *Cyclamen, a Guide for Gardeners, Horticulturists and Botanists* (new edition). B. T. Batsford Ltd., London.

Grey-Wilson, C. & Wilford, R. (1998). *Cyclamen colchicum. Curtis's Bot. Mag.* 15: t. 347.

Hedge, I. C. & Wendelbo, P. (1970). Some remarks on endemism in Afghanistan. *Israel J. Bot.* 19: 401–417.

Holubec, V. & Kfiivka, P. (2006). *The Caucasus and its Flowers*. Loxia, Prague.

Lehmann, J. G. C. (1817). *Monographia generis Primularum*. Leipzig.

Lidén, M. (2007). The genus *Dionysia* (Primulaceae), a synopsis and five new species. *Willldenowia* 37: 37–61.

Lidén, M. & Zetterlund, H. (1997). *Corydalis, a Gardener's Guide and a Monograph of the Tuberous Species*. AGS Publications Ltd., Pershore.

Lièvre, A. le. (1994). A view of Edmond Boissier. *Curtis's Bot. Mag.* 11: 131–143.

Lindley, J. (1846). *Silene schafta. Bot. Reg.* 32: t. 20.

Mathew, B. (1982). *The Crocus: a Revision of the Genus Crocus*. B. T. Batsford Ltd., London.

Mathew, B. (1989). *The Iris* (second edition). B. T. Batsford Ltd., London.

Mathew, B. (1996). *Fritillaria chitralensis. Curtis's Bot. Mag.* 13: t. 288.

Mathew, B. (1998). *Crocus kerndorffiorum. Curtis's Bot. Mag.* 15: t. 342.

Mathew, B. (1999). Reticulate irises. *Quart. Bull. Alpine Gard. Soc. Gr. Brit.* 67: 299–306.

Mathew, B., Petersen, G. & Seberg, O. (2009). A reassessment of *Crocus* based on molecular analysis. *Plantsman* 8: 50–57.

Mathew, B. & Wilford, R. (2001). *Tulipa regelii. Curtis's Bot. Mag.* 18: t. 406

Meikle, D. (1994). Boissier, floras and types: some observations. *Curtis's Bot. Mag.* 11: 143–146.

Özhatay, N., Page, M. & Sinnott, M. (2000). *Paeonia turcica. Curtis's Bot. Mag.* 17: t. 390.

Parsa, A. (1978). *Flora of Iran*. Ministry of Science and Higher Education, Iran.

Phillips, R. & Rix, M. (1989). *Bulbs*. Pan Books Ltd., London.

Regel, E. A. (1881). *Leontice albertii. Gartenflora* 30: 293, t. 1057.

Rix, M. (1994). *Fritillaria*. In: *Alpine Garden Society Encyclopaedia of Alpines*, vol. 1, ed. K. Beckett, pp. 489–505. AGS Publications Ltd., Pershore.

Rix, M. (2000). *Fritillaria uva-vulpis. Curtis's Bot. Mag.* 17: t. 392.

Rix, M. (2007a). *Fritillaria karelinii. Curtis's Bot. Mag.* 24: t. 580.

Rix, M. (2007b). *Fritillaria gibbosa. Curtis's Bot. Mag.* 24: t. 581.

Rolfe, R. (2000). Plant Awards 1998–1999. *Quart. Bull. Alpine Gard. Soc. Gr. Brit.* 68: 202–203.

Schiman-Czeika, H. (1967). *Gentiana*. In: *Flora Iranica*, part 41, ed. K. H. Rechinger, pp. 8–22. Akademische Druck und Verlagsanstalt, Graz, Austria.

Stearn, W. T. (2002). *The Genus Epimedium and other herbaceous Berberidaceae*. Royal Botanic Gardens, Kew.

Stearn, W. T. & Webb, D. A. (1964). *Gymnospermium* Spach. In: *Flora Europaea*, vol. 1, ed. T. G. Tutin *et al.* Cambridge University Press, Cambridge.

Wendelbo, P. (1961). *Studies in Primulaceae. 1. A Monograph of the Genus Dionysia*. Norwegian University Press, Bergen and Oslo.

Wilford, R. (2006). *Tulips; Species and Hybrids for the Gardener*. Timber Press, Portland.

Asphodelus acaulis

Rhodanthemum catananche

Delosperma kofleri

Dietes bicolor

Ixia rapunculoides

Mediterranean Sea

Cape
Blanc

Tangier • **Algiers**
Rif Mts • Tell Atlas • **Tunis**
Rabat •
Middle Atlas
Marrakesh • High Atlas • Saharan Atlas • **Tripoli**
Essaouira •
Jebel Toubkal • Akhdar
Anti Atlas • Mts

MOROCCO • ALGERIA

TUNISIA

Cairo

LIBYA

EGYPT

S a h a r a   D e s e r t

Nile

Al Miska
Mts

ETHIOPIA

KENYA

SOMALIA

Congo

⛰ Mt Kenya

⛰ Mt Kilimanjaro

TANZANIA

Indian
Ocean

Atlantic Ocean

MOZAMBIQUE

MADAGASCAR

N

NAMIBIA

Kalahari
Desert

SOUTH
AFRICA

Johannesburg
•

Thabana
Ntlenyana ⛰
Drakensberg
Mts

Cape Fold
Mts

Cape Town
•

Port Elizabeth
•

Mossel Bay
•

Cape
Agulhas

Chapter 10 **Africa**

The road that joins the Spanish port of Algeciras to the resort town of Tarifa winds through the wooded hills at the southern tip of the Iberian Peninsula. Occasionally, the Straits of Gibraltar, where the Atlantic Ocean meets the Mediterranean, can be seen through the trees but it is the mountains of Morocco that catch your eye, looming on the horizon. This is where Europe comes closest to the vast landmass of Africa; less than 10 miles from Spain is another continent.

Africa covers an area of 30,330,000 square kilometres (11,699,000 sq miles). It spans the equator from Cape Blanc in Tunisia in the north to Cape Agulhas in South Africa at the southern tip. Both these extremes are in mediterranean climate areas, but in between are vast deserts, dense jungles and open savannas, famed for their rich wildlife and stunning scenery. The Sahara Desert is by far the largest in the world, covering a massive 9 million sq. km (3,500,000 sq. miles). The highest point in Africa is Mt Kilimanjaro in Tanzania, which reaches 5,895 m (19,340 ft). This snow covered peak is only 330 km (205 miles) from the equator.

The high mountains near the equator, such as Mt Kilimanjaro and Mt Kenya, have an unusual and distinctive flora, including the remarkable giant groundsels (*Dendrosenecio*) and giant lobelias. Like the plants that grow near the equator in the Andes, the species found in Africa's equatorial mountains are adapted to intense sunlight and high temperatures during the day but, due to the high altitude, very low temperatures at night. These conditions prevail throughout the year without the seasonal changes associated with more temperate climates. Not surprisingly, these 'summer every day and winter every night' conditions are difficult to recreate and there has been limited success in cultivating equatorial alpines. The vast majority of African alpines in cultivation originate in the northern and southern extremes of the continent.

LEFT
South Africa's Table Mountain, surrounded by Cape Town, is at the heart of the Cape Floral Kingdom.

The mediterranean climate regions in the north and south of Africa are both rich in geophytes. The Cape Floral Kingdom of South Africa is one of the world's six floral kingdoms, with around 9,000 species growing in an area of only 90,000 sq km or 0.04% of the earth's land surface (Manning *et al.*, 2002). Some of the bulbs and corms that are found there are well known, such as *Gladiolus* and *Nerine*, but many others are little known outside South Africa, despite 400 years of exploration by European naturalists and horticulturists.

Between the Sahara and the Mediterranean Sea in north-west Africa are the Atlas Mountains. These embrace a series of ranges running roughly parallel to the coast from the Atlantic shores of south-west Morocco to northern Tunisia. The highest of these ranges is the High Atlas or Haut Atlas of central Morocco, which peak at Jebel Toubkal, which at 4,167 m (13,671 feet) is the highest point in northern Africa. North of the High Atlas are the Middle or Moyen Atlas, with peaks rising to over 3,000 m (9,843 feet) and north-facing slopes clothed with cedar forests. South of the High Atlas, on the edge of the Sahara, are the hot, dry mountains of the Anti Atlas. In northern Morocco, south-east of Tangiers, are the Rif Mountains, which reach around 2,500 m (8,202 feet). This mostly limestone range is an extension of the mountains of southern Spain. In Algeria, the Atlas Mountains are split into two main ranges, the Tell Atlas

along the coast and the Saharan Atlas further inland. They meet in north-west Algeria to form the Aurès Mountains, which extend into Tunisia.

There are many similarities in the natural vegetation of southern Europe and North Africa, as might be expected given the shared climate. Even if a genus is present in both regions, however, there are often certain species or subspecies (and sometimes unusual colour forms) that are unique to North Africa. As a result of the high mountains, the flat, fertile valleys, the influence of the Atlantic Ocean and the Mediterranean Sea, and the proximity of the Sahara Desert, Morocco has a diverse range of habitats and consequently the largest and richest flora in North Africa. Around 20% of Morocco's flora is endemic, and there are interesting and unusual plants to be found in the other countries along Africa's northern coast.

North Africa's flora, from the Mediterranean to the mountains

The mediterranean climate region of North Africa mainly covers the coastal portions of Morocco, Algeria and Tunisia, the countries that form the region known as the Maghreb. The Mediterranean coasts of Libya and Egypt are much drier, with the dry season lasting over seven months in most parts and an annual precipitation of less than 250 mm (9.8 inches) (Dallman, 1998). The exception here is the Akhdar Mountains and the adjacent coastline, in the Cyrenaica region of north-east Libya, which are home to such plants as *Arum cyrenaicum*, *Narcissus elegans* and *Cyclamen rohlfsianum*.

Three species of *Cyclamen* are found in the Mediterranean region of North Africa. *Cyclamen rohlfsianum* is endemic to Libya and *C. africanum* grows in Algeria and Tunisia. The third species, *C. persicum*, is mainly a plant of the eastern Mediterranean but can also be found in Algeria and Tunisia, where it may have been introduced by man because it seems to be associated with monasteries and cemeteries (Grey-Wilson, 2002). All three are among the least hardy cyclamen and are best grown in a cool but frost-free glasshouse and allowed to dry off completely in the summer, although they may survive outside in sheltered positions in the mildest parts of Britain.

Cyclamen africanum is closest to the commonly grown and completely hardy, European *C. hederifolium*; both belong to series *Purpurascens* of subgenus *Cyclamen* in Grey-Wilson's classification (Grey-Wilson, 2002). Although variable, *C. africanum* is generally the larger plant, with wide, heart-shaped, glossy leaves that can reach 10 cm across and are held on erect or ascending petioles. The pale to deep pink flowers appear in autumn, usually before the leaves, and have distinct auricles around the mouth. They

LEFT
Arum cyrenaicum was once considered endemic to Libya but has also been found in SW Crete.

are held on erect pedicels that can reach 22 cm in length. This species grows in scrub and rocky gullies in north-east Algeria and north-west Tunisia.

Cyclamen rohlfsianum is a distinctive species found in a small area of north-east Libya, between Benghazi and Derna. Grey-Wilson placed this species in its own series within subgenus *Cyclamen*: series *Rohlfsianum*. It is unique among cyclamen in having a cone of anthers protruding from the mouth of the flower. Like those of *C. africanum*, the leaves can be more than 10 cm wide but they are round to kidney-shaped and have 5–9 broad triangular lobes. They arise from an irregular, knobbly tuber and are often attractively marked with grey-green or silvery patterns on the dark green background. The flowers appear in autumn, as the leaves are unfurling, and they are pink with a darker zone at the mouth and small auricles.

The mediterranean climate region used to extend much further south, and in Somalia an isolated flora exists that has similarities to that of the Mediterranean basin further north. Here is another African cyclamen, only discovered in 1986 and formally described three years later. This rare species was named *Cyclamen somalense* by Mats Thulin and Ahmed Mumin Warfa, who found it at an altitude of 1,250–1,600 m (4,101–5,249 feet) in the Al Miskat

Mountains, in Somalia's Bari region at the tip of the Horn of Africa. Growing at around 11°N of the equator, this species is separated from its nearest relative, *C. persicum*, by more than 2,500 km (1,553 miles). *Cyclamen somalense* is very like *C. persicum* and is placed in subgenus *Persicum*, but it grows from a smaller tuber, the leaves are wider than long and have coarsely toothed margins, and the flowers are small with corolla lobes to only 1.5 cm long. Also, the flowers are

ABOVE
Cyclamen rohlfsianum.

THE MESSINIAN EVENT

Around six million years ago, the Strait of Gibraltar closed up, cutting off the Mediterranean Sea from the Atlantic. This is known as the Messinian Event, named after the Messinian stage of the Miocene epoch. As the sea gradually evaporated, a hot, salty wasteland would have remained, at some points up to 4.9 km (3 miles) below the world sea level. Today, Death Valley in California is probably the closest you will find to the conditions that then existed in the dried-up Mediterranean Basin. Although the environment over much of the basin was largely unsuitable for plant life, there would probably have been certain areas where the vegetation could spread from one continent to the other. Such areas are especially likely where the distances involved were not too great, for example, across the Strait of Gibraltar or between present-day Tunisia and Sicily. Geological evidence suggests that there were several cycles of the Mediterranean Sea drying up and refilling, but eventually the Strait of Gibraltar opened up permanently, flooding the basin around the beginning of the Pliocene epoch, 5.3 million years ago.

Death Valley, California, appears much like the Mediterranean Basin must have looked 6 million years ago.

Iris unguicularis

Iris unguicularis is widely cultivated for its early blooms that generally appear from January to April but can open as early as November. It grows from thin, tough rhizomes with wiry roots and forms dense clumps of linear, evergreen leaves. The flowers are generally lavender-blue, but the falls are white towards their base and this area is patterned with dark veins and a yellow median stripe. These sweet-scented flowers are almost stemless but are held above the leaves by an elongated perianth tube that can reach over 20 cm long.

This iris was described by M. L'Abbé Poiret in *Voyage en Barbarie*, an account of his travels in North Africa that was published in 1789. The name *unguicularis* means 'furnished with a claw' and refers to the long, narrow base of the perianth segments.

For many years, this species was known as *Iris stylosa*, a name given to it by René Louiche Desfontaines in 1798, but the earlier published name of *I. unguicularis* takes precedence. It grows in the Mediterranean regions of North Africa, south-east Europe and western Asia, in dry meadows and rocky places and it varies across its range. On Crete, there are forms with particularly narrow leaves and smaller flowers, which were named *I. cretensis* in 1867. This form is now treated as subsp. *cretensis*. The African plants are subsp. *unguicularis*, and the remaining plants, which occur from Greece to Turkey, Syria and Lebanon, constitute subsp. *carica* (Davis & Jury, 1990).

The plants that occur in Algeria, Tunisia and possibly Morocco are more robust than other forms of *Iris unguicularis*. They can be regarded as 'typical' of the species and this is the form most commonly grown in gardens. They are tolerant of a range of conditions but the soil should be neutral to alkaline and never waterlogged. Good drainage and a hot, sunny position are preferable; it will grow in light-dappled shade but flowering may be poor. All forms of *I. unguicularis* can survive several degrees of frost but they may be damaged if temperatures fall below -8 or -9°C.

Several named forms are available. They include the creamy-white 'Alba', the violet-blue 'Mary Barnard' and the large-flowered, pale lavender-blue 'Walter Butt'. They can be increased easily by division in autumn and replanted with the rhizome near but not at the surface.

FAR LEFT
Iris unguicularis 'Speciosa'.

LEFT
The Cretan *Iris unguicularis* subp. *cretensis*

held on short pedicels and not well above the foliage as they are in *C. persicum*. The existence of this species, and its associated mediterranean-type vegetation, so far south indicates that the Mediterranean region was once far more extensive. Gradually, the arid Sahara pushed north squeezing the mediterranean vegetation into a relatively narrow band along the North African coast and leaving this disjunct flora in the hills of north-east Somalia.

Cyclamen is just one of the genera found in both southern Europe and North Africa. The intermingling of floras has been aided in the past by the Mediterranean Sea periodically drying up, easing the passage of species between Africa, Europe and western Asia. Elements of the African flora that have spread into Europe include the genera *Romulea* and *Androcymbium*. Both are at their most diverse in southern Africa but have representatives in North Africa and southern Europe. *Romulea bulbocodium* is the most widespread northern species in the genus and can be found throughout the Mediterranean region. Although it has funnel-shaped flowers similar to those of *Crocus*, which is in the same family (Iridaceae), *Romulea* can be distinguished mainly by the pedicels (flower stalks) that hold the flowers above the ground. *Romulea bulbocodium* produces white to lilac or violet flowers in early spring but they need some warmth and sunshine to open wide. It makes an attractive rock garden plant.

Androcymbium is in the same family as *Colchicum* (Colchicaceae) and is represented in North Africa, from Morocco to Egypt, by *A. gramineum*. This species is also

found in southern Spain, where it has a narrow distribution near Almeria. It flowers in winter, displaying white blooms, often marked with pink streaks towards the centre, nestling at ground level among narrow lanceolate leaves. In Morocco, it grows from the coast inland to the lower slopes of the High Atlas Mountains. Another example of the African flora spreading into Europe is the occurrence of predominantly African species, such as the yellow-flowered, woody-stemmed *Viola scorpiuroides*, on the island of Crete. Populations of *Arum cyrenaicum*, once thought to be endemic to Libya, occur in south-west Crete.

ABOVE
Romulea bulbocodium.

BELOW LEFT
Androcymbium gramineum in cultivation at Kew.

BELOW RIGHT
Viola scorpiuroides grows in both Crete and North Africa.

Narcissus cantabricus
Family: Amaryllidaceae

Augustin de Candolle described *Narcissus cantabricus* in Volume 8 of Redouté's *Liliacées* in 1815. He placed it in section *Bulbocodii*, along with six other species. The plants in this section have been interpreted in various ways, even being classified in their own genus, *Corbularia*. In the account of *Narcissus* for *Flore de L'Afrique du Nord*, Dr René Maire (1959) treats all the North African forms as subspecies or varieties of *N. bulbocodium*.

In a revision of *Narcissus*, Professor Fernandes (1968) from the Botanical Institute at the University of Coimbra, Portugal, recognised five species of bulbocodiums. All the white-flowered plants, apart from *N. bulbocodium* var. *graellsii* and *N. romieuxii* subsp. *albidus*, are treated as forms of *N. cantabricus*. Fernandes divides *N. cantabricus* into three subspecies: subsp. *cantabricus*, subsp. *tananicus* and subsp. *monophyllus*, with subsp. *cantabricus* further divided into four varieties.

The white flowers of *Narcissus cantabricus* are produced in winter, from as early as November through to February or March. They have inflated coronas and perianth tubes, with a slight constriction where the perianth segments join, and they are 2.8–4.5 cm across and held on stems of 3–10 cm tall. The anthers, which produce yellow pollen, do not usually protrude from the corona and the style and filaments are white. The one or more leaves are long and narrow, only 1–2 mm wide. In the wild, this species is found in the hills and mountains of Morocco, Algeria, the Balearic Islands and the extreme south of Spain. It grows on grassy slopes and at the edges of woodland, often on limestone. One of the most beautiful forms, var. *petunioides*, has a widely expanded corona with the margin rolled outwards.

The painting reproduced here, prepared for *Curtis's Botanical Magazine* in 1870, shows *Narcissus cantabricus* subsp. *monophyllus*. The single, thread-like leaves are only 1 mm wide but up to 27 cm long. The flowers are up to 4.5 cm wide and the perianth segments are about the same length as the corona. It grows naturally in Morocco and the sierras of southernmost Spain.

Although many of the early-flowering daffodils can be grown in the open garden, the bulbs of *Narcissus cantabricus* must be protected from rain when they are dormant. It is a fairly hardy species that is untouched by temperatures of -10°C, so a well-ventilated cold frame in full sun is ideal. The frame lights should be left open as much as possible when the plants are in growth; only close them during bouts of heavy rain, snow or frost. Bulbs can be repotted in late summer, allowing an opportunity to inspect for pests and diseases, such as basal rot and

Narcissus Fly, and to provide fresh soil. They should be replanted in a gritty, loam-based soil mix. Low-nitrogen, high-potash feed should be given with each watering as the roots often spiral round the base of the pot and need to be supplied with plenty of nutrients. *Narcissus* bulbs will produce offsets, but the best method of propagation is from seed. *Narcissus cantabricus* will take around four years to reach flowering size.

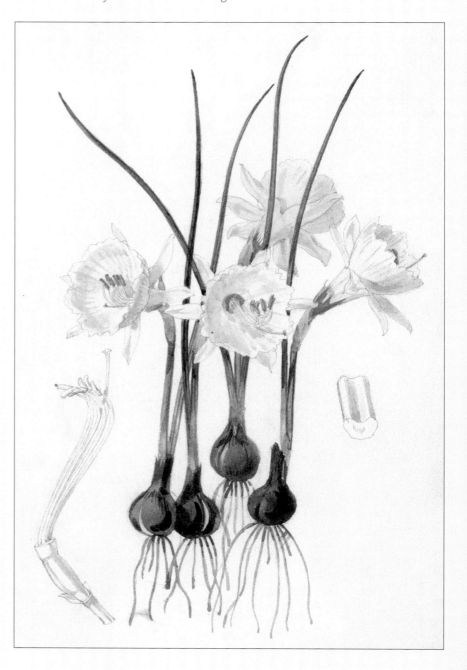

Curtis's Botanical Magazine, plate 5831 (1870). Artist: Walter Hood Fitch.

European plants have also spread south into Africa. Several saxifrages have outlying populations in North Africa, with their main centre of distribution in Europe. Out of the 18 species of African *Saxifraga*, ten are essentially European (Webb & Gornall, 1989). One example is *S. longifolia*. This silver saxifrage chiefly occurs in the Pyrenees, eastern Spain and very locally in south-east Spain, in the mountains above Alicante. The French naturalist Philippe Picot de Lapeyrouse described it in 1801 on the basis of a Pyrenean plant. The solitary rosettes are symmetrical and composed of leaves up to 10 cm long. The inflorescence is a stout panicle of white, occasionally red-spotted flowers that branches from the base and can reach 60 cm tall. The typical form of this species also grows in the Middle Atlas of Morocco, but in the High Atlas it is represented by *S. longifolia* subsp. *gaussenii*, which grows on north-facing cliffs at altitudes of 2,800–3,500 m (9,186–11,483 feet). This subspecies differs mainly in having spathulate rather than linear leaves that are broader at the apex than those of subsp. *longifolia* (Bland, 2000).

Saxifraga pedemontana is a mainly European species in section *Saxifraga* that also has a Moroccan representative. *Saxifraga pedemontana* subsp. *demnatensis* grows in the Middle and High Atlas up to 3,900 m. It is similar to subsp. *cervicornis*, which is found on Corsica and Sardinia, but has larger, more leathery leaves and shorter sepals.

Asphodelus is a genus of Mediterranean plants usually characterised by their tall flower stems, which hold racemes or panicles of starry, white or pale pink flowers. In the hills and mountains of north-west Africa grows *A. acaulis*, which has a very short peduncle so the flowers are held near ground level, peering out from a rosette of long, narrow leaves. These flowers appear in late winter and early spring and are pale to rose pink, and each of the six perianth segments has a narrow, green keel.

In the wild, this species often grows in heavy, red clay soil over limestone (*terra rossa*), which bakes hard in the hot summer sun. Plants are found among stones in fields and forest clearings or growing out of cracks in rocks. By the summer, the leaves have died down and the plant survives underground, sustained by its fleshy roots. Growth begins again with the onset of autumn rains. The hollow, linear leaves can grow to 30 cm long but are only 3 or 4 mm wide. They are usually pressed close to the ground, leaving the flowers free to open wide in the sun.

Asphodelus acaulis was described from Algerian specimens by René Louiche Desfontaines in 1798, in *Flora Atlantica*. In the twentieth century, Dr René Maire (1958) found it in Morocco, listing several locations for it in the Rif Mountains and the Middle and High Atlas. It also occurs in Tunisia.

This species remained rare in cultivation until plants were brought back to England from Morocco by Mrs Robert Lukin in 1935 (Boothman, 1966). It can be grown in the open if planted in a free-draining soil and in full sun. If the soil is too rich, however, masses of upright leaves will be produced and plants grown like this have been likened to a bunch of chives. The pink-flushed blooms clustered in the centre of the rosette will open wide only on sunny days. In the wild, the leaves of *Asphodelus acaulis* die back completely, but in cultivation, it is not uncommon for a few leaves to remain throughout the year.

The genus *Narcissus* has its centre of diversity in the Iberian Peninsula, but species can be found all around the Mediterranean and there is a varied selection, particularly of section *Bulbocodii*, in North Africa. Daffodils that belong to this section, often referred to as 'bulbocodiums' or 'hoop petticoats', are easy to recognise. The corona, which is an extension of the perianth tube that forms the central, cylindrical or cup-shaped part of the flower, is a feature of all *Narcissus* species. In the bulbocodiums, however, it is particularly large and showy and the 'petals' or perianth

BELOW
Asphodelus acaulis.

lobes are small, narrow and sometimes almost insignificant. Among the other characteristics of the bulbocodiums are the anthers fixed at right angles to the filaments and the upward-curving style (Blanchard, 1990). The species in this section are found in south-west Europe from southern France to Spain and Portugal as well as in Morocco and Algeria.

North Africa is also home to some interesting autumn-flowering *Narcissus* species, including *N. serotinus*, *N. elegans* and the unusual green-flowered *N. viridiflorus*. These all occur in Europe too, but another autumnal species, *N. broussonetii*, is endemic to Morocco. This white, multi-flowered daffodil was named in 1815 in honour of the French naturalist Pierre Marie Broussonet. It grows near the coast of western Morocco and inland, as far south as the Anti Atlas. Apart from *N. canariensis*, on the Canary Islands, this is the most southerly *Narcissus*. It is similar in general appearance to *N. papyraceus*, the 'paper white', but it is distinguished by the almost non-existent corona with bright yellow, exerted anthers. In cultivation, it needs frost-free conditions.

Broussonet spent time in Morocco during the last decade of the eighteenth century, exploring around Mogador (Essaouira) and Tangiers and reaching inland as far as Fes. He was one of many European naturalists to explore North Africa in the eighteenth and nineteenth centuries. Nevertheless, in 1871 when Joseph Hooker, then Director of the Royal Botanic Gardens, Kew, travelled to Morocco, much of the country, especially the interior, was still little known. Maps were unreliable and the High Atlas had yet to be ascended by a European. Although the major ports were open to foreigners, it was difficult to gain permission to enter many of the territories inland. Much of the mountainous region was inhabited by independent tribes, who could be hostile to strangers (Ball, 1877).

JOSEPH HOOKER IN MOROCCO

Hooker, through the influence of the English Government, was able to visit Morocco and the Atlas Mountains, exploring around Tangiers and Tétouan before sailing to Essaouira and travelling inland to Marrakech and the slopes of the High Atlas. He travelled between April and June 1871 with the botanist George Maw and a family friend, the senior civil servant and amateur botanist John Ball. The party received valuable information from the French botanist Ernest Cosson, who had a detailed knowledge of the North African flora and who in 1867 had helped the botanical traveller Benedict Balansa obtain permission to travel inland from Essaouira.

Balansa was impeded at every turn, and after a fortnight had to abandon his journey and return to Essaouira, although he was able to collect a large number of

interesting specimens. Hooker was to experience a similar problem, with the guide refusing to allow the party to climb the mountains south of Marrakech, but his determination and the cooperation of a Berber Sheik, allowed them to at least reach the snow. They negotiated an overnight stay in the village of Arround, near the foot of Jebel Toubkal, and on 15 May they began to climb. The Sheik instructed the guides not to let the party climb beyond a stone hut below the pass of Tagherot, but the three English botanists were able to shake off their escorts by asking them to build a fire while they looked for plants. With the guides distracted, they started off up the track. The guides soon realised their intent and tried to persuade them down. John Ball (1877) wrote: "We were overtaken by our guides, who used every means of threat and entreaty to induce us to return: for a time, we silenced them by some silver coins; but they were in a pitiable state as we approached the summit".

Unfortunately, the weather deteriorated and the hunt for plants had to be abandoned in the face of strong winds carrying sleet and snow. George Maw was the only one to reach the crest of the ridge at around 3,500 m (11,483 feet) but he could see little. Only then did the party turn back. A few days later, on 23 May, Hooker and Ball were able to ascend Jebel Tezah (3,649 m), and were rewarded with a view across the Sous Valley to the Anti Atlas.

Hooker and his companions collected few true alpines on their exploration of Morocco because many of the high mountains were still covered in snow, but the valleys, slopes and foothills provided a wealth of plants. One of the most colourful sights was a purple *Linaria* found growing in corn fields at the foot of the High Atlas. The following year, this is was named *Linaria maroccana* by Hooker in *Curtis's Botanical Magazine*. A houseleek was collected in the High Atlas and initially thought to be a form of the variable European species *Sempervivum tectorum*. It flowered at Kew in 1873, and in 1878 Ball described it as a new species, *S. atlanticum*. It is the only African representative of the genus.

One of the most beautiful plants seen near Arround was *Rhodanthemum catananche*, which is endemic to Morocco. The genus *Rhodanthemum* is a group of around 15 species of mostly North African mountain plants, which often form mats at high altitudes. One species, *R. arundanum*, occurs in Spain. The plant Hooker, Maw and Ball found was originally named *Chrysanthemum catananche*, and was seen forming sizable patches of silvery green foliage in rocky valleys and on sunny slopes, at altitudes of 2,100–2,700 m (6,890–8,858 feet) (Hooker, 1874). The solitary flower heads reach 4 or 5 cm across and have pale yellow ray florets that are deep red at their base and purplish on the back. The involucral bracts

are silvery-white and translucent. It is a handsome plant that can be grown in the open garden, given a sunny position and good drainage.

Growing on the lower slopes of the High Atlas, on rocky slopes, screes and river shingle and in forest clearings, at altitudes of 600–2,400 m (1,969–7,874 feet) was *Salvia taraxacifolia*. This unusual sage was discovered by Balansa in 1867, at an altitude of 1,000 m (3,281 feet) on Moulaï Ibrahim (Cosson, 1875). Cosson chose the name *taraxacifolia* because the leaves resemble those of the dandelion (*Taraxacum officinale*). Hooker also collected specimens and featured this plant in *Curtis's Botanical Magazine* in 1872, before Cosson had formerly described it.

Salvia taraxacifolia is only found naturally in south-west Morocco and appears to be a distinct relict species, occupying an isolated position within the genus. Hooker noted that it had no close allies but placed it in section *Eusphace*, which also includes the common sage, *S. officinalis*. The grey-green, hairy leaves of *S. taraxacifolia* are pinnately lobed, often with a large, rounded terminal lobe and their undersides are densely covered in woolly hairs, giving them an almost white appearance. The hairy stems can reach 45 cm tall and hold up to 9 whorls of 6–12 flowers. The flowers are up to 3 cm long and are produced from late spring to summer and sometimes into autumn if in a sheltered position. They come in shades of pink or white with yellow and purplish markings, and make an attractive combination with the grey-green leaves. *Salvia taraxacifolia* will survive several degrees of frost but is best grown in a well-ventilated cold frame or alpine house, to protect it from too much moisture in the autumn and winter.

ABOVE
Salvia taraxacifolia.

BELOW LEFT
Rhodanthemum catananche.

The collections made by Hooker, Maw and Ball on their Moroccan trip were an important contribution to the understanding of the flora of the Atlas Mountains. In the twentieth century, the French botanist Dr René Maire, based at the University of Algiers, worked on the *Flora de L'Afrique du Nord* but Morocco still has no complete Flora of its own and the Atlas Mountains are relatively little visited by botanical travellers. However, the situation is changing and in 1999 the first volume of a new flora of Morocco written by Moroccan botanists, *Flore Pratique du Maroc*, was published. The second volume appeared in 2007 and three volumes in all are planned.

South Africa

At the opposite end of the African continent from Morocco, a Mediterranean-type climate also occurs, in a narrow band along the coast of the Western Cape of South Africa. Centred on Cape Town, this climate region encompasses the Cape Floral Kingdom, where the plants have diversified to a massive extent, resulting in thousands of species that make up an astonishing ten percent of the world's flora, with around 70% of the species being endemic. This mediterranean climate region stretches from Port Elizabeth in the east, to Cape Town at the south-west tip of South Africa. It then reaches northwards along the Atlantic coast, also known as West Coast, as far as the Bokkeveld escarpment, to form a crescent-shaped zone that only reaches inland for about 125 km (75 miles). Inland from the west coast the mountain ranges, such as the Cedarberg,

Roggeveld and Bokkeveld, run north-south but east of Cape Town the ranges, such as the Langeberg and Outeniqua Mountains, run east-west. These are the Cape Fold Mountains, composed largely of Table Mountain sandstone and to a lesser extent quartzite, and they average around 1000 to 1500 m altitude with some peaks reaching over 2,000 m. Between these ranges are more fertile agricultural valleys, famed for their fruit and wine. Near Cape Town itself are the Hottentots Holland Mountains, which have the greatest diversity of plant species in South Africa (Dallman, 1998).

The climate of the south-western Cape is one of mild winters and warm summers. Temperatures average between 7 and 15°C in winter and 15 to 25°C in summer but can exceed 30°C in the inland valleys. Frosts are rare, especially along the coast but snow can fall on the mountains. The predominant vegetation in this region is called fynbos and here is where plant diversity in South Africa reaches its peak.

Cape fynbos is characterised by leathery-leaved, evergreen shrubs, including proteas and ericas, that reach around 1 to 3 m tall, with occasional taller plants but virtually no trees. Between these shrubs are tough, grass-like restios and plenty of bulbs (Manning, 2007). The area around the small town of Nieuwoudtville, on top of the Bokkeveld escarpment, has been called the bulb capital of the world, where approximately half of the species are bulbous. Fynbos vegetation mostly occurs on nutrient poor, acid soils and is reliant on regular fires to maintain the diversity of species. Without fire the flora would become

BELOW
The Franschhoek Valley, in the Hottentots Holland Mountains, is famed for its vineyards.

dominated by trees. Fire also recycles nutrients, which is vital for growth on the poor soils that fynbos colonises. Many species regenerate from seed and there is often a flush of luxuriant growth that takes advantage of the increased light levels and supply of nutrients after a fire. They include annuals and short-lived perennials whose seeds only germinate after being subjected to chemicals found in smoke. Geophytes escape fire by surviving underground as storage organs but the flush of new nutrients in the weeks after a burn promotes flowering in some species that otherwise may rarely flower, normally only growing leaves each year as they are swamped by surrounding vegetation. The clearance of plant cover and the infusion of fresh nutrients, leads to a combination of flowering annuals and bulbs that create a beautiful sight on the scorched ground in the months after a fire.

The Kogelburg Biosphere Reserve, a southern extension of the Hottentots Holland Mountains along the coast to the east of Cape Town, is at the heart of fynbos plant diversity. The slopes of the mountains in this reserve plunge steeply into the sea at the southern tip of Africa and are home to around 1,650 species of which 77 are endemic to the area. South African botanist Dr John Manning describes the relatively moist Kogelburg Mountains as a botanical ark, providing a refuge for ancient species from times when the climate of the Cape was wetter and less seasonal. These

have now died out from mountains further inland where periods of drought are more pronounced (Manning, 2004). Among these relict plants are the only shrubby genera of the *Iris* family and some of the rarest members of the *Protea* family (Proteaceae).

The fynbos vegetation of Western Cape reaches high up the slopes and there is no true alpine zone in the Cape Fold Mountains. However, the plants do experience sub zero temperatures at higher altitudes. The Roggeveld escarpment is one of the coldest parts of South Africa and winter frost and snow is normal, although precipitation is low, reaching only 250 mm on the escarpment itself. Elsewhere in the Cape Fold Mountains there are plenty of rocky crags and crevices to provide the kind of hostile conditions to which alpine plants have become adapted. The species found in these mountains have great potential as garden and alpine house plants.

The region around Cape Town receives very little summer rain but travel east, towards Mossel Bay and beyond to Port Elizabeth, and summer rainfall increases. On the eastern side of South Africa, including Eastern Cape, Kwazulu Natal, Lesotho and the Drakensberg Mountains, rain mostly falls in the summer months. The Drakensberg is the highest mountain range in southern Africa, reaching 3,482 m (11,420 feet) on Thabana Ntlenyana. This escarpment faces east, with dramatic, dark cliffs of black basalt overlying softer-coloured sandstones and shales. Rainfall can reach 2000 mm annually on the escarpment and mostly falls as summer storms. Above an altitude of 1800 m in the high Drakensburg of KwaZulu-Natal is the Drakensberg

LEFT
Moraea ramosissima, in Iridaceae, a fynbos species that only flowers after fire

BELOW
The mountains of Kogelburg Biosphere Reserve, as seen from Harold Porter Botanical Garden

Alpine Centre, home to over 2000 species, of which nearly 400 are endemic (Manning, 2004). Plants from this region include the autumn-flowering amaryllid, *Nerine bowdenii*, the alpine yellow-worts, *Sebaea natalensis* and *S. thomasii* (Gentianaceae), Christmas bells, *Sandersonia aurantiaca* (Colchicaceae), as well as species of *Diascia*, *Glumicalyx* and *Zaluzianskya*, all in Scrophulariaceae.

Plants such as these, from the eastern side of South Africa, will need very different conditions in cultivation to those from Western Cape. Being used to wet summers and rainfall possible all year round, some of these plant are easier to grow in the open garden as they do not need a dry summer rest. Although the eastern half of South Africa has fewer species than the Western Cape, there is a greater diversity of plant families. In the Cape Floral Kingdom, twenty percent of the flora is represented by only two families, Compositae (Asteraceae) and Leguminosae (Fabaceae), and other large families include Aizoaceae, Ericaceae and Iridaceae. In fact, half the flora is represented by only ten families (Moll, 2006). Plant diversity in the west is due to speciation in the region over the past 25 million years so plants are likely to have many close relatives. In the east, the genera are, on average, less closely related to each other (Forest *et al.*, 2007), hence the wider range of plant families.

MASSON AND THUNBERG IN SOUTH AFRICA

Cape Town was established by the Dutch East India Company in 1652 and it became an important stopover on the route from Europe to the East. The Dutch recorded and illustrated the plants found in the area around Cape Town. Some were sent back to Europe, especially bulbous plants including *Nerine sarniensis* and various *Gladiolus* and *Lachenalia*, which were easily transported when dormant. By the late eighteenth century, the authority of the Dutch was weakening and explorers of other nationalities found it easier to travel in the region. During a stopover at Cape Town on the return leg of the voyage of HMS *Endeavour*, Joseph Banks had a brief glimpse of the extraordinary flora of this region. His keen botanical eye must have noted the potential of this flora and in his subsequent role as royal advisor on scientific matters, including the development of the Royal Gardens at Kew, Banks organised for a Kew gardener, the Scotsman Francis Masson, to explore the Cape as Kew's first official plant collector.

Masson joined the first leg of James Cook's second expedition, sailing to Cape Town on board HMS *Resolution*. He landed in October 1772 and remained there for the next three years. His first trip inland took him east of Cape Town as far as Swellendam and then back via the Hottentots Holland Mountains. For a second, longer trip, beginning in September 1773, Masson was invited to join the Swedish

botanist Carl Thunberg. They headed north from Cape Town, as far as the Oliphants River, turned south-east towards Swellendam and then reached Mossel Bay on the south coast. They travelled as far east as Addo on the Zondags River, beyond the limits of Dutch rule (Saltmarsh, 2003), but their guides were unwilling to go any further, fearing attacks by a tribe of Hottentots known as Caffers. They returned to Cape Town via Swellendam, arriving four months and fourteen days after setting out.

Masson joined Thunberg again for a third trip in September 1774. They set off north again but this time travelled beyond the Oliphants River to the Doorn River,

before heading east to present-day Nieuwoudtville. They explored the Bokkeveld and Roggeveld Mountains before returning to Cape Town three months later. The following March, Masson set off for England.

Masson and Thunberg found many new and wonderful flowers on their explorations. Several were illustrated for *Curtis's Botanical Magazine*, including the striking turquoise-green-flowered *Ixia viridiflora*, which Thunberg had originally seen on his first expedition in 1772, before he joined forces with Masson.

After leaving Cape Town in 1775, Thunberg headed east and went on to make his name as the 'Japanese Linnaeus'. Masson continued hunting for plants, visiting the Canary Islands, Madeira, the Azores and the West Indies, as well as south-west Europe and North Africa. Then, towards the end of 1785, he returned to the Cape, this time staying for nine years. In 1797 he travelled to Canada, still collecting for Kew, where he died in 1805, aged 65.

Masson was responsible for introducing many plants to Kew, from where they were subsequently distributed to growers in Britain and elsewhere, but it was the scientist Thunberg, who became Professor of Botany at Uppsala University in 1784, who was responsible for describing many of the new species that they had found. Thunberg eventually published *Flora Capensis* between 1807 and 1820, the first detailed account of the Cape flora. This period, at the end of the eighteenth century and beginning of the nineteenth, has been called the Cape Period in recognition of the intense interest the British had in the Cape flora. Nurseries such as the Vineyard Nursery in Hammersmith, which was founded by James Lee and Lewis Kennedy in 1745, as well as James Knight's Exotic Nursery and the nursery of James Colvill, both on the King's Road, London, specialised in Cape plants.

The plants Masson introduced from South Africa ranged from bulbs and corms to cycads and succulents; he had a particular interest in the succulent genus *Stapelia*, in Asclepiadaceae, and published *Stapeliae novae* in 1796. One of the world's oldest pot plants, the cycad *Encephalartos altensteinii*, is still growing in the Palm House at Kew, having been brought to Kew by Masson in 1775. Among the geophytes sent to Kew Gardens were plants such as the creamy-white, iris-like *Moraea tricuspidata* and the bright pink-flowered *Watsonia marginata*. In December 1775,

Gazania linearis
Family: Compositae (Asteraceae)

The genus *Gazania* is almost entirely South African, with a few species occurring in Namibia and Mozambique and one, *G. krebsiana* subsp. *serrulata*, reaching as far north as Tanzania. The rich, bright colours of the flowers make them popular bedding plants and many cultivars have been produced. The perennial *Gazania linearis* can withstand non-persistent frosts if kept fairly dry and makes an attractive rock garden plant that produces an abundance of golden yellow flowers in early summer. It is endemic to the summer rainfall area of South Africa, occurring from Humansdorp, just west of Port Elizabeth, north to Kwazulu-Natal, growing on grassy slopes and rocky cliffs at altitudes up to 3,050 m (10,007 feet).

Gazania linearis was first described as *Gorteria linearis* by Carl Thunberg in his *Prodromus Plantarum Capensium*, published between 1794 and 1800. In 1917, Claridge Druce transferred *Gorteria linearis* to *Gazania* and published the name *Gazania linearis*.

In a revision of the genus, Helmut Roessler (1959) recognised 16 annual and perennial species of *Gazania* and divided *G. linearis* into two varieties: var. *linearis* and var. *ovalis*. Typically, *G. linearis* has linear to linear-lanceolate leaves of up to 10 mm wide, but in var. *ovalis*, the leaves are broadly lanceolate to elliptic and up to 25 mm wide. In both varieties, the leaves can be pinnately lobed and are held in rosettes arising from a stout, woody crown. The leaves are glabrous on the upper surface but their undersides are thickly covered with soft, white hairs, except around the midrib. The solitary flower head (capitulum) is up to 7 cm wide and held above the leaves on a stem of 10 cm or more in length. The ray florets are generally golden yellow, often with a dark base, but occasionally are white with a yellow band near the base. The disc florets are yellow to reddish-orange.

This species should be planted in a sunny position, in soil that is free-draining but does not dry out completely in the summer. On a rock garden, it benefits from being sited close to large rocks, where the soil retains some moisture, even during hot, dry periods. Older plants will develop many rosettes of long, narrow leaves. They are readily propagated from cuttings taken in mid to late summer; alternatively, sow seed in autumn or winter. Delay pricking out until the plants have formed a small clump with a good root system, thinning where necessary. The strongest seedlings will probably flower in their first year.

Gazania linearis was introduced to cultivation in England in the nineteenth century and was already well-known when mentioned in the *Gardeners' Chronicle*, as *G. longiscapa* (now treated as a synonym), in 1883. Mr J. Medley Wood (1883), writing from the Natal Botanic Garden, describes an unusual use for this plant: "the tomentum found upon the lower side of the leaves forms the only dress worn by a large number of the native Zulu girls...The back of the leaf is scraped with the thumbnail and the woolly covering removed, which is then twisted, soaked in fat, and attached to a string until sufficient is collected to form a thick fringe which is then tied around the loins."

Curtis's Botanical Magazine, plate 9354 (1934). Artist: Lilian Snelling.

Masson wrote to Linnaeus, sending him a specimen of a bulbous plant with a compact inflorescence held between two fleshy leaves. Thunberg thought it should be named after Masson and Linnaeus agreed. Thunberg eventually described the new genus *Massonia* in 1780, in Maarten Houttuyn's *Natuurlijke Historie*.

There are probably six species of *Massonia*, with four being found in the Cape, although opinions vary; for example, Ute and Dietrich Müller-Doblies (1997) recognise 12 species. These plants have a condensed inflorescence made up of small tubular flowers with long, firm stamens. The inflorescence appears from between two wide leaves that are held flat to the ground. Some species, such as *M. pustulata*, have bumps and blisters (pustules) on their leaves. This species flowers in December in Britain and like the others, it is intolerant of water during its dormant season. As the seed pods expand, they dry out and open. The whole inflorescence then becomes detached and in the wild can be blown along the ground, distributing the small, round black seeds as it goes. Interestingly, the first species to be described, *Massonia depressa*, has been found to be pollinated by rodents, which are attracted by its viscous nectar, and transfer pollen from one plant to another on their nose (Johnson *et al.*, 2001).

GROWING SOUTH AFRICAN PLANTS

There are plenty of South African plants in cultivation, including *Pelargonium*, *Crocosmia*, *Agapanthus*, *Kniphofia* and *Osteospermum*, to name a few, but alpines from this part of the world are relatively scarce. One reason for this is that many South African species are not, or are not considered to be, frost hardy. However, a little experimentation, and sometimes a degree of luck, can lead to new plants being found that can happily survive winters in the open garden. Of course, a cold frame or alpine house, especially if kept just frost free, will increase the number of species you are able to grow.

Plants like *Gazania linearis* in Compositae survive outside all year round in milder parts of Britain. Gazanias, like osteospermums, are usually grown as half-hardy bedding or container plants, but the yellow-flowered *G. linearis* has been cultivated on Kew's rock garden for over a decade now. It originates from south-east South Africa so it is used to rain in the summer months; it just needs plenty of sun and free-draining soil that will not stay too wet in the winter.

Berkheya is in the same subtribe of Compositae (subtribe Gorteriinae of the Arctotideae tribe) as *Gazania*. The genus contains around 75 species that are distributed throughout tropical Africa, from Ethiopia and Nigeria southwards, with the greatest concentration of species in southern Africa (Hind, 2006a). The striking *B. purpurea* has tall stems that reach 40–50 cm high, sometimes more. They erupt from dense clumps of thistle-like foliage and display showy, pale

LEFT
Berkheya purpurea.

BELOW
Helichrysum splendidum.

TOP LEFT
Gladiolus tristis.

TOP RIGHT
Ixia rapunculoides.

BOTTOM LEFT
Dierama pulcherrima.

BOTTOM RIGHT
Dietes bicolor.

purple, radiate flower heads (capitula) that reach up to 8 cm across. The main growing season for this species, as for *G. linearis*, is summer and in cultivation it flowers from June to August. It comes from the eastern side of South Africa, growing on grassy slopes at altitudes of 1,500–3,050 m (4,921–10,007 feet). It produces plenty of seed, from which new plants are easily raised, sometimes flowering in their first year. Division is another simple method of propagation.

The genus *Helichrysum* is an important group of African plants in the Compositae, with around 245 of the 600 species known worldwide occurring in South Africa. One of the most reliable outside has proved to be the shrubby, silver-leaved, mound-forming *H. splendidum*. Its small, bright yellow flower heads are clustered together at the tip of each leafy stem in summer. The hairy, silver-grey leaves are almost rectangular, with a rounded tip, and reach around 1.5 cm long and 4 mm wide. This plant needs plenty of sunshine and plenty of space as it can spread to over 1 metre across. It comes from the summer rainfall region of South Africa, from the Swartberg and Outeniqua ranges, through Eastern Cape, Kwazulu-Natal and Lesotho, to Swaziland and into tropical Africa, reaching altitudes of 2,500 m (8,202 feet). According to John Grimshaw (2006), there is some doubt that *H. splendidum* is the correct name for the cultivated plant because the wild specimens are more upright with the capitula held in tight rounded heads. Very similar is *H. trilineatum*, from the Drakensberg. Plants of this species grown on the Rock Garden at Kew have very narrow, linear, sticky green leaves, which are only 2 mm wide, and the whole plant is more lax than the *H. splendidum* of gardens, which forms neater, more dense mounds.

Two other species in this genus that do well in the open are also from the Drakensberg. *Helichrysum basalticum* has softly hairy, rounded, grey leaves held flat to the ground in a loose rosette, which gives rise to a leafy scape holding a domed inflorescence of yellow flower heads. *Helichrysum bellum* has clear white flowers with a yellow centre held 10–15 cm above the lanceolate green leaves.

Cotula is a genus of around 55 species in Compositae of which the majority are South African. *Cotula fallax* is an attractive silvery-leaved species that has been cultivated for many years in the USA, Europe and Japan under the wrong name. For a long time, it was masquerading in the trade as *C. hispida*. The origin of the plant in general cultivation is unknown, but it is almost certain that it too is from South Africa. Kew botanist Dr Nicholas Hind (2006b) attempted to identify this plant using the keys in Harvey and Sonder's *Flora Capensis* from 1865 and Olive Hilliard's *Compositae in Natal* from 1977. He also checked treatments from other areas where cotulas are known to occur, such as the *Flora of Tropical East Africa*. Hind

ABOVE
Kew's plant of *Helichrysum trilineatum*.

LEFT
Cotula fallax on the Rock Garden at Kew.

Oxalis hirta
Family: Oxalidaceae

Oxalis is the seventh largest genus in the Cape Floral Region of South Africa where there are 118 species of which 94, including *O. hirta*, are endemic (Goldblatt & Manning, 2000). This species occurs naturally in south-west South Africa, from the Bokkeveld Mountains south to the Cape Peninsula.

Like all *Oxalis* from South Africa (except the cosmopolitan weed *O. corniculata*), *O. hirta* is a bulbous species. It is dormant throughout the hot, dry summers that are characteristic of the Mediterranean-type climate in Western Cape and growth begins with the onset of winter rains. The branched, leafy shoots are initially erect but tend to flop over as they lengthen. They can eventually reach over 30 cm long. The leaves are almost sessile and divided into three linear-oblong leaflets. The whole plant is softly hairy. The peduncles arise from the upper leaf axils in autumn and early winter and hold solitary flowers in shades of deep magenta-red to violet, purple or unusually white. The flowers have a yellow throat and rarely the whole flower can be yellow. In a revision of South African *Oxalis*, Terence Salter (1944) divides *O. hirta* into seven varieties but admits that these groups are somewhat arbitrarily distinguished by characteristics such as hairiness, leaflet shape and flower colour.

Oxalis hirta was introduced into cultivation in 1793 but has never become a popular plant despite its glorious, sometimes vivid pink, early winter flowers. This is probably due to its unreliable hardiness and often untidy habit. The renowned alpine plantsman and nurseryman Will Ingwersen (1935) wrote of this plant: "...but the flowers, great goblets of glowing portwine ruby, are produced just when winter is in the air, the days at their dullest and the air so full of moisture that the loose, lax stems flop over, and those buds will only unfurl and display their gorgeous beauty when the sun shines during the few scattered hours in November."

Like many of the bulbous species of *Oxalis*, *O. hirta* seems to grow better if pot-bound, as long as the bulbs don't actually touch. After watering in, the soil can be left to dry out before applying more water. Once growth appears, the soil is best kept moist and regular watering is necessary. The leafy stems will initially be erect and the flowers will open in autumn and early winter. Good light is needed to prevent etiolation. The stems continue to elongate during and after flowering, and will all too easily flop over and become straggly. By late spring, they will begin to go brown and watering should be reduced. Once the stems have dried, they can be cut or carefully pulled away and no more water will be needed until the autumn. Propagation is usually from bulb offsets that are separated during repotting and grown on. Seed will only be produced if two clones are present.

The plant illustrated here is the form that gained a Preliminary Commendation from the RHS when exhibited by Kew in October 1984. The flowers are larger and a deeper pink than those of other cultivated forms. As the original material came from Henrik Zetterlund at Gothenburg Botanic Garden, it was given the cultivar name 'Gothenburg'. However, this cultivar easily falls within the morphological range of this variable species. It received an Award of Merit in November 1996.

Curtis's Botanical Magazine, plate 217 (1993). Artist: Mark Fothergill.

concluded that the plant was an undescribed species and named it *C. fallax*, the specific name meaning deceptive or misleading.

Cotula fallax is a low-growing, silky-hairy perennial. The flower heads are like small yellow buttons held 8–10 cm above the foliage on thin, leafless stems. The grey-green leaves are finely divided into short narrow segments, giving the whole plant a soft, feathery feel. Surprisingly considering its hairiness, this species does well in the open garden. In damp situations it will rot off, but given a sunny, airy position and free-draining soil it will survive outside for several years. Propagation is best from cuttings, which are easily rooted in spring or summer. The true *C. hispida* is a larger, more robust plant that is only thinly hairy.

Although South African composites make up a significant part of our garden flora, it is the geophytes from the region that are proving to be of greater interest to alpine gardeners. Apart from a few popular genera, these bulbous plants tend to be grown in specialist collections. Many are not very hardy or need to be kept completely dry during their dormant season, making them unsuitable for general garden situations but, as noted earlier, it is always worth experimenting.

Bulbous plants are found in both the summer and the winter rainfall regions of southern Africa, but it is the mediterranean climate of the Cape that has given rise to the greatest diversity, with around 1,400 geophyte species, most of them endemic (Duncan, 2003). Iridaceae is the third largest family in the Cape Floral Kingdom, with around 670 species (Moll, 2006), and includes such well-known plants as angels fishing rods (*Dierama*) and montbretia (*Crocosmia*). Some genera, like *Gladiolus* and *Romulea*, occur outside the region but are at their most diverse in South Africa. Endemic genera include *Watsonia*, *Sparaxis* and *Ixia*.

Members of Iridaceae that do well outside at Kew include the pale yellow *Gladiolus tristis* and the pink *G. carneus* from Cape Province. In the summer months, the wiry wands of *Dierama pulcherrimum* hold dangling purple blooms one metre or more above the tufts of narrow sword-like leaves. Another summer grower is *Dietes bicolor* from Eastern Cape, which has creamy-white flowers very much like an iris.

Ixia rapunculoides flowers in late March, producing spikes of violet-pink, funnel-shaped blooms. During the Cape Period, ixias were very popular plants. Many appeared in various publications in the late eighteenth and early nineteenth centuries but unfortunately misidentification was common. Hybrids were also being produced in Holland at the time, often causing more confusion (Duncan, 2006). Many of those early ixias have now been transferred to other genera, such as *Sparaxis*, *Tritonia* and *Hesperantha*. Even the Mediterranean *Romulea bulbocodium* appeared as *Ixia*

LEFT
Pale pink flowers of *Rhodohypoxis baurii* var. *confecta*.

bulbocodium in 1794. There are now thought to be around 50 species of these summer-dormant, cormous geophytes, all endemic to South Africa.

Among the most popular cultivated geophytes from South Africa are species of *Rhodohypoxis*. This is a genus of low-growing, starry-flowered perennials in the family Hypoxidaceae, which is centred on the Drakensberg Mountains. They can bloom for several months in the summer and die down completely for the winter. Olive Hilliard and Bill Burtt (1978) recognise six species, of which *R. baurii* is the most widespread in the wild and in cultivation.

Rhodohypoxis baurii is distributed in and around the Drakensberg, in the Eastern Cape, Natal and Lesotho, and possibly further north in Swaziland and the Transvaal. It grows in damp grassland and rocky places, at altitudes of 1,100–2,900 m (3,609–9,514 feet). It reaches 5–15 cm tall, with up to ten narrow, hairy leaves and one or two red, pink or white flowers. As with all species of *Rhodohypoxis*, the three inner perianth segments are sharply bent at the claw and virtually close the mouth of the flower, giving them their characteristic 'blind' appearance.

Rhodohypoxis baurii is a hardy plant that can be grown in well-drained soil, in sun or partial shade, on a rock garden or in an alpine trough. However, the dormant rootstocks are best kept dry during the winter months and a sheet of glass placed over the trough or soil pocket can be used effectively to keep off the rain. *Rhodohypoxis* often do better if grown tightly packed in a pot or pan, in a cold frame or alpine house, which allows the soil to be kept dry when they are dormant. Once in growth, they need plenty of moisture. In the wild, this species is usually found in soil that is damp or almost waterlogged in the summer.

By providing a protected environment, such as a bulb frame or alpine house, the variety of South African plants you can grow can be increased enormously. Cushion plants, like the soft, hairy, grey-leaved *Helichrysum milfordiae* from Lesotho, will do well under glass. Bulbs can be protected from rain during their dormant phase and a little heating will keep frost at bay. This steps make it possible to cultivate the whole range of colourful romuleas, gladioli, ixias and moraeas from the eastern and western sides of South Africa. These plants are not true alpines and some of them stretch the boundaries of even the broadest definition of alpine, but they are among the wide range of plants that just need to be kept dry for a season or only require a free-draining soil to thrive. They are not special plants, they are plants for anyone who wants to have a go at growing them, and they will continue to enrich our gardens from whichever continent they originate.

RIGHT
Helichrysum milfordiae.

Bibliography and references

Ball, J. (1877). Spicilegium Florae Maroccanae. *Bot. J. Linn. Soc.* 16: 281–294.

Blanchard, J. W. (1990). *Narcissus, a Guide to Wild Daffodils*. Alpine Garden Society, Woking, Surrey.

Bland, B. (2000). *Silver Saxifrages*. AGS Publications Ltd. Pershore, Worcs.

Boothman, S. (1966). *Asphodelus acaulis* Desf. *Bull. Alpine Gard. Soc. Gr. Brit.* 34: 173.

Cosson, E. (1875). Index Plantarum in Imperio Maroccano australi recentius a Cl. Balansa et ab indigenis duobus sub auspiciis Cl. Beaumier lectarum. *Bull. Soc. Bot. France* 22: 51–70.

Dallman, P. R. (1998). *Plant Life in the World's Mediterranean Climates*. Oxford University Press.

Davis, A. P. & Jury, S. L. (1990). A taxonomic review of *Iris* L. series *Unguiculares* (Diels) Lawrence. *Bot. J. Linn. Soc.* 103: 281–300.

Duncan, G. (2003). Endangered geophytes of the Cape Floral Kingdom. *Curtis's Bot. Mag.* 20: 245–250.

Duncan, G. (2006). *Ixia tenuifolia*. *Curtis's Bot. Mag.* 23, t. 55.

Fernandes, A. (1968). Keys to the identification of native and naturalized taxa of the genus *Narcissus* L. In: *The Daffodil and Tulip Year Book*, 33. pp. 37–66. Royal Horticultural Society, London.

Forest, F., Grenyer, R., Rouget, M., Davies, T.J., Cowling, R.M., Faith, D.P., Balmford, A., Manning, J.C., Proches, S., van der Bank, M., Reeves, G., Hedderson, T.A.J. & Savolainen, V. (2007). Preserving the evolutionary potential of floras in biodiversity hotspots. *Nature* 445: 757—760.

Goldblatt, P. & Manning, J. (2000). *Cape Plants*: 10–15. National Botanical Institute of South Africa, Missouri Botanical Garden.

Grey-Wilson, C. (2002). *Cyclamen, a Guide for Gardeners, Horticulturists and Botanists* (new edition). B. T. Batsford Ltd. London.

Grimshaw, J. (2006). African Everlastings. *Bull. Alpine Gard. Soc. Gr. Brit.* 74: 369–378.

Hilliard, O. M. & Burtt, B. L. (1978). Notes on some plants from Southern Africa, chiefly from Natal: VII. *Notes Roy. Bot. Gard. Edinburgh* 36: 43–76.

Hind, N. (2006a). *Berkheya purpurea*. *Curtis's Bot. Mag.* 23: t. 568.

Hind, N. (2006b). *Cotula fallax*. *Curtis's Bot. Mag.* 23: t. 570.

Hooker, J. D. (1874). *Chrysanthemum catananche*. *Curtis's Bot. Mag.* 100: t. 6107.

Ingwersen, W. E. (1935). The genus *Oxalis* in the rock garden. *Bull. Alpine Gard. Soc. Gr. Brit.* 3: 81–87.

Johnson, S. D., Pauw, A. & Midgley, J. (2001). Rodent pollination in the African lily *Massonia depressa* (Hyacinthaceae). *Amer. J. Bot.* 88 (10): 1768–1773.

Maire, R. (1958). *Asphodelus* L. In: *Flora de L'Afrique du Nord*, 5, ed. R. Maire. pp. 26–44. Éditions Paul Lechevalier, Paris.

Maire, R. (1959). *Narcissus* L. In: *Flora de L'Afrique du Nord*, 6. ed. R. Maire. pp. 51–76. Éditions Paul Lechevalier, Paris.

Manning, J. (2004). *Southern African Wild Flowers, jewels of the veld*. Struik Publishers, Cape Town.

Manning, J. (2007), *Field Guide to Fynbos*. Struik Nature, Cape Town.

Manning, J., Goldblatt, P. & Snijman, D. (2002). *The Color Encyclopedia of Cape Bulbs*. Timber Press, Portland, Oregon.

Medley Wood, J. (1883). *Gazania longiscapa*. *Gard. Chron.*, ser. 2, 20: 471.

Moll, E. (2006). The Cape Floral Kingdom. *Bull. Alpine Gard. Soc. Gr. Brit.* 74: 278–295.

Müller-Doblies, U. & D. (1997). A partial revision of the tribe Massonieae (Hyacinthaceae). *Feddes Repert.* 108: 49–96.

Roessler, H. (1959). Revision der Arctotideae — Gorteriinae (Compositae). *Mitt. Bot. Staatssamml. München* 3: 377–381.

Salter, T. M. (1944). The genus *Oxalis* in South Africa: a taxonomic revision. *J. S. African Bot.*, Supplementary Volume 1: 238–242.

Saltmarsh, A. C. (2003). Francis Masson: Collecting plants for King and country. *Curtis's Bot. Mag.* 20: 225–244.

Webb, D. A. & Gornall, R. J. (1989). *Saxifrages of Europe*. Christopher Helm Ltd., Bromley, Kent.

Index to scientific names and cultivars

cashmerianum 159, 160
Dendrosenecio 213
Deutzia 134
   crenata 134
   gracilis 134
   scabra 134
Diascia 224
Dianella 121
   tasmanica 108, 120, 121
Dianthus 35, 37
   alpinus 38
   haematocalyx 18
   pavonius 38
Dicentra 61
   canadensis 61
   cucullaria 60, 61
   occidentalis 60
Dierama 231
   pulcherrima 228, 231
Dietes bicolor 214, 228, 231
Dionysia vii, 207–209
   aretioides 176, 206, 207, 209
      'Gravetye' 209
      'Paul Furse' 209
      'Phyllis Carter' 209
   cristagallii 210
   curviflora 209
   involucrata 209
   michauxii 181
   mira 207
   mozaffarianii 207, 210
   odora 209
   sarvestanica 208, 210
   tacamahaca 210
   tapetodes 209
   viva 210
   zetterlundii 210
   zschummelii 210
Diphylleia 146
   grayei 146
Dodecatheon 51, 55–57
   frigidum 55
   meadia 55–57
      subsp. brachycarpum 57
      subsp. meadia 57
      subsp. membranaceum 57
      forma album 57
      'Album' 57
      'Splendidum' 57
   pulchellum 56
Douglasia 74, 77
   montana 48, 75
   nivalis 77

Draba 37, 38, 189
   bryoides 37, 38
   cusickii var. cusickii 50
   dedeana 38
   longisiliqua 38, 189
   mawii 7
   mollissima 38
   rigida 34
Dracophyllum 111
Dryas drummondii 71

Eccremocarpus 85
   scaber 85
Eminium rauwolfii 181
Encephalartos altensteinii 220
Epidendrum 156
   humile 156
   praecox 156
Epimedium 144, 145
   subgenus Epimedium 145
      section Diphyllon 145
      section Epimedium 145
      section Macroceras 145
      section Polyphyllon 145
   subgenus Rhizophyllum 145
   alpinum 145, 146
   colchicum 185
   diphyllum 145, 146
   elatum 145
   grandiflorum 145, 146
   koreanum 145
   macrosepalum 145
   perralderianum 145
   pinnatum 145, 183
      subsp. circinatum 185
      subsp. colchicum 146, 183, 185
      subsp. pinnatum 185
   pubigerum 145, 183
   ×rubrum 146
   sempervirens 145, 146
      var. rugosum 145, 146
      var. sempervirens 146
   trifoliolatobinatum 126, 145
   ×versicolor 146
   ×youngianum 146
Eranthis 141
   hyemalii 141
   pinnatifida 141
Eremurus himalaicus 151
Erigeron 65
   compositus 64, 65
Erinacea anthyllis 43
Eriogonum 63

flavum 63
   jamesii 71
   pauciflorum 70
   umbellatum 71
Eritrichium nanum 17, 38
Erythronium 51, 66
   albidum 48, 51
   americanum 66
   dens-canis 66
   grandiflorum 65, 74
   japonicum 128
   revolutum 66
Eschscholzia californica 78, 79
Espeletia 88, 92
   argentea 92
   corymbosa 92
   grandiflora 92
   schultzii 92
Eulychnia iquiquensis 93
Euphorbia acanthothamnos 39
   griffithii 173
   lactiflua 95
   myrsinites 23
   wallichii 152

Fabiana 85
   imbricata 85
   nana 85
Fraxinus 61
Fritillaria 51, 65, 142, 143, 179, 195–197, 200
   subgenus Petilium 195
   subgenus Rhinopetalum 196
   alburyana vii
   amabilis 144
   ariana 196
   ayakoana 144
   bucharica 196
   camschatcensis 143
   chitralensis 176, 195
   eduardii 195
   gibbosa 196
   imperialis 193, 195, 197
   japonica 143, 144
      var. koidzumiana 143
   kaiensis 144
   karelinii 196
   koidzumiana 143
   meleagris 195
   muraiana 144
   pallidiflora 197
   pudica 65
   raddeana 195
   shikokiana 144

Index to common names

121	
131	
141	142
151	152
161	162
171	172
181	182
191	192
201	202
211	212	213
221	222	
231	232
241	242
251	

N